The Islamic State in Britain

Drawing on extensive field research with activists on the streets of London, Michael Kenney provides the first ethnographic study of a European network implicated in terrorist attacks and sending fighters to the Islamic State. For over twenty years, al-Muhajiroun (Arabic for "the Emigrants") strived to create an Islamic state in Britain through high-risk activism. A number of Emigrants engaged in violence, while others joined the Islamic State in Iraq and Syria. Kenney explains why young Britons joined the Emigrants, how they radicalized and adapted their activism, and why many of them eventually left. Through an innovative mix of ethnography and network analysis, Kenney explains the structure and processes behind this outlawed network and explores its remarkable resilience. What emerges is a complex, nuanced portrait that demystifies the Emigrants while challenging conventional wisdom on radicalization and countering violent extremism.

Michael Kenney is Associate Professor of International Affairs at the University of Pittsburgh. He is the author of *From Pablo to Osama: Trafficking and Terrorist Networks, Government Bureaucracies, and Competitive Adaptation*, among other publications. His new book, *The Islamic State in Britain*, is based on extensive field work on al-Muhajiroun, an outlawed activist network in the United Kingdom. His research has been supported by the National Science Foundation, the Office of Naval Research, the National Institute of Justice, and other institutions.

STRUCTURAL ANALYSIS IN THE SOCIAL SCIENCES

Edited by Mark Granovetter

The series Structural Analysis in the Social Sciences presents studies that analyze social behavior and institutions by reference to relations among such concrete social entities as persons, organizations, and nations. Relational analysis contrasts on the one hand with reductionist methodological individualism and on the other with macro-level determinism, whether based on technology, material conditions, economic conflict, adaptive evolution, or functional imperatives. In this more intellectually flexible, structural middle ground, analysts situate actors and their relations in a variety of contexts. Since the series began in 1987, its authors have variously focused on small groups, history, culture, politics, kinship, aesthetics, economics, and complex organizations, creatively theorizing how these shape and in turn are shaped by social relations. Their style and methods have ranged widely, from intense, long-term ethnographic observation to highly abstract mathematical models. Their disciplinary affiliations have included history, anthropology, sociology, political science, business, economics, mathematics, and computer science. Some have made explicit use of social network analysis, including many of the cutting-edge and standard works of that approach, whereas others have kept formal analysis in the background and used "networks" as a fruitful orienting metaphor. All have in common a sophisticated and revealing approach that forcefully illuminates our complex social world.

Recent Books in the Series

(continued after Index)

The Islamic State in Britain

Radicalization and Resilience in an Activist Network

MICHAEL KENNEY
University of Pittsburgh

 CAMBRIDGE
UNIVERSITY PRESS

CAMBRIDGE
UNIVERSITY PRESS

University Printing House, Cambridge CB2 8BS, United Kingdom

One Liberty Plaza, 20th Floor, New York, NY 10006, USA

477 Williamstown Road, Port Melbourne, VIC 3207, Australia

314–321, 3rd Floor, Plot 3, Splendor Forum, Jasola District Centre, New Delhi – 110025, India

79 Anson Road, #06-04/06, Singapore 079906

Cambridge University Press is part of the University of Cambridge.

It furthers the University's mission by disseminating knowledge in the pursuit of
education, learning, and research at the highest international levels of excellence.

www.cambridge.org
Information on this title: www.cambridge.org/9781108470803
DOI: 10.1017/9781108557108

© Michael Kenney 2018

First published 2018

Printed and bound in Great Britain by Clays Ltd, Elcograf S.p.A.

A catalogue record for this publication is available from the British Library.

Library of Congress Cataloging-in-Publication Data
Names: Kenney, Michael, 1967– author.
Title: The Islamic state in Britain : radicalization and resilience
in an activist network / Michael Kenney.
Description: New York: Cambridge University Press, 2018. |
Series: Structural analysis in the social sciences
Identifiers: LCCN 2018029895 | ISBN 9781108470803 (hardback)
Subjects: LCSH: Muslims – Great Britain – Politics and government. |
Muslims – Political activity – Great Britain. | Islam and politics – Great Britain. |
Jihad. | Islamic fundamentalism – Great Britain. | Radicalism – Great Britain. |
Great Britain – Politics and government – 2007– | Terrorism – Religious aspects – Islam.
Classification: LCC BP65.G7 K46 2018 | DDC 322/.10941–dc23
LC record available at https://lccn.loc.gov/2018029895

ISBN 978-1-108-47080-3 Hardback

For Emilia and Caroline, who make it all worthwhile

Contents

Figures

Tables

Acknowledgments

Any research project that begins at one academic institution and ends at another is bound to accumulate a long list of personal and professional debts. This book is no different.

My research on al-Muhajiroun began in 2007, when I was an assistant professor at the Pennsylvania State University, Harrisburg. Between 2007 and 2009, my research on Islamist militancy in Britain and Spain was supported by the National Institute of Justice. During this period, I met several of the activists who later became instrumental in my research for this book. That field work began in earnest in November 2010, with funding from the Office of Naval Research.

At Penn State Harrisburg, I received tremendous support from Steven Peterson, then Director of its School of Public Affairs, and Marian Walters, Associate Dean for Research and Graduate Studies. After I joined the University of Pittsburgh, John Keeler, Dean of the Graduate School of Public and International Affairs (GSPIA), became an equally enthusiastic champion of my research. In the early stages of this project, I benefitted from collaborating with John Horgan, Mia Bloom, and Cale Horne, then colleagues at Penn State's main campus, and Kathleen Carley and Michael Martin from Carnegie Mellon University. At GSPIA I am surrounded by colleagues who inspire me with their own research, including Phil Williams, Taylor Seybolt, Ryan Grauer, Luke Condra, Meredith Wilf, and Michael Poznansky. During the first year of this project, I received research assistance from several Penn State students, including Kurt Braddock, Peter Vining, Camilla Robinson, and Nicole Zinni. Following my move to GSPIA, many other students provided valuable support, including Stephen Coulthart, Leah Kaufman, Evan Peterson, Rakan Twal, and Stephen Worman.

After finishing the draft of this book, I convened a workshop, or what Martha Crenshaw might call a "murder board," where she, Marc Sageman, Kathleen

Blee, Colin Clarke, and Taylor Seybolt raked over my manuscript with finely toothed intellectual combs. Their unsparing generosity made this a better book. The Matthew B. Ridgway Center for International Security Studies sponsored the workshop and Sandy Monteverde made sure everything ran smoothly. Other researchers who have commented on my research include Mary Beth Altier, Deborah Avant, Jérôme Drevon, Luke Gerdes, Alexander Montgomery, Sarah Parkinson, David Rapoport, Oliver Westerwinter, and Dominick Wright. Mark Granovetter and the anonymous reviewers at Cambridge University Press provided constructive critiques of the manuscript, which I used to sharpen my analysis. Robert Dreesen and Robert Judkins, also at Cambridge, guided me through the review and production process. Some of the material in this book was originally published in the *Journal of Conflict Resolution* ("Structure and Performance in a Violent Extremist Network," co-authored with Stephen Coulthart and Dominick Wright), and *Terrorism and Political Violence*/Taylor & Francis Online ("A Community of True Believers: Learning as Process among 'The Emigrants,'" August 30, 2017, www.tandfonline.com).

Numerous people helped me during my trips to London, including Abdul Haqq Baker, James Brandon, Karen Fields-Roberts, Mary Gadsen, Salam Hafez, Ghaffar Hussein, Abdul Hye Miah, Robert Lambert, Hanif Qadir, Catherine Raymond, Hannah Stuart, and Douglas Weeks. I could not have completed this book without the many people within and outside al-Muhajiroun who shared their insights and expertise with me, often on multiple occasions. I cannot thank them by name, but I am grateful for their help. My activist respondents will not agree with everything I have written, but I hope they feel I have faithfully reported what they told me and what I observed of their activities.

My final and most important debt of gratitude goes to the two people who have sacrificed more for my research than anyone else, my wife and daughter. To them I dedicate this book.

Introduction: Meeting the Emigrants

> The main purpose of the organization is to call society to Islam, command good and forbid evil, and to establish the *khilafah*, which is the Islamic state.
>
> Leading activist

In the early morning of September 25, 2014, dozens of police officers raided the homes of several men in London. They belonged to al-Muhajiroun (Arabic for "the Emigrants"), a banned activist network dedicated to establishing the Islamic caliphate in Britain. The police arrested nine leaders, some of whom called on their followers to support the Islamic State in Iraq and Syria (ISIS), which had recently been outlawed by the British government as a terrorist organization. The charges against several activists were soon dropped. But the authorities continued their investigation of two leaders, Anjem Choudary and Mizanur Rahman, both of whom were later prosecuted – and convicted – for their support of the Islamic State.[1]

This was not the first time British authorities cracked down on al-Muhajiroun. In the aftermath of the London bombings in July 2005, government officials prevented the network's founder and original emir, Omar Bakri Mohammed, from returning to the country, transforming what was supposed to be a temporary visit to Lebanon into his permanent exile from Britain. With Bakri out of the way, officials arrested other network leaders, convicting several of crimes related to their activism. When activists bounced back from

---

[1] Interviews with three leading activists, Ilford, East London, December 9, 2014, Whitechapel, East London, December 11, 2014, and Stratford, East London, December 13, 2014. For more on the arrests, see Dominic Casciani, "Anjem Choudary held in London terror raids," *BBC News* (September 25, 2014), www.bbc.com/news/uk-england-29358758 [Accessed September 25, 2014]; and Vikram Dodd and Josh Halliday, "Anjem Choudary among nine arrested in London anti-terrorism raid," *The Guardian* (September 25, 2014), www.theguardian.com/uk-news/2014/sep/25/nine-arrested-london-anti-terrorism [Accessed September 25, 2014].

these early setbacks to continue their efforts to establish the caliphate through protests and street preaching, the British government formally outlawed al-Muhajiroun, making it a crime for individuals to belong to or support the group in any way. After activists dropped the al-Muhajiroun name, officials outlawed spin-off groups that appeared in its place, like the Saved Sect and al-Ghurabaa ("the Strangers"). The police enforced the bans by disrupting the network's public talks and conferences, pestering activists during their demonstrations and street preaching, and searching their homes and educational centers.

The activists rounded up in September 2014 were veterans of such treatment. They had been raided and arrested many times. In an interview three months after his 2014 arrest, one of them, a leading activist I refer to as "Rohan" in this book, told me that his home had been searched by the British police every year since 2011. Rohan's house was also raided earlier, in 2006, when he was arrested after a provocative, but mostly peaceful, protest. When I asked him whether anything had changed with Abu Bakr al-Baghdadi's recent declaration of the Islamic State, the same goal the Emigrants had been striving towards since 1996, he looked at me and said, "I think the officials are worried. That's why they're stepping things up."[2]

For many years, al-Muhajiroun proved to be remarkably resistant to British officials' periodic attempts to "step things up." The network not only survived the crackdowns. It bounced back from them to recruit new supporters, indoctrinate them in its Salafi-Islamist ideology, and mobilize them into high-risk activism. What explains this puzzle? Why did al-Muhajiroun not crumble after its charismatic emir left Britain? How did activists continue to recruit and radicalize supporters despite government repression? Did pressure from British authorities, along with the rise of the Islamic State in Iraq and Syria, push activists towards political violence? This book sets out to answer these questions through an ethnographic group analysis of an outlawed group that was at the center of London's vibrant Islamist scene from the late 1990s until recently.

---

[2] Interview with "Rohan," leading activist, Whitechapel, East London, December 11, 2014. Also, earlier interview with Rohan in Whitechapel, December 7, 2010, and interviews with different leading and veteran activists, Ilford, East London, December 9, 2014, and Stratford, East London, December 13, 2014. Field notes, Whitechapel, East London, December 11, 2014. Rohan is not this respondent's real name. It is a pseudonym I have given him. In this and the following chapters, I use pseudonyms for a few respondents whose interviews and personal stories I draw on repeatedly. One goal of ethnography is to demystify the extraordinary by revealing its normality. I use pseudonyms to normalize these respondents. All my pseudonyms are fictitious, with no connection to the people they represent. I created these fake names from a list of common Pakistani and Bangladeshi names, reflecting the ethnic heritage and family ties of many, but not all, of these respondents. See "Students of the World," www.studentsoftheworld.info/penpals/stats.php3?Pays=BNG and www.studentsoftheworld.info/penpals/stats.php3?Pays=PAK [Accessed October 1, 2017].

WHY AL-MUHAJIROUN?

This book tells the story of a network of deeply committed activists who sought to replace Great Britain's secular democracy with a religious theocracy based on their interpretation of Salafism and Islamism.[3] The Emigrants never came close to establishing an Islamic caliphate in Britain, but their tale is worth telling for a number of reasons. First, as a proselytization network that recovered from the removal of their original leader, the banning of their organization and other setbacks, al-Muhajiroun is a fascinating case of organizational resilience under pressure. This study contributes to the literature on resilience and organizational adaptation because researchers have largely avoided studies of non-state actors who have been outlawed and repressed by the same governments whose authority they challenge.[4] Drawing on 148

---

[3] Salafism is a puritanical reform movement within Sunni Islam whose followers seek to return the religion to its "purest, most authentic" state, as practiced by the Prophet Mohammed and his contemporaries and the first two generations of Muslims who came after them, known collectively as "the pious predecessors." Salafis base their understanding of the religion on a literal reading of scripture, specifically the Qur'an and hadiths (collected sayings and stories of the Prophet). Drawing on these sources, Salafis seek to emulate Mohammed in all aspects of their daily lives, including dress and physical appearance. While Salafis largely agree on their religious beliefs (*aqeedah*) and matters of jurisprudence (*fiqh*), they often disagree when applying these principles to contemporary life. One point of contention concerns acceptable forms of political engagement in modern society. Mainstream Salafis, variously referred to as "quietists," "purists," or "scholastics," reject political activism as religiously "deviant" and counter-productive, preferring to focus their efforts on personal "purification and education." Other Salafis, called "activists" or "politicos," embrace activism as a way of increasing social justice and implementing Islamic law. A third set of Salafis, often referred to as "Salafi-jihadis," go beyond non-violent activism to support the political violence they believe is necessary to establish God's rule on Earth. Al-Muhajiroun incorporates elements of both the Salafi activist and Salafi-jihadi perspectives. Hizb ut-Tahrir, the Muslim Brotherhood, and other Sunni "Islamists" are similar to Salafi activists in that they engage in social and political activism to establish the *shariah*, or Islamic law, as the basis for organizing political and legal authority in the community. However, Islamists do not follow the Salafi creed and *manhaj*, the practical method of applying these religious beliefs to their daily lives. Al-Muhajiroun activists do. Interviews with leading and veteran activists, Ilford, East London, November 13, 2010, Stratford, East London, November 29, 2010, and Whitechapel, East London, June 22, 2011. For discussion on the different types of Salafism, see Bernard Haykel, "On the Nature of Salafi Thought and Action," in *Global Salafism: Islam's New Religious Movement*, edited by Roel Meijer (New York: Columbia University Press, 2009), pp. 33–57; Quintan Wiktorowicz, "Anatomy of the Salafi Movement," *Studies in Conflict & Terrorism* 29, no. 3 (2006), pp. 207–9; and Shiraz Maher, *Salafi-Jihadism: The History of an Idea* (New York: Oxford University Press, 2016). For more on Islamism, see Mohammed Ayoob, *The Many Faces of Political Islam* (Ann Arbor, MI: University of Michigan Press, 2008); International Crisis Group, "Understanding Islamism," *Middle East/North Africa Report*, No. 37 (March 2, 2005), pp. 1–35; and Shadi Hamid, *The Temptations of Power: Islamists and Illiberal Democracy in a New Middle East* (New York: Oxford University Press, 2014).

[4] Exceptions include Sharon Erickson Nepstad, "Persistent Resistance: Commitment and Community in the Plowshares Movement," *Social Problems* 51, no. 1 (2004), pp. 43–60; Michael Kenney, *From Pablo to Osama: Trafficking and Terrorist Networks, Government Bureaucracies, and Competitive Adaptation* (University Park, PA: Pennsylvania State University Press, 2007);

interviews, hundreds of hours of field work, and thousands of news reports, the following chapters explain how al-Muhajiroun adapted its activism in response to government efforts to destroy it.

These changes include both structural and tactical adaptations. The next chapter uses formal and informal network analysis to explore the Emigrants' main structural change, shifting from a centralized, "scale-free-like" system based on a single leader to a more diffuse "small-world-like" network featuring redundant hubs who bridged different clusters of local activists. Chapter 4 draws on interviews and field observations to examine activists' tactical adaptations, including creating new spin-off groups when British officials outlawed old ones, replacing their original emir with veteran activists after authorities banned "Sheikh Omar" from Britain, and increasing their online activism when officials made it harder for them to secure venues for their public talks and conferences. These structural changes and tactical adaptations allowed activists to continue their activism for many years, despite being targeted for disruption. Al-Muhajiroun's resilience is not just important for network activists and British policy makers. It has implications for other non-state actors, including terrorist groups like al-Qaeda and ISIS that are part of the larger Salafi-jihadi movement to which the network belongs. I revisit these larger questions in the final chapter.

A second reason for focusing on al-Muhajiroun has to do with the network's persistence in Great Britain. Some cases are important enough to understand on their own.[5] Al-Muhajiroun is one such case. Throughout its twenty years of preaching and protesting, it has captured the attention of British society like few other activist groups in the country. It has been the extremist network Britons love to hate. To be sure, other preachers and activist groups have permeated London's Islamist counterculture, including Abu Qatadah, Abdullah Faisal, and Abu Hamza and his Supporters of Shariah group. The Emigrants not only achieved greater notoriety than these other extremists, they outlasted them all. By the summer of 2014, al-Muhajiroun was the last group standing that publicly called for replacing Britain's liberal democracy with an ISIS-style caliphate.

Over the years, Britain's tabloid media has churned out hundreds of reports documenting the Emigrants' most notorious antics, from public conferences celebrating the anniversary of 9/11 to demonstrations against the repatriated remains of fallen British soldiers to "Muslim patrols" enforcing "shariah law

René M. Bakker, Jörg Raab, and H. Brinton Milward, "A Preliminary Theory of Dark Network Resilience," *Journal of Policy Analysis and Management* 31, no. 1 (2012), pp. 33–62; and Nathan P. Jones, *Mexico's Illicit Drug Networks and the State Reaction* (Washington, DC: Georgetown University Press, 2016).

[5] For more on the substantive importance of certain cases in qualitative research, see Gary Goertz and James Mahoney, *A Tale of Two Cultures: Qualitative and Quantitative Research in the Social Sciences* (Princeton, NJ: Princeton University Press, 2012), pp. 184–5.

zones" in East London. Journalists and politicians have frequently depicted leading activists as "hate preachers" and vile layabouts who exploit state benefits to subsidize their activism while converting Britain's impressionable youth into fire-breathing fanatics. Al-Muhajiroun thrived in the glare, using its strategy of "media jihad" to spread its ideology and recruit new supporters. In the process, activists, and the tabloid media that enabled them, inflated themselves into something much bigger than they were: a vanguard movement of thousands of *da'is* (propagators) spread across dozens of cities in the United Kingdom, preparing British society for the inevitable coming of the Islamic state.

In reality, even during its peak in the late 1990s and early 2000s, al-Muhajiroun never numbered more than 150 to 200 dedicated members, what activists refer to as "intellectual affiliates," along with several hundred supporters, known in network circles as "contacts." After the British government cracked down against the Emigrants, first after the 9/11 attacks, and then more systematically after Operation Crevice in March 2004 and the 7/7 bombings in 2005, the number of activists declined to several dozen intellectual affiliates and little more than a hundred contacts.[6] During the years of my field work, when the network came under intense pressure from the authorities, it shrank even more, to a couple dozen intellectual affiliates and several dozen contacts. Leading activists liked to brag to journalists about the network's outsized presence in Britain, but privately they acknowledged their footprint was much smaller. After I had been in London for a couple of months interviewing and observing activists at various events, one leader admitted as much. "You know and I know we're not many in number," he told me at a café near Walthamstow's main square. "But in the media we're big, massive."[7]

Media coverage was essential to maintaining the Emigrants' creative fiction that they were on the verge of bringing the Islamic state to Britain, even as they were dismissed by other British Muslims. Contrary to the impression created by some reports, al-Muhajiroun never enjoyed widespread popular support among Britain's diverse Muslim communities. Although some local mosques and community centers tolerated their presence during the late 1990s, after the 9/11 attacks and the 7/7 bombings a few years later, the Emigrants and their

---

[6] Interviews with "Haroon," former contact, Westminster, Central London, June 14, 2011, "Rashid," former activist, Whitechapel, East London, June 26, 2011, and US official, Mayfair, Central London, December 3, 2010. Also, see Quintan Wiktorowicz, *Radical Islam Rising: Muslim Extremism in the West* (Lanham, MD: Rowman & Littlefield, 2005), p. 10.

[7] Interview with leading activist, Walthamstow, East London, December 2, 2010. In this book, all references to "activists" mean al-Muhajiroun activists, unless stated otherwise. I refer to three types of activists: leading activists, veteran activists, and rank-and-file activists. Leading activists are network leaders who direct its activism and serve as al-Muhajiroun's ideologues. Veterans are experienced activists who have been involved in al-Muhajiroun for years. They often serve as local leaders for the network. Rank-and-file activists are low-level proselytizers who perform much of the network's day-to-day activism. For a list of the interviews in this book, see Appendix: Interviews.

message became increasingly marginalized.[8] Activists themselves acknowledge their isolation. "We do feel ostracized, many times within the society," explains one respondent. "We find that we are outsiders in society because we bring our revolutionary idea."[9] "Sadly, we are a minority in this country," adds a leading activist. "Even within the Muslim community, the vast majority have integrated fully into the idea of British culture and democracy."[10]

At the heart of the Emigrants' paradoxically small presence but large impact on British society, and another reason they are worth studying, has been their success in indoctrinating hundreds of young men and women while maintaining their ideological cohesion. Unlike many Salafi-jihadi groups in the Middle East and Western Europe, the Emigrants of Britain have suffered relatively few ideological splits.[11] This is a reflection of the strong, almost cultish influence Omar Bakri Mohammed exerted over his followers and the network's energetic "community of practice," both of which I explore in Chapter 3. Bakri's followers internalized his ideas and worked hard to prepare British society for the caliphate. His preaching network may have been small and marginalized, but it was also productive, with activists organizing countless *da'wah* stalls and private study circles, along with regular demonstrations and public conferences. Al-Muhajiroun has always specialized in ideological indoctrination and contentious politics, not terrorism. Yet some activists and supporters went beyond activism to become involved in political violence, both within and outside Great Britain. In doing so they amplified the network's impact by transforming themselves from annoying "loudmouths" into a legitimate security threat facing the United Kingdom and other countries where they engaged in violence.

In fact, the Emigrants have long posed a vexing challenge for British policy makers. As one of the world's leading democracies, Britain's legal and political institutions allow the robust, peaceful expression of political dissent. Al-Muhajiroun's activism is repellant to many Britons, but it is grounded in legally protected free speech and association that are a cornerstone of the country's political system. When activists organize da'wah stalls to preach their

---

[8] Interviews with Haroon, Westminster, Central London, June 14, 2011; "Ali" and "Maryam," two other former activists, Hounslow, West London, June 21, 2011; research director, think tank, Bloomsbury, Central London, December 14, 2010; and two London Metropolitan Police officers, Vauxhall, South London, June 15, 2011.

[9] Interview with veteran activist, Skype, March 23, 2011.

[10] Interview with leading activist, Skype, June 26, 2013. Also, interviews with activists in Kensington, Central London, November 11, 2010, Stratford, East London, June 27, 2011, and Southall, West London, June 28, 2011.

[11] For more on the ideological divisions that have plagued Salafi-jihadis in Europe and Egypt, see Brynjar Lia, *Architect of Global Jihad: The Life of al-Qaida Strategist Abu Mus'ab al Suri* (New York: Columbia University Press, 2008); Jérôme Drevon, *Institutionalising Violence: Strategies of Jihad*, unpublished book manuscript; and Lawrence Wright, "The rebellion within: An al Qaeda mastermind questions terrorism," *The New Yorker* (June 2, 2008).

extremist blend of Salafi-Islamism, or stage demonstrations outside foreign embassies to denounce the West's "war on Islam," they are engaging in lawful protest. This raises important questions over the British government's ability to control activist groups that radicalize young men and women, without sacrificing core political values and civil liberties underlying the country's democracy.

Of course, the British are no strangers to dissident politics, even terrorism, having struggled with political violence from Irish nationalists and other terrorist threats in recent decades. Her Majesty's authorities have ample police powers and legislative resources to counter the Emigrants, including the Public Order Act (1986), the Terrorism Acts (2000, 2006), and the Anti-Terrorism, Crime, and Security Act (2001). Over the years British police and prosecutors have used these tools to arrest and convict network activists for public disorder, inciting racial hatred, terrorist fundraising, and soliciting murder at protests that went beyond legally protected speech.[12] On several occasions, they have used the Terrorism Act, as amended in 2006, to outlaw al-Muhajiroun and a number of its spin-off groups. More recently, law enforcers have exploited administrative controls such as the Terror Prevention and Investigation Measures (TPIMs), Anti-Social Behaviour Orders (ASBOs), and Multi-Agency Public Protection Arrangements (MAPPA) to restrict activists' movements and activities, even after they are released from prison.

These counter-terrorism efforts have weakened the Emigrants, but not destroyed them. During the years of my field work, from 2010 to 2015, the network continued its high-risk activism, both locally and internationally, despite being formally outlawed and coming under heavy police pressure. Locally, activists regularly called passersby to Islam in da'wah stalls on some of London's busiest thoroughfares, while protesting everything from the London Summer Olympics to the British government's extradition of Abu Hamza and other terrorism suspects to the United States to alcohol sales in Brick Lane, the popular East London restaurant district.[13] To facilitate their activism,

---

[12] Robin Simcox, Hannah Stuart, and Houriya Ahmed, *Islamist Terrorism: The British Connections* (London: The Centre for Social Cohesion, 2010); Wiktorowicz, *Radical Islam Rising*, pp. 61–67. For a broader discussion of the British government's counter-terrorism institutions and operations, see Frank Foley, *Countering Terrorism in Britain and France: Institutions, Norms and the Shadow of the Past* (Cambridge: Cambridge University Press, 2013).

[13] Field notes, Islington, North London, July 21, 2012; Anjem Choudary, "Demonstration Exposing the Evil of the Olympics," press release (July 26, 2012); Anjem Choudary, "What Every Muslim Should Know About the Evil of the Olympic Games," press release (August 1, 2012); Associated Press, "Police: Small group of Islamist protesters near Olympic Park ahead of closing cere-mony," *Washington Post* (August 12, 2005), www.washingtonpost.com/world/europe/police-small-group-of-islamist-protesters-near-olympic-park-ahead-of-closing-ceremony/2012/08/12/ce4a7ed4-e4b2-11e1-9739-eef99c5fb285_story.html [Accessed August 17, 2002]; Anjem Choudary, "The Real Criminals are the US and UK Regimes Not Abu Hamza!," press release (September 25, 2012); Anjem Choudary, "Stop the Extradition! A Warning to All Muslims in the UK," press release (October 1, 2012); Associated Press, "Hate preacher Abu Hamza

activists continued to create spin-off groups, including Need4Khilafah, Muslim Prisoners, and Islamic Emergency Defence (featuring its provocative acronym, IED).[14] Internationally, activists worked to establish a "fifth column" in Western Europe by assisting groups in Belgium (Shariah4Belgium), Denmark (Kaldet til Islam), and Norway (Prophet's Ummah), among other countries. When British authorities made it harder for activists to host public events at brick-and-mortar venues in London, activists turned to the Internet, posting their lectures and other materials on websites and social media.

In the wake of Abu Bakr al-Baghdadi's proclamation of the Islamic State in June 2014, the Emigrants' environment became even more hostile. At a time when hundreds of young men and women from Britain were traveling overseas to join ISIS and fight against the Bashar al-Assad regime, government authorities struggled to keep their young citizens from leaving. After network leaders declared the new caliphate to be legitimate and activists held rallies declaring their support for the Islamic State, the police cracked down even harder, culminating in the September 2014 raids. Following their arrests, several leading activists were barred by a London magistrate from participating in da'wah stalls. But even this did not stop them. At one event near the Olympic Park in Stratford in December 2014, I saw two of

extradited to US after UK ruling," (October 6, 2012), www.timeslive.co.za/world/2012/10/06/hate-preacher-abu-hamza-extradited-to-us-after-uk-ruling [Accessed October 11, 2012]; Trevor Grundy, "British shop owners threatened with 40 lashes for selling alcohol," *Washington Post* (December 16, 2013), www.washingtonpost.com/national/religion/british-shop-owners-threatened-with-40-lashes-for-selling-alcohol--resend/2013/12/16/7b950054-668b-11e3-997b-9213b17dac97_story.html [December 17, 2013].

[14] Field notes, Islington, North London, July 21, 2012, and personal communications with network activists, various dates; Adam Barnett, "Video: 'Fear Allah', hate preacher Anjem Choudary tells shopkeepers at anti-alcohol march," *East London Advertiser* (December 13, 2013), www.eastlondonadvertiser.co.uk/news/court-crime/video_fear_allah_hate_preacher_anjem_choudary_tells_shopkeepers_at_anti_alcohol_march_1_3111141 [Accessed December 16, 2013]; Daniel Binns, "Waltham Forest: Campaigners to 'shame' kerb crawlers," *Waltham Forest Guardian* (June 19, 2012), www.guardian-series.co.uk/news/9768051.WALTHAM_FOREST__Campaigners_to__shame__kerb_crawlers/?ref=mr [Accessed June 25, 2012]; *Daily Mail*, "Police arrest 20 protesters 'from banned group Muslims Against Crusades' outside US embassy in London," (December 2, 2011), www.dailymail.co.uk/news/article-2069190/Muslims-Against-Crusades-protesters-arrested-outside-U-S-embassy-London.html?ITO=1490 [Accessed December 8, 2011]; Ted Jeory, "Islamic preacher Choudary peddles hatred from a sweet shop," *Sunday Express* (May 26, 2013), www.express.co.uk/news/uk/402663/Islamic-preacher-Choudary-peddles-hatred-from-a-sweet-shop [Accessed June 10, 2013]; Omar Karmi, "'Muslim Patrols' prompt backlash in UK," *The National* (February 22, 2013), www.thenational.ae/news/world/europe/muslim-patrols-prompt-backlash-in-uk [Accessed March 15, 2013]; and Martin Robinson, "Muslim group backed by hate preacher Anjem Choudary called IED 'mocks Britain's war dead' with its name," *Daily Mail* (June 25, 2013), www.dailymail.co.uk/news/article-2347987/Muslim-group-backed-hate-preacher-Anjem-Choudary-called-IED-mocks-Britain-s-war-dead.html [Accessed June 25, 2013].

the arrested activists calling people to Islam with other supporters engaged in public da'wah. When I asked one of them whether the da'wah stall was a violation of his bail conditions he denied it was a stall. "It was not a da'wah stall because there was no table," he explained, in response to my puzzled expression. "If there was a table," he continued, "then it would be a da'wah stall. But there was no table, so it's just da'wah, not a da'wah *stall*."[15] He flashed me a mischievous grin as he said this, as if to underscore his duplicitous remark – and the challenge facing law enforcers who sought to curtail his activism.

The escalation in government pressure against the Emigrants had another unintended consequence. Facing increased pressure from the police at home, some activists decided they could no longer practice their contentious politics in the United Kingdom. With the *khilafah* now declared, they felt obligated to help Abu Bakr al-Baghdadi and his followers build the caliphate. A number of them fled to Iraq and Syria; others were caught trying. Al-Muhajiroun, which helped establish London as the center of the European Salafi-jihadi scene ten years earlier, now emerged as a small, but significant channel in the flow of British citizens to the Islamic State.

A final reason why I focus on the Emigrants is because I can. As a social scientist who combines ethnography, process tracing, and network analysis, I rely on primary source data to document activists' beliefs and behaviors and the cultural processes through which they acquire them. One of the biggest challenges in studying radicalization and political violence is accessing respondents who are willing to discuss their principles and practices – and who can do so in meaningful ways.[16] Those with the right cultural expertise are typically insiders in a group or counterculture that faces substantial pressure. Often these people are suspicious of outsiders who do not share their world views. Nor are they particularly eager to share their hard-wrought experience with them.

As a research subject, al-Muhajiroun largely defies these expectations. I originally accessed the Emigrants in September 2007, hoping to get as close as possible to a cultural group engaged in radicalization, and – if I were "lucky" – political violence. At the time I saw the network as a proxy for al-Qaeda-inspired extremism, given its already well-earned reputation as a militant group seeking to establish the caliphate. When I first met a leading activist and three of his young students at a park in Woolwich, South London, not far from where Michael Adebolajo would later murder Lee Rigby, I could not

---

[15] Interview with leading activist, Stratford, East London, December 13, 2014; field notes, da'wah stall, Stratford, East London, December 13, 2014.

[16] Michael Kenney, "Learning from the 'Dark Side': Identifying, Accessing, and Interviewing Illicit Non-State Actors," in *Conducting Terrorism Field Research: A Guide*, edited by Adam Dolnik (New York: Routledge, 2013), p. 29; Wiktorowicz, *Radical Islam Rising*, pp. 30–31; and H. Russell Bernard, *Research Methods in Anthropology: Qualitative and Quantitative Approaches*, 4th edition (Lanham, MD: Altamira, 2006), p. 146.

have foreseen the rise of the Islamic State and how closely the activist network would come to approximate Salafi-jihadi terrorism and insurgency. What
I could see from my first encounter was that activists were willing to talk with
me. They saw our discussion as a form of da'wah, obligatory preaching for
which they would be rewarded in the afterlife.[17]

When I returned to London three years later, I discovered that all three
students were not only still involved in al-Muhajiroun, each had risen to
become a prominent activist in the network.[18] They remembered me and our
earlier meeting. More importantly, they remembered that I kept my promise of
protecting the confidentiality of what they told me that afternoon.[19] With the
blessing of network leaders, these and other gatekeepers opened their world to
me, introducing me to additional respondents, inviting me to observe them at
da'wah stalls and demonstrations, even tolerating my presence at private talks.
"This is Michael Kenney," one of them said as he introduced me to a small
group of supporters early on in my field work. "It's okay to talk with him. We
have a relationship."[20]

I spent the next four-and-a-half years building my relationship with these
and other respondents. The activists I interviewed and observed during my
trips to London are the experts of their social setting and culture. They understand better than most, certainly better than many of the journalists and think
tank "experts" who write about them, why they do what they do, and how
they do it. In this book, I draw on their interviews and stories to trace the processes by which they join the activist network, how they radicalize into full
membership or "intellectual affiliation," and why so many of them eventually
decide to leave.[21] Before exploring these processes in the following chapters,
in the remainder of this one I elaborate upon al-Muhajiroun's confrontational
activism, discuss activists' decision to ally themselves with the Islamic State,
describe the network's connections to political violence within and outside
Britain, and briefly consider whether, as many believe, the Emigrants are a
"conveyor belt" to political violence.

---

[17] Field notes, Woolwich, South London, September 22, 2007.

[18] Field notes, Leyton, East London, November 6, 2010, Whitechapel, East London, November 9,
2010, and Bethnal Green, East London, November 28, 2010.

[19] I continued to follow this human subjects' protection throughout my field research. This
is why I refer to my respondents anonymously throughout this book. Doing so makes it
difficult, if not impossible, for other researchers to replicate my findings. I accept this as a
necessary trade-off to encourage my respondents to discuss their experiences in high-risk
activism.

[20] Field notes, Whitechapel, East London, November 9, 2010. Also, see Kenney, "Learning from
the 'Dark Side'," p. 30.

[21] For more on process tracing, see Goertz and Mahoney, *A Tale of Two Cultures*, pp. 106–109,
and Alexander L. George and Andrew Bennett, *Case Studies and Theory Development in the
Social Sciences* (Cambridge, MA: MIT Press, 2005). I discuss my research methods and strategy
of analysis in more detail in the methodological appendix.

THE NETWORK'S IDEOLOGICAL STRUGGLE

At the time of the September 2014 police raids, al-Muhajiroun had been calling Britain to the caliphate for over eighteen years. In January 1996, Omar Bakri, Anjem Choudary, and a third activist who later left formed the Emigrants as a splinter group of Hizb ut-Tahrir. Bakri led the British branch of this transnational Islamist party for a decade before falling out with Hizb ut-Tahrir's global leaders over his aggressive activism.[22] In selecting the name of their new group, Bakri and his followers appropriated a term with deep historical significance for Muslims.[23] In the early years of Islam, "the Emigrants" referred to the Prophet Mohammed's companions who accompanied him in exile following his expulsion from Mecca. Just as these original *Muhajiroun* helped Mohammed establish a base for his new religion in Medina, from where he and his followers later conquered Mecca and much of the Arabian peninsula, so Bakri and his followers hoped they might play a similar role in bringing the Islamic state to Britain – and the rest of the world. "The main purpose of the organization," explained a leading activist years before Abu Bakr al-Baghdadi's June 2014 declaration, "is to call society to Islam, command good and forbid evil, and to establish the *khilafah* [caliphate], which is the Islamic state."[24]

Reflecting its origins as an offshoot of Hizb ut-Tahrir, al-Muhajiroun has always displayed Islamist leanings, particularly in its devotion to public activism, which quietist Salafis abhor. After 9/11 Omar Bakri and his followers shifted to a Salafi orientation in their theological beliefs when Bakri became increasingly influenced by Abu Qatadah, Abu Hamza, and other Salafi-jihadi preachers. But Bakri, and by extension the Emigrants, continued to follow some of Hizb ut-Tahrir's views, including the need for a military coup to take power in certain countries, such as Pakistan. Bakri's ability to combine Islamist and Salafi influences while maintaining his network's ideological cohesion was a remarkable achievement and reflects the strong influence he wielded over his followers. Yet, as I discuss in Chapter 5, Bakri's embrace of Salafi fundamentalism was too much for some supporters, who left the network over this. At the same time, his theological transformation from Islamist to Salafi led others to join al-Muhajiroun, including some activists who had been active in Abu Hamza's Supporters of Shariah group.

---

[22] Interviews with leading activists, Ilford, East London, December 12, 2014, Leyton, East London, November 4, 2010, Ilford, East London, November 13, 2010, and Walthamstow, East London, December 2, 2010. Also, see Wiktorowicz, *Radical Islam Rising*, pp. 8–9; and Mahan Abedin, "Al-Muhajiroun in the UK: An Interview with Sheikh Omar Bakri Mohammed," *Jamestown Monitor* (March 23, 2004), www.jamestown.org/news_details.php?news_id=38 [Accessed November 24, 2007].

[23] Interview with leading activist, Ilford, East London, December 12, 2014. Also, interview with Brixton Salafi, Brixton, South London, October 23, 2007; and Kylie Baxter, *British Muslims and the Call to Global Jihad* (Victoria, Australia: Monash University Press, 2007), p. 53.

[24] Interview with leading activist, Leyton, East London, November 4, 2010.

Bakri's Emigrants have always seen themselves as engaged in an ideological battle between their Salafi-Islamist ideology and Western ideas of liberal democracy and free-market capitalism. "Our aim," notes one activist, "is to break down the ideological barrier that the West has put in our way to implement the shariah."[25] "The Americans are not just fighting people," observes a second respondent, referring to the War on Terror. "They're fighting a phenomenon, this ideology... That's why many times you hear reports in the media saying, 'It's a battle of hearts and minds.'"[26] "We can see clearly that there is a war taking place against Islam and Muslims," adds a third activist in a lecture posted on YouTube. "The war against Islam has many fronts. We see the physical warfare taking place against Islam in Afghanistan to Iraq to Syria to Burma to Mali to Somalia and many other places, even right here in the UK, from the arrests of many Muslims. But there is a warfare that is taking place against Islam by the *kuffar* [non-believers] which is not as easy to spot... the ideological warfare."[27]

These allusions to warfare and fighting are not rhetorical slips of the tongue. The Emigrants believe they are engaged in a clash of civilizations between "the camp of truth" and "the camp of falsehood." Anjem Choudary explains what this means in a lecture posted on YouTube: "there are two camps in the world today... There are those people who believe sovereignty and supremacy belongs to Allah and at the head of that is the *Khalifah* [Caliph] Ibrahim, Abu Bakr al-Baghdadi... And in the other camp there are those people who believe sovereignty and supremacy belong to man and at the head of this camp at the current time is Barack Obama." Choudary casts the battle between the two camps in apocalyptic terms: "[T]his struggle will continue... until Yawm al-Din [the Day of Judgment] on every level, intellectual, political, military, economic. And the Muslims, *inshallah* [God willing] will prevail."[28]

As frontline soldiers in this cosmic battle, network activists are taught to "fight for the cause," explains "Abdul," the cause being "to establish Islam everywhere."[29] This involves three forms of activism: *da'wah*, *hisbah*, and *jihad*.[30] Da'wah refers to "calling society to Islam," which for al-Muhajiroun

[25] Interview with activist, Leyton, East London, November 14, 2010.

[26] Interview with activist, Whitechapel, East London, November 9, 2010.

[27] Network activists often use the term "kuffar" in a derogatory way to refer to non-Muslims. Abu Sayfullah, "What is a[n] Extremist Muslim | Abu Sayfullaah," YouTube video (July 24, 2014), www.youtube.com/watch?v=BLUbzbfafQ4&feature=share [Accessed October 8, 2014].

[28] Anjem Choudary, "Duties of the Khalifah and Conditions for his Removal," YouTube video (November 2014). Before "Caliph Ibrahim's" declaration of the Islamic State, Choudary used to say that Osama bin Laden was the leader of the camp of truth.

[29] Interview with "Abdul," former activist, Whitechapel, East London, June 18, 2011.

[30] The Emigrants are not the only Salafi-jihadis who privilege these three forms of activism. For an interesting discussion of how the Egyptian Islamic Group, which assassinated Anwar Sadat in 1981, practiced all three, see Roel Meijer, "Commanding Right and Forbidding Wrong as a

FIGURE O.1 Al-Muhajiroun activists engage passersby at a da'wah stall. Supporters of Sunnah was a spin-off group that focused on street preaching.
Photograph by Michael Kenney.

means preaching its Salafi-Islamist world view to Muslims and non-Muslims alike (see Figure 0.1).[31] Hisbah means "commanding good and forbidding evil," or demonstrating in public on social and political issues activists consider important (see Figure 0.2). And jihad means "fighting in the way of God," supporting the armed *and* ideological struggle of Muslims against non-Muslim oppressors, either to remove the latter from Muslim lands or to impose Islamic law on reluctant populations. Given al-Muhajiroun's adoption of the Salafi creed and methodology and its consistent support for jihad in Afghanistan, Iraq, Syria, and other war zones, I consider its activists to be "Salafi-jihadis."[32]

Principle of Social Action: The Case of the Egyptian al-Jama'a al-Islamiyya," in *Global Salafism*, pp. 189–220.

[31] The da'wah practiced by the Emigrants and other activist groups differs from traditional quietist proselytizing. Unlike quietist Muslims, the religious interpretation promoted by Islamic activists is deeply informed by their political and ideological beliefs. See Wiktorowicz, *Radical Islam Rising*, p. 50, and Janine A. Clark, "Islamist Women in Yemen: Informal Nodes of Activism," in *Islamic Activism: A Social Movement Theory Approach*, edited by Quintan Wiktorowicz (Bloomington, IN: Indiana University Press, 2004), pp. 168–9.

[32] In their interviews and conversations, activists often identify themselves as "Salafis" in their *aqeedah*, or theological beliefs. They also follow the Salafi *manhaj* or methodology in their dress and physical appearance. Interviews with former activist, Walthamstow, East London, July 17, 2012, and several different activists, Woolwich, South London, September 22, 2007 and December 2, 2010, Leyton, East London, November 6, 2010 and December 9, 2010, Lewisham, South London, December 11, 2010 and June 18, 2011, Hounslow, West London, June 28, 2011 and September 4, 2013, Whitechapel, East London, June 22, 2011, Stratford, East London, June 25, 2011, Wembley Central, West London, September 5, 2013, and Skype, March 23, 2011.

FIGURE 0.2 Al-Muhajiroun activists perform "hisbah" near the Lebanese embassy in London. Led by speaker Anjem Choudary, they are protesting Omar Bakri Mohammed's arrest in Lebanon. To Choudary's immediate right is Bakri's son, Mohammed Fostok, who later joined the Islamic State in Iraq and Syria, where he was reportedly killed.
Photograph by Michael Kenney.

But for them jihad is as much an ideological struggle as a military one. Like their companions in the larger Salafi-jihadi movement, activists seek to replace "sovereignty of man," which they view as hopelessly decadent and corrupt, with their utopian vision of "sovereignty of God."[33]

For much of its twenty-year existence, al-Muhajiroun has strived to make God's sovereignty supreme through ideological struggle. This has meant engaging in what activists call "jihad of the tongue," speaking out against what they see as the anti-Islamic policies of Great Britain, the United States, and other countries, rather than jihad of the sword, traveling overseas to participate in actual fighting. "We can't all go to Iraq and Afghanistan," explains a leading activist, highlighting how he and his colleagues have tried to pursue their activism through legal channels. "And we can't give money because we'd

---

Also see Sheikh Omar Bakri Muhammad, *The Islamic Verdict on Jihad and the Methodology to Establish the Khilafah* (n.d.), p. 29; and Muslims Against Crusades, "What is the Meaning of Jihad?," (July 24, 2011), www.muslimsagainstcrusades.com/jihad/what-is-the-meaning-of-jihad [Accessed August 16, 2011].

[33] Interviews with leading activist, Leyton, East London, November 4, 2010, and other activists, Walthamstow, East London, December 2, 2010, Whitechapel, East London, June 16, 2011, and Wembley Central, West London, September 5, 2013. Also, see Fawaz A. Gerges, *ISIS: A History* (Princeton, NJ: Princeton University Press, 2016), p. 223.

be funding terrorism abroad, but what we can do is condemn the British government and their policies."[34]

Wielding the sword of jihad is the duty of groups like al-Qaeda and ISIS, with whom the Emigrants affiliate ideologically, not operationally. "Al-Qaeda is fulfilling its responsibility in Iraq and Afghanistan and elsewhere physically and militarily," observes the same leading activist, in a separate interview. "We believe we're fulfilling our role, not militarily but verbally. Our responsibility is to condemn and expose the foreign policy, condemn the evil taking place... we're singing the same tune as al-Qaeda, verbally."[35] "It's not just a physical thing, there's also an intellectual side to it," clarifies another respondent. "Da'wah and jihad go hand-in-hand."[36] "If a man can't reach the battlefield for security reasons or something like that," adds a third activist, "he will do his utmost to support it verbally, financially, however he can."[37] "That's why Allah said in the Qur'an all of you shouldn't go to the battlefield," notes a different leading activist. "Some of you should remain behind to teach the people about their *deen* [religion]... they are both struggling for the same objective. We're doing it here, in the ideological battlefield. They're doing it in the military battlefield."[38]

Since its creation al-Muhajiroun has waged ideological battle by staging da'wah stalls, demonstrations, and public conferences that push the boundaries of free speech and association in Great Britain. The group's protests and conferences are often deliberately confrontational, to attract attention from the media and provoke "moral shock" among potential supporters and British society.[39] During demonstrations activists express the outrage they feel against British and American foreign policy and the West's perceived "war on Islam." They do this by shouting provocative slogans and displaying gruesome pictures of mutilated and malnourished children, who they claim are victims of Western violence against Muslims. In staging such incendiary displays, activists seek to shock busy shoppers and bystanders and call attention to their cause. "Our policy is to spread Islam to the max," one leading activist explains. Referring to passersby, he adds, "That's why we have to be provocative, to make them

---

[34] Interview with leading activist, Ilford, East London, November 13, 2010. Also, interviews with other activists, Leyton, East London, December 9, 2010, and Whitechapel, East London, November 9, 2010.

[35] Interview with leading activist, Ilford, East London, November 29, 2010.

[36] Interview with rank-and-file activist, Lewisham, South London, December 11, 2010.

[37] Interview with veteran activist, Leyton, East London, November 6, 2010.

[38] Interview with leading activist, Leyton, East London, November 4, 2010.

[39] On moral shock, see James M. Jasper, *The Art of Moral Protest* (Chicago: University of Chicago Press, 1997); James M. Jasper and Jane Poulsen, "Recruiting Strangers and Friends: Moral Shocks and Social Networks in Animal Rights and Antinuclear Protest," *Social Problems* 42 (November 1995), pp. 493–512; Quintan Wiktorowicz and Karl Kaltenthaler, "The Rationality of Radical Islam," *Political Science Quarterly* 121, no. 2 (2006), pp. 295–319.

wake up, to make them think."[40] "We have enough difficulty getting people just to come to demonstrations," confirms a veteran activist, explaining his inflammatory speech at one demonstration, which led to his conviction for inciting murder for terrorist purposes. "We were at the mosque calling for Muslims to support the cause over in Iraq... According to the prosecution, we were calling people to go to Iraq, to become involved in fighting. But I was just hoping to wake them up."[41]

Under the stewardship of Omar Bakri Mohammed and leading activists like Anjem Choudary, Mizanur "Abu Baraa" Rahman, and Omar "Abu Izzadeen" Brooks, the Emigrants mastered the art of waking people up through provocation and moral shock. To mark the first anniversary of the September 11 terrorist attacks, activists staged a conference at the Finsbury Park Mosque, then led by Abu Hamza, Bakri's competitor and sometime collaborator. With its confrontational title, "A Towering Day in History," the event drew substantial media attention, in Britain and internationally.[42] After a similar conference – one called "The Magnificent 19," scheduled for the second anniversary of the attacks – was cancelled, network activists organized a press conference during which one of them spoke of the "good deed" committed by the "magnificent 19 martyrs."[43] British politicians accused activists of glorifying terrorism, which they denied. Years later, mindful that glorifying terrorism was now illegal, in part because of their own provocations, respondents continued to deny they sought to glorify the 9/11 attacks. However, they did acknowledge that they saw these public events as "a marketing tool... a provocation to generate public awareness" and "a way of attracting the media" and young people to their activism.[44]

In keeping with their strategy of media jihad, the Emigrants often sought to manipulate the media when promoting their activism. Prior to hosting their high-profile events, leading activists would text and email their press contacts, encouraging them to attend. This enhanced the spread, if not necessarily the appeal, of their message through broad media coverage. Activists understood that most reporters portrayed them as outrageous fanatics, but they accepted this as a necessary cost for amplifying their message to the widest possible audience, including potential supporters. Early on in my field work, I asked one leading activist about recent press coverage alleging he was

---

[40] Interview with leading activist, Walthamstow, East London, December 2, 2010.

[41] Interview with veteran activist, Stratford, East London, November 29, 2010.

[42] Interviews with veteran and rank-and-file activists, Southall, West London, June 28, 2011, and Wembley Central, West London, September 5, 2013; Sean O'Neill, "'Towering Day' conference at mosque," *Daily Telegraph* (September 9, 2002), p.11; James Abdulaziz Brown, "Muslim radicals plan meeting about 9/11," *Boston Globe* (September 10, 2002), p. A7; *Bristol Evening Post*, "Tense standoff at conference held in mosque," (September 12, 2002), p. 4.

[43] Paul Harris, "September 11 and in the heart of London, the apologists for terror peddle their poison," *Daily Mail* (September 12, 2003), p. 8; Alan Freeman, "19 terrorists Islamic heroes, extremists say," *Globe and Mail* (September 11, 2003).

[44] Interview with veteran activist, Southall, West London, June 28, 2011.

responsible for radicalizing a British-Iraqi suicide bomber who blew himself up in Stockholm. He shrugged off my concern. "There is no such thing as bad press," he responded. "It's all good press because it focuses attention on the cause." When I pressed him, asking if he wasn't worried the media were demonizing him and his followers, he dismissed my suggestion: "Other people… will come forward to verify the press accounts" and see that he and his fellow activists are not the brutes the media have made them out to be.[45]

When these "sincere people" approach the network to verify sensational media reports, activists try to recruit them to the cause. "Ahmed," a veteran activist I interacted with on multiple occasions, claims "the benefit we get from the people we recruit" through news reports "far outweighs the harm that is caused by the people who don't like us."[46] Even the most scandalous reports in British tabloids like *The Sun* and *The Daily Mirror* enhance al-Muhajiroun's media jihad, by creating the misimpression that the activist network is larger than it is and representative of Britain's diverse Muslim communities. "The tabloid media give Anjem Choudary exactly what he wants," complains a US government official who followed the network closely for years. "They give him the attention he needs to make his movement seem larger – and more threatening – than it really is."[47]

In addition to working their press contacts, activists seek to maximize their media coverage by timing their rallies to coincide with major events, such as the London Summer Olympics and the royal wedding of Prince William and Catherine Middleton.[48] To mark the tenth anniversary of the 9/11 attacks, activists demonstrated outside the US embassy, where they burned a replica of the American flag and chanted "burn, burn USA."[49] To protest the 2010 anniversary of Armistice Day, when people across Great Britain and Europe, mourn

---

[45] Field notes, Centre for Islamic Services, Whitechapel, East London, December 16, 2010. Also, interview with veteran activist, Southall, West London, June 28, 2011, and Martin Evans, Gordon Rayner and Andy Bloxham, "Stockholm bomber: family blame Britain for radicalization," *Daily Telegraph* (December 13, 2010), www.telegraph.co.uk/news/uknews/terrorism-in-the-uk/8200044/Stockholm-bomber-family-blame-Britain-for-radicalisation.html [Accessed December 14, 2010].

[46] Interview with "Ahmed," veteran activist, Tottenham, North London, December 4, 2010.

[47] Interview with US government official, Mayfair, Central London, December 3, 2010.

[48] Michael Holden, "Radical Muslims plan opening ceremony protest outside park," *Chicago Tribune* (July 27, 2012), www.chicagotribune.com/sports/olympics/sns-rt-us-oly-ceremony-protest-day0bre86q0zt-20120727,0,3246587.story [Accessed July 27, 2012]; Muslims Against Crusades, press release, "Official Announcement: Muslims to Disrupt Royal Wedding," (March 26, 2011); and Ryan Wilkinson, "'Muslim extremist who warned of terror attack on Kate and William's wedding worked on Tube'," *Daily Mirror* (August 6, 2014), www.mirror.co.uk/news/uk-news/muslim-extremist-who-warned-terror-4007716#.U-VVSqPNO9U [Accessed August 9, 2014].

[49] Andy Bloxham, "9/11 anniversary: Muslim protesters burn US flag outside embassy in London," *Daily Telegraph* (September 11, 2011), www.telegraph.co.uk/news/worldnews/september-11-attacks/8755834/911-anniversary-Muslim-protesters-burn-US-flag-outside-embassy-in-London.html [Accessed September 19, 2011].

the loss of soldiers who have died in war since World War I, activists gathered outside the Royal Albert Hall, where they held signs reading "Afghanistan: The Graveyard of Empires," and "British Soldiers Burn in Hell!" The protest reached its peak when activists chanted "British troops murderers" and "burn, burn murderers," while setting two symbolic poppies on fire.[50] When these incendiary protests received widespread media coverage, as they often did, activists considered it a success, encouraging them to stage even more provocative protests the next time. Ahmed confirmed this when asked whether the media response to the 2010 Armistice Day demonstration, which he helped organize, gave activists an incentive to be provocative: "Yeah, exactly. We can't get to the khilafah [caliphate] without creating the public awareness," including through provocation. "This is one of the ways which has been very successful for us."[51]

Creating the public awareness involves lots of da'wah and hisbah. The Emigrants' activism is relatively cheap, but calling society to Islam and commanding good and forbidding evil still requires resources. The major resource constraint facing the Emigrants is human labor. Fortunately for the network, activists give their labor freely, without receiving a salary or charging for their services. They do this willingly because they are taught by Omar Bakri and other leaders that any action they perform on behalf of their call is "rewardable" in the afterlife.[52] Beyond this free labor, however, "the da'wah still takes money," explains a veteran activist at a stall he is running in Stratford. Printing leaflets for distribution at stalls, creating signs and banners for waving at demonstrations, and renting halls for hosting public conferences all require funds. "It takes money to cover all of this stuff," confirms the da'wah stall emir.[53]

How does al-Muhajiroun cover these costs? Primarily from regular donations by activists and occasional contributions by other supporters.[54] Britain's tabloid media often portray the Emigrants as a bunch of welfare-exploiting slackers who live off state benefits, but many activists in my sample were gainfully employed. One of these respondents was in charge of collecting donations for the network's "halaqah" or study circle in Whitechapel. He

---

[50] The poppy flower is a popular symbol used in Armistice Day ceremonies. Many Britons wear the small red flower on their lapel in the days and weeks leading up to the anniversary. Field notes, Kensington, Central London, November 11, 2010; *BBC News*, "Man guilty of burning poppies at Armistice Day protest," (March 7, 2011), www.bbc.co.uk/news/uk-england-london-12664346 [Accessed March 10, 2011]; Alan Cowell, "100 years after World War I began, Europe remembers its end," *New York Times* (November 11, 2014), www.nytimes.com/2014/11/12/world/europe/europe-armistice-day-world-war.html [Accessed November 12, 2014].

[51] Interview with Ahmed, Tottenham, North London, December 4, 2010.

[52] Interviews with Haroon, Westminster, Central London, June 14, 2011, and rank-and-file activist, Hounslow, West London, September 4, 2013.

[53] Interview with veteran activist, Stratford, East London, December 6, 2010.

[54] Interviews with veteran activist, Whitechapel, East London, June 17, 2011, and different rank-and-file activists, Stratford, East London, June 27, 2011, and Hounslow, West London, September 4, 2013. Also, see Abedin, "Al-Muhajiroun in the UK."

explained how the collections process worked: "I made a list of every member's name. If you were working or not working, you had to give some money." The amount of cash activists gave him depended on how much they worked. "If you were working full time it was £100 a month," around $160 dollars at the time. "If you were working part time, it was £50 a month, if you wasn't working, it was as much as you could give." Activists on welfare gave around "£20 a month." External supporters typically made larger contributions, but less frequently. The respondent gave the example of a local businessman who was an important supporter. "He wasn't a regular giver, but every now and again, he gave £500, or £1000."[55]

Activists also raised money by selling items at da'wah stalls and public conferences. The items they sold included Omar Bakri's self-published booklets, along with cassettes, compact discs, and DVDs of lectures by Bakri and other leading activists. They even sold food, perfume, and clothing at larger public conferences. Activists were allowed to keep some money from these sales, but most of the funds went to al-Muhajiroun.[56] Respondents were unclear about what happened to the money they raised. "I never knew where it went," explains Abdul, the former activist, referring to money from the literature he sold at da'wah stalls in London. "What I knew, it was going to the Muslim countries who were suffering... Or it may have gone in Bakri's pocket, to be honest."[57]

FROM JIHAD OF THE TONGUE TO JIHAD OF THE SWORD

Despite al-Muhajiroun's commitment to peaceful activism and the ideological struggle, a number of activists have gone beyond jihad of the tongue to engage in jihad of the sword. Like other Salafi-jihadis, network activists subscribe to a "covenant of security" that prevents them from attacking the people with whom they live, as long as the British government protects their lives and livelihoods.[58] Yet this verbal agreement does not cover conflicts overseas, particularly when activists believe Western armies have "invaded Muslim lands."

[55] Interview with former activist "Salman," Poplar, East London, July 24, 2015. Also, interviews with former activists Abdul, Whitechapel, East London, June 18, 2011, and Rashid, Whitechapel, East London, June 26, 2011.

[56] Interviews with former activists Ali and Maryam, Hounslow, West London, June 21, 2011, and Rashid, Whitechapel, East London, June 26, 2011.

[57] Interview with Abdul, Whitechapel, East London, June 18, 2011.

[58] This concept comes from Islamic scripture, specifically the sixth verse of the ninth chapter in the Qur'an, where God reportedly commands Mohammed to grant his protection to disbelievers who seek it. See *Interpretation of the Meanings of the Noble Qur'án in the English Language*, revised edition, summarized by Muhammad Taqi-ud-Din Al-Hilali and Muhammad Muhsin Khan (Riyadh, Saudi Arabia: Maktaba Dar-us-Salam, 2007), p. 206. Other Salafi-jihadis, including the prominent al-Qaeda ideologue Sayyid Imam al-Sharif, also accept the covenant of security. See Maher, *Salafi-Jihadism*, p. 48.

This was dramatically revealed to me one night when I was hanging out with activists and supporters at their educational center in Whitechapel, East London. During an interview with one of my gatekeepers, I noticed several young supporters enthusiastically passing around a copy of Abdullah Azzam's *Defence of the Muslim Lands*, which calls on Muslims to join the fighting in Afghanistan and Palestine. My curiosity caught the attention, and wrath, of several activists who angrily questioned me about the purpose of my research. Luckily the gatekeeper came to my defense, calming his colleagues and explaining to me, "Michael, look, here we have the covenant of security, but overseas is another matter. The book refers to situations that are overseas."[59]

A number of activists have pursued these overseas situations by engaging in jihad of the sword in Afghanistan and Palestine. During the run up to the American-led invasion of Afghanistan in 2001, network leaders reportedly encouraged activists to fight on behalf of the Taliban. Some of them took the advice. At the time the Emigrants maintained a branch in Lahore, Pakistan, where activists allegedly provided shelter to British militants on their way to fight in Afghanistan. According to news reports, several activists who reached the battlefield and fought on behalf of the Taliban were later killed or wounded in American airstrikes.[60] These included Afzal Munir and Aftab Manzoor, both of whom had been active in the network's Luton branch before leaving al-Muhajiroun and ridiculing its leaders.

Other activists engaged in attacks outside war zones. In April 2003, Omar Sharif, a British Muslim who distributed leaflets at al-Muhajiroun events in Derby, and Asif Hanif, a young man from Hounslow who was friends with Sharif, journeyed to the Gaza Strip, where they met with members of Hamas' military wing, the Izz al-Din al-Qassem Brigades. During the Second Intifada, the Qassem Brigades carried out dozens of suicide bombings in Israel and the West Bank. A week after entering Gaza, the two British citizens traveled to Mike's Place, a popular bar in Tel Aviv. They waited outside the bar until it filled with patrons before executing their attack. Hanif successfully detonated his suicide bomb at the bar's entrance, ripping his body to shreds and killing two musicians and a bartender. Dozens more were injured. Sharif tried to detonate his bomb vest but it failed to explode. He assaulted a security guard and fled. Twelve days later, local officials pulled his body from the Mediterranean Sea.[61]

---

[59] Field notes, Centre for Islamic Services, Whitechapel, East London, June 16, 2011.

[60] Wiktorowicz, *Radical Islam Rising*: p. 7; Simcox, Stuart, and Ahmed, *Islamist Terrorism*, pp. 377–83; Paul Harris, Martin Bright, and Burhan Wazir, "Five Britons killed in 'jihad brigade'," *The Observer* (27 October 2001), www.guardian.co.uk/world/2001/oct/28/terrorism .afghanistan3 [Accessed August 9, 2012]; Danielle Demetriou and Patrick Sawer, "'More British Muslims to fight for the Taliban,'" *The Evening Standard* (October 29, 2001), p. 1.

[61] Stephanie Clifford, "At Arab bank's terrorism trial, victim recalls seeing suicide bomber's body," *New York Times* (August 21, 2014), www.nytimes.com/2014/08/22/nyregion/at-banks-terrorism-trial-victim-testifies-about-suicide-bombing-in-israeli-bar.html [Accessed August 22, 2014]; Sue Clough, "Suicide bomber made will before Israel mission," *Daily Telegraph*

In recent years the flow of British activists to foreign lands increased from a periodic drip to a steady dribble. Contributing to activists' willingness to emigrate was not only the escalation of the civil war in Syria and the reemergence of ISIS, but legal problems related to their activism in the United Kingdom. As government authorities turned up the heat against the Emigrants, more and more activists became convinced they could no longer call society to Islam and command good and forbid evil in Britain. "People who are in that situation need to go to a place where they can fulfill their duty," explains a leading activist. "Because if you can't carry da'wah in England then you will go somewhere else where you can."[62] In March 2014, several months before ISIS declared its caliphate, Abu Rahin Aziz, a prominent activist who participated in the network's da'wah stalls and protests and maintained one of its most popular websites, fled to Syria while on bail for assaulting a bystander at a stall in London's West End.[63] The following month, another activist, Mirza Tariq Ali, skipped bail over a similar violent disorder offense stemming from his activism. He headed to Iraq. Unlike his friend, Ali did not reach his destination. He was caught in Croatia and deported to his native Pakistan, where he soon became a commander for the Pakistani Taliban. After the Taliban massacred 132 children by attacking a school in Ali and other Taliban fighters were killed in a series of counter-terrorism operations in March 2015.[64] Meanwhile Aziz joined ISIS after reaching Syria, becoming a fighter in one of its paramilitary units. He fought in several battles and repeatedly used his social media accounts to threaten terrorist attacks in Britain. In July 2015 he was reportedly killed by an American drone strike near Raqqa.[65]

(April 29, 2004), www.telegraph.co.uk/news/uknews/1460565/Suicide-bomber-made-will-before-Israel-mission.html [Accessed October 9, 2014]; and Wiktorowicz, *Radical Islam Rising*, p. 1.

[62] Author interview with leading activist, Skype, August 28, 2014.

[63] Steve Swann and Secunder Kermani, "Pair under police investigation skip bail 'to fight in Syria'," *BBC News* (June 18, 2014), www.bbc.com/news/uk-27911081 [Accessed June 23, 2014]; Julia Sutton, "Luton Muslims preachers, including ringleader Abu Aziz, face jail after being found guilty of affray at the Old Bailey," *Luton on Sunday* (June 19, 2014), www.luton-dunstable.co.uk/Luton-Muslims-preachers-including-ringleader-Abu-Aziz-face-jail-guilty-affray-Old-Bailey/story-21703392-detail/story.html [Accessed May 15, 2015]; *Luton On Sunday*, "Luton radical Abu Aziz has joined ISIS in Syria," (January 20, 2015), www.luton-dunstable.co.uk/Luton-radical-Abu-Aziz-joined-ISIS-Syria/story-25892785-detail/story.html [Accessed May 15, 2015].

[64] Robert Mendick, Robert Verkaik, and Duncan Gardham, "NHS doctor flees UK to join Taliban," *Daily Telegraph* (November 15, 2014), www.telegraph.co.uk/news/uknews/terrorism-in-the-uk/11233736/NHS-doctor-flees-UK-to-join-Taliban.html [Accessed December 11, 2016]; Robert Verkaik and Robert Mendick, "NHS doctor who became Taliban commander killed 'in drone strike'," *Daily Telegraph* (March 14, 2015), www.telegraph.co.uk/news/worldnews/islamic-state/11472703/NHS-doctor-who-became-Taliban-commander-killed-in-drone-strike.html [Accessed May 27, 2015].

[65] Alice Ross, "Death of British jihadi in July drone strike raises 'kill list' questions," *The Guardian* (September 8, 2015), www.theguardian.com/uk-news/2015/sep/08/death-british-jihadi-july-drone-strike-raises-kill-list-questions [Accessed December 11, 2016].

SUPPORTING THE CALIPHATE

When Abu Bakr al-Baghdadi announced the reestablishment of the caliphate on June 29, 2014, it was a watershed moment for al-Muhajiroun. Like Salafi-jihadis throughout the global movement, the Emigrants had to decide whether ISIS's caliphate was authentic and deserving of their support. In Britain, activists had been striving for the caliphate for over eighteen years when Baghdadi declared himself caliph at the Great Mosque in Mosul. After determining that "Caliph Ibrahim" and his organization satisfied the necessary requirements, the Emigrants accepted his leadership unequivocally. "Like it or not he's the leader of all the Muslims," explained a leading activist, referring to the new caliph. "He meets the conditions, so he's a legitimate leader."[66]

In accepting the legitimacy of Baghdadi and the Islamic State, activists stood in stark contrast to Salafi-jihadi preachers like Abu Qatadah al-Filistini, Abu Muhammad al-Maqdisi, and Abu Bashir al-Tartusi, all of who denounced ISIS and its self-declared leader as profane deviations from the prophetic tradition. But the Emigrants prided themselves on their interpretation, which they tied to their long-standing activism. Another leading activist put it this way: "If people who have been working for the khilafah [caliphate] for the past twenty years as their main objective cannot recognize the khalifah [caliph] when he is appointed, then I'm afraid that nobody is going to be able to recognize him."[67]

Indeed, leading activists may have felt that the credibility of their network was at stake in recognizing ISIS. After all, they had been working to establish the Islamic caliphate for years – and now here it was. If al-Muhajiroun failed to support Baghdadi's nascent proto-state, it would have damaged its reputation as being on the vanguard of the Salafi-jihadi movement in Europe. Some network activists appear to have recognized this. In the days leading up to their declaration of support, Anjem Choudary and Mizanur Rahman were urged by influential activists like Siddhartha "Abu Rumaysah" Dhar to proclaim their loyalty to Baghdadi and the Islamic State on social media, saying it would be good for them and the Emigrants. Adding a sense of urgency to their pleas was activists' belief that they needed to declare their support within three days of Baghdadi's announcement. Failing to do so may have risked damaging not only al-Muhajiroun's reputation, but its internal cohesion as well.

Once they decided to support ISIS, Choudary and Rahman recorded separate lectures in which they extolled the virtues of the new state and explained why the juristic and practical conditions for the caliphate and its caliph had been met. Consistent with their nearly twenty years of activism, the Emigrants held rallies and handed out leaflets announcing their support.[68] One of the

[66] Interview with leading activist, Stratford, East London, December 13, 2014.
[67] Interview with leading activist, Skype, August 28, 2014.
[68] LBC News, "Leaflets promoting ISIS handed out in West End," *LBC* (August 13, 2014), www .lbc.co.uk/leaflets-promoting-isis-handed-out-in-west-end-95375 [Accessed August 13, 2014]; Brian Whelan, "The British Muslims who want to live under an Islamic State," *Channel*

network's most visible supporters for the new caliphate was none other than Siddhartha Dhar. Dhar was a key coordinator who served as Choudary's right-hand-man. He was also a close friend and colleague of Mizanur Rahman's. During my field work, Dhar organized many of the network's prominent events and campaigns. After Abu Bakr al-Baghdadi announced the caliphate, Dhar pressured Choudary to support it. He also increased his own media profile, appearing on numerous television programs to express his support for the Islamic State and his desire to emigrate to Syria.[69]

Along with Choudary and his childhood friend Rahman, Dhar was arrested in the September 2014 roundup of al-Muhajiroun leaders. Unlike his two colleagues, however, he fled Britain after being released on bail. Before the authorities realized he was missing, Dhar traveled to Syria with his young family, where he became an insurgent and propagandist for the Islamic State. Like his friend Abu Rahin Aziz, who fled to Syria months earlier and also joined the Islamic State, Dhar became a hero to activists in Britain, who envied him for his ability to reach the caliphate. "I think he's living a much safer, freer life now than any of us," one of these activists told me. "Now he doesn't have to worry about police harassment... every time there's a knock on my door, my children are scared it's the police again... It's a bit ironic, but that's how it is. People don't feel safe here, they feel safer there."[70] When asked if other activists should emigrate to Iraq and Syria, given the establishment of the Islamic State and the continued repression they faced in Britain, this leading activist didn't hesitate to respond: "Absolutely! I don't see any reason why they shouldn't."[71]

Other activists shared these sentiments, transforming themselves from metaphorical "emigrants" into real ones. Around the same time that Siddhartha Dhar made it to the caliphate, one of his fellow activists, Mohammed Haque, traveled to Syria, where he also joined the Islamic State. During my field work, Haque was a regular presence at da'wah stalls and demonstrations. With his large size and intimidating demeanor, he was often assigned to work security. He also acted as a bodyguard for network leaders. Haque was arrested for public disorder at the 2010 Armistice Day demonstration, where he fought

4 *News* (August 15, 2014), www.channel4.com/news/radical-british-muslims-islamic-state-caliphate-iraq-syria [Accessed June 9, 2015].

[69] *BBC News*, "Islamic State: Young British Muslims debate Caliphate," (August 14, 2014), www.bbc.com/news/uk-28772646 [Accessed June 9, 2015]; BBC, "Why are Muslims migrating to the Caliphate?," *News at Six* (August 22, 2014), www.youtube.com/watch?v=3AYo4jAvpYY [Accessed June 9, 2015]; BBC, "What should be done about British Islamic extremists?," *Sunday Morning Live* (August 24, 2014), www.youtube.com/watch?v=ANLmn4iAmYk [Accessed June 9, 2015]; and Whelan, "The British Muslims who want to live under an Islamic state."

[70] Interview with leading activist, Whitechapel, East London, December 11, 2014. Also, interviews with another leading activist, Stratford, East London, December 13, 2014, and veteran activist, Whitechapel, East London, December 14, 2014.

[71] Interview with leading activist, Whitechapel, East London, December 11, 2014.

with several police officers.[72] In Syria, he reportedly became a soldier for the Islamic State and was identified as one of the masked executioners in a propaganda video also featuring Dhar. Haque later appeared in a second ISIS video, allegedly beheading another victim.[73] Haroon Khurshid and Bilal Safdar, two British cousins who attended da'wah stalls and other network events in London, also traveled to Syria during this period, where, like Dhar and Haque, they joined ISIS. Both Khurshid and Safdar were reportedly killed fighting on behalf of the Islamic State.[74] Finally, two of Omar Bakri's own sons, Mohammed and Bilal, emigrated to Syria, where they also became insurgents for the caliphate. In Britain, both sons had been involved in al-Muhajiroun. Mohammed, Bakri's oldest child, was a veteran activist who was highly regarded by his colleagues. He regularly attended da'wah stalls and protests around London, along with Siddhartha Dhar, Abu Rahin Aziz, and Mohammed Haque. The two Bakri brothers reportedly traveled together to Syria, where, like Khurshid and Safdar, they died fighting for the Islamic State.[75]

These are not the only Emigrants to attain "martyrdom" in Iraq and Syria. In February 2014, Abdul Waheed Majeed drove a truck packed with explosives into a prison in Aleppo, killing dozens of people on behalf of *Jabhat al-Nusra*, al-Qaeda's Syrian affiliate. Years earlier, the former activist had been a regular at network events in Crawley, West Sussex, where he organized Omar Bakri's talks, drove him to local venues, and recorded his lectures.[76] In November 2014, Kabir Ahmed drove a truck packed with explosives into an Iraqi police

---

[72] Field notes, Kensington, Central London, November 11, 2010; *BBC News*, "Two men charged over poppy burning protest in London," (December 13, 2010), www.bbc.co.uk/news/uk-england-london-11987236 [Accessed December 13, 2010].

[73] Josh Barrie, "'The Giant': Second British extremist 'identified in ISIS video'," *The Independent* (January 17, 2016), www.independent.co.uk/news/uk/home-news/the-giant-second-british-extremist-identified-in-isis-video-a6818151.html [Accessed October 27, 2016]; Ben Farmer, "Anjem Choudary's bodyguard could be in horrific Islamic State beheading video," *Daily Telegraph* (December 18, 2016), www.telegraph.co.uk/news/2016/12/18/anjem-choudarys-bodyguard-could-horrific-islamic-state-beheading/ [Accessed December 21, 2016].

[74] Field notes, Whitechapel, East London, September 4, 2013, and Westminster, Central London, September 6, 2013; Omar Wahid, "Cousins killed within months of each other in Syria after being radicalised by Anjem Choudary shared a British bride," *Sunday Mail* (August 20, 2016), www.dailymail.co.uk/news/article-3751063/Cousins-killed-months-Syria-radicalised-Choudary-shared-British-bride.html [Accessed August 22, 2016].

[75] Agence France-Presse, "Son of radical cleric Omar Bakri believed killed in Iraq fighting for ISIS," *The Guardian* (December 29, 2015), www.theguardian.com/world/2015/dec/30/omar-bakri-son-killed-iraq-fighting-for-isis-report [Accessed December 12, 2016].

[76] Kirin Randhawa, Justin Davenport, and David Churchill, "Suicide bomber Brit worked as driver for hate cleric Omar Bakri," *The Evening Standard* (February 13, 2014), www.standard.co.uk/news/crime/exclusive-suicide-bomber-brit-worked-as-driver-for-hate-cleric-omar-bakri-9125787.html [Accessed September 22, 2014]; Edward Malnick, "Suspected Syria bomber 'was driver to extremist preacher'," *Daily Telegraph* (February 13, 2014), www.telegraph.co.uk/news/uknews/law-and-order/10636571/Suspected-Syria-bomber-was-driver-to-extremist-preacher.html [Accessed March 16, 2014].

convoy in Baiji, north of Baghdad, killing eight and injuring fifteen more. Before traveling to Syria, where he first joined Jund al-Sham and later switched to ISIS, Ahmed had been active in al-Muhajiroun circles in Derby, East Midlands, distributing leaflets at da'wah stalls in the city.[77] And in November 2016, as the Islamic State sought to defend its shrinking caliphate, Terrence "Khalid" Kelly, drove a truck packed with explosives into an Iraqi Shia militia outside Mosul, killing himself and injuring others. Before blowing himself up on behalf of ISIS, Kelly, a convert to Islam, had been active in al-Muhajiroun for years. He regularly appeared at da'wah stalls and protests around London before returning to his native Dublin, where he led a small group of supporters.[78]

WHEN THE COVENANT OF SECURITY NO LONGER APPLIES

Network leaders stress that they accept the covenant of security in Britain, preventing them from attacking the people with whom they live. But they also insist that abiding by this agreement is an "individual" choice, to be made by each activist. Over the years, a number of activists have decided that the covenant is no longer valid, freeing them to engage in political violence in the United Kingdom. In Operation Crevice, a year before the 7/7 bombings, British authorities disrupted a major terrorist plot involving several former Emigrants, including Omar Khyam and Mohammed Junaid Babar, who later turned state's evidence and testified against Khyam and his colleagues. Khyam became involved in al-Muhajiroun as a teenager in the late 1990s. He attended the group's circles in Crawley, where he studied with Omar Bakri, watched videos of Muslims being killed in Bosnia, and made friends with other activists, several of whom later participated in his bombing plot. In January 2001, Babar joined the Emigrants' small branch in New York City, composed of just a handful of activists. Babar organized group meetings in the basement of his parents' home in Queens, coordinated lectures and demonstrations around New York City, and wrote and distributed leaflets advocating the establishment of a caliphate throughout the West. After 9/11 he moved to Pakistan and later made a fund-raising trip to London, where he attended network events

---

[77] Karen McVeigh and John Plunkett, "Derby mother 'distraught' over reports of jihadi son's death in Iraq," *The Guardian* (November 10, 2014), www.theguardian.com/uk-news/2014/nov/10/kabir-ahmed-mother-distraught-isis-bbc-criticised [Accessed June 2, 2015]; Lucy Osborne, Paul Bentley, and Damien Gayle, "Muslim fundamentalist who was jailed in Britain for saying gays should be stoned to death kills eight in ISIS suicide attack," *Daily Mail* (November 8, 2014), www.dailymail.co.uk/news/article-2826693/British-jihadist-convicted-gay-hate-crimes-blows-ISIS-suicide-mission-Iraq.html [Accessed November 12, 2014].

[78] Interview with veteran activist, Ilford, East London, November 13, 2010; Raf Sanchez, "Irish jihadist 'Khalid Kelly' blows himself up in ISIL suicide bombing near Mosul," *Daily Telegraph* (November 5, 2016), www.telegraph.co.uk/news/2016/11/05/irish-jihadist-khalid-kelly-blows-himself-up-in-islamic-state-su/ [Accessed November 7, 2016]; Peter Stanford, "Preaching from the converted," *The Independent on Sunday* (May 16, 2004), pp. 14–15 and 17–18.

and met some of al-Muhajiroun's British activists. After traveling to Pakistan to receive training in weapons and fertilizer-based explosives, Khyam and the other perpetrators returned to Britain, where they stockpiled over half a ton of ammonium nitrate they planned to use in a series of truck bombings around London. Fortunately, the fertilizer bomb plot was disrupted by the police before Khyam and his colleagues could carry it out.[79]

Several years later, in December 2010, British security forces disrupted another plot involving al-Muhajiroun activists. Still in the early stages of preparation, the plan called for attacks on numerous targets, including Westminster Abbey, the US embassy, and the London Stock Exchange. Several members of the conspiracy attended protests and da'wah stalls organized by Islam4UK and Muslims Against Crusades, two al-Muhajiroun spin-off groups. One perpetrator, Mohammed Rahman Choudury, was deeply involved in Muslims Against Crusades and the Emigrants' halaqah in Whitechapel. He recorded videos documenting protests and provided technical support for lectures by leading activists. I saw him at numerous events during my field work, including a talk by Anjem Choudary at the network's Centre for Islamic Services in Whitechapel only days before authorities disrupted his terrorist plot.[80]

In the run up to the London Summer Olympics in 2012, British authorities uncovered another terrorist conspiracy involving al-Muhajiroun activists. Also, at an early stage of planning, this plot included activists who traveled to Pakistan to receive explosives training and discussed an attack targeting Wootton Bassett, a market town near London where parades were held to honor British troops killed in Afghanistan. Islam4UK and Muslims Against Crusades staged high-profile demonstrations against British troops in the town. Two perpetrators from the Summer Games plot, Jahangir Alom, a former community support officer for the London Metropolitan Police, and Richard Dart,

---

[79] Interviews with leading activists, Leyton, East London, November 4, 2010, Ilford, East London, November 29, 2010, and Walthamstow, East London, December 2, 2010. Also, see "Testimony of Mohammed Junaid Babar," Proceedings at Trial, Superior Court of Justice, Her Majesty the Queen against Mohammad Momin Khawaja, Indictment No. 04-G30282, Volume 1 (June 23, 2008) and Volume 4 (July 2, 2008); Preet Bharara, US Attorney, Southern District of New York, United States v. Mohammed Junaid Babar, 04 Cr. 528 (VM), sentencing request letter (November 23, 2010); *The Guardian*, "UK terror plot: The five found guilty yesterday portrait of an extremist cell," (May 1, 2007), p. 4; Jamie Doward and Andrew Wander, "Terror links: The network," *The Observer* (May 6, 2007), p. 26; and Raffaello Pantucci, *'We Love Death as You Love Life': Britain's Suburban Terrorists* (London: Hurst & Company, 2015), pp. 152–3, 164–72.

[80] Field notes, Kensington, Central London, November 11, 2010, Lewisham, South London, December 11, 2010, and Whitechapel, East London, December 16, 2010; *BBC News*, "Terror suspects in custody over 'pre-Christmas plot'," (December 27, 2010), www.bbc.co.uk/news/uk-12081828 [Accessed January 3, 2011]; John F. Burns and Alan Cowell, "Militants plead guilty in plan to bomb London stock exchange," *New York Times* (February 1, 2012), www.nytimes.com/2012/02/02/world/europe/militants-admit-plan-to-bomb-london-stock-exchange.html [Accessed January 31, 2013].

a recent convert whose radicalization was featured in the BBC documentary, *My Brother the Islamist*, were active in both spin-off groups. Like Mohammed Choudury, Alom and Dart participated in da'wah stalls and demonstrations organized by the activist network in Wootton Bassett and elsewhere until shortly before their arrests.[81]

Tragically, not all terrorist plots in Britain involving the Emigrants were disrupted by the authorities. In May 2013, two former activists shocked Britain by running over Lee Rigby, an off-duty British soldier, with their car before stabbing him to death with butcher knives and a meat cleaver. The younger attacker, Michael Adebowale, participated in network demonstrations outside the US embassy and St Paul's Cathedral only months before the gruesome murder.[82] The older terrorist, Michael Adebolajo, who took the lead in killing and nearly decapitating Rigby, was involved in al-Muhajiroun, on and off, for several years. He participated in a local study circle in Woolwich and attended talks by Omar Bakri and Anjem Choudary. Respondents deny that Adebolajo was a fully committed intellectual affiliate, but they acknowledge that his religious and political views were influenced by his activism.[83]

More recently, another activist, Khurram Butt, reportedly led the terrorist attack on the London Bridge and Borough Market in June 2017. Butt and two accomplices drove a rental van into pedestrians on the bridge on a busy Saturday night before getting out of their vehicle and stabbing customers in nearby bars and restaurants. Prior to his attack, Butt had been a regular at network da'wah stalls, protests, and online chat rooms. He also appeared in a British television documentary featuring other activists, including Siddhartha

---

[81] Field notes, Ilford, East London, November 13, 2010, Kensington, Central London, November 15, 2010, Stratford, East London, November 29, 2010, and Stratford, East London, December 6, 2010. Also, see Shiv Malik, "Muslim convert from BBC documentary pleads guilty to terrorism charges," *The Guardian* (March 15, 2013), www.guardian.co.uk/uk/2013/mar/15/muslim-convert-bbc-documentary-terrorism [Accessed March 15, 2013]; and Vikram Dodd, "Three jailed for discussing possible terror attack," *The Guardian* (April 25, 2013), www.guardian.co.uk/uk/2013/apr/25/three-jailed-possible-terror-attack [Accessed June 11, 2013].

[82] Sean O'Neill, "Cameron confronts 'extremist narrative'," *The Times* (London) (December 20, 2013), p. 9; BBC One, "From jail to jihad?," *Panorama* (May 12, 2014), www.youtube.com/watch?v=_-GJtgGywWc#t=52 [Accessed August 2, 2014].

[83] Interviews with leading and veteran activists, Skype, June 26, 2013, Whitechapel, East London, September 4, 2013, and Wembley Central, West London, September 5, 2013. Also, see Esther Addley and Josh Halliday, "Lee Rigby murder: Adebolajo tells court soldier killed in 'military attack'," *The Guardian* (December 9, 2013), www.theguardian.com/uk-news/2013/dec/09/lee-rigby-murder-accused-adebolajo-religion-is-everything [Accessed December 16, 2013]; Andrew Gilligan, "Woolwich attack: 'Lone wolves' who run with the pack," *Sunday Telegraph* (May 25, 2013), www.telegraph.co.uk/news/uknews/terrorism-in-the-uk/10080864/Woolwich-attack-Lone-wolves-who-run-with-the-pack.html [Accessed June 10, 2013]; Sandra Laville, Peter Walker and Vikram Dodd, "Woolwich attack suspect identified as Michael Adebolajo," *The Guardian* (May 23, 2013), www.guardian.co.uk/uk/2013/may/23/woolwich-attack-suspect-michael-adebolajo [Accessed May 28, 2013]; and Jason Burke, *The New Threat: The Past, Present, and Future of Islamic Militancy* (New York: The New Press, 2015), pp. 172–3.

Dhar, Ricardo MacFarlane, and Mohammed Shamsuddin.[84] Along with his fellow attackers, Butt was shot dead by responding police officers with minutes of initiating the rampage, but not before they killed eight people and wounded at least forty-eight others.[85]

Many observers see these violent plots and attacks as proof that al-Muhajiroun is a "gateway" and "conveyor belt" to violent jihad and terrorism.[86] In making this argument, however, they only consider the few activists and former activists who radicalized to violence, disregarding the many who did not. By focusing exclusively on violent perpetrators, these observers overstate the connection between radicalization and violence in al-Muhajiroun. In the following chapters, I avoid this "selection bias" by including respondents in my interview sample who did not radicalize or become involved in political violence.[87]

This variation is critical to understanding why the Emigrants were not a conveyor belt to violence for two reasons. First, many people who heard al-Muhajiroun's message did not join the activist network. In the late 1990s and early 2000s, thousands of Britons were exposed to the network's public conferences, demonstrations, and da'wah stalls. Few of them became involved in the Emigrants' high-risk activism. Among those who did some

---

[84] Lizzie Dearden, "London attack linked to hate preacher Anjem Choudary's extremist network," *The Independent* (June 6, 2017), www.independent.co.uk/news/uk/home-news/london-attack-bridge-borough-isis-perpetrators-khuram-butt-links-anjem-choudary-documentary-jihadis-a7776101.html [Accessed June 6, 2017]; William Booth and Rick Noack, "Man featured in a documentary called 'The Jihadis Next Door' was one of London attackers," *Washington Post* (June 5, 2017), www.washingtonpost.com/world/europe/man-featured-in-a-documentary-called-the-jihadis-next-door-was-one-of-london-attackers/2017/06/05/6d47f918-49ed-11e7-987c-42ab5745db2e_story.html [Accessed June 6, 2017]; Rukmini Callimachi and Katrin Bennhold, "London attackers slipped by despite an avalanche of warnings," *New York Times* (June 6, 2017), www.nytimes.com/2017/06/06/world/europe/london-assailants-terrorism-warning-signs-fbi.html [Accessed June 7, 2017].

[85] Lizzie Dearden, "London attack: CCTV footage shows terrorists running towards armed police before being shot dead," *The Independent* (June 8, 2017), www.independent.co.uk/News/uk/home-news/london-attack-cctv-footage-police-shot-dead-terrorists-bridge-borough-market-stabbing-isis-khuram-a7778941.html [Accessed June 8, 2017]; Robert Booth, Ian Cobain, Vikram Dodd, Matthew Taylor, and Lisa O'Carroll, "London Bridge attacker named as Khuram Butt," *The Guardian* (June 6, 2017), www.theguardian.com/uk-news/2017/jun/05/london-bridge-attacker-named-as-khuram-butt [Accessed June 6, 2017].

[86] See, for example, Nick Lowles and Joe Mulhall, *Gateway to Terror: Anjem Choudary and the al-Muhajiroun Network* (London: HOPE not hate, 2013); Vikram Dodd and Jamie Grierson, "Revealed: How Anjem Choudary influenced at least 100 British jihadis," *The Guardian* (August 16, 2016), www.theguardian.com/uk-news/2016/aug/16/revealed-how-anjem-choudary-inspired-at-least-100-british-jihadis [Accessed December 21, 2017]; and Richard Watson, "Has al-Muhajiroun been underestimated?," *BBC Newsnight* (June 27, 2017), www.bbc.com/news/uk-40355491 [Accessed December 21, 2017].

[87] For more on selection bias, see Gary King, Robert O. Keohane, and Sidney Verba, *Designing Social Inquiry: Scientific Inference in Qualitative Research* (Princeton, NJ: Princeton University Press, 1994), pp. 128–37.

participated in the network without internalizing its Salafi-Islamist ideology and becoming full members or intellectual affiliates.

The second reason why the Emigrants were not a conveyor belt to terrorism was that many activists eventually quit the network – without escalating to political violence. For every Michael Adebolajo and Khurram Butt, many more activists left al-Muhajiroun and moved on with their lives, without radicalizing further. If al-Muhajiroun is a conveyor belt to terrorism, why do so many people leave without progressing to violence? I return to this question later in the book, showing that radicalization into violence is not as simple as the conveyor-belt analogy would have it. Activists who escalate to violence are influenced by a number of factors beyond their participation in al-Muhajiroun. Rarely, if ever, are phenomena as complex as an individual's journey to violent extremism and terrorism determined by a single cause or event, even one that appears in multiple cases, as it does with the Emigrants.

GLANCING AHEAD

In the chapters that follow, I unpack this and other complexities to tell more nuanced stories about al-Muhajiroun. These interpretations are organized around multiple themes, including resilience, recruitment, learning, leaving – and the limitations of all these processes. In the next chapter, I begin at the macro-structural level, joining forces with two colleagues to offer a mixed methods account that combines "thin" network analysis with "thick" ethnographic description. Our analysis draws on news reports, interviews, and participant observation to explain how the Emigrants evolved from a centralized "scale-free-like" network centered around Omar Bakri to a smaller, more decentralized, "small-world-like" network led by numerous activists. This small-world system allowed the Emigrants to survive a hostile law enforcement environment, but also made it less likely that they would create an Islamic state in Britain. To support our argument, the chapter includes several measures of network structure. Readers may find this chapter less accessible than the ones that follow it. In our pursuit of clarity, however, we save many of the technical details of our methods and measures for the methodological appendix at the end of this book.

Chapter 2 moves beyond formal network analysis to tell the stories of how and why young Britons join al-Muhajiroun. Drawing on interviews, and insights from research in social movements and religious cults, I identify several factors that lead people to the Emigrants, including biographical availability, turning points, ideological affinity, social networks, charismatic leadership, and prior involvement in other activist groups. I also highlight the importance of al-Muhajiroun's strategy of recruitment, which includes activists' use of da'wah stalls and personal friendships to draw people in. I identify common factors in my respondents' journeys, but I refrain from reducing their stories to a single theory or model of joining. Instead, I call attention to the diversity of their experiences, which combine in unique ways for different individuals to produce the same outcome, participation in the Emigrants' high-risk activism.

Once they become involved in al-Muhajiroun, participants learn to become competent activists. In Chapter 3, I use the concept of communities of practice to explain how recruits master the skills and knowledge they need to become committed insiders. Much of their learning comes from watching more experienced activists perform da'wah and hisbah and then engaging in these activities themselves. In addition to learning by doing, novices learn through companionship with experienced activists and by participating in halaqahs, where they study with small groups of fellow activists. Through all these interactions, novices internalize al-Muhajiroun's ideology, build friendships with other activists, and deepen their commitment to the network. The Emigrants' community of practice has allowed them to indoctrinate hundreds of young Britons, and maintain the network's ideological cohesion. But it has also created a narrow, dogmatic culture that sometimes hampers their ability to respond to pressure. Similar to religious cults, al-Muhajiroun is insulated from alternative views and resistant to change, including change that would help activists survive their increasingly hostile environment.

Chapter 4 focuses on the Emigrants' resilience. Notwithstanding their dogmatic culture, over the years activists have made a number of simple, but effective changes to their activism. These tactical adaptations, which are different from the structural changes described in Chapter 1, allowed them to bounce back from government pressure and other setbacks to continue their da'wah and hisbah. When the government outlawed their spin-off groups, activists created new ones or revived old platforms that were not banned. When the government cracked down on their street preaching, activists moved their stalls, took down their most provocative signs, and emphasized the religious nature of their da'wah. When the government restricted their access to large halls, activists engaged in deception to reserve different venues, moved their public talks to smaller sites, and posted their talks online. British counter-terrorism pressure succeeded in weakening the Emigrants, but it did not eliminate them. Al-Muhajiroun's resilience allowed activists to remain relevant in the global jihadi movement, even as they became increasingly marginalized in Britain.

There are as many exits from al-Muhajiroun as there are pathways to it. Chapter 5 examines how and why activists leave. For many, involvement with the activist network is a passing phase of adolescence. As they age into adulthood these individuals mature out of the Emigrants. Many eventually tire from the network's demands on their time and personal finances, especially when the opportunities and responsibilities of adulthood limit their availability for high-risk activism. But leaving the Emigrants is hard, especially for those remain devoted to their fellow activists. Like joining the network and becoming committed insiders in its community of practice, exiting is a process, typically unfolds over many weeks and months. Those who complete this process experience different outcomes. Many leave and become productive citizens, holding jobs, raising families, and making other contributions to British society. Others leave only to radicalize further into political violence. In recent years, some activists fled Britain to wield the sword of jihad in Iraq and Syria. A number of these individuals faced legal problems in Britain, suggesting that authorities' efforts to stop their activism may have had unintended, and tragic, consequences.

I conclude this study by exploring the larger implications of my research, including two phenomena that may not be as important as commonly thought: online radicalization and countering violent extremism (CVE) programs. I also revisit the debate raised earlier in this chapter, namely whether the Emigrants are a conveyor belt to political violence or a safety valve for disgruntled youth. In discussing the current state of al-Muhajiroun, I credit British authorities for disrupting the activist network and fragmenting its small-world-like structure. But I also recall an earlier period when the network was down but not out, only to reemerge as an even more notorious player in Britain's Islamist scene. Today, vestiges of a weakened al-Muhajiroun remain, sustained by its resilient ideology and small group halaqahs. Whether the Emigrants rebound from their latest setbacks or remain dormant depends in no small part on its most persistent activists, especially leaders who have recently been released from prison.

I end this chapter with a caveat, to help readers understand the limits of what I offer. The following chapters are a case study of one outlawed network, which I explore through ethnographic network analysis and process tracing. I do not pretend to uncover timeless truths about al-Muhajiroun or universal laws about Salafi-jihadism. My aim is to understand the Emigrants and their high-risk activism, to make them less "strange" and more accessible by interpreting what activists say and do. Like all ethnographies, steeped in network analysis or not, my account is limited by the time and place of my field work, and by my ability to understand what I saw and experienced. In the following chapters, I present these interpretations, grounded in the observable implications of my data, in the hope of improving our grasp of this often sensationalized, poorly understood network. If this book contributes to our knowledge of the Emigrants, and the larger Salafi-jihadi movement to which they belong, it does so modestly, with the limitations all case studies confront. My findings are not privileged, just particular. To the extent that I draw larger conclusions, and I do, I infer "from small... densely textured facts."[88] The

---

[88] Clifford Geertz, "Thick Description: Toward an Interpretive Theory of Culture," in *The Interpretation of Cultures: Selected Essays by Clifford Geertz* (New York: Basic Books, 1973), pp. 20, 23, and 28; Michael Kenney, "Hotbed of Radicalization or Something Else?: An Ethnographic Exploration of a Muslim Neighborhood in Ceuta," *Terrorism and Political Violence* 23, no. 4 (Fall 2011), pp. 537–59.

broader reach of my findings will have to be confirmed, or discounted, through additional research.

I suspect that such efforts, both interpretive and nomothetic, will be valuable for scholars and government officials alike. Our interest in studying al-Muhajiroun is not merely academic. Unless we understand why some young men and women in Britain, and the West more broadly, embrace extremist cultures, and why a smaller subset of them mobilize to violence, we are not likely to prevent these processes from continuing in the future. And this has consequences for all of us.

1

Al-Muhajiroun's Small-World Solution

With Stephen Coulthart and Dominick Wright

> You need help in the organization. You want somebody to be in charge of the demonstration, but because of the police pressure it's more spontaneous than before the banning.
>
> Veteran activist

On a freezing cold afternoon in December 2010, the leader of a da'wah stall described a dilemma confronting the Emigrants as his fellow activists handed out leaflets to shoppers outside a mall in Stratford. "I can invite an individual to Islam, but to make an impact on society – I can't do that by myself."[1] No matter how dedicated they are to their cause, no matter how much they are willing to sacrifice for it, activists cannot bring the Islamic state to Britain by working alone. To "make an impact on society" they must coordinate their activism with like-minded companions. But as members of a proselytization network that has been outlawed by the British government, the da'wah stall emir and his colleagues face numerous challenges, not least of which is performing their activism while avoiding arrest and prosecution.

How have activists organized in this environment? What collective forms have they taken to pursue their contentious politics? Did the structure of their network change over time, and, if so, how? Did their network structure influence their ability to engage in high-risk activism? In this chapter, two co-authors and I combine our skills in ethnography and network science to answer these questions. In the sections below, Stephen Coulthart, Dominick Wright, and I analyze news reports, interviews, and field notes using a combination

---

[1] Interview with veteran activist, Stratford, East London, December 6, 2010. Also, field notes, da'wah stall, Stratford, East London, December 6, 2010 and interview with leading activist, Leyton, East London, November 8, 2010.

of social network analysis and qualitative content analysis to explore al-Muhajiroun's structure and performance.

Our mixed methods analysis suggests that al-Muhajiroun's structure and power relations did change over time and that these changes had important implications for its activism. What began as a centralized, "scale-free-like" network centered on a charismatic leader gradually evolved into a more decentralized "small-world-like" network. This small-world network featured clusters of local activists who organized into neighborhood-based study groups called halaqahs. Multiple leading and veteran activists connected these local halaqahs into a larger, cohesive network that proved resistant to external pressure.

These structural changes were not part of some grand strategy by leading activists. Instead, the shift to a more clustered yet cohesive structure evolved over time, as activists struggled to respond to their increasingly hostile environment, exemplified in the removal of their founder and charismatic emir, Omar Bakri, and the British government's banning of their most prominent protest platforms. Chapter 4 discusses the tactical adaptations activists made in response to these pressures. In this chapter we focus on the network's most important structural change. Al-Muhajiroun's decentralized, small-world structure was essential to activists, allowing them to absorb and bounce back from Bakri's "decapitation" and other setbacks by mobilizing their supporters and continuing their activism. Our analysis explores the relationship between network structure and performance. In doing so, we contribute to a growing body of work on networks in international relations and older research on networks and social movements.[2] We do not suggest that small-worlds are superior to other networks, or that decentralization is always preferable to centralization. In fact, the Emigrants' shift to a smaller, more decentralized network made

---

[2] We discuss the international relations research below. Examples of network analysis in the literature on social movements and protest mobilization include David E. Snow, Louis Zurcher Jr., and Sheldon Ekland-Olson, "Social Networks and Social Movements: A Micro-structural Approach to Differential Recruitment," *American Sociological Review* 45, no. 5 (1980), pp. 787–801; Roger V. Gould, "Multiple Networks and Mobilization in the Paris Commune, 1871," *American Sociological Review* 56, no. 6 (December 1991), pp. 716–29; Doug McAdam and Ronnelle Paulsen, "Specifying the Relationship between Social Ties and Activism," *American Journal of Sociology* 99, no. 3 (November 1993), pp. 640–67; Hyojoung Kim and Peter S. Bearman, "The Structure and Dynamics of Movement Participation," *American Sociological Review* 62, no. 1 (February 1997), pp. 70–93; Karen Barkey and Ronan Van Rossem, "Networks of Contention: Villages and Regional Structure in the Seventeenth Century Ottoman Empire," *American Journal of Sociology* 102, no. 5 (1997), pp. 1345–82; Ann Mische, *Partisan Publics: Communication and Contention Across Brazilian Youth Activist Networks* (Princeton, NJ: Princeton University Press, 2008); Dan J. Wang and Sarah A. Soule, "Social Movement Organizational Collaboration: Networks of Learning and the Diffusion of Protest Tactics, 1960–1995," *American Journal of Sociology* 117, no. 6 (May 2012), pp. 1674–722; and Christopher Bail, *Terrified: How Anti-Muslim Fringe Organizations Became Mainstream* (Princeton, NJ: Princeton University Press, 2014).

it less likely activists would achieve their ultimate objective, establishing the caliphate in Britain.

NETWORK ANALYSIS IN INTERNATIONAL RELATIONS

Reflecting their growing importance in world politics, networks have recently received substantial attention from students of international relations.[3] Following the appearance of Margaret Keck's and Kathryn Sikkink's study, *Activists Beyond Borders*, a growing number of scholars have shown how transnational advocacy networks influence state behavior on human rights through lobbying, shaming, and other activities.[4] Hoping to demonstrate that the power of such networks is not limited to "low" politics, security scholars have examined how networks of intergovernmental organizations shape conflict and cooperation among participating states.[5] In the aftermath of 9/11, scholars turned their attention to non-state actors, seeking to understand how networks of terrorists, insurgents, criminals, ethnonationalists, nuclear proliferators, and small arms traders engage in collective action, often as they confront government efforts to disrupt their activities.[6]

[3] In this literature, a network refers to a system of "nodes" and the "ties" that bind them. Nodes can be individuals, organizations, even nations. Ties refer to the social relations that connect different nodes, making them part of a larger whole. See Scott D. McClurg and David M. J. Lazer, "Political Networks," *Social Networks* 36 (2014), pp. 1–4; Scott D. McClurg and Joseph K. Young, "Editors' Introduction: A Relational Political Science," *PS: Political Science and Politics* 41, no. 1 (2011), pp. 39–43; and Stanley Wasserman and Katherine Faust, *Social Network Analysis: Methods and Applications* (New York: Cambridge University Press, 1994).

[4] Margaret E. Keck and Kathryn Sikkink, *Activists Beyond Borders: Advocacy Networks in International Politics* (Ithaca, NY: Cornell University Press, 1998); Charli Carpenter, *"Lost" Causes: Agenda Vetting in Global Issue Networks and the Shaping of Human Security* (Ithaca, NY: Cornell University Press, 2014); Sanjeev Khagram, James Riker, and Kathryn Sikkink, eds., *Restructuring World Politics: Transnational Social Movements, Networks, and Norms* (Minneapolis, MN: University of Minnesota Press, 2002); Wendy H. Wong, *Internal Affairs: How the Structure of NGOs Transforms Human Rights* (Ithaca, NY: Cornell University Press, 2012); and Jennifer Hadden, *Networks in Contention: The Divisive Politics of Climate Change* (New York: Cambridge University Press, 2015).

[5] Emilie M. Hafner-Burton and Alexander H. Montgomery, "Power Positions: International Organizations, Social Networks, and Conflict," *Journal of Conflict Resolution* 50, no. 1 (February 2006), pp. 3–27; Han Dorussen and Hugh Ward, "Intergovernmental Organizations and the Kantian Peace: A Network Perspective," *Journal of Conflict Resolution* 52, no. 2 (2008), pp. 189–212; Zeev Maoz, *Networks of Nations: The Evolution, Structure, and Impact of International Networks, 1816–2001* (New York: Cambridge University Press, 2010), and Mette Eilstrup-Sangiovanni, "Varieties of Cooperation: Government Networks in International Security," in *Networked Politics: Agency, Power, and Governance*, ed. Miles Kahler (Ithaca, NY: Cornell University Press, 2009), pp. 194–227.

[6] Sean F. Everton, *Disrupting Dark Networks* (New York: Cambridge University Press, 2012); Ami Pedahzur and Arie Perliger, "The Changing Nature of Suicide Attacks: A Social Network Perspective," *Social Forces* 84, no. 4 (June 2006), pp. 1987–2008; Paul Staniland, *Networks of Rebellion: Explaining Insurgent Cohesion and Collapse* (Ithaca, NY: Cornell University Press, 2014); Phil Williams, "Transnational Criminal Networks," in *Networks and Netwars*, edited

Whether they study networks from the perspective of low or high politics, international relations scholars highlight the importance of "power" in their analyses. In doing so, they expand upon conventional understandings of this concept in world politics.[7] Rather than conceptualizing power primarily as a material attribute that actors possess, such as the size of a nation's army or its annual gross domestic product, network scholars understand power as inherently relational. Power emerges not solely from individual actors but from the relationships they form with others. Through their social ties, actors gain access to information and other scarce resources.[8] Actors' relative position within the network – what scholars typically refer to as their "centrality" – shapes their ability to access, share, and potentially manipulate these resources. Prominently positioned actors often enjoy access to more information and resources than those on the periphery. For this reason an actor's centrality is critical to its ability to influence others and to shape outcomes to its liking.

Analysts use a variety of concepts to measure network centrality. The most common node-level measure is degree centrality. Actors that rank high in degree centrality have more connections, and therefore greater access, to other nodes in the network. International relations scholars treat access as a proxy for social power.[9] A second node-level measure of centrality is betweenness. Actors that score high in betweenness centrality bridge gaps in network structure by connecting nodes that otherwise would not be connected. This becomes a source of influence when brokers exploit their exclusive, non-redundant ties to direct the flow of information and resources.[10] Researchers use betweenness as a proxy for brokerage power.[11]

by John Arquilla and David Ronfeldt (Santa Monica, CA: RAND, 2001), pp. 61–97; Arjun Chowdhury and Ronald R. Krebs, "Making and Mobilizing Moderates: Rhetorical Strategy, Political Networks, and Counterterrorism," *Security Studies* 18, no. 3 (2009), pp. 371–99; Alexander H. Montgomery, "Ringing in Proliferation: How to Dismantle an Atomic Bomb Network," *International Security* 30, no. 2 (Fall 2005), pp. 153–87; and David Kinsella, "The Black Market in Small Arms: Examining a Social Network," *Contemporary Security Policy* 27, no. 1 (2006), pp. 100–17.

[7] Hafner-Burton, Kahler, and Montgomery, "Network Analysis for International Relations," p. 570; Kahler, "Networked Politics," pp. 11–12; and Deborah Avant and Oliver Westerwinter, "Introduction: Networks and Transnational Security Governance," in *The New Power Politics: Networks and Transnational Security Governance* (New York: Oxford University Press, 2016), eds. Deborah Avant and Oliver Westerwinter, pp. 9–12.

[8] David Knoke, *Political Networks: The Structural Perspective* (New York: Cambridge University Press, 1990), p. 9.

[9] Hafner-Burton and Montgomery, "Power Positions"; Avant and Westerwinter, *The New Power Politics*; and Charli Carpenter, "Governing the Global Agenda: 'Gatekeepers' and 'Issue Adoption'," in *Who Governs the Globe?*, eds. Deborah Avant, Martha Finnemore, and Susan Sell (Cambridge: Cambridge University Press, 2010), pp. 202–37.

[10] Hafner-Burton, Kahler, and Montgomery, "Network Analysis for International Relations," pp. 571–72.

[11] Stacie E. Goddard, "Brokering Peace: Networks, Legitimacy, and the Northern Ireland Peace Process," *International Studies Quarterly* 56 (2012), pp. 501–15; Daniel H. Nexon and Thomas

SCALE-FREE AND SMALL-WORLD NETWORKS

International relations scholars have paid considerable attention to explaining how node-level centrality affects networks' ability to achieve favorable outcomes. They have shown less interest in examining variation among network-level structures – and exploring how these structures change over time and shape performance. Scholars who do focus on network topologies commonly identify three types: distributed, scale-free, and small-world.[12] These types are not mutually exclusive, though they are distinct. Some distributed networks contain small-world-like clusters, and many scale-free networks are small-worlds writ large.[13] Despite the overlap, these types are still useful because each contains properties that distinguish it from others. Of course, many networks, including the one featured in this book, contain features of more than one ideal type. As we show below, al-Muhajiroun's proxy networks displayed elements of both scale-free-like and small-world topologies during its early years, when the network was growing rapidly.

Theories about network structures often begin with distributed networks, also known as random or Erdös-Rényi networks. In distributed systems, connections between nodes occur at random, according to a uniform probability. Several features flow from this. In distributed networks most nodes have around the same number of connections.[14] There are no hubs with many connections, and few brokers to join otherwise unconnected nodes. In such networks power, typically defined in terms of a node's centrality in the network, is evenly distributed, while hierarchy, conceived as the centrality rankings of all nodes in the network, is decentralized.[15] Distributed networks often contain little clustering, though not always. In most distributed systems, two connected nodes do not have a higher probability of sharing connections to other nodes. Moreover, in distributed networks, the diameter, which refers to the largest number of links separating two nodes, is usually large compared to other types of networks. These features influence network behavior and performance. For example, diffusion tends to be slow in distributed systems as information

---

Wright, "What's at Stake in the American Empire Debate," *American Political Science Review* 101, no. 2 (May, 2007), pp. 253–71; and Avant and Westerwinter, *The New Power Politics*.

[12] David A. Lake and Wendy Wong, "The Politics of Networks: Interests, Power, and Human Rights Norms," in *Networked Politics: Agency, Power, and Governance*, edited by Miles Kahler (Ithaca, NY: Cornell University Press, 2009), p. 129; Albert-László Barabási, *Linked: The New Science of Networks* (Cambridge, MA: Perseus Press, 2002); Duncan J. Watts, *Six Degrees: The Science of a Connected Age* (New York: Norton, 2003); and Nicholas A. Christakis and James H. Fowler, *Connected: How Your Friends' Friends' Friends Affect Everything You Feel, Think, and Do* (New York: Little, Brown and Company, 2009).

[13] Luis A. Nunes Amaral, Antonio Scala, Marc Barthelemy, and H. Eugene Stanley, "Classes of Small-World Networks," *Proceedings of the National Academy of Sciences* 97, no. 21 (October 2000), pp. 11149–52.

[14] Lake and Wong, "The Politics of Networks," p. 129.

[15] Hafner-Burton, Kahler, and Montgomery, "Network Analysis for International Relations."

or other resources must travel relatively long paths to spread across the network. If distributed networks are not particularly efficient, they are resistant to attacks against specific nodes. These networks contain no hubs and few brokers that will devastate the network's performance if they are removed.[16]

In scale-free networks, connections between nodes are not randomly distributed. Scale-free networks grow when nodes preferentially attach themselves to well-connected nodes. This "rich get richer" phenomenon creates centralized networks that follow a power law distribution of ties where a few highly connected hubs link to many poorly connected nodes. Hubs enjoy a preponderance of power through their central position. This allows them to shape the flow of information and resources in the network. As in distributed systems, these features impact network behavior and performance. Information and other resources spread rapidly in scale-free systems because they pass through highly connected hubs. Scale-free networks are efficient, powerful engines of diffusion. But this strength becomes a weakness when scale-free networks are targeted for selective, as opposed to random, disruption. The select removal of a small number of hubs can significantly degrade the performance of scale-free systems. Without hubs to unite the network, the network may break into isolated parts.[17]

Small-world networks are distinguished by two features: high local clustering and short path lengths.[18] In small worlds, two connected nodes often share ties to other nodes. These overlapping connections create clusters of nodes that connect tightly to each other but loosely to the rest of the network. Ties that bridge different clusters provide shortcuts that allow information and other resources to flow from cluster to cluster. These shortcuts give small-world networks their short average path lengths and "small world" feel.

As with distributed and scale-free systems, the structural properties of small-world networks affect network behavior and performance. In small worlds, information and resources travel the entire network in relatively few steps. This allows for faster diffusion than distributed systems, but slower diffusion than centralized scale-free networks. In small-world networks resources do not necessarily flow through hubs that dominate the entire system, as they do in scale-free systems. Instead, in small worlds resources flow through nodes that "bridge" or span different clusters. Such nodes are not necessarily hubs

---

[16] Watts, *Six Degrees.*

[17] Albert-László Barabási, *Linked: The New Science of Networks* (Cambridge, MA: Perseus Press, 2002); Albert-László Barabási and Réka Albert, "Emergence of Scaling in Random Networks," *Science* 286 (October 15, 1999), pp. 509–12.

[18] Path length refers to the average number of nodes that must be crossed in the shortest path between any two nodes in the network. Duncan J. Watts and Steven H. Strogatz, "Collective Dynamics of 'Small-World' Networks," *Nature* 393 (1998), pp. 440–2; Duncan J. Watts, "Networks, Dynamics, and the Small-World Phenomenon," *American Journal of Sociology* 105, no. 2 (1999), pp. 493–527; and Thomas W. Valente, *Social Networks and Health: Models, Methods, and Applications* (New York: Oxford University Press, 2010).

because they may have as little as two links, one to each cluster they connect.[19] A hub, in contrast, has many links. Unlike a scale-free network, which can be eliminated through the removal of its hubs, small worlds can exist with or without hubs, as long as there are nodes that bridge different clusters.[20] When small-world networks have multiple nodes spanning different clusters they cannot be fragmented by removing a single node because other nodes remain to bridge the clusters.[21] This makes small worlds more resistant to the elimination of hubs than scale-free systems.[22] In fact, a scale-free network that has its hub removed may transform into a more decentralized small-world network with multiple nodes that bridge different clusters. This is essentially what happened to the Emigrants after Omar Bakri Mohammed left Great Britain, as we show below.

One final clarification. When discussing the aggregate structure of al-Muhajiroun's proxy networks we use the terms 'scale-free-like' and 'small-world-like' to emphasize that our observed networks do not perfectly fit these ideal types. We do so because we recognize that networks are sometimes reported as being scale-free or small world when they could more accurately be described as similar to, or "like," these ideal types. Often a network's distribution of nodes might be close – but not identical – to a power-law distribution, indicating a scale-free network. Clauset, Shalizi, and Newman examine twenty-four datasets describing real-world phenomena that have been characterized in the research literature as having power-law distributions. They find that most do not, though many are close.[23]

The three types of network structure described above have not received a great deal of attention from international relations and social movement scholars. This is surprising given the ubiquity of scale-free and small-world systems in discussions of real-world networks, including commercial airlines, Hollywood actors, and corporate alliances.[24] Focusing on topology helps researchers understand the relationship between network structure and behavior. This is important to understanding how structural changes impact performance. We address this gap by exploring how changes in al-Muhajiroun's topology affected its ability to continue its activism in an increasingly hostile

---

[19] Jennifer Xu and Hsinchun Chen, "The Topology of Dark Networks," *Communications of the ACM* 51, no. 10 (October 2008), p. 64.

[20] Marc Sageman, *Understanding Terror Networks* (Philadelphia, PA: University of Pennsylvania Press, 2004), p. 140.

[21] Xu and Chen, "The Topology of Dark Networks," p. 64.

[22] Duncan J. Watts, "The 'New' Science of Networks," *Annual Review of Sociology* 30 (2004), pp. 243–70.

[23] Aaron Clauset, Cosma Rohilla Shalizi, and M.E.J. Newman, "Power Law Distributions in Empirical Data," *SIAM Review* 51 (2009), pp. 661–703.

[24] Brian Uzzi and Jarret Spiro, "Collaboration and Creativity," *American Journal of Sociology*, Vol. 111, No. 2 (September 2005), p. 492; Watts and Strogatz, "Collective Dynamics of 'Small-World' Networks"; Barabási, *Linked*.

environment. Drawing on our network analysis and thick description we argue that the Emigrants' shift from a centralized "scale-free-like" network to a more decentralized small-world system featuring local halaqahs allowed activists to overcome police pressure and other setbacks to their activism.

NETWORK ANALYSIS AND THE STUDY OF ILLICIT ACTORS

Unlike international relations scholars, students of terrorist and criminal networks have shown considerable interest in their scale-free and small-world properties. In his early analysis of the 9/11 attack network, Vladis Krebs argues that Mohammed Atta and other al-Qaeda operatives formed a small-world system that contained high local clustering and short path lengths. Krebs argues that this structure was essential to the attacks, allowing the geographically dispersed network to coordinate its activities and carry out the operation.[25] In his influential analysis of al-Qaeda, Marc Sageman repeatedly characterizes the transnational network as a small-world system featuring dense clusters of friends who interact frequently with each other. Sageman argues that al-Qaeda's "dense interactivity" makes it resistant to leadership decapitation. However, he also acknowledges that if the authorities remove enough nodes that bridge different clusters, the terrorist network will split apart into "isolated, noncommunicating islands of nodes."[26]

Sageman does not provide statistical measures in support of his analysis, but Xu and Chen measure al-Qaeda using his original data, along with three other underground networks, for average path lengths, clustering coefficients, and power-law degree distributions. After comparing these networks against simulations of distributed networks of the same size, they conclude that all four networks are both scale-free and small-world. By their own admission, Xu and Chen's findings are based on a static view of the clandestine networks they studied.[27] Yet like their "bright" counterparts, "dark networks" are not static. They change over time, often in response to internal and external pressure, including government efforts to destroy them.

Hoping to measure changes in network structures over time, a small number of scholars build longitudinal designs in their studies.[28] We contribute to this research by analyzing the structure of al-Muhajiroun during three time periods corresponding to major events in its history. Not all dark networks respond to

[25] Valdis E. Krebs, "Mapping Networks of Terrorist Cells," *Connections* 24, no. 3 (2002), pp. 43–52. However, Krebs' measures only support his small-world claim after he adds several shortcuts to the original data, reducing the average path length from 4.75 to 2.79.
[26] Sageman, *Understanding Terror Networks*, p. 140.
[27] Xu and Chen, "The Topology of Dark Networks," p. 65.
[28] Kathleen M. Carley, Ju-Sung Lee, and David Krackhardt, "Destabilizing Networks," *Connections* 24(3) (2002), pp. 79–92; Sean F. Everton and Daniel Cunningham, "Terrorist Network Adaptation to a Changing Environment," in *Crime and Networks*, edited by Carlo Morselli (London: Routledge, 2013), pp. 287–308.

external pressure the same way, but the Emigrants' structure clearly changed as its environment became more hostile. During al-Muhajiroun's early years, when police repression was low, the network assumed a more centralized structure, revolving around its charismatic emir. Expressed in terms of the topologies we are using, the activist network was "scale-free-like" before the British government cracked down against it. Afterwards, the Emigrants became more decentralized and small-world-like.

In exploring al-Muhajiroun's proxy networks for their scale-free and small-world properties, we contribute to the literature on dark networks. But this tells only part of our story. Measures of topology do not explain much about how network nodes actually mobilize and engage in contentious politics. Despite their interest in network types, few dark network scholars link structural properties to performance outcomes. Recognizing this shortcoming, researchers have begun to explore the relationship between structure and performance. Sean Everton and Daniel Cunningham note that when resilient terrorist groups are confronted with hostile environments they become more decentralized. This allows them to continue their operations despite state pressure.[29] We draw on Everton's and Cunningham's insight to argue that al-Muhajiroun's shift from a scale-free-like to a more decentralized small-world network facilitated its activism. The shift allowed the Emigrants to bounce back from setbacks, including Omar Bakri's removal from Britain, and mobilize for collective action in an increasingly hostile environment.

AL-MUHAJIROUN'S EARLY YEARS: A SCALE-FREE-LIKE, SMALL-WORLD NETWORK

Many studies of networks in international relations rely exclusively on either "thin" quantitative analyses of network structures using large datasets or "thick" qualitative descriptions of network processes using case studies and process tracing. In this chapter we combine these methods to engage in what we call ethnographic network analysis. We use thin network analysis to measure relationships and structure in al-Muhajiroun at both the node and network levels of analysis. And we use thick description and process tracing to peer inside the outlawed network, deepening our understanding of how activists make decisions, exchange influence, and engage in collective action. In merging these methods we leverage the measurement precision and statistical validity of social network analysis with in-depth knowledge of a specific case grounded in ethnographic field research.[30]

---

[29] Everton and Cunningham, "Terrorist Network Adaptation to a Changing Environment."

[30] Other studies that combine "thin" and "thick" methods of network analysis, without using ethnography, include John F. Padgett and Christopher K. Ansell, "Robust Action and the Rise of the Medici," *American Journal of Sociology* 98, no. 6 (May 1993), pp. 1259–319; Gould, "Multiple Networks and Mobilization in the Paris Commune, 1871"; Carpenter, *"Lost" Causes*; and Hadden, *Networks in Contention*. For more on ethnography and thick description,

TABLE I.I *Time Periods for Measuring al-Muhajiroun's Proxy Networks*

Time Period	Dates	Events
1	January 1, 1996 to August 5, 2005	From al-Muhajiroun's founding in Britain to day before Omar Bakri Mohammed leaves Great Britain for Lebanon (shortly after 7/7 attacks in London)
2	August 6, 2005 to May 30, 2009	Day Bakri leaves for Lebanon to the day activists announce the relaunch of al-Muhajiroun
3	May 31, 2009 to November 30, 2012	Day after al-Muhajiroun relaunch to end of data collection

In order to measure changes in the Emigrants' structure over time, we separate the data for our social network analysis into three time periods corresponding to major events in the network's history (see Table 1.1). Along with our primary source data, gathered over a period of five years, this adds an essential dynamic component to our understanding of al-Muhajiroun. The data for our thin network analysis comes from a sample of over 3000 news reports on the Emigrants, published by a variety of newspapers from January 1996 through November 2012. The networks we draw from these news reports are approximations of real-world networks based on imperfect data. This is why we refer to them as proxy networks. We present these data to make descriptive inferences about the Emigrants' node and network-level structure over these three time periods. We do not suggest the news reports perfectly capture al-Muhajiroun's real-world networks during these years. The news reports, for example, are biased towards leading and veteran activists at the expense of rank-and-file activists. This is because network leaders and veterans are more willing to be interviewed and quoted by reporters who cover the network's public events. Rank-and-file activists, in contrast, often wish to remain anonymous.

The data for our thick network analysis come from interviews and participant observation I conducted during seven research trips to Great Britain between November 2010 and July 2015. Consistent with interpretive analysis, I read, coded, and reflected on my interviews and field notes using *NVivo*, a qualitative data analysis program. For more discussion of our methods, including how we sampled respondents and news reports, extracted network nodes, and measured ties in our proxy networks, see our methodological appendix.

see Clifford Geertz, "Thick Description: Toward an Interpretive Theory of Culture," in *The Interpretation of Cultures: Selected Essays by Clifford Geertz* (New York: Basic Books, 1973), pp. 3–30.

The Emigrants have engaged in collective action through a variety of network structures. In the network's early years, Omar Bakri Mohammed, Anjem Choudary, and other leaders exploited Great Britain's democratic system to organize a network of activists centered around Bakri. This period dates from when Bakri and his students created al-Muhajiroun as a spin-off of Hizbut-Tahrir in early 1996 to the day before Bakri permanently left Britain, almost one month after the 7/7 bombings in London. During this period, al-Muhajiroun contained several well-connected hubs, foremost among them Omar Bakri, who connected the network into a coherent whole. Bakri's centrality in the proxy network is illustrated in the node-level degree and betweenness measures in Table 1.2.

The measures in this table suggest that Omar Bakri, Anjem Choudary, and other hubs enjoyed greater access and brokerage than other nodes in al-Muhajiroun during the network's early years. By these measures, Bakri was considerably more powerful than other nodes in the proxy network. His degree centrality, interpreted here as a measure of access power, was .898, more than double Anjem Choudary's degree centrality of 0.341. Most other nodes in the network connected to fewer neighbors. Indeed, the average total degree centrality for all nodes in the proxy network was just 0.077. These measures suggest that Bakri and Choudary were substantially more "powerful" than peripheral nodes in the network.

Bakri and the other hubs also possessed substantial brokerage, as measured by their betweenness centrality. Nodes that score high in betweenness often serve as brokers of information and other resources by connecting otherwise unconnected nodes to the network. At 0.751 Bakri's betweenness was exceptionally high, suggesting that he enjoyed significantly more brokerage power than other nodes in the proxy network during this period. Even Anjem Choudary, the third most influential broker, had a betweenness centrality of 0.076, just one-tenth of Bakri's. The average betweenness centrality for the top five ranked hubs was 0.198. Although this may seem low, the average betweenness for all of the nodes in the network was 0.012, considerably less than the hubs' average. According to these measures, hubs in this proxy network brokered significantly more connections than other nodes, and Bakri contained more brokerage power than any of them, underscoring his centrality. During this period, al-Muhajiroun's proxy network was characterized by several well-connected hubs, foremost among them Omar Bakri. In combination with the above scores for degree centrality, these betweenness measures support our argument that the Emigrants contained a relatively centralized structure during this period.

These node-level measures also suggest that al-Muhajiroun's proxy network may have contained a scale-free and small-world structure. As we stated earlier, some networks contain properties of more than one ideal type and many scale-free networks are also small worlds. We need additional measures at the network-level to confirm whether this is true for al-Muhajiroun. Table 1.3

TABLE I.2 *Al-Muhajiroun during the Early Years (January 1, 1996–August 5, 2005), Node-Level Degree and Betweenness Centrality, Top 10 Agents and Network Average*[31]

Agent	Degree Centrality	Agent	Betweenness Centrality
Omar Bakri	0.898	Omar Bakri	0.751
Anjem Choudary	0.341	Abu Hamza*	0.088
Abu Hamza*	0.307	Anjem Choudary	0.076
Hassan Butt	0.273	Hassan Butt	0.048
Afzal Munir*	0.205	Abu Izzadeen Brooks	0.028
Aftab Manzoor*	0.193	Afzal Munir*	0.016
Asif Hanif*	0.182	Aftab Manzoor*	0.013
Yassir Khan	0.170	Mohammed Omar*	0.009
Rubana Akghar	0.159	Asif Hanif*	0.007
Ibrahim Hassan	0.148	Abdul Rahman Saleem	0.007
Node Average	0.077	Node Average	0.012

Note: Asterisk indicates that this node is a "false positive."[32]

provides several relevant measures, including degree centralization, betweenness centralization, average path length, and clustering coefficient.[33]

Consistent with a scale-free topology, al-Muhajiroun's proxy network displayed exceptionally high values for network-level degree centralization

[31] The measures in this table and the tables below only include nodes that are connected to the proxy networks. They do not include "isolates" that by definition are not tied to the network. Also, the values for all centrality measures presented in this chapter are normalized.

[32] Several individuals in this table, and Tables 1.5 and 1.6, are "false positives." We identify these individuals with an asterisk. Despite their high values for degree and betweenness centrality, these people were not leaders in al-Muhajiroun. Some were frequently mentioned in news reports on the Emigrants, but they never enjoyed the prominent positions within the activist network implied by their centrality rankings in these proxy networks. Abu Hamza al-Masri, for example, was a Salafi-jihadi preacher in London who participated in some al-Muhajiroun protests and conferences during the network's early years. He was associated with the network, but he was not a leading activist. Instead, he was a rival to Omar Bakri in radical circles in London. Abu Hamza had his own group of followers, called Supporters of Shariah, who competed with the Emigrants for recruits. Other false positives, including Asif Hanif, Afzal Munir, Aftab Manzoor, and Mohammed Omar, ranked high in node-level centrality not because of their importance in the network, but because they were implicated in acts of political violence that received extensive media coverage. For more discussion of the challenges in performing valid social network analysis on the Emigrants using news reports, and the importance of first-hand knowledge from field work in identifying false positives, see Michael Kenney and Stephen Coulthart, "The Methodological Challenges of Extracting Dark Networks," in *Illuminating Dark Networks: The Study of Clandestine Groups and Organizations*, edited by Luke M. Gerdes (New York: Cambridge University Press, 2015), pp. 52–70.

[33] For more discussion of these measures, see our methodological appendix.

TABLE 1.3 *Network-Level Measures in al-Muhajiroun during the Early Years (January 1, 1996–August 5, 2005)*

Measure	Value
Number of nodes	89
Degree centralization	0.840
Betweenness centralization	0.747
Average path length	2.057
Clustering coefficient	0.744

(0.840) and betweenness centralization (0.747) during this period. This is not surprising given Bakri's dominance in the network. Many of the network's connections and most efficient paths flowed through him. He was the star around which the Emigrants revolved. Al-Muhajiroun also displayed an average path length of 2.057 during this period. This is a short path length for a network of eighty-nine agents. This suggests that ideas and other resources passed through the proxy network in just over two steps, facilitating information sharing and learning. Networks with long average path lengths tend to be less efficient learners because information has to pass through more nodes. Finally, the proxy network's clustering coefficient was 0.744, another high value. This indicates that al-Muhajiroun contained tightly bound clusters revolving around Omar Bakri and other hubs, such as Anjem Choudary. The Emigrants' short average path length suggests that rather than fragmenting into isolated clusters, the proxy network was cohesive. With its high local clustering and short average path length the network contained the distinctive features of a small-world system.

Al-Muhajiroun's values for network-level centralization, average path lengths and local clustering are consistent with both scale-free and small-world networks. However, these measures alone are not enough to determine whether the proxy network is scale-free, small-world, or both. For this we turn to additional measures of network topology, including the relative distribution of node degree in the network and the Humphries and Gurney (HG) small-world score.[34] These measures of network structure show al-Muhajiroun's proxy to be scale-free or nearly scale-free in the first time period, depending on the x-floor value set for estimating node degree distribution in the network. When the x-floor is set at 2, the estimated exponent value, $\hat{\alpha}$, for al-Muhajiroun is 1.84 (K-S stat = 0.14, p value = 0.085). This is just outside the power law distribution range identified by Clauset, Shalizi, and Newman.[35] When the x-floor

---

[34] More information on how we calculate these measures of network structure can be found in our methodological appendix.

[35] Clauset, Shalizi, and Newman, "Power Law Distributions in Empirical Data," p. 662.

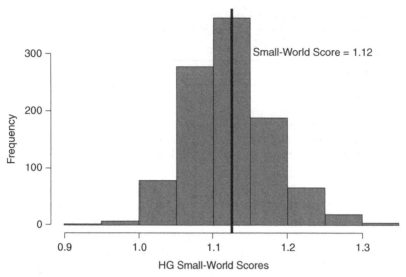

FIGURE 1.1 HG Small-World Test during Time Period 1, Trials = 1,000

is set at 3, the estimated exponent value, $\hat{\alpha}$, is 2.02, just within scale-free range (K-S Stat = 0.17. p value = 0.05).[36] Translated into English, this means that in the first period the network is scale-free-like.

Al-Muhajiroun's proxy network during these years also displayed properties of small-world systems. As shown in Figure 1.1, the network's HG score in Period 1 was greater than one. This means that the proxy network's average path length was short enough and its clustering high enough for it to be classified as a small-world system. The results also confirm that the Emigrants' proxy was not a distributed or random network during this period.

These structural measures provide important insights into the topology of the activist network during its formative years. At a time when the Emigrants operated relatively unhindered in Great Britain, activists developed a centralized network around Omar Bakri. During this period al-Muhajiroun resembled a "scale-free-like" and small-world network characterized by a dominant, highly connected hub linked to a large number of moderately connected nodes. As with other scale-free systems, it was the hub – Bakri – that largely defined the network's structure.

These results are consistent with our argument, but they do not tell us much about how al-Muhajiroun's structure affected its internal relations and

---

[36] As an additional check on these results we compared the distribution of connections using the two different x-floor values to simulated networks undergoing preferential attachment processes parameterized at $\hat{\alpha}$ = 1.84 and 2.02, respectively. In both cases, our results rejected the possibility that the two samples came from different distributions.

performance. To get a better handle on this, we turn to our interviews with current and former activists in the network. Thick description of these primary sources confirms and extends the findings from our social network analysis of the Emigrants' structure.

INSIDE AL-MUHAJIROUN'S SCALE-FREE-LIKE, SMALL-WORLD NETWORK

During al-Muhajiroun's early years, the activist network essentially revolved around its charismatic leader and central hub. Omar Bakri "was the main person," observes Abdul, a former activist. "Everyone used to go to him to make any decisions on any activities or anything that they wanted to happen." His remark echoes other respondents who were active in the network.[37] Bakri's influence was rooted not only in his central position in the network, but in the leadership roles he performed and his relations with activists. From the network's founding as a spin-off group of Hizb ut-Tahrir in 1996 to his departure from Britain almost ten years later, Bakri was al-Muhajiroun's religious authority and global leader, as well as its national *emir* in the United Kingdom. In fulfilling these roles, Bakri set al-Muhajiroun's agenda, crafted its ideological vision, and indoctrinated activists in private study circles and public talks.[38] He also served as the network's primary point of contact with the media, frequently appearing on radio and television programs and speaking with journalists.

Befitting his central role in the network, Omar Bakri Mohammed exerted substantial authority over his followers. He was respected by activists for his knowledge of Islamic scripture, his ability to connect with them on a personal level, and his willingness to engage them for extended periods, often stretching late into the night.[39] "Sheikh Omar" inspired his followers. Activists who studied with him recall the paternal sway he held over them. "He was our scholar," remembers the former activist "Ali," expressing the feelings many respondents had towards Bakri. "He was our leader. He became our big brother, our dad. He was everything."[40] In a separate interview, "Rashid,"

---

[37] Interview with Abdul, Whitechapel, East London, June 18, 2011. Also, interviews with former activists, Ali and Maryam, Hounslow, West London, December 13, 2010 and June 21, 2011.

[38] Interviews with Maryam, Hounslow, West London, June 21, 2011, and Haroon, former supporter, Westminster, Central London, June 14, 2011. Also, see Quintan Wiktorowicz, *Radical Islam Rising: Muslim Extremism in the West* (Lanham, MD: Rowman & Littlefield, 2005), pp. 51 and 106.

[39] Interviews with Ali and Maryam, Hounslow, West London, June 21, 2011. Also, interviews with Rashid, another former activist, Whitechapel, East London, June 26, 2011, and Rohan, a leading activist, Whitechapel, East London, December 7, 2010. For more on Bakri's personal charisma and accessibility, see Wiktorowicz, *Radical Islam Rising*, pp. 147–8, and Jon Ronson, *Them: Adventures with Extremists* (London: Picador, 2001).

[40] Interview with Ali, Hounslow, West London, June 13, 2010. Also, interviews with Rohan, Whitechapel, East London, December 7, 2010, and veteran activist, Wembley Central, West London, June 25, 2011.

another former activist explains, "I was young and I wanted to have someone to follow and respect and look up to as a father figure."[41]

Notwithstanding the father-like authority he exerted over his young followers, Omar Bakri and his top students administered their network loosely. Bakri's strengths lay in communicating al-Muhajiroun's vision and ideology to his students. He preferred to delegate administrative tasks to others. In this, he was ably assisted by Anjem Choudary, who acted as his subordinate and the day-to-day administrator of al-Muhajiroun in the United Kingdom. But like his mentor, Choudary was more interested in calling society to Islam and commanding good and forbidding evil than managing activists. Both leaders regularly visited local study circles or halaqahs, but the purpose of their visits was to deliver lectures rather than manage people. "There wasn't a lot of checking up on people," explains Abdul, when asked whether Bakri or Anjem Choudary supervised the halaqahs. "It was mostly just trusting them to do what they had to do."[42]

Capitalizing on Omar Bakri's relationship with his students, the Emigrants expanded rapidly during these years.[43] Similar to other scale-free networks, al-Muhajiroun grew from a handful of followers to several hundred supporters, as participants preferentially attached themselves to their charismatic hub. This included old students who followed Bakri to his new group after he left Hizb ut-Tahrir and new supporters who were attracted to his confrontational activism. Many British Muslims were repelled by Bakri's message, but young recruits flocked to his fiery lectures, delivered in mosques and community centers throughout the country, and the network's high-profile events, including the "Rally for Islam" held in London's Trafalgar Square in 1998. Activists recruited aggressively during the late 1990s, exploiting their networks of friends and family members, and reaching out to other recruits through da'wah stalls, often held in local neighborhoods during market days. Finishing each other's sentences, Abdul and "Haroon" recall how quickly al-Muhajiroun grew in their neighborhood during this period.

ABDUL: "It was the big thing... We were actively part of them [al-Muhajiroun]... it was the thing to do because it was growing at that time... everyone used to be involved."
HAROON: "It proliferated rather quickly in local mosques."
ABDUL: "Rapidly, rapidly."
HAROON: "Communities had to put a stop to it because everyone who was under 20, 21 was involved, or knew of it or attended events or was sympathetic to" –

---

[41] Interview with Rashid, Whitechapel, East London, June 26, 2011.

[42] Interview with Abdul, Whitechapel, East London, June 18, 2011. Also, interviews with Haroon, Westminster, Central London, June 14, 2011, and Ali, Hounslow, West London, June 21, 2011.

[43] For discussion of the importance of the student-teacher relationship to the growth of religious networks more generally, see Quintan Wiktorowicz, "The Salafi Movement: Violence and the Fragmentation of Community," in *Muslim Networks: From Hajj to Hip Hop*, edited by Miriam Cooke and Bruce B. Lawrence (Chapel Hill, NC: University of North Carolina Press, 2005), pp. 208–34.

ABDUL: "To the cause. We all used to agree with it."

HAROON: "We were very young and the whole community was electrically charged with it."

ABDUL: "It was a buzz. We all got a buzz out of it. The kind of events we used to have, the talks and the demonstrations we used to do. Everyone used to get a buzz out of it. It was like a kid with a new toy... It was brilliant."[44]

If al-Muhajiroun's rapid expansion and Omar Bakri's dominance captured the activist network's scale-free nature during this period, the halaqah epitomized its small-world-ness. These neighborhood-based, invitation-only study circles doubled as the Emigrants' administrative vehicle. Study circles, which met weekly to discuss Bakri's teachings, contained tightly-knit clusters of local activists who performed much of the network's daily activism.[45] The groups were small, with anywhere from half a dozen to two dozen participants, depending on activists' ability to recruit new supporters and keep them involved.[46] "There used to be about twenty to thirty people in my halaqah," recalls Abdul, who attended a study circle in Tottenham, North London, where Omar Bakri maintained his headquarters. "The same people week after week, plus new people coming in."[47]

Attendance at halaqah meetings was mandatory. "Once you become a member," notes the former activist Ali, "you have to turn up once a week for your closed halaqah."[48] In addition to these closed meetings, halaqah members were expected to attend other weekly meetings, including an open circle that allowed outsiders, and at least one da'wah stall. Activists from the same group often formed intense friendship bonds with each other, developed over time through repeated face-to-face interaction. "You would always be together," explains Rashid, who was deeply involved in al-Muhajiroun during these years. "You'd spend time together, even socially. You'd hang out together, maybe at each other's houses, or at events, or just hanging out."[49] "It's lots of face-to-face interaction, lots of camaraderie and spending time together," adds Haroon, who was also active in the network during this period. "There were always social gatherings. Three, four, five times a week. Some of them saw each other

---

[44] Interview with Abdul, Whitechapel, East London, June 18, 2011.

[45] Such discussion circles are not unique to al-Muhajiroun. Other Islamic networks also rely on local circles of participants who meet regularly to study scripture, share ideas, and organize activities. For discussion of the role these circles play in the Turkish social movement inspired by Fethullah Gülen and his teachings, see Helen Rose Ebaugh, *The Gülen Movement: A Sociological Analysis of a Civic Movement Rooted in Moderate Islam* (London: Springer, 2010), pp. 47–64.

[46] Interviews with leading activist, Leyton, East London, November 6, 2010, and Ali and Maryam, Hounslow, West London, December 13, 2010.

[47] Interview with Abdul, Whitechapel, East London, June 18, 2011.

[48] Interview with Ali, Hounslow, West London, December 13, 2010.

[49] Interview with Rashid, Whitechapel, East London, June 26, 2011. Also, interviews with activists in Mile End, East London, June 26, 2011, Lewisham, South London, June 18, 2011 and Stratford, East London, June 27, 2011.

every day."[50] The purpose of all this hanging out was to develop strong ties with fellow activists in order to deepen their commitment to the cause, build in-group solidarity, and mobilize participants for high-risk activism. This was something that Omar Bakri himself encouraged. Bakri instructed his charges "to spend time with each other," according to one respondent with strong ties to the network leader. "Keep close to your brother so it will build a bond between you."[51]

Halaqah leaders mobilized their study circles for collective action, including da'wah stalls and demonstrations. "A lot of it would be down to the local halaqahs," explains Haroon, highlighting the decentralized nature of the network's daily activism. "Decisions on da'wah stalls, all that kind of stuff were decided on by the emir [halaqah leader]."[52] In reflection of some centralization during these years, high-profile protests like the Rally for Islam were organized through Bakri's headquarters in Tottenham, which also produced the leaflets and other materials used by activists. Network leaders Omar Bakri and Anjem Choudary regularly bridged the different halaqahs by delivering talks and loosely overseeing their activities.

In this fashion, al-Muhajiroun's scale-free-like, small-world structure mobilized top-down, through Bakri's authority and leadership, and bottom-up, through the halaqahs. The network's authority was centralized in Bakri's charismatic figure, but the administration of its activism was largely delegated to local halaqahs, with their rank-and-file activists. This structure produced a high level of performance, resulting in extensive activism. Rank-and-file activists organized da'wah stalls, public conferences, and demonstrations on a regular basis. "We used to go to so many conferences," recalls Abdul. "There was always something going on."[53] "There was a point in the late 1990s," adds a leading activist, "where we did more demonstrations than any other street movement in Britain."[54]

THE LATER YEARS: CHANGING TO A SMALL-WORLD-LIKE NETWORK

Al-Muhajiroun might have continued to flourish in this centrally authorized, loosely administered fashion had its environment not become increasingly hostile. However, in the wake of the London Underground bombings in July 2005 and other terrorist attacks, British authorities increased the pressure on the network and activists suffered a series of setbacks. These included "Sheikh

---

[50] Interview with Haroon, Westminster, Central London, June 14, 2011.

[51] Interview with veteran activist, Whitechapel, East London, June 17, 2011.

[52] Interview with Haroon, Westminster, Central London, June 14, 2011. Also, interview with Ali, Hounslow, West London, June 21, 2011.

[53] Interview with Abdul, Whitechapel, East London, June 18, 2011.

[54] Interview with leading activist, Skype, June 26, 2013.

TABLE 1.4 *Network-Level Measures in al-Muhajiroun during Three Time Periods*

Measures	Time Period 1	Time Period 2	Time Period 3
Number of nodes	89	82	75
Degree centralization	0.840	0.737	0.599
Betweenness centralization	0.747	0. 614	0.357
Average path length	2.057	2.124	2.108
Clustering coefficient	0.744	0.702	0.718

Omar's" move to Lebanon shortly after the London bombings, the convictions of several prominent activists on criminal charges, and the banning of different spin-off groups that publicized the network's activism. Some activist networks may have folded under such intense pressure. The Emigrants did not. Instead, the network shed its scale-free-like structure and evolved into a smaller, more decentralized small-world-like network.

The same network and node-level measures of al-Muhajiroun's centrality and topology can be used to test our argument. Now, however, we apply these measures to proxy networks we extracted from the newspaper data after Omar Bakri left Britain in the wake of the 7/7 bombings (Time Period 2), and after activists publicly relaunched al-Muhajiroun several years later (Time Period 3). We begin at the network-level of analysis, where we examine a range of structural properties for the proxy networks during each time period, including size, degree centralization, betweenness centralization, average path length, and clustering coefficient (see Table 1.4).

The network-level measures in Table 1.4 suggest that al-Muhajiroun's proxy networks became smaller, less centralized, and more clustered over time, while maintaining their cohesiveness. Before Omar Bakri left Britain there were 89 nodes in the network from the newspaper data.[55] In Time Period 2, measured when Bakri no longer resided in Britain, the proxy network contained 82 nodes. In the third and final time period, measured after al-Muhajiroun resurrected its original name, the network contained 75 nodes. Over the three periods observed here the proxy networks declined by 14 nodes, or nearly 16 percent.

[55] We repeat our earlier caveat about interpreting these results too precisely. The newspaper data from which we derive our proxy networks undercount the number of nodes because many rank-and-file activists are not mentioned by name in press accounts of al-Muhajiroun. During the late 1990s, the real network contained several hundred activists and supporters throughout Great Britain, far larger than the 89 nodes in Time Period 1. While the Emigrants' were smaller by the time of my field work, many rank-and-file activists I interviewed were not mentioned in press accounts. This suggests that the real network was larger than the 75 nodes in the proxy network for Time Period 3, which ends in 2012. We use these measures to highlight trends in al-Muhajiroun, such as its declining size and greater decentralization. We do not suggest the newspaper data perfectly represent this outlawed activist network.

In addition to suggesting that the Emigrants shrank, the network-level measures show the proxy networks decentralized over time. The network's degree centralization drops from 0.840 in the first period to 0.599 in the third, a decline of 29 percent. The fall in network-level betweenness is even more pronounced, declining 52 percent from 0.747 in the first period to 0.357 in the third. These results suggest that as al-Muhajiroun's external environment became increasingly hostile, the proxy networks were becoming less centralized around Omar Bakri and the other leading activists.

Even as the Emigrants' proxy networks became smaller and less centralized, they remained tightly clustered, as shown in their clustering coefficients. During the three time periods, the clustering coefficient fell slightly from 0.744 in the first to 0.702 in the second before rising to 0.718 in the third. The increasing hostility faced by al-Muhajiroun did not exert a significant impact on its clustering, at least according to this measure. The proxy networks contained tight clusters whether the law enforcement environment was congenial to the Emigrants' activism – or not. High clustering can lead to fragmentation, particularly when clusters are poorly connected to the rest of the network. In al-Muhajiroun this effect was offset by the network's low average path length, which increased marginally from 2.057 in the first period to 2.108 in the last. In all three periods, nodes in the proxy networks connect to other nodes by an average of just over two steps. These are short path lengths for networks of nearly 100 nodes, suggesting that information continued to move through al-Muhajiroun in few steps, irrespective of environmental hostility. The short path lengths indicate the proxy networks remained cohesive even as British authorities intensified their pressure and the Emigrants' local clustering increased slightly in the final period.

The short path lengths, high local clustering, and declining centralization of the three proxy networks suggest that al-Muhajiroun was changing from a centralized network revolving around Omar Bakri Mohammed to a decentralized, yet cohesive network with local clusters organized around a larger number of hubs. This is consistent with our argument that the Emigrants shifted to a more decentralized, small-world-like structure as its environment became increasingly hostile. To explore this further, and to better understand power relations within al-Muhajiroun, we examine node-level measures during all three time periods, focusing on degree centrality and betweenness centrality (see Tables 1.5 and 1.6).

The measures in Tables 1.5 and 1.6 suggest that power relations in al-Muhajiroun underwent three important changes over time. First, following his move to Lebanon and the network's continued activism in Great Britain, Omar Bakri Mohammed slowly lost access and brokerage power among the Emigrants. In the early years the activist network centered on Omar Bakri, as reflected in his remarkably high centrality scores. Although his node-level values and rankings held steady in Time Period 2, by the final period, measured several years after his departure from Britain, Bakri was

TABLE 1.5 *Node-Level Degree Centrality in al-Muhajiroun during Three Time Periods*

Time Period 1		Time Period 2		Time Period 3	
Omar Bakri	0.898	Omar Bakri	0.802	Anjem Choudary	0.716
Anjem Choudary	0.341	Anjem Choudary	0.481	Omar Bakri	0.554
Abu Hamza*	0.307	Abdul Rahman Saleem	0.321	Abu Hamza*	0.473
Hassan Butt	0.273	Abu Izzadeen Brooks	0.309	Abu Izzadeen Brooks	0.459
Afzal Munir*	0.205	Abu Hamza*	0.210	Abdul Rahman Saleem	0.405
Aftab Manoor*	0.193	Omar Khyam*	0.173	Abdul Muhid	0.365
Asif Hanif*	0.182	Mohammed Babar*	0.160	Ali Beheshti*	0.297
Yassir Khan	0.170	Abdul Muhid	0.136	Ibrahim Hassan	0.284
Rubana Akghar	0.159	Abu Uzair Sharif	0.136	Mizanur Rahman	0.284
Ibrahim Hassan	0.148	Mohammed Alamgir	0.123	Afzal Munir*	0.270
Node average	0.077	Node average	0.083	Node average	0.133

Note: Asterisk indicates that this node is a "false positive."

TABLE 1.6 *Node-Level Betweenness Centrality in al-Muhajiroun during Three Time Periods*

Time Period 1		Time Period 2		Time Period 3	
Omar Bakri	0.751	Omar Bakri	0.620	Anjem Choudary	0.367
Abu Hamza*	0.088	Anjem Choudary	0.198	Omar Bakri	0.214
Anjem Choudary	0.076	Abdul Rahman Saleem	0.117	Abdul Rahman Saleem	0.120
Hassan Butt	0.048	Abu Izzadeen Brooks	0.054	Abu Hamza*	0.102
Abu Izzadeen Brooks	0.028	Mohammed Babar*	0.044	Abu Izzadeen Brooks	0.064
Afzal Munir*	0.016	Omar Khyam*	0.030	Abdul Muhid	0.038
Aftab Manzoor*	0.013	Abu Abbas	0.011	Afsor Ali	0.034
Mohammed Omar*	0.009	Abu Hamza*	0.011	Mohammed Shamsuddin	0.028
Asif Hanif*	0.007	Khalid Kelly	0.010	Omar Khyam*	0.024
Abdul Rahman Saleem	0.007	Omar Sharif	0.009	Afzal Munir*	0.018
Node average	0.012	Node average	0.014	Node average	0.015

Note: Asterisk indicates that this node is a "false positive."

just one hub among several. No longer was "Sheikh Omar" the most powerful node with the most connections in the proxy network, as measured in degree centrality; nor was he the most important broker, as measured in betweenness centrality.

For both measures, Omar Bakri's former student, Anjem Choudary, emerged as the top-ranked node in Time Period 3. This underscores the second major change in power relations in al-Muhajiroun: Anjem Choudary's ascendance. As Bakri's sun set, Choudary's star rose. He became the most accessible hub in the final proxy network, with more connections to other nodes, and greater brokerage than other hubs, including Bakri. Significantly, the rise in Choudary's centrality measures and rankings occurred after he and other activists tried to revitalize the network by resurrecting the original al-Muhajiroun banner following the British government's banning of several spin-off groups.

Yet unlike the first period, when Omar Bakri Mohammed towered above the other nodes, Choudary was merely first among equals in Time Period 3. This illustrates the third, most consequential change in al-Muhajiroun's power relations: the more equal distribution of access and brokerage in the last proxy network. In the final period no single hub dominated the way Bakri did during the first two. Instead ties were more evenly distributed across numerous hubs, starting with Choudary, whose degree centrality was 0.716, and continuing with Bakri (0.554), Abu Izzadeen Brooks (0.459), Abdul Rahman Saleem (0.405), and Abdul Muhid (0.365). In this proxy network, six nodes possessed degree centrality scores of 0.365 or higher; in the first one, only Bakri did. Across the entire proxy network, the node average for degree centrality in Period 3 (0.133) was nearly double the node average in Period 1 (0.077). Rather than simply replacing one dominant hub (Bakri) with another (Choudary), the final proxy network featured several hubs, all of whom played important roles for the Emigrants.

The emergence of these nodes in the last period suggests that al-Muhajiroun was evolving from a centralized network dominated by Omar Bakri to a more decentralized proxy, with different local clusters connected by multiple hubs. This structure maintained the network's overall coherence and gave the Emigrants their small-world feel. Several of these nodes, including Omar "Abu Izzadeen" Brooks, Abdul Muhid, and Abdul Rahman Saleem, were released from prison during this period, having completed their sentences for various criminal offenses. Each of them continued their activism, drawing on the "street cred" prison gave them to re-establish themselves in the activist network. All of them became prominent in the more decentralized proxy network, reinforcing each other by bridging the clusters. Their emergence helps explain why the Emigrants were able to adapt to the loss of the network's founder and spiritual leader, an issue I explore more in Chapter 4.

These measures suggest that al-Muhajiroun was evolving from a scale-free-like network to more decentralized small-world. To explore this possibility further, we return to the structural measures we used for the proxy networks'

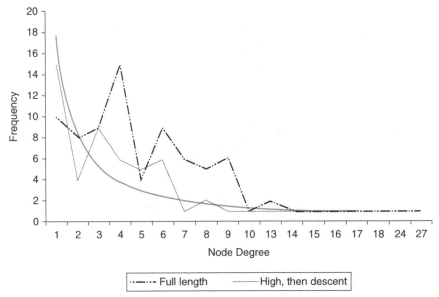

FIGURE 1.2 Node Distribution in Time Period 2

scale-free and small-world properties, applying them to the final two time periods. Figure 1.2 shows the results of our scale-free tests during Time Period 2. Similar to the first proxy network, the node degree distribution in this period resembles a power-law. Few nodes have many connections while many nodes have few, as indicated in the "long tail" of the distribution. This appears to show that the proxy network remained scale-free after the intensification of state power against it. Unlike the early years, however, the Emigrants' power law distribution in Time Period 2 is ambiguous. When we set the x-floor at 4, the estimated exponent value, $\hat{\alpha}$, for al-Muhajiroun is 2.43 (K-S stat = 0.13, p value = 0.34), within the established range of a power law distribution. But the degree distribution's tail declines unevenly. The proxy network's degree distribution does not significantly resemble a power law, even when we set the x-floor value at 9, near the end of the distribution ($R^2 = 0.778$).

If al-Muhajiroun was no longer unambiguously scale-free in Time Period 2, what was it? Did the proxy network retain its small-world structure, despite being under pressure from the authorities? Results from the HG test of small-world properties, shown in Figure 1.3, suggest that it did. During the second period al-Muhajiroun still approximates a small-world network, despite experiencing a decline in its small-world score, from 1.12 in the first period to 0.997 in the second.

The persistence of al-Muhajiroun's small-world-ness in Time Period 2 is impressive given the pressure from British authorities on the activist network during these years. Did the changes experienced by the Emigrants in the

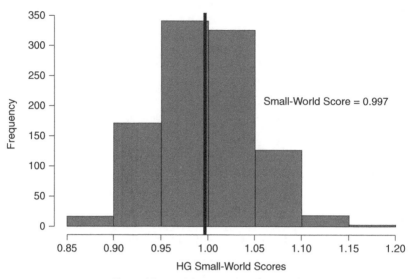

FIGURE 1.3   HG Small-World Test for Time Period 2, Trials = 1,000

aftermath of Omar Bakri's exile represent a short-term departure from its tradition of revolving around a central figure or did the activist network continue
down a different structural path? To answer this question we apply the tests of
al-Muhajiroun's scale-free properties to the final time period in our data, measured several years after Bakri left Britain and shortly after activists relaunched
the al-Muhajiroun platform in 2009 (Time Period 3). If al-Muhajiroun fully
recovered by this time and re-established its previous pattern of organization,
we would expect to see the proxy network become scale-free again while continuing to maintain its small-world properties.

However, our results suggest that the Emigrants did not return to their scale-
free-like form following the application of state power. With an x-floor set to
3, the estimated exponent value, $\hat{\alpha}$, was 0.667 (K-S stat = 0.15, p value = 0.14).
This is well below the minimum threshold value of 2. Instead of containing a
few hubs with many connections and many nodes with few connections, the
proxy network contained many hubs with modest amounts of connections.
Well-connected nodes still existed, Omar Bakri among them, but no hubs
dominated the way Bakri had during the first period. Social power spread
throughout the network, with ties becoming more evenly distributed across
numerous hubs, some of which bridged different clusters.

Does the persistence of well-connected hubs in al-Muhajiroun suggest
that it retained its small-world character during the final period? According
to results from the HG test (Figure 1.4), the proxy network's small-world
score declined slightly, from 0.997 in the second period to 0.92 in the third.
This suggests that al-Muhajiroun remained "small-world-like" as it evolved

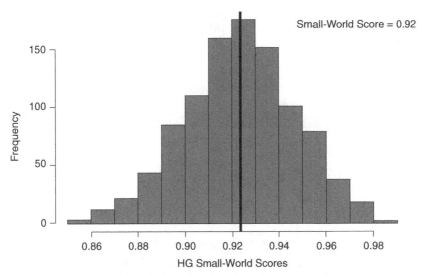

FIGURE I.4 HG Small-World Test for Time Period 3, Trials = 1,000

from a centralized network with scale-free and small-world properties to a more dispersed, small-world system with multiple, moderately connected hubs. As we emphasized earlier, many scale-free networks are also small worlds. Some networks may lose their scale-free properties while remaining small worlds. Our results confirm that the Emigrants' final proxy network shed its scale-free-like properties, but retained its small-world-ness. This structure allowed activists to continue their da'wah stalls and protests in a more hostile environment.

We can summarize our network-level results by plotting al-Muhajiroun's scale-free and small-world properties during all three time periods on a single graph. Our analysis distinguishes between "scale-free" and "scale-free-like" and between "small-world" and "small-world-like" networks. These distinctions are based on the assumption that many networks are not purely scale-free or small-world but exhibit structural properties that are close enough to be "like" them. Consequently, our two "likeness" categories extend the range of the pure types, but only slightly. To be considered scale-free or small-world, the proxy network must have a parameter value that falls within specific boundaries of the node degree distribution or the HG small-world score. As defined above, scale-free networks have a degree distribution exponent, α, that falls in the range $2 < \alpha < 3$. Small-world networks have an HG score, S^Δ, greater than 1. Scale-free "likeness" and small-world "likeness" each contain an interval that extends the boundaries for both types of structures. We define "small-world-like" by extending the $S^\Delta > 1$ boundary to values falling within one standard deviation (i.e. mean − 1SD) of the measure using

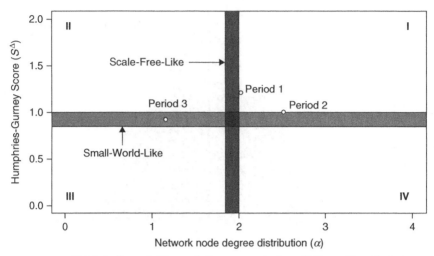

FIGURE 1.5 Al-Muhajiroun's Network Structures during all Three Time Periods

our 1000 simulation networks sample. If the network's HG score is less than but within one standard deviation of 1, we consider it to be "small-world-like." We consider the network to be "scale-free-like" if its observed and simulated degree distributions are not significantly different, but the estimated exponent falls outside the range $2 < \alpha < 3$.[56]

We plot al-Muhajiroun's proxy networks for each time period using these definitions. In Figure 1.5, the vertical axis corresponds to the network's HG score, S^Δ, while the horizontal axis corresponds to the network's node degree distribution exponent, α. The bold lines that mark S^Δ at the value 1 and α at the value 2 represent the minimal conditions for placement in the scale-free or small-world categories. In the figure, Quadrant I is scale-free and small-world, Quadrant II is small-world only, Quadrant III is neither scale-free nor small-world, and Quadrant IV is scale-free only. The shaded areas in the graph correspond to the "likeness" extensions for each structure. The horizontal shaded area represents "small-world-like" and the vertical shaded area signifies "scale-free-like."

As shown in the graph, the first proxy network (Period 1) displayed scale-free-like and small-world properties during the Emigrants' early years, before law enforcement pressure intensified. This supports our argument that al-Muhajiroun, like other dark networks, was scale-free-like before the British government exerted significant pressure against it. In this period, the activist network displayed a power law distribution of ties. A few highly connected hubs, led by Omar Bakri, dominated the network through their access power

[56] Our methodological appendix contains more information on how we calculate the observed and simulated distributions of this scaling parameter.

and brokerage. In Period 2, the proxy network exhibited both scale-free and small-world-like properties. On the surface, this appears to contradict our claim that al-Muhajiroun would decentralize and lose its scale-free form after the government cracked down against it. But as we discussed, the scale-free results for this period are ambiguous: the network tail's uneven decline suggests that the degree distribution does not resemble a power law, a defining attribute of scale-free networks. Finally, the proxy network for Period 3 contained properties of a small-world-like network only. Even as its scale-free properties declined, al-Muhajiroun remained small-world-like. Instead of a single hub which dominated the system, the Emigrants contained multiple hubs that bridged different clusters. This structure produced high local clustering with short path lengths across the network, allowing activists from different clusters to share information and other resources across the redundant bridges that linked them.

Even though activists would have preferred that Omar Bakri Mohammed remained in Britain to guide their activism, moving from a scale-free-like structure to a more decentralized small-world system helps explain why the Emigrants became so resilient in the face of intense counter-terrorism pressure. This structure allowed activists to mobilize in an increasingly hostile environment. Exploring this argument requires that we go beyond measuring the Emigrants' structural properties to observe how activists actually organized their contentious politics. To better understand this crucial link between network structure and performance, we return to our ethnographic data.

INSIDE THE EMIGRANTS' DECENTRALIZED SMALL-WORLD-LIKE NETWORK

The formal network analysis above is consistent with my interviews and participant observation. For many years following Omar Bakri's departure from Britain, al-Muhajiroun continued to function as a transnational advocacy network, with activists and supporters coordinating their activities in pursuit of shared goals and principled beliefs. Interviews with network leaders, activists, and other respondents confirm that Omar Bakri no longer dominated the network during these years. Bakri remained an important figure but his role in the network was limited, in part due to legal problems he faced in Lebanon, culminating in his imprisonment for promoting extremist ideologies and inciting violence.[57] Several of Bakri's long-standing students responded to

---

[57] Ian Johnston, "Banned radical cleric Sheikh Omar Bakri Mohamed arrested in Lebanon over 'links to terrorism'," *The Independent* (May 26, 2014), www.independent.co.uk/news/world/middle-east/banned-radical-cleric-sheikh-omar-bakri-mohamed-arrested-in-lebanon-over-links-to-terrorism-9434213.html [Accessed July 7, 2014]; *Daily Star*, "Lebanon sentences 5 over terror charges," (April 20, 2015), www.dailystar.com.lb/News/Lebanon-News/2015/Apr-20/295139-lebanon-sentences-5-over-terror-charges.ashx [Accessed June 26, 2015].

this setback by picking up his mantle. Chapter 3 describes how these activists increased their leadership in the network, delivering lectures that Bakri himself once gave and mentoring newcomers who continued to join al-Muhajiroun's "community of practice."

As important as they were to the activist network, none of these emergent leaders enjoyed Omar Bakri's authority or religious credentials. Consequently, power relations within the activist network became more diffuse and its organization even more decentralized. Some respondents go so far as to claim that their network lacked any formal organization, even as they continued to follow its culture, including the principled beliefs and ideology that Anjem Choudary and other hubs propagated. "The culture's the same," explains one leading activist who has been with the network since the late 1990s, "we haven't changed our culture, but there's just no organization. If you look at the materials that are being used by our group, we don't necessarily call them al-Muhajiroun, but the theme is more or less the same. The ideas are more or less the same, the *fiqh* [Islamic jurisprudence], in terms of the rulings, is still the same. It's just that we don't have an organization."[58]

"We don't need to be part of an organization anyway," claims another leading activist, "because there are personalities in the UK that have so much popularity and notoriety they don't need organizations. They can act as individuals and see the impact on society." He himself is one of these "popular" activists who contributed to al-Muhajiroun's notoriety in Britain and internationally after Omar Bakri's departure. "I can say my name in the papers and I can still have the impact," he adds, acknowledging this point. But even he admits that his colleagues still have to coordinate with each other to have an impact on British society. I pushed him on this point: "You can say who and you get the attention, but you alone cannot organize demonstrations. If you want to actually engage in collective action like we're talking about, you need others, right?"

"Of course," he concedes, "because collective activity by definition means more than one."

"Exactly. So that group there, whatever you want to call it."

"Collective," he responds. "Movement. I prayed before I came here. That was collective activity. We all come together around a common cause and a common objective with someone in charge... So you're fine on demonstrations. It could be that 97 percent of the people at the demonstration, you've never met them before. But the cause and the objective – they all appear for. So with demonstrations, rallies, it's about getting the people to support the cause and if they agree they will come. And if they don't maybe they won't come. Or sometimes they agree but their fear of speaking out in society will keep them from coming."[59]

The research director of a London-based think tank that has followed the Emigrants closely for years makes a similar point. "It operates much more

---

[58] Interview with leading activist, Ilford, East London, November 13, 2010.
[59] Interview with leading activist, Leyton, East London, November 8, 2010.

like a group of like-minded people," he says, describing the activist network. "They turn up when they want to turn up and don't turn up when they don't want to turn up."[60] This fluid, almost ad hoc structure was confirmed by other respondents within and outside al-Muhajiroun, some of whom juxtaposed the network's formal lack of "organization" with its need for leaders to organize the group's activism. "There isn't an organization so it's not easy to get somebody in charge," explains one veteran activist, adding, "You need help in the organization. You want somebody to be in charge of the demonstration, but because of the police pressure it's more spontaneous than before the banning."[61] "As far as structure goes," confirms an officer who specializes in al-Muhajiroun for the London Metropolitan Police, "it's not as rigid as it once was. Dominant personalities almost outweigh rank." His colleague agrees: "There are some really strong personalities within the group now. There's quite a few of them."[62]

These leading and veteran activists run network activities in different areas. Moreover, they provide essential bridging connections between local clusters. The new leaders work together to ensure a sense of continuity and cohesiveness that continues even a decade after Bakri left Britain. In each area, leaders form groups of activists who organize da'wah stalls and demonstrations. The basic unit of organization remains the small, local group, in the form of the halaqah. At the time of my field work, groups in East, West, and South London had their own study circles, composed of local activists and their recruits who met regularly to indoctrinate each other, and plan and carry out activities. Different leaders and veterans act as redundant bridges between the halaqahs, allowing information and resources to flow from cluster to cluster. In addition to organizing local activities, halaqahs also mobilize participants for special events involving different study circles. These include large da'wah stalls activists call "Islamic roadshows" and political protests in London and other cities.

As they did when Omar Bakri was still around, halaqah members form strong friendship bonds by hanging out with each other at study sessions, da'wah stalls, and other social activities. Similar to the Salafi-jihadi cliques studied by Marc Sageman, activists create a "collective social identity and strong emotional feelings for the in-group" through "intense face-to-face interaction."[63] This collective identity, grounded in the network's vision of establishing the Islamic caliphate in Britain and elsewhere, provides, as Haroon explains, "a sense of camaraderie, a reason for doing something."[64] This sense

---

[60] Interview with research director, think tank, Bloomsbury, Central London, December 14, 2010.

[61] Interview with veteran activist, Walthamstow, East London, November 16, 2010.

[62] Interview with two London Metropolitan Police officers, Westminster, Central London, June 29, 2011.

[63] Sageman, *Understanding Terror Networks*, p. 154. Sageman adds, "This process is not well studied empirically because it would involve long-term observation of groups of friends." Fortunately, this book *is* based on long-term observation of al-Muhajiroun activists and, as such, provides support for Sageman's claim. I explore this process in greater detail in Chapters 2 and 3.

[64] Interview with Haroon, Westminster, Central London, June 14, 2011.

of camaraderie is evident at network events, where activists work together to set up tables and tents, make protest signs, distribute literature and compact discs, and record their activities to post on the Internet. "We're close brothers," explains one respondent while handing out leaflets with several activists at a da'wah stall in Ilford, "we don't have to be flesh and blood, we're brothers and we just help each other out with what needs to be done."[65]

Al-Muhajiroun's small-world-ness is frequently on display at such events, particularly large gatherings involving activists from different clusters. Consistent with the network's small-world orientation, activists often arrive in small groups of people from their halaqah. At one demonstration I observed, outside the Saudi embassy in Mayfair, one of the network's leading activists from Whitechapel appeared with a group of halaqah brothers in tow, all of them chanting protest slogans.[66] A week later, different clusters of activists arrived separately at an Islamic roadshow on the High Road near Wembley Stadium.[67] Before, during, and after these events, activists socialized mostly with other brothers from their halaqahs. Cross-cluster contact was freely permitted, but only leading and veteran activists tended to engage supporters from different groups, whom they knew from delivering talks and participating in other events run by the local halaqahs. At the conclusion of the larger roadshows and demonstrations, groups often left the same way they arrived, in unison with their halaqah brothers.

In recent years al-Muhajiroun has not been as active as it was during Omar Bakri's tenure in Britain.[68] Activists organize fewer protests and da'wah stalls and their events are often poorly attended. In this sense, the network's performance has declined as it has become more diffuse and decentralized. Yet the network continues to mobilize its followers and recruit new supporters. During my field work I saw activists calling people to Islam in da'wah stalls and roadshows on some of London's busiest streets, while protesting a variety of issues, including the Lebanese government's arrest of Omar Bakri in 2010, the London Olympic Games in 2012, and the British Parliament's discussion of a burka banning bill in 2013.[69] Many of the same leading and veteran activists participated in these events, but each year new supporters appeared, joining their persistent colleagues to command good and forbid evil. The tenacity of al-Muhajiroun's activism highlights the resilience of its decentralized,

---

[65] Interview with rank-and-file activist, Ilford, East London, November 13, 2010; field notes from Supporters of Sunnah da'wah stall in Ilford, East London, November 13, 2010.

[66] Field notes from protest at the Royal Embassy of Saudi Arabia, Mayfair, Central London, June 17, 2011.

[67] Field notes from Islamic roadshow in Wembley Central, West London, June 25, 2011.

[68] Interviews with several activists, Whitechapel, East London, September 4, 2013, Rashid, Whitechapel, East London, June 26, 2011, and US government official, Mayfair, Central London, December 3, 2010.

[69] Field notes from different locations in London, November 15, 2010, June 17, 2011, June 25, 2011, July 21, 2012, and September 6, 2013.

small-world-like form. The network's shift to a more distributed, yet clustered structure facilitated its ability to mobilize supporters even as British authorities arrested its activists, disrupted its protests, outlawed its spin-off groups, and forbade its leaders from engaging in public da'wah.

At least two mechanisms help explain the Emigrants' persistence as a small-world network and its performance in recent years. The first mechanism linking the network's structure to its performance was the emergence of several nodes that bridged different clusters. These leading and veteran activists essentially replaced al-Muhajiroun's original emir and centralized hub. Clusters were connected not by a single node but by multiple ones. This allowed information and other resources to spread throughout the network even after Omar Bakri fled Britain. Anjem Choudary, Abu Izzadeen Brooks, Abdul Muhid, Mizanur Rahman, and other leading activists connected to the same local clusters, providing redundant links between them. These activists were less connected than Bakri had been during the early years, but connected enough to provide robust shortcuts between clusters. This prevented clusters from fragmenting into isolated islands of nodes when people like Choudary were arrested and, in some cases, convicted of criminal offenses.

The second mechanism linking al-Muhajiroun's small-world-like structure to its performance was the neighborhood-based study circle. These local groups remained the organizational vehicle through which activists engaged in high-risk activism and recruited new supporters. Halaqahs in different London neighborhoods formed tight clusters of activists who met regularly to interact, hear private talks, and absorb the network's ideology. These clusters organized da'wah stalls in their neighborhoods and coordinated with other halaqahs during larger events. As I will show in the next chapter, halaqahs also served as an entry point for recruits who approached activists at da'wah stalls and public conferences. Through these small groups, the network continued to attract newcomers and mobilize them for collective action even as British authorities arrested their leaders and banned their spin-off groups.

CONCLUSION

In recent years, the British government has confronted a weakened, but resilient, al-Muhajiroun network, one that bounced back from numerous setbacks to continue to indoctrinate young men and women into its Salafi-Islamist ideology. Following an escalation in law enforcement pressure, the Emigrants evolved from a centralized scale-free-like network to a smaller, more decentralized, small-world-like system. This structure offered an organizational "solution" to the activist network's collective action dilemma through two mechanisms. First, the small-world configuration allowed multiple leading and veteran activists to connect different clusters. Through these bridging connections, information and other resources spread through the network, even when individual leaders were removed from the system. Second, the local halaqahs' small-group structure allowed activists to interact frequently, coordinate their activities, and recruit new followers to replace participants who were removed because of state pressure.

These findings suggest that network structure has important implications for performance. Small-world networks with multiple nodes spanning different clusters are self-healing.[70] When one node – even a hub as centralized as Omar Bakri – crumples, others emerge to bridge the gap and keep the resources flowing, allowing the network to overcome the disruption. Al-Muhajiroun's "small-world-ness" enabled its survival after Bakri's departure, allowing it to mobilize followers and engage in contentious politics in a hostile environment.

Significantly, the Emigrants' shift to a smaller, more decentralized network was not the result of Bakri's or Anjem Choudary's overarching strategy or vision. Rather, this transformation was the unintended result of dozens, if not hundreds, of small changes made without much thought other than getting through another day in the land of disbelief (*dar al-kuffar*) so that activists could continue to call Britons to their interpretation of Islam. The moral of this story is not the triumph of networks over hierarchies. Nor do we want to suggest that small-worlds are inherently superior to scale-free and distributed networks, in hostile environments or otherwise. If the small-world network became al-Muhajiroun's default structure, it was not its chosen one. Omar Bakri Mohammed would have preferred to remain in Britain, calling for the caliphate through an expanding scale-free network centered on him and his ambitious vision. Alas, Her Majesty's Government had other plans. As Bakri's successors have undoubtedly learned, it's hard to overthrow one government and build another without a large, formal organization to marshal resources, command followers, and resolve disputes. Evolving into a small-world network may have helped the Emigrants weather their turbulent environment, but it also made it increasingly unlikely that Bakri's followers would ever achieve their ultimate objective: creating the Islamic state in Great Britain.

---

[70] Christakis and Fowler, *Connected*, p. 293.

2

Joining the Emigrants

> Straight away when I sat down, they all surrounded me and started talking. They were very welcoming, very friendly. They made me feel wanted.
>
> Ali, former activist

Early on in my field research, I met one of al-Muhajiroun's leaders near his home in Leyton, East London. He had been with the Emigrants since the beginning, and served as a gatekeeper for my research, giving me access to many of his followers. After talking at length about his own journey to Islamic activism, he chuckled at my question about how people become involved in al-Muhajiroun. "There's no one way you see, Michael," he explained. "People sometimes appear at stalls and they start distributing leaflets with us. Sometimes they attend our lectures and end up wanting to be a part of it. Other times they'll be studying and they come across our YouTube videos or other things and they communicate with us. There's 101 ways in which someone can start participating in the activities of the organization, the *jama'ah*."[1]

In the following months and years, I interviewed dozens of activists, many of whom described their own journeys to al-Muhajiroun, sundry experiences that supported this leader's insight. Some were recruited to the network through its da'wah stalls in London and other British cities. Others learned about the network through one of its high-profile protests, its online videos, or leaders' frequent appearances in the media. Some joined the Emigrants after becoming disenchanted with other groups, including the Tablighi Jama'at and Hizb ut-Tahrir. Many were drawn in through family connections and friendship ties. Some married into the activist network. Several were recruited in prison. Listening to the narratives of dozens of respondents who became involved in the network's activism, I came to realize that there is no single pathway to

---

[1] Interview with leading activist, Leyton, East London, November 4, 2010.

al-Muhajiroun, just as others observe there is no royal road to radicalization or terrorism more broadly.[2] The paths to al-Muhajiroun are as complex and diverse as the individuals who walk them.

And yet certain patterns do emerge from activists' stories. These patterns became increasingly clear to me as I reflected on their narratives about how and why they joined their companions and mobilized to high-risk activism. Da'wah stalls and public talks *are* essential to drawing in new participants, as are activists' family and friendship ties, and the accessibility, charisma, and perceived knowledge of leaders like Omar Bakri Mohammed. Although activists prefer to think of their ideology as representing the "pure" form of Islam, irresistible to anyone ready to receive it, in practice the Emigrants rely on a strategy of recruitment to pull people in. This strategy is tailored to young men and women who seek identity and belonging, and who are becoming more politically engaged with their world. Over the years, activists have become adept at identifying potential recruits, often from their own social networks. Through sustained interaction they seek to exploit recruits' need for fellowship with like-minded peers and their desire to build meaningful lives.

In this chapter, I describe this recruiting process and other factors that "push and pull" people into al-Muhajiroun. However, readers looking for a simple model of sequential "steps" to the activist network or irreversible "stages" of development will be disappointed.[3] Joining the Emigrants is a complex process that cannot be reliably reduced to models depicting compulsory steps and stages. In analyzing my respondents' narratives, I do not present a single theory or causal explanation for joining. Individuals who experience many of the conditions described below may experience other factors I do not document, which also contribute to their mobilization.[4] But even if the patterns and

---

[2] For discussion of the various pathways to violent radicalization and terrorism, see Clark McCauley and Sophia Moskalenko, *Friction: How Radicalization Happens to Them and US* (New York: Oxford University Press, 2011), pp. 218–19; John Horgan, *The Psychology of Terrorism* (New York: Routledge, 2005), pp. 80–106; Peter R. Neumann, "The Trouble with Radicalization," *International Affairs* 89, no. 4 (2013), pp. 873–93; and Marc Sageman, *Misunderstanding Terrorism* (Philadelphia, PA: University of Pennsylvania Press, 2017), pp. 89–109.

[3] Prominent examples of the stage-theory approach to radicalization include Fathali Moghaddam's "staircase to terrorism" metaphor and the New York Police Department's oft-cited model of "Salafi-jihadi radicalization." See Fathali M. Moghaddam, "The Staircase to Terrorism: A Psychological Exploration," *American Psychologist* 60, no. 2 (February–March 2005), pp. 161–9; and Mitchell D. Silber and Arvin Bhatt, *Radicalization in the West: The Homegrown Threat* (New York: Police Department, City of New York, NYPD Intelligence Division, 2007).

[4] For similar observations, see Clark McCauley and Sophia Moskalenko, "Mechanisms of Political Radicalization: Pathways Toward Terrorism," *Terrorism and Political Violence* 20, no. 3 (2008), p. 429; and John Horgan, *The Psychology of Terrorism* (New York: Routledge, 2005), pp. 105–6.

conditions I describe in this chapter are not sufficient, many of them do contribute to my respondents' decisions to join the activist network. These contributing factors are well-known to scholars of social movements and religious sects, and to help me make sense of them I draw on their studies of recruitment.[5] Many of my findings on al-Muhajiroun are consistent with this literature, lending further support to those studies, and underscoring the broader significance of my own.

SEARCHING FOR ANSWERS

Individuals who become involved in al-Muhajiroun must be receptive to its culture and ideology. This requires openness to ideas and worldviews that many Muslims and non-Muslims, even some who eventually become activists, find excessive, even offensive. Describing his own journey to al-Muhajiroun, one respondent who I call "Salman" recalls his first lecture: "I came out of the talk and said to myself, 'A bunch of extremists! There's no way Islam is like that.'"[6] Yet within a matter of months, Salman accepted many of the ideas he heard in that talk. How do individuals become receptive to ideas and beliefs that many British citizens consider repugnant?

A number of respondents described their embrace of al-Muhajiroun as part of a broader process of self-discovery that began when they questioned themselves about their religious beliefs and the meaning of life. As is common among young people, this period of self-discovery and "soul searching" typically occurred during adolescence and young adulthood. "When I was fourteen or fifteen I was wondering, 'Why did God create me?'" explains one young activist. Repeating a common complaint from respondents against what they describe as the decadence and materialism of British society, he continues, "What does society have to offer? It offered drugs, sex, rock and roll, and all this, but I thought maybe there's more."[7] "As you grow up you start realizing

---

[5] See, for example, Doug McAdam, "Recruitment to High-Risk Activism: The Case of the Freedom Summer," *American Journal of Sociology* 92, no. 1 (July 1986), pp. 64–90; Donatella della Porta, *Social Movements, Political Violence and the State: A Comparative Analysis of Italy and Germany* (New York: Cambridge University Press, 1995); James A. Aho, *The Politics of Righteousness: Idaho Christian Patriotism* (Seattle: University of Washington Press, 1990); Kathleen M. Blee, *Inside Organized Racism: Women in the Hate Movement* (Berkeley, CA: University of California Press, 2002); John Lofland and Rodney Stark, "Becoming a World-Saver: A Theory of Conversion to a Deviant Perspective," *American Sociological Review* 30, no. 6 (December 1965), pp. 862–75; and Rodney Stark and William Sims Bainbridge, "Networks of Faith: Interpersonal Bonds and Recruitment to Cults and Sects," *American Journal of Sociology* 85, no. 6 (May 1980), pp. 1376–95.

[6] Interview with Salman, Leyton, East London, December 9, 2010. Salman was not the only activist who viewed al-Muhajiroun as extremist before joining. Interview with veteran activist, Whitechapel, East London, November 9, 2010.

[7] Interview with rank-and-file activist, Skype, June 26, 2013.

there's more to life," observes another activist. "I just wanted to know what am I doing? Is life just about making money?"[8]

Although several respondents became involved in the Emigrants after converting to Islam, many activists in my sample were raised in Muslim households that followed beliefs and practices associated with the *Barelwi* tradition of Sufi Islam.[9] These respondents did not characterize their families or their upbringings as particularly devout. This bothered some of them and they rebelled against it. Turning to al-Muhajiroun was a way for these youngsters to build their own identities by exploring religious ideas that stood in contrast to the Islam practiced by their parents.[10] "I was raised in a Muslim family, but my mum and dad weren't all that practicing," explains one respondent, echoing a common complaint among his fellow activists. "When I turned sixteen or seventeen, I started asking myself, 'What am I going to do with my life?'"[11] "I was born a Muslim but I wasn't practicing Islam," adds a veteran activist. "The point came where I started to ask what my purpose in life was and this led me to look into my way of life and from there I started to rediscover my roots."[12] "I grew up in a very secular household," notes a third activist, who was raised by his single mother. "The only thing I knew about Islam when I was growing up was the month of Ramadan." He recalls how he took "advantage" of his mother's "easy going" parenting to experience "whatever culture the West has to offer." He adds, "I became very disillusioned with this in my mid-teens and late-teens."[13]

Numerous respondents emphasize that "identity crises" they faced as children of South Asian immigrants influenced their decision to rediscover their roots. Many children in bicultural families struggle with "dual" identities without embracing high-risk activism, but these activists played up the cultural conflicts they experienced growing up in Pakistani and Bangladeshi households in Great Britain. This is consistent with the writings of former Hizb ut-Tahrir activists who argue that identity crises experienced by young British Muslims are a major factor in pushing them towards involvement in extremist groups like al-Muhajiroun and Hizb ut-Tahrir.[14]

---

[8] Interview with veteran activist, Whitechapel, East London, November 9, 2010.

[9] For more on the Barelwi tradition of Islam in Britain, see Sophie Gilliat-Ray, *Muslims in Britain: An Introduction* (Cambridge: Cambridge University Press, 2010), pp. 92–8.

[10] In his study of al-Muhajiroun during the network's early years, Quintan Wiktorowicz also characterizes most of his sample of network respondents as "irreligious prior to their seeking and involvement in the movement." Quintan Wiktorowicz, *Radical Islam Rising: Muslim Extremism in the West* (Lanham, MD: Rowman & Littlefield, 2005), p. 102.

[11] Interview with rank-and-file activist, Ilford, East London, November 13, 2010.

[12] Interview with veteran activist, Skype, March 23, 2011.

[13] Interview with veteran activist, Wembley Central, West London, June 25, 2011.

[14] See, for example, Ed Husain, *The Islamist: Why I Joined Radical Islam in Britain, What I Saw Inside and Why I left* (London: Penguin, 2007); and Maajid Nawaz, *Radical: My Journey from Islamist Extremism to a Democratic Awakening* (London: WH Allen, 2012).

When discussing al-Muhajiroun activists, however, these recollections should be tempered with the indoctrination they receive from Omar Bakri and other ideologues. In their public talks and halaqah sessions, Bakri and other leading activists stress the importance of cross-cultural conflicts in Britain. They see these conflicts as part of a broader incompatibility between their interpretation of Islam and secular British society.[15] Respondents' comments about identity crises reflect their indoctrination in al-Muhajiroun's teachings as much as their own journeys to the activist network.[16] "The environment you live in is so incompatible sometimes," explains one respondent from a Pakistani family. "We go through a lot of different stuff, especially with the different cultures. We're exposed to a lot of things in this country. We start to question our identity. There's an identity crisis. We start to think to ourselves, 'Hang on a moment, what is this culture I am following?'"[17] Among the "different stuff" that this and other respondents highlight is struggling with racism and cultural integration in Britain. "We face discrimination," observes another activist of Pakistani heritage. "We face a massive clash of identity. In the schools we are taught you need to adopt the hip-hop culture of the West and Britain. But we are also told you need to be Pakistani, you need to be Asian, so we find ourselves completely lost. Are we Pakistani? Are we Muslim? Are we British? So we start to question, 'Hold on, who am I? What am I doing here?'"[18]

Respondents' references to the more indefinite "we" in these statements are telling. When asked whether they themselves experienced racial abuse or discrimination while growing up in Britain, many of these same individuals said no. Catherine Zara Raymond makes a similar point in her interviews with network activists.[19] Reflecting on his own experience in the late 1990s, former activist Abdul recalls, "There wasn't that much racism against Muslims. It was very relaxed here." These respondents insist they were not personally affected by racial discrimination or conflicts in cultural integration.[20]

Although some respondents do experience discrimination or deprivation, such first-hand experience was not a necessary condition for individuals to join the Emigrants. "I come from a good background," declares one respondent of

---

[15] For more on the importance of identity crises in al-Muhajiroun's teachings, see Wiktorowicz, *Radical Islam Rising*, pp. 87–92; and Catherine Zara Raymond, "Al Muhajiroun and Islam4UK: The Group Behind the Ban," (London: International Centre for the Study of Radicalisation and Political Violence, King's College, 2010), pp. 20–1.

[16] Kathleen Blee makes a similar point when discussing her female respondents' stories about how they became racist activists. See Blee, *Inside Organized Racism*, p. 35. Also, see Eileen Barker, *The Making of a Moonie: Choice or Brainwashing?* (Oxford: Basil Blackwell, 1984).

[17] Interview with veteran activist, Whitechapel, East London, November 9, 2010.

[18] Interview with rank-and-file activist, Southall, West London, June 28, 2011.

[19] Raymond, "Al Muhajiroun and Islam4UK," p. 20.

[20] However, Abdul also points out that "tensions" against Muslim communities have risen since he left al-Muhajiroun. Other respondents insist they did experience racism growing up and that this contributed to their alienation and journey to the activist network. Interviews with Abdul, Whitechapel, East London, June 18, 2011, and Maryam, Skype, November 20, 2012.

Bangladeshi heritage, stressing that no abuse or deprivations pushed him to al-Muhajiroun. "I received a good education, a good upbringing. I was working and I had money in my pocket. Whatever I wanted, I had."[21] "I don't think I had any kind of personal insecurities or anything like that," adds Ahmed, another activist of South Asian descent. Ahmed describes his receptivity to the network's ideas as due to his youthful questioning about life rather than direct experience with discrimination. "I was more like, 'what is my purpose in life?'" Later, he elaborates: "I mean at that age you're insecure, you're thinking, 'what is your purpose in life? What is your career going to be? What are you going to do with your life?'"[22] Whether or not they suffered from racism or identity crises, many respondents insist it was their personal search for meaning that led them to the activist network.

BIOGRAPHICAL AVAILABILITY AND TURNING POINTS

Reflecting their "biographical availability" for high-risk activism, young people are particularly susceptible to the lure of al-Muhajiroun. Doug McAdam's description of American college students who participated in voter registration drives in Mississippi during the "freedom summer" of 1964 is applicable to many British Emigrants forty-five years later. These young men and women "are simply free, to a unique degree, of constraints that tend to make activism too time consuming or risky for other groups to engage in," McAdam writes. Released from "the demands of family, marriage, and full-time employment," they have more time and face fewer risks for engaging in high-risk activism.[23] Young recruits to al-Muhajiroun, who are often still in school or have only just left, are also free of such constraints. Their greater availability helps explain why so many Emigrants tend to be young, typically in their late teens and early twenties. But their biographical availability is fleeting.[24] As I will show in Chapter 5, many activists leave the network after a few years of intense participation, in part because their availability declines as they mature into adulthood.

In addition to being biographically available for high-risk activism, recruits to al-Muhajiroun have often reached a point in their lives when they are ready to try something different. Scholars of social movements and religious cults have long highlighted the importance of "turning points" as catalysts for religious seeking.[25] Involvement in a new social or religious group, no matter

[21] Interview with rank-and-file activist, Leyton, East London, November 14, 2010.
[22] Interview with Ahmed, Tottenham, North London, December 4, 2010. Also, interview with rank-and-file activist Stratford, East London, June 20, 2011.
[23] McAdam, "Recruitment to High-Risk Activism," p. 85.
[24] Doug McAdam, *Freedom Summer* (New York: Oxford University Press, 1988), p. 44; also McAdam, "Recruitment to High-Risk Activism," pp. 70, 85.
[25] For the classic discussion, see John Lofland and Rodney Stark, "Becoming a World-Saver: A Theory of Conversion to a Deviant Perspective," *American Sociological Review* 30, no. 6 (December 1965), pp. 862–75. Also, see John Lofland, *Doomsday Cult: A Study of Conversion,*

how "strange" it may appear to outsiders, provides people who are at a crossroads the opportunity to explore something new. Not unlike recruits to the Unification Church, or "Moonies," studied by John Lofland and Rodney Stark many years ago, teenagers and young adults who embrace the Emigrants often identify turning points in their education as the trigger to their soul searching.[26] One respondent, who grew up in a conservative Muslim household and had strong family ties to the network, described his exposure to post-secondary education as a turning point that led him *back* to al-Muhajiroun, following a youthful period of rebellion against his father, a leading figure in the network. "When I went to university and saw the corruption that's what basically triggered me off," he recalls. "When I saw they were offering free alcohol, free condoms... and later on, when I was invited to night clubs and pubs, it was a problem 'cause all of my friends were doing that and I was left out, so I felt isolated. I realized these were not my friends. That's when I snapped out of it."[27]

Other recruits question whether their formal schooling will provide them with a satisfying job and a meaningful life. The leading activist "Rohan" recalls questioning the value of his education, and a professional career more generally, while preparing for Britain's university entrance examination. "I was at college doing my A-levels, studying to go on to university when I started to think more about life in general. 'What is the purpose of life? Why am I here?'"[28] Asked whether anything prompted his reflections, Rohan mentions the pressure he felt from his father to measure up to his older brothers:

I wasn't sure what to do at university, what to study. My father was asking me, "What do you want to become?" My brother had already gone to medical school. So he had already defined a clear path for himself. Another brother had also finished his degree and was quite focused on his work already. So my father wanted me to really put myself forward. That was quite confusing for me. This led me to think a lot more about what do I want to do with my life?[29]

At this point, Rohan began to think seriously about the role of religion in his life, even though neither he nor his family was particularly observant. "I was never very religious, but when it came to that point in my life where I was really looking into what is the purpose of life, that's when I started

Proselytization, and Maintenance of Faith (Englewood Cliffs, NJ: Prentice-Hall, 1966); and Michael D. Langone, "Responding to Jihadism: A Cultic Studies Perspective," *Cultic Studies Review* 5, no. 2 (2006), pp. 268–306.

26 Lofland and Stark, "Becoming a World-Saver," p. 870; Lofland, *Doomsday Cult*, p. 51. Also, see Barker, *The Making of a Moonie*.

27 Interview with veteran activist, Whitechapel, East London, June 17, 2011. Also, interview with rank-and-file activist, Stratford, East London, June 20, 2011.

28 In the British educational system, "college" refers to the two-year equivalent of an American student's junior and senior years in high school, while "university" is equivalent to the post-secondary education provided at American colleges and universities.

29 Interview with Rohan, leading activist, Whitechapel, East London, December 7, 2010.

to really think about Islam." Around this time, Rohan was leaving a mosque after Friday prayers when he took a leaflet at a da'wah stall run by network activists outside the building. The leaflet discussed the need for a united global community and an Islamic caliphate to bring this about. The idea appealed to him: "I thought that seemed like a good idea. Why aren't we one united *ummah* [Muslim community]? Why shouldn't we have an Islamic state? It just seemed like common sense."[30] Eager to learn more, he began to attend lectures by "Sheikh Omar Bakri Mohammed," which he heard about from activists at the da'wah stall.

Before he got far in his new studies, Rohan traveled to his father's home country for an extended period. "I had a lot of time to sit and think," he recalls of his visit to Bangladesh. "I took some books with me and I was able to read and change some things, like perfect my prayer." Six months later, when he returned to Britain, Rohan described himself as "a lot more religious, a lot more practicing, and thinking more Islamically." As a young, single, unemployed man, he was also biographically available for activism. Rather than following his brothers' professional paths, Rohan decided to look for the activists at the stall: "I knew where they were. So when I came back I went to visit the da'wah stall and then I started going to some more of the talks."[31] Rohan's studies with Omar Bakri and other network leaders progressed from there. He eventually became one of Bakri's closest students and a leading activist in al-Muhajiroun.

TURNING AWAY FROM GANGS AND CRIME

For some respondents, searching for the meaning of life has less to do with turning points in their formal education and more with turning away from delinquency. "You've got a lot of youth who have lost their identity, who have no future, they're unemployed, they're regularly into crime," explains a leading activist. "Many of the people who joined us over the years used to be in that kind of lifestyle."[32] Indeed, several respondents emphasized that their criminal behavior and the legal consequences stemming from it led them to become involved in al-Muhajiroun. "I had a number of court cases pending," explains one veteran activist, "I was involved in a few things, nothing to be proud of, some violence, some theft and burglary. I found it quite disturbing that I could face the possibility of a prison sentence... So I started to look towards God."[33] This religious seeker's journey of self-discovery did not take him directly to al-Muhajiroun, but he did end up joining the activist network after participating

---

[30] Interview with Rohan, Whitechapel, East London, December 7, 2010.
[31] Interview with Rohan, Whitechapel, East London, December 7, 2010.
[32] Interview with leading activist, Ilford, East London, December 12, 2014.
[33] Interview with veteran activist, Wembley Central, West London, June 25, 2011.

in Abu Hamza's Supporters of Shariah group. I return to his story later in the chapter.

The path from criminality to al-Muhajiroun was straighter for other respondents. "I was drug dealing. I used to be in gangs, used to do all this stuff," recalls one activist. After talking with an activist at a da'wah stall, he realized, "I wanted to change. I sat and I contemplated, 'Truly, what am I doing here? What is the purpose of my life?'"[34] He began listening to online lectures by Anjem Choudary, attended a halaqah organized by activists, and joined his new companions at their da'wah stalls. Another respondent who had been involved in gangs also attributes his rejection of crime to the Emigrants. The network, he explains, "took me away from that. It showed me that life is not about drugs and gangs."[35]

Other respondents credit al-Muhajiroun with turning them away from "immoral" lifestyles, even if they were not necessarily involved in crime. "My lifestyle before joining wasn't very good," explained Salman, in one of our interviews when he was still active in the network. "I used to get in trouble a lot. I used to do a lot of things I shouldn't be doing."[36] In a follow-up interview four-and-a-half years later, Salman clarified what he meant: "I went out with friends, drank. I went pubbing … I was a bit of a rebel. I enjoyed drinking."[37] Another respondent who worked as a disc jockey emphasized the tension he felt between his "hip hop" lifestyle and his Muslim upbringing. "I was in and out of clubs and it was taking a toll on me. I was raised as a Muslim and we were always told, 'You have to do good,' and, 'don't do this and don't do that.' So I knew the basics." This tension, he continues, caused him to turn towards al-Muhajiroun. "Near the end of my involvement in the music scene I was like, 'Half the things I'm doing are completely against what I'm supposed to believe.'"[38]

Whether stimulated by their immoral lifestyles, involvement in crime, frustration with formal schooling, or merely intellectual curiosity, network activists often search their souls on their way to al-Muhajiroun. Virtually all of the activists I interviewed who joined the network during their adolescence or early adulthood identified religious seeking as an important reason for their openness to the Emigrants.

To introduce variation on the dependent variable of entering al-Muhajiroun, I also interviewed respondents who dabbled in the activist network but never joined. Significantly, these respondents did not experience the same need to search for life's meaning through religion. Unlike his friends who were deeply involved in al-Muhajiroun, Haroon, a former contact who participated in

---

[34] Interview with rank-and-file activist, Lewisham, South London, December 11, 2010.
[35] Interview with veteran activist, Walthamstow, East London, November 16, 2010.
[36] Interview with Salman, Leyton, East London, December 9, 2010.
[37] Interview with Salman, Poplar, East London, July 24, 2015.
[38] Interview with rank-and-file activist, Southall, West London, June 28, 2011.

network events for two years, already had a strong identity and sense of purpose. He was committed to completing his education and preparing for a career in journalism. Indeed, Haroon's interest in the activist network was not only related to his desire to hang out with his friends, but to engage in the sort of investigative work he believed would help him prepare for his career: "I was quite fortunate because I knew I wanted to be a journalist and I knew al-Muhajiroun would be great to write about. I had done this before with [mentions another religious group]."[39] While he regularly attended his local mosque and practiced his religion, Haroon was not at a turning point in his life, nor was he seeking a greater purpose through religion. His lack of religious seeking, along with his educational and professional goals, help explain why he ultimately rejected the activist network.

BECOMING MORE POLITICALLY AWARE

In addition to their religious seeking, several respondents highlight their emerging political awareness as an important reason for their receptivity to al-Muhajiroun's ideology. Like other college and university students in Britain, these individuals are exposed to new political ideas and issues in pursuing their formal education. One veteran activist recalls how his growing interest in politics during college lead him to the Emigrants. "I began to become more interested in international affairs," he explained. "I studied politics, media studies, and business, so I had a lot of interest in politics in general. And when I was seventeen years old I began to hear the lectures of Sheikh Omar Bakri Mohammed."[40] Salman also highlights his growing interest in history and politics shortly before becoming involved in the activist network: "I started reading up on Palestine, I started looking into politics, I started looking into history. It went from there."[41] Ahmed recalls how his childhood friend, Rohan, first drew him to the network by emphasizing the political dimensions of al-Muhajiroun's worldview: "I wasn't Muslim at the time, so it wasn't something that I was interested in. But when he started to talk about these concepts, the shariah, khilafah, jihad, and then 9/11 happened, I was curious."[42] Ahmed engaged in many conversations with Rohan over a period of several months before progressing from mere curiosity to actually joining the activist network. But his initial interest was sparked less by his own religious seeking and

---

[39] Interview with Haroon, former contact, Westminster, Central London, June 14, 2011.
[40] Interview with veteran activist, Walthamstow, East London, November 16, 2010.
[41] Interview with Salman, Poplar, East London, July 24, 2015.
[42] Interview with Ahmed, Tottenham, North London, December 4, 2010. Other respondents also emphasized how their growing political awareness made them open to al-Muhajiroun's ideology. Interviews with Abdul, Whitechapel, East London, June 18, 2011, and activists, Whitechapel, East London, November 9, 2010, Lewisham, South London, December 11, 2010, and Stratford, East London, June 20, 2011.

more by his connection to Rohan and his curiosity about the Emigrants' political ideas.

Respondents' political awareness made them more open to the grievances expressed by al-Muhajiroun, along with its proposed solution to these "injustices." The activist network's ideology includes a long list of complaints against Western foreign policy, starting from the Sykes–Picot Agreement in 1916 that divided portions of the Ottoman Empire's Middle Eastern territories into areas of British and French colonial influence to the US-led coalition's military campaign against the Islamic State in Iraq and Syria. The thrust of this grievance narrative is that the West destroyed the last Islamic caliphate and is determined to keep another from forming because it is incompatible with capitalism and democracy. As one leading activist puts it, "the real reason" why the United States and other Western powers are involved in Iraq, Afghanistan, Somalia, and other countries is "because they understand if the shariah is implemented, if you once again have a khilafah, with a foreign policy of annexing land and spreading the shariah around the world, that will be the beginning of the end of liberty, democracy, and freedom."[43] For this and other respondents, the revival of the Islamic state is the only solution to the problems of "man-made law" and corruption that plague all Western and "non-Muslim" countries today. "All of them need to be removed," explains a veteran activist, referring to the governments of non-Muslim and Muslim majority countries, "and be replaced with an Islamic state, the khilafah system." Only this, he adds, "will bring about the true justice and tranquility that people are seeking."[44]

This sweeping, if simplistic, vision appeals to many politically-minded respondents, including one leading activist who became involved in the network relatively late in his personal journey, after completing his post-secondary education:

When the Caliphate was created, stretching from the heart of Europe to Africa and the Middle East, Islam – as a political system, a judicial system, a social-economic system – had the answers to all of society's problems. This is really something that opens your eyes and that's what happened to me. Having grown up in Britain, having received a secular education… I never came across Islam as anything more than ritual acts: praying, fasting, going on a pilgrimage one day. When you talk about Islam as an ideology, as a complete way of life, in the sense of a spiritual way of life and a political way of life, something which could replace capitalism and democracy, this is what really opened my eyes.[45]

The Emigrants' interpretation of Islam as a political, economic, and judicial system, and not merely a set of religious beliefs and "ritual acts," attracted

[43] Interview with leading activist, Skype, November 8, 2011.
[44] Interview with veteran activist, Wembley Central, West London, September 5, 2013.
[45] Interview with leading activist, Skype, June 26, 2013.

this and other respondents to the activist network. Once made, this intellectual connection deepened their engagement in al-Muhajiroun's culture and ideology, leading many to sustained involvement in the network.

SOCIAL NETWORKS AND PAST INVOLVEMENT WITH OTHER GROUPS

For all their youthful struggles, identity crises, and turning points, al-Muhajiroun activists do not have a monopoly on adolescent soul searching. Most teenagers and young adults go through a period of self-discovery and exploration without becoming involved in high-risk activism, let alone activism that seeks to transform Western society into an Islamic caliphate. Nor is al-Muhajiroun the only option available for young, politically active Muslims who wish to become involved in London's vibrant Islamist scene. For years a number of different Salafi and Islamist groups have been active in Great Britain, including Hizb ut-Tahrir, the Tablighi Jama'at, the Muslim Association of Britain, the Young Muslim Organisation, and the Society for the Revival of the Prophetic Way (better known by its Arabic acronym, JIMAS).[46] In addition to these formal organizations, informal groups and networks have proliferated in the United Kingdom. Some of these networks have centered on Salafi-jihadi preachers based in London, including Abu Qatadah al-Filastini, Abdullah Faisal, Abu Hamza al-Masri, Abu Bashir al-Tartusi, and Anwar al-Awlaki.[47] Over the years the Emigrants have competed with these groups for followers in what Quintan Wiktorowicz calls a "competitive marketplace of ideas."[48]

Why did the respondents in my sample end up in al-Muhajiroun and not one of their competitors? In fact, consistent with research on high-risk activism, numerous respondents were involved with other groups before they joined the Emigrants.[49] When explaining why they chose to join al-Muhajiroun

---

[46] Philip Lewis, *Young, British and Muslim* (London: Continuum, 2007); Gilliat-Ray, *Muslims in Britain*; and Sadek Hamid, "The Attraction of 'Authentic' Islam: Salafism and British Muslim Youth," in *Global Salafism: Islam's New Religious Movement*, edited by Roel Meijer (New York: Columbia University Press, 2009), pp. 384–403.

[47] Hamid, "The Attraction of 'Authentic' Islam," p. 396; Lewis, *Young, British and Muslim*, pp. 130–1; Robert Lambert, *Countering Al-Qaeda in London: Police and Muslims in Partnership* (New York: Columbia University Press, 2013); Duncan Gardham, "The Poplar preacher leading an armed gang of jihadis in Syria," *Daily Telegraph* (7:42PM BST October 19, 2012), www.telegraph.co.uk/news/worldnews/middleeast/syria/9621352/The-Poplar-preacher-leading-an-armed-gang-of-jihadis-in-Syria.html [Accessed December 12, 2014]; and Scott Shane, *Objective Troy: A Terrorist, A President, and the Rise of the Drone* (New York: Tim Duggan Books, 2015): pp. 145–9.

[48] Wiktorowicz, *Radical Islam Rising*, p. 86.

[49] McAdam, "Recruitment to High-Risk Activism"; della Porta, *Social Movements, Political Violence and the State*; and Gregory L. Wiltfang and Doug McAdam, "The Costs and Risks of Social Activism: A Study of Sanctuary Movement Activism," *Social Forces* 69, no. 4 (June 1991), pp. 987–1010.

rather than one of these other groups, respondents emphasized their attraction to the activist network's ideology, declaring that only the Emigrants followed the "true path" of Islam. But ideological affinity – and youthful soul searching – alone do not explain why people joined. Also consistent with research on social movements and high-risk activism, respondents who became involved with the activist network often had family or friendship ties that pulled them in.[50]

The biggest organizational pathway to al-Muhajiroun, particularly during its early years, was Hizb ut-Tahrir, a transnational Islamist party formed by several disillusioned Muslim Brotherhood members in the early 1950s.[51] The flow of activists from this Islamist party to al-Muhajiroun is not surprising given that Omar Bakri was the leader of Hizb ut-Tahrir in Britain for ten years. Bakri eventually left the party after fighting with its global leaders. When Bakri, Anjem Choudary, and another supporter created al-Muhajiroun as a splinter group of Hizb ut-Tahrir in January 1996, a number of activists followed their emir to his new venture. The relationship between Bakri and his students was a strong draw for Hizb ut-Tahrir activists, allowing the Emigrants to grow rapidly in its first months.

Social movement theory suggests that this exodus could be explained largely by social ties between defectors from Hizb ut-Tahrir and participants in the new group. There is ample evidence to support this. In his early study of al-Muhajiroun, Wiktorowicz observes that Bakri's new group "sent shockwaves" throughout Hizb ut-Tahrir (HT) and "quickly attracted disaffected HT followers and Omar's former students."[52] Rashid was one of these students. He belonged to Hizb ut-Tahrir and studied with Bakri before following him to the Emigrants. According to Rashid, the immediate catalyst of his departure from Hizb ut-Tahrir was his attendance at the wedding of Bakri's daughter, who "was marrying a friend of mine." The wedding took place shortly after Bakri left his old group, when Hizb ut-Tahrir viewed him, as Rashid recalls, "as a threat because he could take people away to his new party." In response, the party ordered "their members not to have any contact" with Bakri. By attending the wedding, Rashid had broken this rule, which led to a confrontation with his emir in South London: "He said to me, 'You need to obey this or you have to leave the party.' I said, 'You don't leave me no choice.'" Rashid's strong ties to Bakri's new group made his decision an easy one: "I just jumped onto the bandwagon of al-Muhajiroun."[53]

---

[50] David E. Snow, Louis Zurcher Jr., and Sheldon Ekland-Olson, "Social Networks and Social Movements: A Micro-structural Approach to Differential Recruitment," *American Sociological Review* 45, no. 5 (1980), pp. 787–801.

[51] Suha Taji-Farouki, *A Fundamental Quest: Hizb al-Tahrir and the Search for the Islamic Caliphate* (London: Grey Seal, 1996), pp. 5–6.

[52] Wiktorowicz, *Radical Islam Rising*, p. 10.

[53] Interview with Rashid, Whitechapel, East London, June 26, 2011.

Rashid was not the only former Hizb ut-Tahrir activist I interviewed to jump on al-Muhajiroun's bandwagon during its heady early days. As shown in the social network analysis in the previous chapter, the Emigrants grew rapidly into a scale-free-like network during this period as people followed their friends and relatives into the new group. "Suddenly al-Muhajiroun just came out of nowhere," recalls Abdul, who also participated in Hizb ut-Tahrir before joining Bakri's new venture. "I knew Anjem [Choudary], and because al-Muhajiroun was forming in our area, I just followed the crowd from my area. All the young kids followed the crowd." Among the kids following the crowd was Abdul's own sister: "I was the oldest in my family. Everything revolved around me. Whatever I did my younger sibling did. She followed me in about a year before I left."[54]

Hizb ut-Tahrir was not the only organizational path to al-Muhajiroun. Several respondents mentioned that they had participated in the Tablighi Jama'at, the Young Muslim Organisation, and Abu Hamza's Supporters of Shariah network before joining the Emigrants.[55] The level of involvement in these groups varies across respondents. Some respondents spent time with them briefly as part of their religious seeking, when they were still exploring different organizations; others became deeply involved in them before moving on to al-Muhajiroun.

One veteran activist describes how he came to the Emigrants by way of two notorious preachers outside the network, Abdullah Faisal and Abu Hamza. Faisal was a firebrand cleric who served a five-year prison sentence in Britain for incitement to murder before being deported to his home country, Jamaica. Abu Hamza was the leader of the Supporters of Shariah network who was found guilty of inciting violence in Britain before being extradited to the United States, where he was convicted of eleven terrorism-related crimes and sentenced to life in prison.[56] After being "absolutely captivated" by one of Faisal's videotaped lectures, the respondent contacted him and began attending his study circles. Soon he "met Sheikh Abu Hamza at the Finsbury Park Mosque" and became involved in Supporters of Shariah. Then, "I came across Sheikh Omar Bakri Mohammad." Despite feeling "very inclined towards Sheikh Omar," the respondent refused to study with him because Bakri had not yet adopted a "Salafi orientation" in his *aqeedah* or creed, like his teachers Faisal

[54] Interview with Abdul, Whitechapel, East London, June 18, 2011.
[55] Interviews with activists, Ilford, East London, November 13, 2010, Leyton, East London, December 9, 2010, Wembley Central, West London, June 25, 2011, and Southall, West London, June 28, 2011; interview with Maryam, former female activist, Hounslow, West London, December 13, 2010.
[56] Sean O'Neill and Daniel McGrory, *The Suicide Factory: Abu Hamza and the Finsbury Park Mosque* (London: Harper Perennial, 2006); Lambert, *Countering Al-Qaeda in London*; and *BBC News*, "Radical cleric Abu Hamza jailed for life by US court," (January 9, 2015), www.bbc.com/news/world-us-canada-30754959 [Accessed December 11, 2015].

and Hamza. However, after Bakri embraced Salafism a year or two later, "I immediately joined al-Muhajiroun, and then I went on to join the successor organizations of al-Ghurabaa and the Saved Sect. I have been involved with al-Muhajiroun and studying with Sheikh Omar Bakri Mohammed for maybe eleven, twelve years now."[57]

Salman, the respondent who initially dismissed al-Muhajiroun as a "bunch of extremists," joined the network following his exposure to several different groups. Interestingly, Salman found all of these groups lacking in their interpretation or practice of the religion, despite having family ties to some of them. His journey to the Emigrants suggests that social ties to activists are not enough to draw some people in. These seekers require more than shared social relationships. The beliefs articulated by the new group must resonate with their own. It must offer a vision they identify with and are willing to commit themselves to.[58]

The first group that Salman encountered during his religious seeking was the Tablighi Jama'at, a quietist, Sufi-inspired movement known for its missionary work. The Tablighis were active in his neighborhood, and he spent a couple of months going around with their missionaries, "from this mosque to that mosque... I even preached for them."[59] Gradually, Salman became dissatisfied with some of the Tablighis' religious practices, as well as their answers to his questions. "They were not really answering everything according to the Qur'an or *sunnah*," he explained, articulating a common fundamentalist critique of the movement. "They were using a lot of ration and logic. So I didn't spend a lot of time with them."[60]

Next, Salman explored the Young Muslim Organisation (YMO), an Islamist group his uncle belonged to and which engaged in extensive youth outreach in the Tower Hamlets borough of East London, where he lived.[61] Despite his family connection and the YMO's reputation for following a conservative interpretation of shariah, Salman found the group too "secular" and apolitical. "Their Islam wasn't really Islam," he recalled. "They prayed five times a day, but everything was allowed for them. Joining the Metropolitan Police was

---

[57] Interview with veteran activist, Wembley Central, West London, June 25, 2011.
[58] For similar arguments on the necessary, but insufficient, influence of social ties on mobilization to high-risk activism, see Doug McAdam and Ronnelle Paulsen, "Specifying the Relationship between Social Ties and Activism," *American Journal of Sociology* 99, no. 3 (November 1993), pp. 640–67; and Roger V. Gould, "Multiple Networks and Mobilization in the Paris Commune, 1871," *American Sociological Review* 56, no. 6 (December 1991), pp. 716–29.
[59] Interview with Salman, Poplar, East London, July 24, 2015.
[60] Interview with Salman, Leyton, East London, December 9, 2010.
[61] Sadek Hamid, "Mapping Youth Work and Muslims in Britain," in *Youth Work and Islam: A Leap of Faith for Young People*, edited by Brian Belton and Sadek Hamid (Rotterdam: Sense Publishers, 2011), pp. 83–97; Ed Husain, *The Islamist: Why I Joined Radical Islam in Britain, What I Saw Inside and Why I left* (London: Penguin, 2007).

allowed. Spying on your Muslim brothers was allowed."[62] He was offended by these views because they contradicted his religious and political beliefs.

Salman had even stronger family ties to the more political Hizb ut-Tahrir. These included several relatives he identified as "speakers" for the organization.[63] He often interacted with these relatives at family gatherings. Notwithstanding his family connections, Salman complained that Hizb ut-Tahrir members also used "a lot of ration, a lot of logic" in their interpretation of Islam, rather than accepting scripture literally. Although he accepted much of Hizb ut-Tahrir's political ideology, which was similar to al-Muhajiroun's, he criticized the party's strategy of not working to establish the Islamic state in Britain: "Even for establishing shariah, they used ration to say, 'We need to establish it in Muslim land rather than in the UK.'"[64]

Still searching for answers, Salman attended an al-Muhajiroun talk with two acquaintances from Bethnal Green, an East London neighborhood in Tower Hamlets and Hackney. This was when he had his initial "bunch of extremists" reaction. "They were talking about 9/11. They were talking about the 'Magnificent 19,'" he recalled, referring to al-Muhajiroun's incendiary description of the 9/11 hijackers. "We came out of there before they finished the lecture. We looked at each other and said, 'This is not Islam, man. This is too extreme.'"[65] After this lecture Salman decided to research the religion on his own. "I started picking up books," he recalls. "Salafi books. I started reading about the aqeedah," theological beliefs, as interpreted by fundamentalist Salafi scholars.[66]

In the meantime, Salman continued to attend Omar Bakri's talks with his two acquaintances, "off and on." One talk in particular made a strong impression on them: "It was about giving da'wah. They were saying that it was an

---

[62] Interview with Salman, Leyton, East London, December 9, 2010.

[63] Interview with Salman, Poplar, East London, July 24, 2015.

[64] Interview with Salman, Leyton, East London, December 9, 2010. Here Salman identifies one of the main differences between al-Muhajiroun and Hizb ut-Tahrir. Both groups believe that establishing the Islamic state is part of the "divine method" described in the Qur'an, but Hizb ut-Tahrir does not call for achieving this objective in Western countries like Britain. Al-Muhajiroun does. For discussion of this and other differences between the two groups, see Mahan Abedin, "Al-Muhajiroun in the UK: An Interview with Sheikh Omar Bakri Mohammed," *Jamestown Monitor* (March 23, 2004), www.jamestown.org/news_details.php?news_id=38 [Accessed November 24, 2007].

[65] Interview with Salman, Poplar, East London, July 24, 2015. Such experiences are not unique to al-Muhajiroun. Rodney Stark recalls how many recruits to the American branch of the Unification Church, better known as the Moonies, initially regarded the group's theological beliefs as "quite odd": "I recall one who told me that he was puzzled that such nice people could get so worked up about 'some guy in Korea' who claimed to be the Lord of the Second Advent. Then, one day, he got worked up about this guy too. I suggest that this is also how people in the first century got themselves worked up about someone who claimed to be the Lord of the First Advent." Rodney Stark, *The Rise of Christianity: A Sociologist Reconsiders History* (Princeton, NJ: Princeton University Press, 1996), pp. 19–20.

[66] Interview with Salman, Leyton, East London, December 9, 2010.

obligation... it was like a completely different spin to what I was hearing from their 9/11 talk. And we thought, 'This sounds different from what they did before.' Maybe it was a smart move by them, putting in this lecture."[67] The da'wah lecture impressed Salman because it resonated with his growing identity as a Salafi. He and his acquaintances began attending more al-Muhajiroun talks, during which Salman compared Bakri's teachings with the "ration and logic" he was hearing from his relatives in the Young Muslim Organisation and Hizb ut-Tahrir. By then, Bakri had completed his "conversion" to Salafi Islam, which I discuss in more detail in Chapter 5, and Salman found his message consistent with the literalist interpretation of Islam he himself embraced. The affinity between Salman's views and Omar Bakri's, and Salman's identity as a Salafi, were essential to his acceptance of Bakri's teachings. "I realized that Sheikh Omar was speaking the truth," he recalls. "Because every time he spoke he gave strong evidence" for what he was saying based on the Qur'an and sunnah.[68]

Once Salman and his associates accepted Bakri as a legitimate scholar, they decided to explore al-Muhajiroun further. They began to participate in da'wah stalls in East Ham and Whitechapel, while also continuing to attend public talks by Bakri, Anjem Choudary, and other speakers. "We started enjoying it," he explains. "We thought, 'This is the way forward.' And then they said to us, 'Look, we have a private halaqah. We would like you guys to attend.'"[69] In the private study circle, Salman and his friends learned more about the Emigrants' blend of Salafism and Islamism, which appealed to them. They also deepened their friendship with each other and other activists they met in the halaqah. The three recruits continued their involvement in the network, attending da'wah stalls and halaqah discussions, eventually becoming fully committed activists.

Part of what makes Salman's journey to al-Muhajiroun so interesting is that he favored his ideological affinity with Omar Bakri and other network leaders over his family ties to other groups, whose views did not resonate with his fundamentalist identity. Yet even Salman required an "in" to the Emigrants, someone who could introduce him to other activists. His connection turned out to be fairly weak, an acquaintance he'd "seen around" the neighborhood, one of the two associates who accompanied him to his first lectures.[70] "We weren't friends before," he emphasizes, describing his relationship with this person. "We knew each other. I lived in Bethnal Green and he lived on the other side of Bethnal Green, so we used to see each other in the neighborhood."

---

[67] Interview with Salman, Poplar, East London, July 24, 2015.
[68] Interview with Salman, Leyton, East London, December 9, 2010.
[69] Interview with Salman, Poplar, East London, July 24, 2015.
[70] For the seminal analysis on the role of "weak ties" in providing people with new opportunities and linking them to larger communities, see Mark S. Granovetter, "The Strength of Weak Ties," *American Journal of Sociology* 78, no. 6 (May, 1973), pp. 1360–80.

"But," he continues, we "never knew each other on a personal level, never any friendship level."[71]

This is consistent with other respondents whose initial link to al-Muhajiroun came from activists they had met at da'wah stalls. Rohan describes how he "met some brothers at a da'wah stall" months before he joined and how this was enough for him to reestablish contact with them, when he was ready: "I knew they used to do da'wah stalls, so I went to them. There's one local stall that I had always known about... I went to visit the da'wah stall and asked, 'What kind of things are you doing? Are you doing any talks?' Then I started going to some of the talks."[72]

Even if weak ties suffice for establishing the introduction to al-Muhajiroun, many respondents enjoy stronger bonds to the activist network before joining. These bonds are often based on family relations and friendships. "I have an old friend who I knew from childhood," explains Ahmed, describing his initial contact in al-Muhajiroun. This friend turned out to be Rohan, with whom he grew up in the same London neighborhood.[73] "I knew the brothers for a very long time before," remarks another respondent, explaining how he met his "brothers" in al-Muhajiroun through "my older brother and my friend's older brothers."[74] Sibling ties are common among the Emigrants, as are spousal ones. "I married into a family that [name of prominent activist] is married into," says a former activist, noting his matrimonial ties to the network.[75] "I've always seen brothers, from a young age," adds a final respondent, who grew up in a family with deep ties to the network. "They've always told me you should stick to your father and soak up the knowledge."[76]

In the last chapter, my colleagues and I used social network analysis to show how power relations and social structures changed in al-Muhajiroun over time. Here my network analysis is less formal, but no less insightful. As the examples above suggest, respondents connect to the Emigrants through strong and weak ties of varying intensity and duration. Whether through a parent or an in-law, a close childhood friend or a neighborhood acquaintance, these interpersonal relationships not only link individuals to the activist network, they prime them for accepting its ideology. "I was familiar with them," concedes the respondent who grew up in an al-Muhajiroun family, describing how his close ties help explain his attraction to the network. "I know you could say it's a biased view."[77] But strong ties are important even outside network

[71] Interview with Salman, Bethnal Green, East London, November 28, 2010.

[72] Interview with Rohan, Whitechapel, East London, December 7, 2010.

[73] Interview with Ahmed, Tottenham, North London, December 4, 2010. I was able to verify Ahmed's claim in a separate interview with Rohan several years later. Interview with Rohan, Whitechapel, East London, December 11, 2014.

[74] Interview with rank-and-file activist, Leyton, East London, November 14, 2010.

[75] Interview with former activist, Walthamstow, East London, July 17, 2012.

[76] Interview with veteran activist, Whitechapel, East London, June 17, 2011.

[77] Interview with veteran activist, Whitechapel, East London, June 17, 2011.

families. "At first I was a bit irritated," recalls Ahmed, whose connection to the Emigrants was through his childhood friend Rohan, rather than family members. "I was like, 'Go away, don't bother me.' But then I thought, 'Let me give him a chance.'... And I found that a lot of the stuff he was saying was right."[78] The more embedded Ahmed and others became within the network, the more likely they were to accept its beliefs and practices, even those they once considered "too extreme." These social relationships not only gave people like Ahmed the connections they needed to the activist network, they increased their confidence in the information they received. Ahmed accepted the information about al-Muhajiroun's ideology because it came from Rohan, someone he knew – and trusted. Through his repeated conversations with Rohan, Ahmed began to acquire a political identity that corresponded with al-Muhajiroun's world view. From here it was just a matter of more interactions with Rohan and other activists before Ahmed joined the Emigrants.

ATTRACTION OF OMAR BAKRI MOHAMMED AND OTHER LEADERS

Hizb ut-Tahrir's leaders had reason to worry when Omar Bakri left. With his contacts to local youths in Britain, his knowledge of Islamic scripture, his passionate speeches, and his accessible, engaging personality, Bakri was bound to draw activists to his new group – and he did. Consistent with Weber's theory of charismatic authority, Bakri's leadership was based on his followers' recognition of his "exceptional powers or qualities."[79] "He was the only known charismatic gentleman in the movement," recalls one former Hizb ut-Tahrir activist who followed Bakri to his new group. "The rest were not as charismatic as him."[80] "He was an extremely powerful speaker," observes another respondent. "I've seen people crying, even my father used to cry. He [Bakri] used to have such a big impact upon him, talking about the struggle happening around the world and that kind of thing. This is a large part of the reason why he could attract a lot of people."[81]

Other respondents also praised Bakri's captivating speeches and charisma, which they contrasted with the brusque formality of local imams. These immigrant clerics often preached in the native tongue of their older South Asian congregants. They struggled to connect with the young, second- and

---

[78] Interview with Ahmed, Tottenham, North London, December 4, 2010.

[79] Max Weber, *The Theory of Economic and Social Organization*, translated by A. M. Henderson and Talcott Parsons, edited with an introduction by Parsons (New York: Free Press, 1964), pp. 358–9.

[80] Interview with former Hizb ut-Tahrir and al-Muhajiroun activist, Walthamstow, East London, July 17, 2012.

[81] Interview with leading activist, Ilford, East London, December 12, 2014.

third-generation British Muslims who also attended their sermons.[82] "We didn't see the imams as people who could relate to us," explains Rashid, the former Hizb ut-Tahrir activist-turned-Emigrant. "They spoke in Urdu or Bengali or Arabic. They weren't able to relate to the issues we faced here." Then, he adds, "Omar Bakri came along. He was very charismatic and he spoke English."[83] "Many of the imams are a little bit aloof," notes another respondent. "They just recite the Qur'an before they disappear, and they don't like you to ask questions." Bakri, in contrast, encouraged questions and would spend hours talking with his supporters. He "used to be a 24/7 guide... he'd hardly sleep sometimes."[84] "What I found so fascinating about Sheikh Omar was his charisma with the youth," recalls a veteran activist. "Not like some preachers, where the youth fall asleep within five minutes, Sheikh Omar kept you engaged for hours."[85]

Reflecting the breadth of London's Islamist scene, many of Bakri's students had access to other extremist preachers in London, including Abu Hamza, Abdullah Faisal, Abu Qatadah, Abu Bashir al-Tartusi, and Anwar al-Awlaki. Some of these speakers, such as Hamza and Awlaki, were known for their personal charisma and engaging speaking style, while others, including Faisal, Qatadah, and Tartusi were respected for their knowledge of Islamic scripture and jurisprudence. What separated Bakri from these preachers was his focus on the political, economic, and social systems of the Islamic state, as grounded in his blend of Salafi theology and Islamist ideology. One convert who became a prominent activist recalls how Bakri "had a solution to every single aspect of society, whether socially, judicially, politically. And that was part of what guided me towards becoming a Muslim."[86]

Omar Bakri also distinguished his network from others, including Hamza's Supporters of Shariah and Bakri's own Hizb ut-Tahrir, by insisting that his followers actually work towards establishing the Islamic state in Britain through public da'wah and hisbah, as opposed to merely culturing activists in closed halaqahs.[87] "Allah's rule is everywhere, so you work wherever you are," explains one respondent who was previously involved with Hizb ut-Tahrir. "That doesn't necessarily mean you believe it's going to come to Britain first, but you work wherever you are, according to the method of the Prophet. Meaning call society to Islam, command good, forbid evil, and get enough

---

[82] Interviews with Rohan, Whitechapel, East London, December 7, 2010, and another leading activist, Leyton, East London, November 4, 2010.

[83] Interview with Rashid, Whitechapel, East London, June 26, 2011.

[84] Interview with leading activist, Ilford, East London, December 9, 2014.

[85] Interview with veteran activist, Wembley Central, West London, June 25, 2011.

[86] Interview with veteran activist, Walthamstow, East London, November 16, 2010.

[87] Interviews with different leading and veteran activists, Leyton, East London, November 4, 2010 and November 6, 2010; Whitechapel, East London, November 9, 2010, December 7, 2010, and June 17, 2011; and Wembley Central, West London, September 5, 2013. Also, see Wiktorowicz, *Radical Islam Rising*, pp. 141–2.

support to one day take the authority."[88] "I decided I would part company with HT," explains another former Hizb ut-Tahrir activist, "because they were talkers as opposed to doers. I was fed up with that."[89]

Moreover, unlike some influential Salafi-jihadi preachers based in the United Kingdom such as Abu Qatadah and Abu Bashir, "Sheikh Omar" delivered his talks in colloquial English, using his relative command of the language to share jokes and funny stories that delighted his young listeners. "The Sheikh's a very funny character," emphasizes one leading activist.[90] "He was a joker," notes Abdul, recalling his days in the activist network. "There was always humor. His favorite term was 'disaster.' We always used to break out in laughter." "He'd say, 'Disaster!'," he adds, mimicking Bakri's voice. "It was funny."[91]

As humorous, charismatic, and engaging as Omar Bakri could be, he was not the only one who drew young people to al-Muhajiroun. Respondents in my sample also mentioned other leaders who influenced their decision to become involved, including Anjem Choudary, Abu Izzadeen Brooks, Mizanur Rahman, and Abu Uzair Sharif.[92] One long-standing activist, who was based in the English coastal city of Southampton at the time, recalls how "the moment my life changed is when Anjem came down" to lecture his small group of fellow activists. "He had a couple of sessions with us, and he blew me away, basically."[93] Another respondent emphasizes Choudary's influence on his decision to join the activist network: "I just had that zeal to study under Anjem. I was going to all his classes and stuff and I thought that Anjem was someone who was following Islam, without changing or compromising, just following it as it should be. Ever since I've been studying with him, joining him in the da'wah."[94] A prominent young activist recalls the impact several leaders had on his activism: "Much of my influence has come from Sheikh

---

[88] According to al-Muhajiroun's doctrine, "taking the authority" in Britain and other countries may occur peacefully or violently, including by military *coup*, if possible. Interview with rank-and-file activist, Hounslow, West London, September 4, 2013. Also, interview with leading activist, Ilford, East London, December 12, 2014.

[89] Interview with former Hizb ut-Tahrir and al-Muhajiroun activist, Walthamstow, East London, July 17, 2012. For more on how al-Muhajiroun characterizes itself as "people of action" rather than "people of words," see Suha Taji-Farouki, "Islamists and the Threat of *Jihad*: Hizb al-Tahrir and al-Muhajiroun on Israel and the Jews," *Middle Eastern Studies* 36, no. 4 (October 2000), p. 32.

[90] Interview with leading activist, Ilford, East London, December 12, 2014.

[91] Interview with Abdul, Whitechapel, East London, June 18, 2011.

[92] Interviews with activists, Leyton, East London, November 6, 2010, Ilford, East London, November 13, 2010, Bethnal Green, East London, November 28, 2010, Lewisham, South London, December 11, 2010, Whitechapel, East London, June 17, 2011, Wembley Central, West London, June 25, 2011, and Southall, West London, June 28, 2011.

[93] Interview with leading activist, Ilford, East London, November 13, 2010.

[94] Interview with rank-and-file activist, Mile End, East London, June 26, 2011.

Omar and from people like Anjem Choudary, Abu Izzadeen, even Brother Mizanur [Rahman]."[95]

RECRUITING FOR AL-MUHAJIROUN

Religious seekers who are ideologically inclined towards al-Muhajiroun and inspired by network leaders still need someone to "pull" them into the activist network. As with other forms of high-risk activism, recruits require contact with someone who can explain the Emigrants' vision and ideology in a way they can understand, introduce them to other activists, and bring them to events.[96] Recruiters may be family members, childhood friends, neighborhood acquaintances, co-workers, even activists they meet at one of the network's da'wah stalls and public lectures. Leaders encourage rank-and-file activists to seek new recruits when performing their da'wah and to tap into their own networks of friends, family members, and acquaintances.

One activist I interviewed at a da'wah stall in Stratford, East London recalls how he was recruited into the activist network, nearly two years before, at the same stall where we spoke: "I was with a group of twenty people, heading off somewhere, up to no good. Then a group of three Muslims in this exact space, doing a da'wah stall, they stopped us." The respondent identified his interlocutor, who was one of the network's top recruiters and a leader of the spin-off group, Muslims Against Crusades. "He stopped me… and he said, 'Look, why are you here?'" In addition to questioning him about the meaning of life, this recruiter also engaged the young man in a discussion about what was "going on in Iraq and Afghanistan." Sensing the young respondent's interest, the recruiter "invited me to come down to a lecture or class."[97]

The respondent was indeed interested and he accepted his recruiter's invitation. "The first speaker I went to was Anjem Choudary," he recalled. "In those days, I didn't know who Anjem Choudary was. I just sat in one of his lectures and after that I started coming down to hear other speakers." Asked how he knew when and where the talks would be, the respondent said "one of them took my number and he kept me informed by texting me." In addition to attending talks, he continued to visit his recruiter at different da'wah stalls: "I'd just stick around and I was always asking questions. For a good two or three months, I used to come down to his stalls, even roadshows. I didn't engage in the da'wah myself. I used to just keep asking questions." Emphasizing the extended period that passed between his initial encounter at the da'wah stall and his final decision to become an activist, he adds, "It took me half a year to get involved completely, to put my heart into the da'wah."[98]

[95] Interview with leading activist, Whitechapel, East London, June 17, 2011.
[96] McAdam, "Recruitment to High-Risk Activism," p. 65; Snow, Zurcher, Jr., and Ekland-Olson, "Social Networks and Social Movements."
[97] Interview with rank-and-file activist, Stratford, East London, June 27, 2011.
[98] Interview with rank-and-file activist, Stratford, East London, June 27, 2011.

FIGURE 2.1 Activist talks to community support officer at da'wah stall.
Photograph by Michael Kenney.

This young activist's experience illustrates the importance of da'wah stalls
to al-Muhajiroun's recruitment. Other respondents also emphasize how they
were connected to the network through da'wah stalls. "For me it was a stall,
same as this one," observes an activist at a stall in Ilford. After activists at the
stall explained their beliefs to him, "something clicked in me and from that
day I started coming to the brothers. I started going to the talks."[99] "They
were in Stratford," recalls another respondent, who worked for the London
Metropolitan Police at the time. "They had a stall there and I met them because
I used to patrol up and down that area. I used to see them a lot and I used to
love interacting with them and talking to them."[100] Apparently the da'wah
had a strong impact on him: he eventually quit his job and became a full-time
activist. Activists targeted other police officers as well. On several occasions
I saw activists giving da'wah to community support officers who were monitoring their stalls and roadshows (see Figure 2.1).[101]

Al-Muhajiroun has long recognized the importance of recruiting new activists
through da'wah. Some respondents even speak of the network's recruitment
strategy and methods. Referring to a recent recruit I was interviewing, one
veteran activist explains, "He is actually proof of what I was saying about

[99] Interview with activist, Ilford, East London, November 13, 2010. Also, interview with another
activist at the same da'wah stall, November 13, 2010, and interview with activist, Lewisham,
South London, December 11, 2010.
[100] Interview with different activist at the same da'wah stall, Ilford, East London, November
13, 2010.
[101] Field notes, al-Muhajiroun da'wah stalls, Stratford, East London, November 29, 2010 and June
20, 2011, and Islamic roadshow, Wembley Central, West London, June 25, 2011.

the recruiting policy. He saw us at a talk, asked us questions and when his misconceptions were all cleared up, he understood there's something good here. And that's how we're on the work of recruiting."[102] "Maryam," a former female activist, adds, "Methods of recruiting members included da'wah stalls on the Hounslow High Street in West London."[103] While Maryam was referring to her own activism in al-Muhajiroun years earlier, during my field work I often saw activists recruiting people at stalls in Hounslow and other London neighborhoods, including Ilford, Islington, Lewisham, Stratford, Tottenham, and Wembley.[104]

To attract attention to their street preaching, activists often call out to passersby, hand them leaflets, and engage the few people who stop to talk. To encourage busy pedestrians to stop or at least slow down, activists sometimes shout their message through loud speakers or display eye-catching – and provocative – posters and banners. Ali, a former activist who ran da'wah stalls in West London recalls how he and his companions displayed grisly photos of bombing victims at their stalls. The idea was to shock young bystanders and interest them in their activism:

On the da'wah stall you get new young people coming in. They look and see a big picture. "Oh, this is bad," they say. "These are our brothers and sisters getting bombed every day?" So you start hitting this point and these young people are interested now. "Who are you? You're different from other Islamic organizations. Why don't they tell us this in the mosque? You guys are very knowledgeable. You know what's happening. We like you. Can we come and see you?" "Yeah, no problem," we tell them. "We have an open discussion circle. Come in, bring your friend, bring your neighbor, bring whoever you want to bring. It doesn't matter what they look like. We don't judge them. Bring them."[105]

Activists are encouraged to bring their recruits or "contacts" to open discussion circles and public talks. "You have to work on your contacts," explains Ali, "Try to recruit five people. Bring them in, let them talk to us. Make them feel comfortable and let them ask questions and express their opinions, their interests."[106] "We contact them," adds a current activist, describing the follow-up work that's done with new recruits. "We have them come to one of our events if we're having a talk or conference, or we even invite them to a da'wah stall to see how we give da'wah."[107]

---

[102] Interview with veteran activist, Leyton, East London, November 14, 2010.

[103] Interview with Maryam, Hounslow, West London, December 13, 2010. Also, interview with Haroon, Westminster, Central London, June 14, 2011.

[104] Field notes, da'wah stalls in Hounslow, West London, June 28, 2011 and September 4, 2013, Ilford, East London, November 13, 2010, Tottenham, North London, December 4, 2010, Bethnal Green, East London, December 5, 2010, Lewisham, South London, December 11, 2010, Wembley Central, West London, June 25, 2011, Islington, North London, July 21, 2012, and Stratford, East London, December 13, 2014.

[105] Interview with Ali, Hounslow, West London, December 13, 2010.

[106] Interview with Ali, Hounslow, West London, December 13, 2010.

[107] Interview with rank-and-file activist Hounslow, West London, September 4, 2013.

The purpose of inviting people to open discussions, public talks, and preaching stalls "is to engage them and get them into closed study circles," notes a former activist who worked as a recruiter for al-Muhajiroun.[108] When recruits express interest in learning more, "we put them into halaqahs," adds a leading activist. As I will show in the next chapter, activists are indoctrinated in the Emigrants' ideology in these invitation-only study circles. "At the end of the day," the leading activist continues, "our aim is to create more da'is, people that carry da'wah. That's what we want to do. We want to make the jama'ah [group] bigger."[109]

Recruitment is not limited to da'wah stall contacts. Activists are expected to draw on their personal networks of friends, family members, and acquaintances for potential newcomers. The former recruiter recalls how, apart from engaging people at al-Muhajiroun events, recruiting "was done very informally through networks of friends and peers."[110] An officer who specializes in the Emigrants for the London Metropolitan Police agrees. Recruitment often occurs through "word of mouth and family links and friendship," he explains, giving an example: "once you get [name of prominent activist] in, he's gonna bring in his friends, and they're gonna bring in their friends."[111] Along with Omar Bakri's charisma, this dynamic of friends recruiting friends helps explain why the Emigrants grew so rapidly into a scale-free-like network during its early years.

Earlier in this chapter, I highlighted several examples of people who were pulled into the activist network through friends, family members, classmates, and other associates. Although they didn't necessarily realize it at the time, many of these people were recruited into al-Muhajiroun by the same activists who introduced them to its ideology. Ahmed, who later became a prominent activist before leaving Britain to join ISIS, was one of these recruits. He was drawn into al-Muhajiroun by Rohan, his close childhood friend. "I knew him since I was a young child of about eight or nine," he recalled in an interview. "We grew up together in the neighborhood." Initially, according to Ahmed, he was not interested in Rohan's attempts to recruit him: "It had nothing to do with me and my course of life. But he kept challenging me and he kept confronting me."[112]

Over a period of several months the two friends met "regularly, about once a week," during which they engaged in long conversations about shariah, the khilafah, the meaning of life. Gradually, after five to six months of intense, weekly "debates and discussions," Ahmed, who had been raised in a non-Muslim household, was ready to embrace al-Muhajiroun's interpretation of

---

108 Interview with former activist, Walthamstow, East London, July 17, 2012.

109 Interview with leading activist, Walthamstow, East London, June 22, 2011.

110 Interview with former activist, Walthamstow, East London, July 17, 2012.

111 Interview with London Metropolitan Police officer, Westminster, Central London, June 29, 2011.

112 Interview with Ahmed, Tottenham, North London, December 4, 2010.

Islam. "Prior to that I never had that kind of desire to become a Muslim," he recalls. "It was not in my agenda at all." "You needed your friend to help pull you in?" I asked. "Yes," he replied. "He was the one who forced me to think about my role in life."[113]

Later, during the same interview, Ahmed reflected on the importance of these face-to-face discussions for his recruitment to al-Muhajiroun. "The way it happened, the indoctrination, if you can call it that, was through interaction, one-to-one interaction" between him and Rohan. Attempting to generalize from his experience to recruiting others into al-Muhajiroun, Ahmed adds, "The way it works with the organization is that we have one-to-one interaction. I'm doing that right now."[114] Indeed, following our interview Ahmed and I continued our conversation at the da'wah stall, during which he asked me about my background and life in the United States in an attempt to make a personal connection with me.[115]

This happened often during my field work. So often, in fact, that I developed the habit of allowing respondents to proselytize to me. This helped me develop a rapport with them, while giving them the opportunity to perform their activism. One reason activists were willing to interact with me was that it fulfilled their obligation to engage in da'wah. This is an essential act for them, one that is "rewardable" in the afterlife. Another motivation was their desire to "convert" me. Converts are prized recruits in al-Muhajiroun, in part because they do not have a thorough understanding of the religion and they often lack strong ties to local Muslim communities.[116] Indoctrination into the network's Salafi-Islamist worldview is easier when recruits do not have the knowledge to question what they are being told and the connections to Muslims outside the network who can put the Emigrants' ideas into perspective.

My interviews often ended with activists "inviting" me to accept their interpretation of Islam, so that I might save my soul and enter paradise after death. "You don't want to die a kafir," a leader in the network once warned, using a derogatory term for non-Muslim.[117] On another, more thoughtful occasion, he explained his rationale for meeting with me during my numerous trips to London: "When you come, I always try to give you the time. You can ask

---

[113] Interview with Ahmed, Tottenham, North London, December 4, 2010. Ahmed's story is reminiscent of Rodney Stark's experience interviewing members of the Unification Church: "many claimed they had not been particularly interested in religion before. One man told me, "If anybody had said I was going to join up and become a missionary I would have laughed my head off. I had no use for church at all." Rodney Stark, *The Rise of Christianity: A Sociologist Reconsiders History* (Princeton, NJ: Princeton University Press, 1996), p. 16.

[114] Interview with Ahmed, Tottenham, North London, December 4, 2010.

[115] Field notes from al-Muhajiroun da'wah stall in Tottenham, North London, December 4, 2010.

[116] Interviews with Abdul, Whitechapel, East London, June 18, 2011, and Maryam, Hounslow, West London, December 13, 2010.

[117] Interview with leading activist, Whitechapel, East London, September 4, 2013.

questions about this, that and the other and I'll answer them, but my main purpose is to invite you to Islam." I wasn't unique in this respect. "I do this with everyone," he added, at least among people who were willing to engage with him.[118] But as a middle-aged university professor, I was a little older than his typical recruit, who tended to be younger and less educated. My own perspective as a religiously agnostic social scientist engaged in field research helps explain why I did not accept my respondent's cause and join his activism. I simply did not identify with him or his network of supporters. Had I been younger, however, and still in the process of forming my own identity, I would have been more susceptible to his personal charisma, which was considerable.

This may help explain why activists often direct their recruitment towards young people. "They used to focus on the young for recruitment," emphasizes Abdul, the former activist. "Because they knew the young were more vulnerable... they tried to get as many youngsters as possible."[119] "After the talk," notes a leading activist, explaining how activists would approach young audience members who attended lectures by Anjem Choudary and other leaders, "we'd grab the youngsters and we'd speak to them at their level. That's the way it should be done."[120] "I would try to find people who had a sense of grievance, a sense of longing for identity and belonging," adds the former recruiter.[121] In practice, this meant focusing on youth, particularly young men and women who lacked firm personal identities, and the religious knowledge and rhetorical skills to effectively counter al-Muhajiroun's message. Such youngsters "don't know what they want to be," explains Maryam. "They're confused." In contrast, network recruiters come across as confident and knowledgeable: "They think they have the answer to everything, which is really convincing to young people who lack the critical knowledge and skills" to refute what they are being told.[122] "We stuck to a certain script and didn't get into sounding like we were divisive or subversive," adds the former recruiter. "I would befriend, I would discuss. It was very much countless friendly da'wah."[123]

Befriending recruits is another important feature of al-Muhajiroun's recruitment strategy. It's not enough for recruiters to draw people to network events and expose them to the Emigrants' ideology. While activists take pride in the perceived supremacy of their beliefs, they understand the need to build friendships with people they hope will return. "When we saw young people coming to the stall," explains the former activist Ali, "we tried to build a relationship with them. We tried to listen to them and talk to their level."[124] Ali's insight mirrors a key finding from decades of research on cults,

---

[118] Interview with leading activist, Ilford, East London, December 9, 2014.
[119] Interview with Abdul, Whitechapel, East London, June 18, 2011.
[120] Interview with leading activist, Walthamstow, East London, June 22, 2011.
[121] Interview with former activist, Walthamstow, East London, July 17, 2012.
[122] Interview with Maryam, Hounslow, West London, June 21, 2011.
[123] Interview with former activist, Walthamstow, East London, July 17, 2012.
[124] Interview with Ali, Hounslow, West London, December 13, 2010.

social movements, guerrilla groups, and terrorist networks: developing strong affective ties – friendships – with recruits is often essential to getting them to join.[125]

When I asked Abdul what drew him to al-Muhajiroun he remarked, without hesitation, "I had friendships. I had a lot of friends. We used to go and have food all the time and stuff. It was a completely different atmosphere for me, an enjoyable atmosphere. I enjoyed it and at the same time I felt for the cause."[126] Ali also highlights his fellowship with "the brothers," which began as soon as he started attending their events: "Straight away when I sat down, they all surrounded me and started talking. They were very welcoming, very friendly. They made me feel wanted."[127]

This was something I experienced first-hand during my field work, especially once I became known among activists. Respondents greeted me with friendly smiles and firm handshakes. They offered me tea when I visited their center in Whitechapel. They engaged me in light-hearted banter and asked how they could help my research. They praised my wispy beard and "humble" demeanor, which they contrasted with the "arrogance" of other academics. And they told me how happy I would make them, if only I converted.[128]

To make recruits feel wanted and build a sense of shared identity, activists organize social activities that give them the opportunity to hang-out with each other. "It's not just Islamic stuff," notes the research director of a London think tank, "it's football and other things as well."[129] These other things include sharing meals in local restaurants, organizing barbeques and other get-togethers, playing soccer and other sports, or simply traveling together to net-work events around Britain.[130] "Someone will give a class and afterwards we eat together and socialize," explains an activist, describing the small gatherings

---

[125] Lofland and Stark, "Becoming a World-Saver"; Rodney Stark and William Sims Bainbridge, "Networks of Faith: Interpersonal Bonds and Recruitment to Cults and Sects," *American Journal of Sociology* 85, no. 6 (May 1980), pp. 1376–95; Rodney Stark, *The Rise of Christianity: A Sociologist Reconsiders History* (Princeton, NJ: Princeton University Press, 1996); Langone, "Responding to Jihadism: A Cultic Studies Perspective"; McAdam, "Recruitment to High-Risk Activism"; Timothy P. Wickham-Crowley, *Guerrillas and Revolution in Latin America: A Comparative Study of Insurgents and Regimes Since 1956* (Princeton, NJ: Princeton University Press, 1992); della Porta, *Social Movements, Political Violence and the State*; Aho *The Politics of Righteousness*; and Marc Sageman, *Turning to Political Violence: The Emergence of Terrorism* (Philadelphia, PA: University of Pennsylvania Press, 2017).

[126] Interview with Abdul, Whitechapel, East London, June 18, 2011.

[127] Interview with Ali, Hounslow, West London, December 13, 2010.

[128] Field notes Bethnal Green, East London, November 28, 2010, Whitechapel, East London, June 16, 2011, Islington, North London, July 21, 2012, Whitechapel, East London, September 4, 2013; and interview with veteran activist, Edgware Road, West London, July 24, 2015.

[129] Interview with research director, think tank, Bloomsbury, Central London, December 14, 2010.

[130] Interviews with activists, Leyton, East London, November 6, 2010 (two separate interviews), Whitechapel, East London, November 9, 2010, Lewisham, South London, December 11, 2010; interviews with London Metropolitan Police officer, Westminster, Central London, June 29, 2011, and research director, think tank, Bloomsbury, Central London, December 14, 2010.

that happen every week. "We get on well together."[131] Haroon, the former supporter who spent two years hanging out with al-Muhajiroun off-and-on, recalls how Anjem Choudary "would flash his credit card and say, 'Let's all go to BiBi's' [a local chicken restaurant]. He would treat people, take them out." Generalizing beyond Choudary to other leaders, including Omar Bakri Mohammed and Abu Izzadeen Brooks, he adds, "they would hang out with the youth and slowly, slowly break them in. 'We are your brothers, look around you, no one cares for you. We're teaching you how to wrestle, to play table tennis, go to the gym, we're taking you on trips. All you need to do is spread the da'wah, spread the faith.'"[132] The key was to make it fun for people, so they would increase their involvement in the network and come together to build a shared political identity and community. This recruitment strategy was effective, helping activists recruit hundreds of new supporters over the years, and have fun while doing it. "We were having a lot of fun and enjoying ourselves," recalls Abdul, who became deeply involved in the network.[133] "This is the same method used today," adds Ali. "It's very good. It works."[134]

MARRYING IN

Another recruitment strategy that works for al-Muhajiroun is marrying people into the activist network. Leading activists have long sought to expand the network and build trust among activists by encouraging members to marry other activists or, when they marry outside the network, to recruit their spouses.[135] Omar Bakri and other leaders promoted this strategy during the Emigrants' early years, when it was expanding rapidly into a scale-free-like network. Bakri was not shy about using the promise of marriage to interest young people in his network and he performed numerous wedding ceremonies.[136] "Marriage was another way of recruiting," explains Maryam, the former female activist, who was active in this period.[137] Abdul, who was also active during these years,

---

[131] Interview with rank-and-file activist, Mile End, East London, June 26, 2011. Also, interviews with other activists, Lewisham, South London, June 18, 2011 and Stratford, East London, June 27, 2011.

[132] Interview with Haroon, Westminster, Central London, June 14, 2011.

[133] Interview with Abdul, Whitechapel, East London, June 18, 2011.

[134] Interview with Ali, Hounslow, West London, December 13, 2010. Also, interview with another former activist, Walthamstow, East London, July 17, 2012.

[135] Some terrorist organizations, including al-Qaeda and Jemaah Islamiyah, have also used marriage to build trust and ties among members' families. See Jacob N. Shapiro, *The Terrorist's Dilemma: Managing Violent Covert Organizations* (Princeton, NJ: Princeton University Press, 2013), pp. 51–2.

[136] Interview with veteran activist, Stratford, East London, November 29, 2010. Also see Ruth Manning and Courtney La Bau, *In and Out of Extremism* (London: Quilliam Foundation, August 2015), p. 43.

[137] Interview with Maryam, Hounslow, West London, December 13, 2010.

recalls how "everyone started getting married and we started seeing a lot more female members in al-Muhajiroun."[138]

This practice continued during the network's later years, when it was decentralizing into a small-world-like network. Activists who were interested in marrying would tell their network colleagues, who would help them find a suitable spouse. When I interviewed him after he left the network, Salman described how it worked for him: "Before I got married I looked for a wife who covered, I looked for a wife who was practicing. I found her through al-Muhajiroun. They found a sister. I asked the brothers, and they looked around. That's how it works. They found a wife, gave me a wife."[139] Salman had been involved in al-Muhajiroun for several years when he married a female activist. However, other respondents, including recent converts, were approached about finding a spouse sooner. "It was quite an eventful week," recalls one convert. "I'd just become Muslim and then a week later the brothers linked me up with someone. They were trying to help me get married."[140] Left unsaid by this respondent is the prospect that his new "brothers" were trying to solidify his involvement by marrying him to another activist.

Not all activists marry inside the movement, however. Some activists find their spouses through family networks and other ties outside al-Muhajiroun. "I don't have to marry one of the sisters," explains a young respondent, referring to female activists. "That's completely up to me and whoever I marry."[141] The Emigrants' flexibility on this point suggests that leading activists understand the value of marrying outside the network. When activists marry outside, they often recruit their spouse for membership. "When they got married, men would bring their wives in to be the new recruits," explains Maryam. "If they married a new woman, they'd ring up the masoul [halaqah leader] and say, 'I've gotten married. My wife is a bit isolated. Could you get her involved in whatever you're doing?'"[142]

"I used to get my wife to go and speak to some sisters," observes Maryam's husband, Ali, who was himself involved in al-Muhajiroun. "The married brother would come up to me and say his wife is being isolated, 'can you bring others?'" "I would go and visit them," Maryam clarifies. "Yeah, chat and recruit," adds Ali. "The trust was there," Maryam replies. "It was like a win-win for us to get women in." Ali and Maryam were already married when Ali joined al-Muhajiroun, so he recruited her. "My husband came home and said,

---

[138] Interview with Abdul, Whitechapel, East London, June 18, 2011.

[139] Interview with Salman, Poplar, East London, July 24, 2015.

[140] Interview with rank-and-file activist, Mile End, East London, June 26, 2011.

[141] Interview with contact, Wembley Central, West London, June 25, 2011. Also, interview with rank-and-file activist, Stratford, East London, June 27, 2011.

[142] Interview with Maryam, Hounslow, West London, December 13, 2010.

'Look, they're going to start a sisters' circle," recalls Maryam. "And I thought, 'Okay, let me join the bandwagon and see what I can do.'"[143] Over the next several years they both became deeply involved in the Emigrants, with Maryam developing into a leading activist in her sisters' group and Ali rising to become masoul in his London neighborhood.

MAKING FRIENDS IN PRISON

While some respondents claim that al-Muhajiroun steered them away from petty crime and debauchery, numerous activists have been convicted of crimes related to their activism, including terrorism fundraising, soliciting murder for terrorist purposes, and encouraging support for ISIS. Individuals who have been imprisoned for these crimes are among the most dedicated and articulate activists. Leaders like Anjem Choudary, Abu Izzadeen Brooks, and Abdul Muhid have used their time in British prisons to connect with other inmates and preach their ideology to them. When asked whether imprisoned activists try to recruit other inmates to al-Muhajiroun, one London Metropolitan Police officer replies, "What we're seeing is they're trying to convert their cellmates in the prison yard," he concedes. "When they come out of prison we've seen them coming to demonstrations as well, so yeah."[144] Ali, who now counsels prison inmates at risk of radicalization, agrees. Using Abu Izzadeen as an example, he explains, "He made so many friends inside... When he was in prison, he used to talk to inmates... He believed in his cause and for him it makes no difference, 'I'll sit inside or outside and I'll still earn my rewards. I'll still do the da'wah. I'll still convince people.' And he will because he's a very charismatic speaker, very convincing."[145]

Activists admit that they try to recruit people in prison. They see no problem with this. For them it is simply another form of da'wah.[146] A leading activist who communicates regularly with inmates gives the example of a younger colleague who spent time in youthful offender and adult prisons:

He's a very active individual on the streets, going to mosques, going to markets, schools, inviting people to Islam, and that hasn't stopped since he's been in prison. He's been in prison for four months. But regardless, he's brought at least twelve people to become

[143] Interview with Ali and Maryam, Hounslow, West London, December 13, 2010.
[144] Interview with London Metropolitan Police officer, Westminster, Central London, June 29, 2011.
[145] Interview with Ali, Hounslow, West London, June 21, 2011.
[146] Interviews with activists, Stratford, East London, November 29, 2010, and Whitechapel, East London, September 4, 2013. Also see Nic Robertson and Paul Cruickshank, "Cagefighter 'cures' terrorists," *CNN* (July 23, 2012), www.cnn.com/2012/07/20/world/europe/uk-caging-terror-main/index.html [Accessed July 28, 2012].

Muslim from his activities inside prison. In one prison, they couldn't accept the fact that so many people were becoming Muslim every time they came in contact with him, so they moved him from the prison for that sole purpose.[147]

Activists like to brag about all the inmates they have converted to Islam, but it is not clear how many have been swayed, let alone recruited to al-Muhajiroun behind bars. There are, however, cases where activists have successfully mobilized inmates they met in prison.[148] One prominent example is Michael Coe, a former gang member who was sentenced to eight years in prison in 2006 for threatening police officers with a shotgun.[149] In prison, Coe befriended Abdul Muhid, a long-time activist then serving time for soliciting murder and terrorism fundraising for a speech he made at a protest outside the Danish Embassy in 2006. Speaking to a reporter from the BBC television program, *Panorama*, Coe described how Muhid took him under his wing: "we just became friends... he started teaching me about stuff... He's much more knowledgeable than me. He taught me some of the stuff I didn't know."[150]

When Coe was released from Manchester Prison, Abdul Muhid, who had already completed his sentence, met him outside the prison gates, along with other activists, including Mizanur Rahman and future ISIS fighter Abu Rahin Aziz. Back in London, Coe devoted himself to his activism, attending rallies and da'wah stalls on a regular basis. An avid weightlifter, he also served as bodyguard for leading activists like Choudary and Brooks. Under the influence of his new companions, Coe embraced his activism. Several months after his release from prison he revealed his commitment in an interview with BBC reporter Raphael Rowe: "I have a cause. I want to see the establishment of [the] khilafah. I want to see an Islamic state."[151] Coe was not merely playing to

---

[147] Interview with leading activist, Whitechapel, East London, September 4, 2013. Also, see "From jail to jihad?," *Panorama* television program shown on *BBC One* (May 12, 2014).

[148] Of course, "prison radicalization" is a problem that goes well beyond al-Muhajiroun. For research on this phenomenon in British, French, and American prisons, see Imran Awan, "Muslim Prisoners, Radicalization and Rehabilitation in British Prisons," *Journal of Muslim Minority Affairs* 33, no. 3 (2013), pp. 371–84; Farhad Khosrokhavar, "Radicalization in Prison: The French Case," *Politics, Religion & Ideology* 14, no. 2 (2013), 284–306; and Mark S. Hamm, *The Spectacular Few: Prisoner Radicalization and the Evolving Terrorist Threat* (New York: New York University Press, 2013).

[149] Raphael Rowe, "From jail to jihad? The threat of prison radicalization," *BBC Panorama* (May 11, 2014), www.bbc.com/news/uk-27357208 [Accessed August 5, 2014]; Raffaello Pantucci, *'We Love Death as You Love Life': Britain's Suburban Terrorists* (London: Hurst, 2015), pp. 182–3.

[150] *BBC One*, "From jail to jihad?," (May 12, 2014). Also, interview with veteran activist, Stratford, East London, December 13, 2014.

[151] *BBC One*, "From jail to jihad?," (May 12, 2014); Rowe, "From jail to jihad?" Also, interview with veteran activist, Stratford, East London, December 13, 2014, and field notes, Wembley Central, West London, June 25, 2011, and Islington, North London, July 21, 2012.

the camera. Months after the BBC documentary aired, he was arrested along with Simon Keeler, a long-time activist who served his own prison sentence for crimes related to his activism, when they tried to leave Britain illegally, hidden in the back of a tractor-trailer. According to the police, both men were on their way to Syria, where they planned to fight on behalf of ISIS. They were acquitted of these charges. However, both activists pled guilty to possessing false travel documents and were jailed for fifteen months, giving them the opportunity to befriend more inmates.[152]

CONCLUSION

The interviews in this chapter, with current and former activists alike, explain how and why some people join al-Muhajiroun's high-risk activism. In reporting what my respondents told me, I have tried to trace the processes through which they entered the Emigrants.

A number of contributing factors emerge from their stories. Many recruits are young and biographically available for high-risk activism. Some also face a turning point in their lives, making them more receptive to new opportunities and experiences. Some are searching for identity and meaning, which they find in al-Muhajiroun, sometimes after going through other groups first. Some are pulled in through the persistent efforts of trusted intermediaries who extol the virtues of their activism and the eternal rewards for those who join. And some are impressed by the activists they meet at da'wah stalls and the charismatic leaders whose talks they attend. At these talks and other events they begin to develop relationships with activists. When these friendships deepen it solidifies their identity and facilitates their acceptance of the Emigrants' ideology, no matter how odd it initially appeared to them.

These and other contributing factors do not form a single theory of "radicalization" or a deterministic model of joining al-Muhajiroun. I hesitate to identify these conditions as necessary, let alone sufficient, for joining, given the small size of my sample and the possibility that my analysis, however intuitive it may be, could be missing other factors. But the conditions described in this chapter do reveal the basic process through which some young men and women decide to become involved in al-Muhajiroun. My findings also confirm the long-standing consensus among scholars of religious cults, social movements, and terrorist groups about the importance of

---

[152] *BBC News*, "Boxing champion Anthony Small cleared of plotting to join IS," (July 28, 2015), www.bbc.com/news/uk-england-london-33689764 [Accessed August 4, 2015]; *BBC News*, "Five men in court on Syria-related terror and fraud charges," (December 15, 2014), www.bbc .com/news/uk-30477881 [Accessed December 16, 2014]; *Court News UK*, "Keeler: Extremists jailed after trying to sneak out of UK," (July 31, 2015), http://courtnewsuk.co.uk/ [Accessed February 8, 2016]. Also, interviews with activists, Stratford, East London, November 29, 2011 and Wembley Central, West London, June 25, 2011; Simcox, Stuart, and Ahmed, *Islamist Terrorism*, p. 174; and Pantucci, *'We Love Death as You Love Life'*, p. 119.

social relationships for pulling people into these risky pursuits. The Emigrants' leaders are certainly aware of these factors – and their importance for the network's strategy of recruitment. This is why they encourage their followers to organize da'wah stalls and cultivate relationships with recruits. Building these friendships and shared identities is essential for transforming recruits into full-blown activists. In the next chapter, I explore how this process unfolds.

3

A Community of True Believers

We don't need to adapt and change that much because we believe Allah's will is there to protect us.

Leading activist

When activists join al-Muhajiroun they not only become part of a network trying to establish a global Islamic state, they enter a group of like-minded people who learn from each other through collaboration and performance. They join, in other words, a "community of practice." Introduced by cognitive anthropologists and expanded upon by organizational sociologists, the concept explains how people learn the practices behind their shared concerns, ranging from craft professions such as midwifery and meat cutting, to sundry legal and extra-legal pursuits, like parenting, insurance claim processing, and drug trafficking.[1] These informal communities exist within larger networks and formal organizations. In communities of practice, veterans interact with newcomers to share stories, solve problems, and build shared identities. Through these interactions, novices absorb the community's culture and master the

---

[1] The concept originates in the work of Jean Lave and Etienne Wenger, particularly their co-authored book, *Situated Learning: Legitimate Peripheral Participation* (New York: Cambridge University Press, 1991), and Wenger's subsequent publications, including *Communities of Practice: Learning, Meaning, and Identity* (New York: Cambridge University Press, 1998). Subsequent applications include John Seely Brown and Paul Duguid, "Organizational Learning and Communities-of-Practice: Toward a Unified View of Working, Learning, and Innovation," *Organization Science* 2, no. 1 (1991), pp. 40–57; Wanda J. Orlikowski, "Knowing in Practice: Enacting a Collective Capability in Distributed Organizing," *Organization Science* 13, no. 3 (May–June 2002), pp. 249–73; Davide Nicolini, Silvia Gherardi, and Dvora Yanow, eds., *Knowing in Organizations: A Practice-Based Approach* (Armonk, NY: M.E. Sharpe, 2003); and Michael Kenney, *From Pablo to Osama: Trafficking and Terrorist Networks, Government Bureaucracies, and Competitive Adaptation* (University Park, PA: Pennsylvania State University Press, 2007).

knowledge and practical skills they need to become competent practitioners. In the process, they form identities as valued members of a common enterprise, transforming themselves into committed insiders willing to share their knowledge with new supporters.

In contrast to the literature on social networks and social movements, communities of practice have not been widely discussed among scholars of political violence.[2] Instead researchers have produced a growing body of literature on terrorism learning and adaptation.[3] These studies have improved our understanding for how terrorists train, innovate, and adopt new technologies. But few researchers exploit primary source data, including interviews and field work, to uncover the processes through which extremists learn the beliefs and skills they need to become competent practitioners. This suggests that communities of practice holds unfulfilled promise for the field. Realizing this promise means that scholars should focus less on the outputs of learning, attributing changes in terrorist behavior to tactical or strategic "adaptation," and more on the processes through which participants acquire knowledge and experience.

This chapter embraces this change in orientation by applying communities of practice to the Emigrants. Like other communities of practice, al-Muhajiroun's community is not static. It changes over time as new participants join and become socialized in the network's norms and customs. These ways of believing and doing provide a set of shared principles and practices that have largely endured as the network evolves in response to internal and external pressures. They have also allowed the Emigrants to transform young recruits into competent activists, while maintaining their ideological cohesion.

---

[2] This is despite the efforts of two prominent scholars, Max Taylor and John Horgan, who introduced the concept to readers of the leading terrorism studies journal in 2006. See Max Taylor and John Horgan, "A Conceptual Framework for Addressing Psychological Process in the Development of the Terrorist," *Terrorism and Political Violence* 18, no. 4 (2006), pp. 585–601. Taylor and Horgan's discussion of communities of practice, draws heavily on Karsten Hundeide, "Becoming a Committed Insider," *Culture and Psychology* 9, no. 2 (2003), pp. 107–27.

[3] Some of the more prominent examples of this literature include Brian A. Jackson, John C. Baker, Kim Cragin, John Parachini, Horacio R. Trujillo, and Peter Chalk, *Aptitude for Destruction, Volume 1: Organizational Learning in Terrorist Groups and Its Implications for Combating Terrorism* and *Aptitude for Destruction, Volume 2: Case Studies of Organizational Learning in Five Terrorist Groups* (Santa Monica, CA: RAND Corporation, 2005); James J.F. Forest, ed., *Teaching Terror: Knowledge Transfer in the Terrorist World* (Lanham, MD: Rowman & Littlefield, May 2006); Adam Dolnik, *Understanding Terrorist Innovation: Technologies, Tactics and Global Trends* (London: Routledge, 2007); Maria J. Rasmussen and Mohammed M. Hafez, eds., *Terrorist Innovations in Weapons of Mass Effect: Preconditions, Causes, and Predictive Indicators* (Ft. Belvoir, VA: Defense Threat Reduction Agency, 2010); and Magnus Ranstorp and Magnus Normark, eds., *Understanding Terrorism Innovation and Learning: Al-Qaeda and Beyond* (Abingdon: Routledge, 2015). For a recent review, see Louise Kettle and Andrew Mumford, "Terrorist Learning: A New Analytical Framework," *Studies in Conflict & Terrorism* 40, no. 7 (2017), pp. 523–38.

Like other such communities, al-Muhajiroun's community of practice is not self-evident to its practitioners.[4] This is neither surprising nor disconfirming. After all my respondents are Islamist activists, not organization theorists, and the concept enjoys limited reach in Salafi-jihadi circles. Activists do not speak of the Emigrants' community of practice in their interviews. But they do identify themselves as "students" of their religion and "intellectual affiliates" in the activist network. They explain how they learn the network's ideology through "companionship" with more experienced activists, and they describe their activism as a "learning process" that never ends. Respondents stress the need to "account" for themselves and "review" their behavior so that they can improve their da'wah and hisbah. At the same time they are so confident in the power of their ideology and their status among God's chosen ones that they have convinced themselves they don't always need to adapt because He will protect them. In this chapter I unpack these themes and paradoxes, tracing the processes through which activists develop into competent practitioners by observing experienced activists and engaging in high-risk activism, while letting their insularity and dogmatism limit their ability to learn.

INTELLECTUAL AFFILIATION IN AL-MUHAJIROUN'S COMMUNITY OF PRACTICE

As befitting their participation in an illicit network that has been outlawed by British authorities, membership in al-Muhajiroun – and its community of practice – is fluid and informal. When activists become involved in the network, they do not sign a contract identifying themselves as members, nor do they perform initiation rites or swear their allegiance to a leader or organization. "There are many movements out there which have a *bayat*, like a pledge, or a contract, or a promise to abide by the rules of the emir and so on," explains a leading activist, distinguishing al-Muhajiroun from other Islamist groups like Hizb ut-Tahrir and the Muslim Brotherhood. "We have never had anything like that."[5]

If activists don't sign membership contracts, or even pledge loyalty to an emir, on what, if anything, is their membership based? Respondents identify two sources of "membership in al-Muhajiroun": administrative affiliation and intellectual affiliation. People affiliate "administratively" by participating in al-Muhajiroun's activities; they affiliate "intellectually" by internalizing its ideology and culture. The first requires that activists "attend the various lectures, demonstrations, processions, and so on."[6] The second requires that they go

---

[4] Joanne Roberts, "Limits to Communities of Practice," *Journal of Management Studies* 43, no. 3. (May 2006), p. 625; and Wenger, *Communities of Practice*, p. 125.

[5] Interview with leading activist, Leyton, East London, November 4, 2010.

[6] Interview with leading activist, Skype, June 26, 2013. Also, see Quintan Wiktorowicz, *Radical Islam Rising: Muslim Extremism in the West* (Lanham, MD: Rowman & Littlefield, 2005), pp. 190–1.

beyond this to join a halaqah and study the beliefs and concepts that form the basis of the Emigrants' activism. Administrative affiliation means participating in al-Muhajiroun's activist network; intellectual affiliation means participating in its community of practice.

Like other communities of practice, membership in al-Muhajiroun's community is grounded in the shared culture of its insiders, and their willingness to apply this culture to their activities.[7] Intellectual affiliation includes a commitment to acquiring the values and ideas that form the basis of the Emigrants' activism. As one activist puts it, "intellectual affiliation is about gaining the knowledge."[8] Activists gain the knowledge by attending talks, participating in halaqah discussions, and interacting with their companions. Through engagement they develop "the necessary culture, the understanding of why they're rising as a movement," observes a leading activist.[9] This understanding is based on participants' shared knowledge, rather than a pledge of loyalty to a specific leader such as Omar Bakri or Anjem Choudary. "Those who are with you have the same understanding and the same concepts," adds a leading activist. "We base it [membership] on whether someone has the same understanding. Do they really understand… and how much does that understanding have an impact in their life?"[10]

As this rhetorical question suggests, acquiring al-Muhajiroun's shared understanding is only the first step towards intellectual affiliation and membership in its community of practice. To become full participants, activists must apply the knowledge they have learned to their activism. Another leading activist puts it this way: "Intellectual affiliation is we study the same culture of understanding and that culture will push me and motivate me to act in a particular way, to interact and call society towards Islam, and to challenge the dominant forces and ideas in society." "The culture we share will motivate us to act in the same way," he adds. "Therefore, you'll see us as a collective group."[11] Shared culture, enacted through collective action, forms the basis of al-Muhajiroun's community, and membership within it. The more activists "engage with the culture, the more we will consider them to be with us," confirms the first leading activist. "They would have intellectual affiliation with our group and be considered members."[12]

This adds another layer of complexity to my interpretation of the Emigrants. Al-Muhajiroun is not just a network of individuals, connected through social ties. It is a community of "true believers" bound together through their shared

---

7   Lave and Wenger, *Situated Learning*, and Wenger, *Communities of Practice*.

8   Interview with veteran activist, Whitechapel, East London, November 9, 2010.

9   Interview with leading activist, Skype, June 26, 2013.

10 Interview with leading activist, Leyton, East London, November 4, 2010.

11 Interview with leading activist, Leyton, East London, November 8, 2010.

12 Interview with leading activist, Leyton, East London, November 4, 2010. Also, interview with same respondent, Skype, June 26, 2013.

identity and their common understanding of the world, and their role within it.[13] Intellectual affiliation forms the basis of this shared identity and understanding. "The affiliation isn't because we're just a group of brothers," explains a respondent, "the affiliation is ideological... the bond between the brothers isn't just a mere brotherhood, it is on an ideological level as well, meaning that our thought process is the same."[14]

Al-Muhajiroun's ideological bonds serve as a marker of identity and a boundary for the network, distinguishing its community of practice from other groups engaged in Islamist activism. "Not everyone can just become part of the group," explains a respondent, "people are cultured in."[15] People are cultured in when they internalize the network's ideology and engage in its activism. "All the brothers that come out and give da'wah today are affiliated," notes another activist. He elaborates while handing out leaflets at a stall outside a shopping mall in South London: "The difference between us and other groups is that we are affiliated with the same understanding. If you ask me and you ask any of these brothers, they will give you the same views as me because we do not differ in the intellectual aspect." He continues, drawing the intellectual boundary between al-Muhajiroun and other groups: "If you go to someone at another organization, the Tablighi Jama'at, or the Salafis, or the Islamic Association for Palestinian Youths, he would tell you his belief of jihad is this, his belief of da'wah is that. He believes democracy is acceptable. I believe democracy is wrong. They differ in their intellectual understanding." But al-Muhajiroun's differences with these other groups are not merely intellectual. They manifest themselves in action as well: "You wouldn't see them with me out here at the stall because they believe they can't be here. They believe in the other aspects of Islam. But *we* [motions to his fellow activists at the stall] are affiliated under the same understanding."[16]

Along with their shared intellectual affiliation, the Emigrants are also bound by their participation in a joint enterprise, building an Islamic state in Britain and globally. Working together to achieve this goal forms a critical part of their identity. "They're united by this common vision," explains the research director of a London-based think tank. "They get their sense of belonging out of it, a sense of, 'We're part of a movement, we're going somewhere, we've got vision, we've got an agenda.'" This agenda includes a special role for activists, who are told, "'You're part of this divine movement and we're going to change the world. We're going to restore our religion and bring Muslims back to their rightful place. And you're going to be a key part of it.'"[17] "We're part of the struggle," confirms Rashid, who spent several years in the network. "We're

[13] Wiktorowicz, *Radical Islam Rising*, pp. 17, 191.
[14] Interview with activist, Leyton, East London, November 14, 2010.
[15] Interview with veteran activist, Leyton, East London, November 6, 2010.
[16] Interview with rank-and-file activist, Lewisham, South London, December 11, 2010.
[17] Interview with research director, think tank, Bloomsbury, Central London, December 14, 2010.

all in it together." This sense of collective identity, he explains, contributes to "a strong bond between the brothers."[18] "It's about identity, about a sense of belonging," adds Maryam, another former activist. "It gave us structure, it gave us a vision."[19] "It's like joining a gang, or a fraternity," adds Haroon, a former supporter who affiliated administratively, but not intellectually, with the network. "You just feel you belong somewhere, like you have a brotherhood."[20]

Like others I met in London, Haroon spent a lot of time with activists but never joined the community. Called "contacts" in al-Muhajiroun, these individuals affiliate administratively with the Emigrants, but not intellectually. They attend network events, interact with intellectual affiliates, and even agree on certain issues, such as the perceived oppression of Muslims by Western governments. But they do not systematically study, nor fully internalize, the Emigrants' ideology.[21] Haroon went to many da'wah stalls and protests during his two years in the network. He also attended private study sessions in a local halaqah led by Omar Bakri himself. He even helped activists vandalize property by plastering stickers advertising al-Muhajiroun events. Despite his sustained involvement in the network, Haroon insists that he never accepted his friends' extremist beliefs and would even question them privately about the ideas they were learning: "I wouldn't confront them openly, but on the side I'd say, 'Yeah, this is whack. Why are you doing it?' And they're like, 'you don't believe in it, you don't understand.'"[22]

Indeed, he didn't believe in it. Like other administrative affiliates, Haroon was part of al-Muhajiroun's activist network, but not its community. Only those who internalize the network's ideology, and who manifest these beliefs in their actions, truly radicalize and become devoted members of its community of practice.

FROM NOVICE TO PRACTITIONER

When novices join a community of practice, they interact with experienced practitioners who socialize them to the community's norms and practices. In some communities, this process occurs through formal apprenticeships that match beginners with knowledgeable veterans; in others, the process unfolds informally, with novices seeking out mentors on their own. In both cases,

---

[18] Interview with Rashid, Whitechapel, East London, June 26, 2011.
[19] Interview with Maryam, Skype, November 20, 2012.
[20] Interview with Haroon, Westminster, Central London, June 14, 2011.
[21] Interview with Haroon, Westminster, Central London, June 14, 2011, and two other contacts, Wembley Central, West London, June 25, 2011.
[22] Interview with Haroon, Westminster, Central London, June 14, 2011. Some readers may suspect that Haroon was trying to downplay his intellectual commitment to al-Muhajiroun. However, I was able to confirm his account with another respondent, Abdul, a former activist who was his closest friend in the network. Interview with Abdul, Whitechapel, East London, June 18, 2011.

newcomers seek to learn from old-timers by watching them, asking them questions, and imitating their behavior.[23]

Al-Muhajiroun does not have a formal apprenticeship program, but recruits still learn from experienced activists. "The best way to learn is to get amongst the brothers and watch them," explains one respondent at a busy Saturday afternoon da'wah stall. "Most of the brothers have experience, so you watch and you listen."[24] "My mentor is the brother there," adds another rank-and-file activist at the same stall, pointing to the emir running their da'wah. "Any question I have I will call on him. I don't have the full knowledge of how this works. I'm still learning. But any question I've got, I'll ask him."[25] "We watch and we learn, like an apprenticeship," confirms another respondent, explaining how he and his colleagues observe activists perform da'wah. "It's a learning process. You're constantly learning."[26]

Activists also learn from instructors who deliver lectures on the network's ideology in private talks and public lectures. The student–teacher relationship is important in al-Muhajiroun, and grounded in activists' understanding of Islamic tradition and scripture. "We see from history that even with the Prophet, *Aleyhi al Salam* [Peace Be Upon Him/PBUH], he learned from the Angel Gabriel," explains an activist. "Gabriel called to him and God guided him. And then the Prophet was an example for his companions. And it carried on like that. They had students and then the students had students. And this is how Islam was passed through the generations."[27] Something similar happens in al-Muhajiroun's community of practice, which is dynamic and changes over time. Veteran ideologues share their expertise with novices who gradually develop their own knowledge and experience. Once these novices develop into full participants, they pass along their knowledge to the next "generation" of recruits.

The original emir, Omar Bakri Mohammed, was the first and most important teacher. Virtually all of al-Muhajiroun's ideology is based on Bakri's teachings and writings, which reflect his Salafi-inspired interpretation of religious theology mixed with an Islamist ideology that borrows heavily from Hizb ut-Tahrir. Bakri communicated his blend of Salafi-Islamism to his students through formal lectures and private talks, many of which were recorded and later posted on the Internet, and in self-published booklets, such as *The Islamic Standard*, *The Road to Jannah*, and *The Islamic Verdict on Jihad and the Method to Establish the Khilafah*. These writings and

[23] Lave and Wenger, *Situated Learning*, p. 95, and Wenger, *Communities of Practice*, p. 100.

[24] Interview with rank-and-file activist, Ilford, East London, November 13, 2010.

[25] Interview with different rank-and-file activist, Ilford, East London, November 13, 2010. Also, interview with Abdul, Whitechapel, East London, June 18, 2011.

[26] Interview with leading activist, Leyton, East London, November 6, 2010.

[27] Interview with veteran activist, Leyton, East London, November 6, 2010. Also, interview with another activist, Ilford, East London, November 13, 2010.

recordings, along with activists' own notes from Bakri's talks, comprise the shared body of al-Muhajiroun's knowledge-based artifacts.[28] They contain the language, concepts, scriptural quotes, and interpretations that represent Bakri's, and by extension the network's, world view. Students must learn this knowledge to become intellectually affiliated with the Emigrant's community of practice. They do this by attending public lectures and private halaqahs, and through "self-study," reading the booklets and watching or listening to the lectures on their own.[29]

When Omar Bakri left Britain in 2005, under intense pressure after the 7/7 bombings in London, activists lost face-to-face access to their main teacher. Fortunately for them, several of Bakri's closest students had mastered his teachings and emerged as effective preachers by then. Long-time activists such as Anjem Choudary, Mizanur Rahman, and Abu Izzadeen Brooks not only assumed leadership of al-Muhajiroun's decentralized, "small-world-like" network, they took over Bakri's teaching responsibilities. These and other leaders traveled around London and Great Britain to deliver public talks and halaqah lectures, often working from notes of their mentor's speeches. When Bakri failed to return to Britain, they replaced him as the network's leading ideologues and instructors. "Sheikh Bakri's not here anymore, he's in Lebanon," explains one activist at a da'wah stall in Ilford, East London, "but his students are here, and I learn from them."[30] Referring to one of these students, another respondent elaborates: "The Sheikh's moved on, but now Anjem has learnt enough that he can teach. He studied his notes. Everything Sheikh Omar learned, he passed on to Anjem, and now Anjem is our teacher."[31]

As Anjem Choudary and other network leaders learned from Omar Bakri, so did the next generation of activists learn from them, underscoring the dynamism of al-Muhajiroun's community. By watching Choudary, Rahman, and Brooks present talks and engage in da'wah, these activists acquired the ideological knowledge and practical skills they needed to become competent practitioners. Eventually, some of them became teachers themselves, delivering talks to activists around Britain. "We ourselves started teaching," notes one such respondent, who became a leading activist for the network in East London.

---

[28] Roberts, "Limits to Communities of Practice," pp. 624–5; Wenger, *Communities of Practice*, pp. 125–6; Martha S. Feldman, "Organizational Routines as a Source of Continuous Change," *Organization Science* 11, no. 6 (November-December 2000), pp. 611–29; and Lynn Eden, *Whole World on Fire: Organizations, Knowledge, & Nuclear Weapons Devastation* (Ithaca, NY: Cornell University Press, 2004).

[29] Interviews with activists, Leyton, East London, December 9, 2010, and Stratford, East London, June 20, 2011.

[30] Interview with rank-and-file activist, Ilford, East London, November 13, 2010.

[31] Interview with different rank-and-file activist, Ilford, East London, November 13, 2010. Also, interviews with other activists, Stratford, East London, December 6, 2010, and Lewisham, South London, December 11, 2010.

Motioning to another activist at the table where we were sitting, he adds, "I teach and the brother here teaches. We propagate Islam to the community."[32]
One evening I observed one of the network's younger teachers propagate Islam to the community by lecturing on the "heroes of Islam." Much of this activist's involvement in al-Muhajiroun occurred after Bakri had left Britain. Consequently, his primary teachers were people like Choudary, Brooks, and Rahman. But he was a quick learner with a knack for Arabic. Within a few years of joining the community he was delivering his own talks, incorporating his own innovations into his delivery.[33] On a warm night in June 2011, he lectured for ninety minutes to over thirty students packed into a small classroom in the network's educational center in Whitechapel, East London. "We're not going to get the global domination of Islam without a community," he told his listeners. "We need to establish a community."[34] I was surprised by one of his innovations. Rather than using hand-written notes, as I had seen his teachers do during their talks, he used his iPhone.[35]
In addition to lecturing, this activist led a spin-off group he helped create called Muslims Against Crusades. As I will show in the next chapter, Muslims Against Crusades was composed of dedicated activists who specialized in confrontational demonstrations, including the infamous poppy-burning protest on Armistice Day in 2010. Beyond his leadership role, the young teacher also regularly engaged in da'wah and recruited new activists to al-Muhajiroun. In a separate interview, one of his recruits talked to me about learning from his mentor: "He and other brothers in the *jama'ah* [group] are very knowledgeable, especially in history. I asked him what the poppy symbolizes and why we had a poppy-burning day and he enlightened me."[36] Indeed, the young teacher's knowledge of the Emigrants' Islamist ideology and Salafi theology, help explain his rise to a leadership position in the network. Like other rising stars in al-Muhajiroun, and his teachers in the network before them, he developed from a novice to a competent practitioner and leading activist in his own right. During my field work, I observed three "generations" of activists, all of whom carefully cultivated their recruits and shared their knowledge and experience with them. This helped the new recruits develop into competent practitioners who passed along their own expertise to those who came after them. Such cross-generational learning enhanced the Emigrants' resilience by allowing them to spread their ideology to newly committed insiders even when original leaders like Omar Bakri were no longer around to guide them.

---

[32] Interview with leading activist, Leyton, East London, November 6, 2010.
[33] Interviews with veteran activist, Whitechapel, East London, November 9, 2010, June 17, 2011, and December 4, 2013.
[34] Field notes and audio recording of lecture, Whitechapel, East London, June 16, 2011.
[35] Field notes, Whitechapel, East London, June 16, 2011.
[36] Interview with rank-and-file activist, Stratford, East London, June 27, 2011.

SUHBA: LEARNING FROM COMPANIONSHIP

In communities of practice novices learn by accompanying experienced practitioners, watching how they "talk, walk, work, and generally conduct their lives."[37] Learning through companionship is essential to the Emigrants. Respondents believe it is even more important than studying in the classroom or reading books. "It's called "suhba in Arabic," explains a leading activist. "It's when you accompany somebody. It's not about sitting down in the classroom and taking notes, it's about following someone and listening to them and taking notes."[38] "You can only learn so much from lectures and in a classroom environment," remarks another leading activist. "The real way you will educate yourself is by accompanying someone and seeing how they live their life, their character and their behavior. You can learn more in a day in this kind of companionship than you could attending lectures for a whole year."[39] Almost four years later, in an online lecture delivered to thirty listeners, he made the same point: "The best way to learn is not by books but through suhba, companionship."[40] In a follow-up interview two days later, he elaborated: "It's difficult to know where the emphasis is when you're reading a book. When you have companionship with a teacher, you can gain the knowledge properly, because you know where the emphasis is… otherwise it's very difficult."[41] Respondents emphasize that the practice of suhba, like much of their activism, stems from the example of the Prophet Mohammed and his own companions. "The Prophet [PBUH] used to accompany his own sahabah, his companions," the leading activist notes in a different interview, "and they would spend time together, accompanying him."[42]

Al-Muhajiroun does not have a monopoly on suhba. Quintan Wiktorowicz, a leading authority on contemporary Salafism, identifies the student-teacher relationship as "the most important social tie in the Salafi community."[43] But this tie is not just important to Salafis. Many scholars in both the Sunni and Shia traditions emphasize the importance of learning by accompanying and observing more knowledgeable sheikhs or teachers.[44] This traditional

[37] Lave and Wenger, Situated Learning, p. 95.
[38] Interview with leading activist, Leyton, East London, November 8, 2010.
[39] Interview with leading activist, Leyton, East London, November 4, 2010.
[40] Notes from lecture delivered online in PalTalk room, "Road to Jannah," (August 26, 2014), www.paltalk.com/g2/paltalk/1183046821 [Accessed August 26, 2014].
[41] Interview with leading activist, Skype, August 28, 2014.
[42] Interview with leading activist, Ilford, East London, December 9, 2014. Also, interviews with another leading activist, Leyton, East London, November 8, 2010, and veteran activist, Southall, West London, June 28, 2011.
[43] Quintan Wiktorowicz, "The Salafi Movement: Violence and the Fragmentation of Community," in Muslim Networks: From Hajj to Hip Hop, edited by Miriam Cooke and Bruce B. Lawrence (Chapel Hill, NC: University of North Carolina Press, 2005), p. 213.
[44] See Jonathan Porter Berkey, The Transmission of Knowledge in Medieval Cairo: A Social History of Islamic Education (Princeton, NJ: Princeton University Press, 1992); Jamil M. Abun-Nasr, Muslim Communities of Grace: The Sufi Brotherhoods in Islamic Religious Life

model of Islamic learning continues today, as seen in the practice of many contemporary religious schools or *madrassas*. Reflecting the importance of suhba in al-Muhajiroun, networks activists often accompany their teachers, like Omar Bakri and Anjem Choudary, as they travel around Britain delivering talks. "I accompanied him on many tours around England when he was teaching, giving seminar lectures," explains one of Bakri's oldest students, himself a leading activist in the network. "Many people wanted to travel with him and follow him around."[45] "I was going with him everywhere I could to attend all of his lectures," recalls Rohan, another leading activist who studied closely with Bakri. "If that meant driving him or accompanying him in the car, I'd jump in. He used to give lectures all over the UK: Luton, Derby, Birmingham."[46] "Brother Anjem gives about thirteen classes a week around the country, if not more," explains a third respondent, referring to activists' suhba with Bakri's protégé, Anjem Choudary, years later. "Many brothers go with him."[47] "We travelled around together," adds another activist, discussing his own companionship with Choudary. "He could see I was eager to learn so he took me around with him a lot. We'd go to different classes. It was intensive learning."[48]

Activists fortunate enough to travel with their teachers do not limit their learning to listening to lectures and writing notes. These trips give novices the opportunity to soak up the Emigrants' norms and practices by spending time and interacting with their mentors. Students ask questions about doctrinal issues, such as the difference between suicide and "self-sacrifice," and practical matters, like how to determine whether a potential spouse has the "right personality."[49] They also observe how their teachers interact with others, Muslims and non-Muslims alike, and model their behavior based on what they see. Recalling his travels with Omar Bakri, one leading activist explains, "Being in that vehicle with him really was an incredible experience. You could learn just by watching his behavior. To be with him, travel around with him, and look at the way he dealt with things was an education in itself."[50] Referring to his own "constant travels" with Bakri, another respondent elaborates, "We were learning things in the car, sitting in the restaurant with him, sleeping in

(New York: Columbia University Press, 2007); and Smita Tewari Jassal, "The Sohbet: Talking Islam in Turkey," *Sociology of Islam* 1, nos. 3–4 (2014), pp. 188–208.

[45] Interview with leading activist, Leyton, East London, November 4, 2010. Also, interview with Abdul, Whitechapel, East London, June 18, 2011.

[46] Interview with Rohan, Whitechapel, East London, December 7, 2010.

[47] Interview with veteran activist, Leyton, East London, December 9, 2010.

[48] Interview with rank-and-file activist, Mile End, East London, June 26, 2011.

[49] Interviews with two activists, Leyton, East London, November 6, 2010, and a third in Wembley Central, West London, June 25, 2011.

[50] Interview with leading activist, Ilford, East London, December 9, 2014. And interviews with same activist, Leyton, East London, November 4, 2010, and another leading activist, Leyton, East London, November 8, 2010.

the same house. Having that constant companionship with him, he taught us everything."[51]

This last respondent grew up in a single-parent household and saw "Sheikh Omar" as a father figure. Initially, he was devastated when Bakri left Britain, but he continued his suhba with other leading activists in al-Muhajiroun. In a separate interview, he discusses his "companionship with Abu Izzadeen and Brother Anjem," two of the activists who replaced Bakri on the network's lecture circuit: "By spending time on the road with them, you pick up a lot, like how they took up certain rulings [from scripture], and a lot of techniques, like how to speak to the media."[52] "We'd always be chatting and having food," adds another activist, reflecting on his travels with Anjem Choudary. "He'd always be talking to me about giving da'wah, commanding good, forbidding evil. He'd teach me so much stuff."[53]

Traditionally, suhba refers to the relationship between a "sheikh" and his "disciples," but in al-Muhajiroun activists also learn from their companionship with other experienced activists.[54] These interactions build friendships, enhance group solidarity, and deepen newcomers' commitment to the cause. As part of this companionship, novices supplement what they learn from their teacher's lectures with ideological and practical knowledge they accumulate from talking with their peers. "We're constantly learning from each other," explains one activist. Asked to specify how this happens, he adds, "through companionship, through traveling, through gatherings and meetings, even having some food together."[55] Another rank-and-file activist elaborates: "Companionship is very important. You learn from the people who have more experience. They've faced different situations which you've never faced because you are new." He gives an example from his initial forays in street da'wah: "I started to engage and if I had any trouble I would refer to someone else who knew. It's like when you go into a job and you learn from your peers who have more experience."[56]

To facilitate their companionship, and the learning that comes with it, activists spend lots of time together. They hang out at halaqah sessions, da'wah stalls, and public protests. They interact socially outside of their formal activism, dining at cafés and restaurants, playing sports and exercising at the gym, and visiting each other at their homes. Like their activism more broadly, these interactions are time consuming and limit activists' availability for other pursuits, including education and employment. But the interactions serve a larger purpose. "We never hang out just for the sake of it," explains one

---

[51] Interview with veteran activist, Wembley Central, West London, June 25, 2011.

[52] Interview with veteran activist, Southall, West London, June 28, 2011.

[53] Interview with rank-and-file activist, Mile End, East London, June 26, 2011. Also, interview with another activist, Leyton, East London, November 14, 2010.

[54] Berkey, *The Transmission of Knowledge in Medieval Cairo*, p. 34; Abun-Nasr, *Muslim Communities of Grace*, p. 60.

[55] Interview with rank-and-file activist, Lewisham, South London, June 18, 2011.

[56] Interview with rank-and-file activist, Southall, West London, June 28, 2011.

veteran activist.[57] Instead, hanging out reinforces al-Muhajiroun's ideology and collective identity by allowing activists to share information and experience whenever they get together. "This is how they exchange information, mainly in person," adds Haroon. "You've gotta be in the circle."[58] Asked how he acquires information about his activism, another respondent underlines the importance of peer-to-peer interactions among activists throughout the country: "Everyone shares through our networks of brothers in other parts of the UK. All the brothers involved in the da'wah, they always share information with each other."[59]

But what exactly do activists talk about when hanging out? "Well, a lot," replies another respondent. "We talk about the world we live in. Some brothers talk about football [soccer], 'This player is good' and so on." "But," he adds, "we always end up talking about Islam."[60] "We discuss ideas," adds a veteran activist. "We talk about doing da'wah. And we always talk about politics, what's happening here, what's happening there. We're not isolated like other Europeans who get lost in themselves."[61]

They also discuss the theological foundations of their activism, sharing verses from scripture and stories from history to convince themselves that they are following the prophetic tradition. These discussions help newcomers overcome their reservations about participating in certain activities, like protests.[62] One respondent describes how he resolved his doubts about protesting by asking his companions whether their activism was grounded in divine canon: "I always wanted to know is this the best way to do it, how are you supposed to do it, and stuff like this." "So the brothers advised me," he continues. "They gave me evidence from 1,400 years ago about how the Prophet [PBUH] and the companions dealt with things until I was pretty much satisfied."[63]

In addition to sharing their ideas about politics and Islamic activism, participants use their companionship to share skills that enhance their day-to-day activism. "Whenever we learn a skill we want to share it with one another," explains one respondent. "Whenever we come across something new, maybe a new technique, we teach each other what we've learned."[64] A veteran activist

---

[57] Interview with veteran activist, Whitechapel, East London, June 17, 2011.

[58] Interview with Haroon, Westminster, Central London, June 14, 2011.

[59] Interview with rank-and-file activist, Ilford, East London, November 13, 2010.

[60] Interview with rank-and-file activist, Stratford, East London, June 27, 2011.

[61] Interview with veteran activist, Whitechapel, East London, June 17, 2011.

[62] Activists from other religious traditions also engage in group discussions to fortify their resolve. Sharon Nepstad observed this among activists in the Catholic Plowshares movement: "The belief that they are part of a prophetic tradition helps Plowshares activists overcome doubts about the importance of their sacrifices and the need for ongoing resistance." Sharon Erickson Nepstad, "Persistent Resistance: Commitment and Community in the Plowshares Movement," *Social Problems* 51, no. 1 (2004), p. 54.

[63] Interview with rank-and-file activist, Southall, West London, June 28, 2011.

[64] Interview with rank-and-file activist, Leyton, East London, November 14, 2010.

gives an example: "Some of us have professional backgrounds. I'm a graphic designer." Graphic design, in both print and online formats, is a sought after skill among the Emigrants. Activists use it to create eye-catching pamphlets and banners for their da'wah stalls and demonstrations, along with attractive websites that communicate the network's ideology. Referring to fellow activists who want to tap into his skill set, the respondent explains, "They want to study with me so they can do the same thing." Rather than hoarding his expertise or charging his companions, he shares his technical knowledge with them, freely and without reservation. "I teach them Photoshop and I teach them web design. I'll help them out because at the end of the day, we're all in the same boat. That's how knowledge spreads."[65]

LEARNING BY DOING

In communities of practice, novices learn through participation. They develop their skills and build their identities by performing the activity, be it delivering babies, fixing Xerox copiers, or engaging in high-risk activism.[66] Newcomers to al-Muhajiroun develop their skills and build their identities by watching and listening to more experienced activists as they perform the network's contentious activism and then joining the action themselves. "The only real way to learn the da'wah is to get out there," explains an activist at a stall outside a popular shopping mall on Ilford's High Street. "You just have to get out there and watch and listen to the brothers, see how they give da'wah, and do it."[67] "You learn by doing," confirms another respondent at a stall near the Brick Lane market in Tower Hamlets. "It's learning on the job."[68]

For many activists, learning on the job begins soon after they begin. "You start straight away," notes one respondent at a da'wah stall in Stratford, explaining how he became involved in street preaching right after joining al-Muhajiroun's community of practice.[69] "From day one, pretty much," adds an activist at a stall on Lewisham's High Street. "The important thing is to act upon the knowledge as you go along."[70] When asked why he started da'wah

---

[65] Interview with veteran activist, Whitechapel, East London, June 17, 2011.

[66] Lave and Wenger, *Situated Learning*; Brown and Duguid, "Organizational Learning and Communities-of-Practice"; Orlikowski, "Knowing in Practice," p. 250; and Julian E. Orr, *Talking about Machines: An Ethnography of a Modern Job* (Ithaca, NY: Cornell University Press, 1996).

[67] Interview with rank-and-file activist, Ilford, East London, November 13, 2010; field notes from Supporters of Sunnah da'wah stall, Ilford, East London, November 13, 2010.

[68] Interview with rank-and-file activist, Bethnal Green, East London, December 5, 2010.

[69] Interview with rank-and-file activist, Stratford, East London, November 29, 2010; field notes from Supporters of Sunnah da'wah stall, Stratford, East London, November 29, 2010.

[70] Interview with rank-and-file activist, Lewisham, South London, June 18, 2011; field notes from Convert2Islam da'wah stall, Lewisham, South London, June 18, 2011.

so early in his activism, he cites the network's interpretation of scripture: "The Prophet [PBUH] commanded us to convey, even if you know only one verse. This is enough for me to pass it on to people."[71]

Novices receive little formal training on how to engage in da'wah or carry out protests. "There wasn't a lot of training," confirms one respondent. "I was just watching the actions of my peers and my elders. I followed in their footsteps because I trust them and I trust what they're doing."[72] "It's not like you get a certification or permit or permission from anyone to do da'wah," explains a veteran activist at a stall he is running on Hounslow's High Street in West London. Speaking with me on a nearby bench as he keeps an eye on his companions, he elaborates: "Whether you're good at it or not will come from time and experience. You don't have to be the best speaker in the world. You just come out and give da'wah to your ability."[73]

Learning by doing is not limited to da'wah. Activists also learn to "command good and forbid evil" by participating in demonstrations. Like first-timers on the stall, novices begin their immersion in hisbah by silently observing protests, standing among their fellow activists and asking questions, but not doing much else. Following their initial exposure to the network's rallies, they progress to waving protest signs and chanting slogans like "British soldiers go to hell" and "burn, burn USA," sometimes while surrounded by riot police and counter-protestors from the English Defence League and Britain First. If their enthusiasm hasn't waned after their introduction to al-Muhajiroun's contentious politics, they advance to greater involvement. This may include serving as protest stewards, making impromptu speeches, and organizing demonstrations.[74]

One respondent describes his own progression from nervous bystander to sign-waving fanatic to head of protest security. "I would go to demonstrations with my face covered," he recalls, referring to his early involvement in network protests, including one against British soldiers who were returning from Afghanistan. "I had a strong fear about this demonstration." Inspired by what he was learning from Anjem Choudary and other activists, he overcame his fear and participated in this and other protests organized by the Emigrants' spin-off group, Muslims Against Crusades. "One day I was in

---

[71] Interview with rank-and-file activist, Lewisham, South London, June 18, 2011. Also, interviews with activists, Leyton, East London, November 6, 2010 and November 14, 2010, Lewisham, South London, December 11, 2010, and Stratford, East London, November 29, 2010.

[72] Interview with rank-and-file activist, Southall, West London, June 28, 2011.

[73] Interview with veteran activist, Hounslow, West London, September 4, 2013; field notes from da'wah stall, Hounslow, West London, September 4, 2013. Also, interview with rank-and-file activist, Ilford, East London, November 13, 2010.

[74] Interviews with activists: Whitechapel, East London, November 9, 2010, Kensington, Central London, November 11, 2010, Leyton, East London, November 14, 2010, and Wembley Central, West London, June 25, 2011. Field notes from network protests at Kensington, Central London, November 11, 2010, Mayfair, Central London, June 17, 2011, and Westminster, Central London, September 6, 2013.

security at a demonstration, just helping out," he explains. He liked the role, which allowed him to tap into his well-honed "fighting intellect." Afterwards, he continued to work in security at different demonstrations: "It became a regular practice for me to do security."[75] As he accumulated experience with his new role, and gained the trust of leading activists, he was asked to handle security at high-profile protests, including the Armistice Day poppy-burning demonstration in 2010. He also developed into one of the network's most outspoken activists, drawing on his rhetorical skills and knowledge of the network's ideology to deliver fiery speeches at private halaqahs and public protests.[76]

The more they preach al-Muhajiroun's blend of Salafi-Islamism at da'wah stalls, the more they protest British and American foreign policy at demonstrations, the better activists become at their provocative activism. "They say practice makes perfect," explains a veteran, when asked whether his activism improved over time. "With practice, you get more confidence and you learn more things, like how to counter particular arguments."[77] Another activist agrees, highlighting how he and his companions benefit from the challenges that arise at different stalls and protests. "If the police come and ask questions, or if a fight breaks out, it's good for us," he emphasizes. "It's a learning experience because we see how to deal with that situation the next time."[78] In performing their activism repeatedly under challenging circumstances, activists transform themselves from raw novices into experienced practitioners.

LEARNING IN HALAQAHS

At the same time they are becoming competent practitioners and committed insiders by performing da'wah and hisbah, activists are also acquiring the basic concepts underlying al-Muhajiroun's activism. Newcomers may initiate themselves into the network's community of practice by participating in its activism, but to comprehend the meaning of their actions, and to progress from administrative to intellectual affiliation, they must develop a basic understanding of its doctrine and ideology. Acquiring this ideological knowledge deepens their commitment to the network and gives direction to their activism.[79] "They've got to know the good in order to command it," explains a leading activist. "They've

---

[75] Interview with veteran activist, Wembley Central, West London, June 25, 2011.

[76] Interviews with veteran activist, Kensington, Central London, November 11, 2010 and Wembley Central, West London, June 25, 2011. Also, interviews with activists, Lewisham, South London, June 18, 2011, and Wembley Central, West London, June 25, 2011 and two London Metropolitan Police officers, Westminster, Central London, June 29, 2011. Field notes, Kensington, Central London, November 11, 2010 and Mayfair, Central London, June 17, 2011.

[77] Interview with veteran activist, Walthamstow, East London, November 16, 2010.

[78] Interview with veteran activist, Leyton, East London, December 9, 2010.

[79] Taylor and Horgan, "A Conceptual Framework for Addressing Psychological Process in the Development of the Terrorist," p. 594.

got to know the evil to forbid it." Acknowledging that not all newcomers know about "concepts like shariah and democracy" when they join the Emigrants, he continues, "a priority for us is to give them the culture in order to achieve our activities: the processions, demonstrations, conferences and seminars."[80] As we have seen, novices absorb this culture through suhba or companionship with their peers and teachers. But much of their ideological "culturing" occurs in halaqahs, neighborhood-based discussion circles where activists come together on a regular basis to learn, build friendships, and deepen their commitment to al-Muhajiroun. "The best way to study is together," remarks a rank-and-file activist, referring to the learning and fellowship within his own circle. "It gets me closer to the brothers and builds my brotherhood."[81]

Chapter 1 describes halaqahs as the local clusters within al-Muhajiroun's small-world network that organize and perform much of its day-to-day activism. As important as these small groups are to the network's structure and performance, in this chapter I focus on halaqahs' doctrinal role: to instruct activists in the network's ideology and strengthen their commitment to its community of practice. Similar to other social movements and religious cults, the small group structure provided by the halaqahs allows activists to meet with like-minded participants on a regular basis and reinforce their convictions through discussion and emotional support. These interactions not only strengthen social ties among activists, they deepen their commitment to beliefs many Muslims find objectionable, even dangerous. The Emigrants' ideological cohesion is not surprising given long-standing scholarship that emphasizes the importance of small, tight-knit groups for indoctrinating participants in "deviant" beliefs outside mainstream religious traditions.[82] "Community," as one social movement scholar puts it, "can sustain even highly improbable beliefs,"[83] such as creating an Islamic state in Britain.

When newcomers are recruited to al-Muhajiroun they are placed in one of these invitation-only study circles, where they meet weekly with other activists and a masoul who leads their discussion for at least two hours, sometimes more.[84] Halaqahs are located in different neighborhoods in London and in other cities where the Emigrants have traditionally enjoyed a strong presence,

---

[80] Interview with leading activist, Leyton, East London, November 4, 2010.

[81] Interview with rank-and-file activist, Lewisham, South London, December 11, 2010.

[82] See, for example, Leon Festinger, Henry W. Riecken, and Stanley Schacter, *When Prophecy Fails* (London: Pinter & Martin, 2008 [1956]); John Lofland, *Doomsday Cult: A Study of Conversion, Proselytization, and Maintenance of Faith* (Englewood Cliffs, NJ: Prentice-Hall, 1966); and Peter Berger, *A Rumor of Angels* (Garden City, NY: Doubleday, 1969).

[83] Nepstad, "Persistent Resistance," p. 51. Nepstad also discusses Berger and Festinger and his colleagues in this context.

[84] Interviews with leading activist, Walthamstow, East London, June 22, 2011, Ali and Maryam, Hounslow, West London, December 13, 2010, Abdul, Whitechapel, East London, June 18, 2011, Rashid, Whitechapel, East London, June 26, 2011, and another former activist, Walthamstow, East London, July 17, 2012. Also, see Wiktorowicz, *Radical Islam Rising*, p. 47.

including Luton, Derby, Cardiff, and Bedford.[85] While the masoul enjoys some discretion in choosing discussion topics, all halaqahs follow the same general course of study. "The reason we have these halaqahs," explains a leading activist, "is because we wanna teach them sequentially."[86]

Reflecting different influences on Omar Bakri's teachings, the network's course of study combines Salafi religious doctrine with an Islamist political ideology derived from Hizb ut-Tahrir. Like other Salafi-inspired fundamentalists, al-Muhajiroun emphasizes *tawheed*, or belief in monotheism, along with a literal interpretation of the Qu'ran and the traditions of the Prophet Mohammed known as the sunnah. "We start off with tawheed and the aqeedah [theological creed]," explains the leading activist, emphasizing the network's puritanical interpretation of Islamic scripture.[87] However, unlike most Salafis, who believe that involvement in protest politics is forbidden, halaqah lessons emphasize the need for al-Muhajiroun's confrontational style of da'wah and hisbah.[88] "We then work our way through the methodology of how to carry da'wah," continues the respondent, describing the network's course of study. "Eventually students become fully fledged da'is," activists who prepare society for the Islamic state by propagating the network's ideology. "It's a circle," he adds, observing how some da'is eventually become teachers in their own right.[89]

Illustrating Hizb ut-Tahrir's influence on its ideology, halaqah lessons also address how the caliphate will govern once it has been re-established, including how its leaders will be selected, how its tax revenues will be levied, how its laws will be applied and adjudicated. Describing the closed circle where he used to receive "deep culturing from Omar Bakri himself," Ali, the former activist, explains, "we were studying the same books that Hizb ut-Tahrir uses, *The Islamic State* and *The Ruling System*, which are written by Sheikh Taqi al-Din al-Nabhani," the founder and chief ideologue of Hizb ut-Tahrir.[90] Another

---

[85] Interviews with Ali and Maryam, Hounslow, West London, December 13, 2010, Salman, Poplar, East London, July 24, 2015, and Haroon, Westminster, Central London, June 14, 2011.

[86] Interview with leading activist, Walthamstow, East London, June 22, 2011. Also, interview with former activist, Walthamstow, East London, July 17, 2012.

[87] Interview with leading activist, Walthamstow, East London, June 22, 2011. Also, interviews with veteran activists, Hounslow, West London, September 4, 2013 and Wembley Central, West London, September 5, 2013.

[88] For more on the "quietist" stance of most Salafis, see Bernard Haykel, "On the Nature of Salafi Thought and Action," in *Global Salafism: Islam's New Religious Movement*, edited by Roel Meijer (Columbia University Press, 2009), pp. 34–5. For discussion of a more nuanced stance taken by some London Salafis, see Robert Lambert, *Countering Al-Qaeda in London: Police and Muslims in Partnership* (New York: Columbia University Press, 2013), pp. 215–16.

[89] Interview with leading activist, Walthamstow, East London, June 22, 2011. Also, interviews with other veteran activist, Hounslow, West London, September 4, 2013 and leading activist, Wembley Central, West London, September 5, 2013.

[90] Interview with Ali, Hounslow, West London, December 13, 2010. The books mentioned by Ali are Taqiuddin an-Nabhani, *The Islamic State* (London: Khilafah Publications, n.d.) and Taqiuddin an-Nabhani, *The Ruling System in Islam (Nidham ul-Hukm fil Islam*, fifth edition (London: Khilafah Publications, n.d.). For more on Taqi al-Din al-Nabhani and the transnational

respondent, a long-time activist who studied with Bakri for many years, mentions several topics that "Sheikh Omar" covered in his halaqah, which also reflected his grounding in Hizb ut-Tahrir's political ideology, including "the judicial system, the economic system, foreign policy. He referred to Nabhani's books, but we studied from Sheikh Omar himself."[91]

During the Emigrants' early years, many halaqahs studied directly with Omar Bakri. To ensure his students received the proper grounding in the network's religious doctrine and political ideology, Bakri met with different halaqahs on a regular basis, delivering private talks to these closed, members-only discussions. He was particularly vigilant during a new halaqah's formative months. "At the beginning, Sheikh Omar was the head of the halaqah," recalls Ali, who belonged to the network's West London halaqah at the time. "He came and gave us a good culturing for three, four months." Once Bakri was satisfied his students had a basic understanding of his ideas, he turned over leadership of the halaqah to a reliable follower who became its regular masoul. "He knew we would be okay by then," explains Ali. But he continued to visit and lecture his students in the circle, to make sure their culturing continued.[92]

After Bakri left Britain, responsibility for culturing halaqah members passed to several of his most trusted and knowledgeable students, including Anjem Choudary, Mizanur Rahman, and Abu Izzadeen Brooks. These activists continued their mentor's practice of visiting different circles within and outside London, lecturing them on tawheed, *usul-al-fiqh* (Islamic jurisprudence) and other topics. Reflecting the cross-generational nature of learning within al-Muhajiroun's community of practice, some of Choudary's students, who developed into intellectual affiliates after Bakri's departure, also delivered talks at study circles. "My friend, who was a senior guy amongst us, gave lectures up north," explains Salman, the former activist, "He used to travel up to Bedford and Derby. A group of twenty people would sit in, and he would give lectures and halaqah talks to the brothers."[93]

The purpose of delivering halaqah talks is not to teach activists for its own sake. It is to give intellectual affiliates the knowledge they need to engage in

Islamist movement he created, see Suha Taji-Farouki, *A Fundamental Quest: Hizb al-Tahrir and the Search for the Islamic Caliphate* (London: Grey Seal, 1996) and Kathleen Collins, "Ideas, Networks and Islamist Movements: Evidence from Central Asia and the Caucasus," *World Politics* 60 (October 2007), pp. 64–96.

[91] Interview with veteran activist, Stratford, East London, November 29, 2010. Also, interviews with Maryam, Hounslow, West London, December 13, 2010, and with activists in Ilford, East London, November 13, 2010 and Tottenham, North London, December 4, 2010.

[92] Interview with Ali, Hounslow, West London, December 13, 2010. Also, interviews with Abdul, Whitechapel, East London, June 18, 2011, and Rashid, Whitechapel, East London, June 26, 2011.

[93] Interview with Salman, Poplar, East London, July 24, 2015. Also, interviews with veteran activist, Leyton, East London, December 9, 2010, and Haroon, Westminster, Central London, June 14, 2011.

activism. "Private halaqahs are the preparation for the real work, the public da'wah," explains a leading activist. "The halaqah is the life and blood of the organization's culture, but we didn't arise to culture people. Rather we rose to command good and forbid evil, to bring about the shariah, and to change society."[94] Al-Muhajiroun's commitment to the "real work" of da'wah and hisbah distinguishes it from other Islamist organizations in the United Kingdom, including Hizb ut-Tahrir, and deepens halaqah members' identity as Emigrants.

Al-Muhajiroun's commitment to activism is also reflected in halaqah discussion topics. While many study circles focus on indoctrinating participants in the network's culture and ideology, explaining *why* the Emigrants engage in hisbah and da'wah, other talks focus on the practical side of the network's activism, addressing *how* to command good, forbid evil, and call society to Islam.[95] "We would ask the masoul questions," explains Maryam, describing how some sessions focused on answering difficult questions during da'wah stalls: "What if this question came up?... So we would learn the tactics of countering arguments."[96] Another respondent, Ahmed, refers to this as the "secondary aspect" of the network's teaching, giving activists "the tools to know how to deal with people, the method in calling people to Islam."[97] Tools covered in these classes include rhetorical techniques for debating non-Muslims, to help activists engage them at stalls.[98] "We teach people in the halaqah how to deal with Christians," explains a leading activist, "We teach them how to deal with the society of Western civilization, or evolution."[99] "This is how to debate a Jewish person," adds Haroon, listing different topics covered in these practical discussions. "This is how to debate an atheist. These are the questions they're likely to ask and these are the answers. It's almost like being a sales person."[100]

"ACCOUNTING" AND LEARNING FROM MISTAKES

In communities of practice members come together to discuss and review their activities.[101] They do this by meeting regularly to talk about their performance,

---

[94] Interview with leading activist, Ilford, East London, December 9, 2014. Also, interviews with another leading activist, Leyton, East London, November 8, 2010, and Ali, Hounslow, West London, December 13, 2010.

[95] Interviews with activists, Bethnal Green, East London, December 5, 2010, and Islington, North London, July 21, 2012.

[96] Interview with Maryam, Hounslow, West London, June 21, 2011.

[97] Interview with Ahmed, veteran activist, Tottenham, North London, December 4, 2010.

[98] Wiktorowicz, *Radical Islam Rising*, p. 195.

[99] Interview with leading activist, Walthamstow, East London, June 22, 2011. Also, interview with former activist, Walthamstow, East London, July 17, 2012.

[100] Interview with Haroon, Westminster, Central London, June 14, 2011.

[101] Wenger, *Communities of Practice*, p. 125; Roberts, "Limits to Communities of Practice," pp. 624–5.

identify problems and opportunities, and share ideas for how to improve. While the Emigrants have little interest in organization theory, they do appreciate the importance of getting together to review and improve their activities. As with so many elements of their activism, their justification for doing so is based on their reading of scripture, as interpreted by Omar Bakri. During interviews, respondents cite sayings attributed to Mohammed about the necessity of "accounting," holding themselves responsible for their behavior at the end of each day. "The Prophet Mohammed [PBUH] said that the Muslim always accounts himself," explains one veteran activist. "Every time I go home, before I go to sleep, I need to account myself, to see how I can improve. We always need improvement."[102] Accounting is necessary, according to this and other respondents, to help them recognize their mistakes – and learn from them. "Mohammed said that every son of Adam makes mistakes and the best of them always rectify themselves."[103] "This is what you call accounting," adds a leading activist. "We're humans and we make mistakes, but we always try to learn from those mistakes."[104]

Accounting is not limited to activists' personal lives. It forms an essential part of their activism. "It is as important as carrying the message of Islam, openly and publicly," emphasizes a leading activist.[105] Indeed, the practice of accounting and learning from mistakes informs how activists carry their message. They learn from their mistakes by getting together after da'wah stalls, demonstrations, and other events and discussing how it went. "We would have a review and say, 'Look, these are the mistakes,'" notes a leading activist. "It's called constructive criticism. We'll say, 'Next time this should not happen.' It's just like a company."[106] "Think of it like a business," adds Ahmed, continuing the corporate analogy. "When a business is failing, you will have a meeting and

---

102 Interview with veteran activist, Whitechapel, East London, November 9, 2010.

103 Interview with veteran activist, Whitechapel, East London, November 9, 2010. Also interviews with two leading activists, Leyton, East London, November 4, 2010 and November 8, 2010, and another activist, Stratford, East London, June 27, 2011.

104 Interview with leading activist, Walthamstow, East London, December 2, 2010.

105 Interview with leading activist, Leyton, East London, November 8, 2010.

106 Interview with leading activist, Walthamstow, East London, June 22, 2011. It is also just like some terrorist groups and social movement organizations. In his discussion on maintaining discipline through indoctrination, Jacob Shapiro highlights the role of "self-criticism sessions" in some social revolutionary groups: "These were essentially group meetings, at which everyone would discuss each other's failures." Similarly, Clark McCauley and Sophia Moskalenko discuss "the constant round of meetings and discussions" devoted to "criticism and self-criticism" in the Weather Underground, which they argue had a radicalizing effect on the group. And Sharon Nepstad describes a retreat she observed of activists from the pacifist Plowshares movement, when "the group reconvened to evaluate" a protest and vigil they staged outside the White House. See Jacob N. Shapiro, *The Terrorist's Dilemma: Managing Violent Covert Organizations* (Princeton, NJ: Princeton University Press, 2013), p. 80; Clark McCauley and Sophia Moskalenko, *Friction: How Radicalization Happens to Them and US* (New York: Oxford University Press, 2011), p. 143; and Sharon Nepstad, "Persistent Resistance," p. 56.

ask, 'Why are we failing?' Or when you want to market a new product, you have a meeting to see what's the best way to market this product. We do all of that." Ahmed continues, moving from analogy to practice: "We have a meeting and we basically discuss. We brainstorm. 'How could it have been better? How could we have maybe solved that problem?' We need this. Otherwise we don't learn from our mistakes."[107]

These brainstorming sessions occur during meetings scheduled for this purpose, and more informally, on the phone or over a meal at a restaurant. "Sometimes the brothers will call a specific meeting about something they were not happy with and we try and rectify it for the next time," explains a respondent.[108] "We meet up with him once a week," notes another rank-and-file activist, referring to regular meetings with his halaqah masoul. "We discuss what we did in the week and how we can improve results."[109] A third activist describes how his da'wah stall leader would convene informal meetings to discuss their activities: "The emir would send out a text, 'Meet me at this café or this place. We're going to have a general meeting on how we can improve the da'wah.' So we'd just get together. It wasn't really a fixed date."[110] "Sometimes in our halaqah or sometimes on the phone, it depends," adds Maryam, describing how it worked in her sisters-only circle. "We weren't as organized as we should have been. It was just, 'How'd you think it went?' A lot of informal discussions."[111]

Whether these discussions take place on the phone, in restaurants, or in more formal settings, both leading and rank-and-file activists take the opportunity to express themselves. Like other communities of practice, al-Muhajiroun seeks to capture different voices in its deliberations, under the assumption that activists will be able to identify solutions by sharing different ideas and experiences. "We need suggestions from everyone in the group," explains one activist. "We sit down and we talk about how we can improve. Everyone gives their opinion and feedback and we base our response on that."[112] "Everyone has a chance to share their points of view," confirms another respondent. "We gather round during lunch or dinner and we just talk about what could be improved."[113]

These discussions can become contentious, with activists disagreeing over problems and solutions. "We often have differences of opinion, over what was beneficial and what was not," notes Ahmed, referring to group discussions after da'wah stalls and demonstrations.[114] Disagreements should be expected in any

---

107 Interview with Ahmed, Tottenham, North London, December 4, 2010. Also, interview with leading activist, Leyton, East London, November 6, 2010.
108 Interview with rank-and-file activist, Mile End, East London, June 26, 2011.
109 Interview with rank-and-file activist, Stratford, East London, June 27, 2011.
110 Interview with rank-and-file activist, Ilford, East London, November 13, 2010.
111 Interview with Maryam, Hounslow, West London, June 21, 2011.
112 Interview with rank-and-file activist, Ilford, East London, November 13, 2010.
113 Interview with different rank-and-file activist, Ilford, East London, November 13, 2010.
114 Interview with Ahmed, Tottenham, North London, December 4, 2010.

community of practice that allows for a robust exchange of ideas among veteran and novice practitioners, as al-Muhajiroun does.[115] One leading activist describes how in his East London halaqah the emir would sometimes question ideas raised by novices over where to hold their da'wah stalls: "When we discussed where we should do da'wah with the youngsters, they would say, 'Let's do this, let's do that.' But the emir would say, 'Okay, why here though? Tell me why we should open it here?' Then another person would say, 'This is the reason.'" The emir's questioning was designed to elicit further discussion within the group, so activists could decide how they wanted to address the issue collectively: "This is how we come to a conclusion. 'Okay, this is how we will do it.'"[116]

Notwithstanding their spirited discussions, there are strict limits to dissent within al-Muhajiroun. Acceptable disagreements are restricted to everyday practices, or what respondents refer to as the "styles and means" of their activism. Questioning the effectiveness of the Emigrants' activism or the legitimacy of its ideology is off-limits. These are "just minor disagreements, nothing that will take you out of the fold of Islam," clarifies a respondent. "In terms of the main issues, there's no disagreement."[117] Ahmed elaborates with an example: "I can't have a meeting saying, 'Maybe we should not call for the khilafah.' That's not acceptable. But I can say, "Maybe our leaflet should be yellow because I think yellow will attract people."[118] "These are styles and means," confirms a leading activist. "A person might believe there is a better way. As long as it's not prohibited, not un-Islamic, we don't have a problem with it." Referring to what he calls the "constant wave" of suggestions that come from his discussions with activists, he adds, "We review them but the general foundations don't change."[119]

Consistent with their discussions, activists apply the ideas they generate from brainstorming to the styles and means of their activism. They tweak their da'wah stalls and demonstrations in response to their group discussions, but they do not fundamentally alter their strategy of activism. Many of these adaptations, which I describe in the next chapter, represent minor improvements, not major changes. "We'll try one technique for a little while," explains a respondent. "If it doesn't work, we'll try a new one."[120]

A leading activist offers an example from an al-Muhajiroun protest outside the Israeli embassy in South Kensington, London. In planning the

---

[115] Lave and Wenger, *Situated Learning*, p. 116. Disagreements are also common in terrorist organizations, a point emphasized by Shapiro in his comparative study, *The Terrorist's Dilemma*.

[116] Interview with leading activist, Leyton, East London, November 6, 2010.

[117] Interview with rank-and-file activist, Ilford, East London, November 13, 2010.

[118] Interview with Ahmed, Tottenham, North London, December 4, 2010.

[119] Interview with leading activist, Leyton, East London, November 6, 2010. Also, interview with Rashid, Whitechapel, East London, June 26, 2011.

[120] Interview with rank-and-file activist, Stratford, East London, June 27, 2011.

demonstration, he and his colleagues faced a challenge. The embassy, which has been targeted by violent protests and bombings over the years, is protected by security barriers in an area adjacent to Kensington Palace Gardens.[121] The embassy's location and security restrict public access to the building. This made it difficult for activists to broadcast their message to their intended audience, the diplomats inside. In brainstorming how to address this problem, the respondent and his colleagues came up with an innovative solution. They decided to construct a tripod scaffold to elevate a single activist above the security barriers, 15 ft off the ground, so that the diplomats would see him and hear his message. On the day of the protest, several activists in "workman outfits" set up the makeshift scaffold and halted traffic on the Kensington High Street, one of central London's busiest roads, while another "climbed to the top" of the scaffold and "addressed the behavior of the Israeli authorities in Palestine with a loudspeaker."[122]

According to the respondent, the police were caught off guard and did not know how to handle the activist on top of the scaffold: "They couldn't take him down, in case he'd fall." Their hesitation allowed the activist to finish his speech before climbing down the scaffold. The spectacle attracted significant attention from people passing by, and the respondent and his colleagues considered the demonstration to be a big success. "It was amazing," he recalls. "They stopped the streets to talk about Palestine. It was the best demonstration I've ever seen in my life." Afterwards, activists tried to learn from their triumph by discussing their innovation together, in an informal after action review. "We reviewed it for how to improve it," he continues. "'How do you think things went? What could we have done better?'"[123]

They decided to build on their success by replicating the scaffold at another protest, this one planned for Marble Arch, one of London's most iconic landmarks and busiest locations. This time, however, they were stymied by the London Metropolitan Police, who were determined not to get outsmarted again. "The police tried to knock over the scaffold with someone on top of it," explains the leading activist, highlighting how law enforcers responded to activists' adaptation with a simple, if potentially dangerous, adjustment of their own. Reflecting on the broader implications of his story, he continues, "Even the police reviewed their own behavior. Everyone reviews their behavior. The police do, governments do, we do. Everyone reviews the whole time."[124] As I will discuss in the next chapter, activists do not adapt their practices in isolation, but through interaction with law enforcers who

---

121 *BBC News*, "On this day—1972: Parcel bomb attack on Israeli embassy," (September 19, 1972), http://news.bbc.co.uk/onthisday/hi/dates/stories/september/19/newsid_2523000/2523027.stm [Accessed September 9, 2016].

122 Interview with leading activist, Leyton, East London, November 8, 2010.

123 Interview with leading activist, Leyton, East London, November 8, 2010.

124 Interview with leading activist, Leyton, East London, November 8, 2010.

seek to control them. On this day at least, the police's counter-adaptation was enough to disrupt the protest and keep activists from commanding good and forbidding evil. They did not attempt the scaffolding trick again. But they did rebound from this setback and continue to learn from their successes and failures, developing more innovations in the months and years ahead.

ON THE STRAIGHT AND NARROW PATH

For all its benefits, al-Muhajiroun's community of practice should not be romanticized. While the community builds companionship, fosters know-ledge sharing and ideological cohesion, and helps activists fix mistakes, it also hampers their activism by limiting their ability to learn. Perhaps the biggest shortcoming in the network's community of practice is its insularity and dogmatism. Like other ideologically driven communities, the Emigrants display an "unbending commitment to established canons and methods."[125] Once they acquire their ideology and develop into competent practitioners, activists often become "static" in their knowledge and "resistant to change."[126] Not unlike members of religious cults, they become isolated from different beliefs and worldviews.[127]

The Emigrants' exclusive reliance on Omar Bakri Mohammed's teachings and their efforts to ignore outside voices adds a cultish dimension to their community. Becoming an intellectual affiliate means accepting, absolutely and without reservation, the network's improbable blend of Salafi-inspired theology and Hizb ut-Tahrir-inspired ideology. Preachers outside the network who have not studied with Bakri or his students are viewed with suspicion, even when they follow a similar understanding of scripture. Network activists not only consider the teachings of these preachers to be "deviant," they refer to some of them as "murtad," apostates who have committed the major sin of rejecting the Islamic creed – and against whom violence is acceptable.[128]

To protect the cohesion of their community, network leaders zealously limit the influence of outside ideologues. Rashid, who referenced writings by non-al-Muhajiroun preachers in the halaqah sessions he led, "just to give it another flavor," was admonished by Anjem Choudary for using an external source to teach his students. "Anjem said to me, 'Oh, no, you should

---

[125] Etienne Wenger, Richard McDermott, and William M. Snyder, *Cultivating Communities of Practice: A Guide to Managing Knowledge* (Boston, MA: Harvard Business School, 2002), p. 149.

[126] Roberts, "Limits to Communities of Practice," pp. 629–30.

[127] See John Lofland and Rodney Stark, "Becoming a World-Saver: A Theory of Conversion to a Deviant Perspective," *American Sociological Review* 30, no. 6 (December 1965), p. 870, and Michael D. Langone, "Responding to Jihadism: A Cultic Studies Perspective," *Cultic Studies Review* 5, no. 2 (2006), pp. 268–306.

[128] Interviews with Salman, Poplar, East London, July 24, 2015, and Rashid, Whitechapel, East London, June 26, 2011.

only use our books,' which I thought was quite narrow because you should be able to refer to other materials as well."[129] The Emigrants' prohibition on external materials is not limited to halaqah lessons. "You're not allowed to have anybody's lectures or talks, audios or leaflets at any of their centers or da'wah tables," adds Salman. "So no scholars, no literature by any other people, apart from al-Muhajiroun speakers. That was the rule. It was their speakers, their leaflets, their talks. Everything has to be in house, nothing from outside."[130] This rule is so important that, as I will discuss in Chapter 5, a number of activists have been removed from the network for failing to follow it.

Al-Muhajiroun's insularity and dogmatism is steeped in its conviction that it is one of the few Islamic groups in the West following the "true path" of Islam. Activists believe that most Muslims living in Britain, and the West more broadly, have watered down their faith, practicing a cultural form of Islam that does not follow the teachings of the Prophet Mohammed and his companions. "The vast majority of the Muslim community doesn't really practice their religion," explains a leading activist. "Either you're a Muslim and you believe in the shariah and the khilafah and jihad and you live by it, or you've got to compromise."[131] Any compromise of the network's beliefs is unacceptable to activists. After all, their activism is "a complete way of life," as another leading activist puts it. Mindful of outsiders' tendency to dismiss their devotion as evidence of cult programming, he adds, "Many people would say that I've become brainwashed." He offers a ready response to such dismissals, one that I heard from other activists as well. "I would say to them, 'Of course. My brain was dirty. And after this process of Islam and this learning, it's been very nicely washed for me.'"[132]

Many activists consider Muslims who compromise their faith, and non-Muslims who have not found the path to "salvation," to be inferior. "I felt like I was superman and that non-Muslims were insects," observes a former activist. "I felt I was superior to other Muslims, like I was the only one who could be righteous. I was untouchable. It was like God had authorized me to behave this way."[133] I observed such arrogance during my field work. When interviewing respondents, or just hanging out with them, some activists treated me with barely disguised scorn. Others made jokes at my expense. During one passionate talk I attended at the network's center in Whitechapel, a leading activist compared the humiliation experienced by Muslims in the West with the degradation awaiting non-Muslims living under the Islamic state.

[129] Interview with Rashid, Whitechapel, East London, June 26, 2011.
[130] Interview with Salman, Poplar, East London, July 24, 2015.
[131] Interview with leading activist, Skype, November 8, 2011.
[132] Interview with leading activist, Leyton, East London, November 6, 2010. Also, interview with rank-and-file activist, Leyton, East London, November 14, 2010.
[133] Nick Lowles and Joe Mulhall, *Gateway to Terror: Anjem Choudary and the al-Muhajiroun Network* (London: HOPE not hate, 2013), p. 54.

"They will be humiliated under the khilafah, not because of their race or their nationality but their *deen* [religion]." "Like the stupid Americans," he added, nodding his head in my direction. As intended, his joke was met with hearty laughter from his young, largely male audience.[134] In addition to their occasional jokes and disparaging remarks, a number of activists refused to use their right hands when shaking mine, as a way of signaling their contempt for my "dirty" non-Muslim status. This practice was based on their view that they should only use their left hands when greeting non-believers because this is the "unclean" hand, the one reserved for the toilet.[135]

The Emigrants' superiority has created problems for them beyond dealing with plucky ethnographers. Activists' dogmatism has hampered their ability to adapt their practices in an increasingly hostile environment. During the network's early years, when Omar Bakri and his supporters were establishing their identity as a worthy inheritor of the Prophet's banner in a country with many Salafi and Islamist competitors, it made sense for them to proclaim their ideological purity and exceptionalism, as a way of "outbidding" other groups in the competition for recruits.[136] Al-Muhajiroun's strategy of convincing recruits it deserved their support worked, as long as British authorities did not trouble themselves with the activist network and the master himself was around to indoctrinate his charges.

These conditions changed after the September 11 attacks, the fertilizer bomb plot in 2004, and the London tube and bus bombings in 2005. British authorities no longer viewed Bakri and other "radical preachers" as harmless fabulists and increased the pressure against them. When Bakri unexpectedly fled Britain after the 2005 attacks, his followers were left to pick up the ideological pieces. In one sense the transition was relatively smooth. As

---

[134] Recording of private talk by leading activist, Centre for Islamic Services, Whitechapel, East London, June 23, 2011; field notes, Whitechapel, East London, June 23, 2011.

[135] Not all activists agreed with this interpretation of handshaking. These respondents had no problem with using their right hands to shake mine and they did so on many occasions. I should also mention that not all activists treated me like an "insect." I enjoyed pleasant interactions with many of my respondents, including several who later became involved in acts of political violence or left Britain to join the Islamic State in Iraq and Syria. These individuals showed me the same courtesy and respect I gave them. Field notes, Stratford, East London, November 29, 2010 and December 6, 2010; Whitechapel, East London, December 16, 2010, June 16, 2011, June 23, 2011, and July 24, 2015; Islington, North London, July 21, 2012; Hounslow, West London, September 4, 2013, and interview with rank-and-file activist, Mile End, East London, June 26, 2011.

[136] For more on outbidding by Islamist parties see Shadi Hamid, *The Temptations of Power: Islamists and Illiberal Democracy in a New Middle East* (New York: Oxford University Press, 2014). For discussion on outbidding by terrorist groups see Mia Bloom, *Dying to Kill: The Allure of Suicide Terror* (New York: Columbia University Press, 2005); Andrew H. Kydd and Barbara F. Walter, "The Strategies of Terrorism," *International Security* 31, no. 1 (Summer 2006), pp. 49–80; and Michael G. Findley and Joseph K. Young, "More Combatant Groups, More Terror?: Empirical Tests of an Outbidding Logic," *Terrorism and Political Violence* 24, no. 5 (2012), pp. 706–21.

shown in Chapter 1, numerous veteran activists like Anjem Choudary and Abu Izzadeen Brooks replaced Bakri as the administrative leaders of the activist network, which became more decentralized and small-world-like. These leaders, who comprised Bakri's most trusted and knowledgeable students, continued to lecture on his behalf, working from their notes of his old talks. They were lucid and engaging, but they were not as fluent in Arabic, nor as well versed in Islamic scripture and Islamist ideology as their teacher.

This led to pressure from Salman and other activists in the network's Whitechapel halaqah to invite other preachers to lecture, including Anwar al-Awlaki and Abu Bashir al-Tartusi. Both preachers were highly regarded and known for their Salafi-jihadi leanings. After delivering a series of popular lectures on Islamic history and jihad in London and other British cities, Anwar al-Awlaki returned to his ancestral home in Yemen, where he reportedly helped plan terrorist attacks for al-Qaeda in the Arabian Peninsula before being killed by a CIA drone strike in 2011.[137] Far from permitting such figures to strengthen al-Muhajiroun's bonafides, Anjem Choudary, Bakri's leading representative in Britain, considered their preaching a threat to the Emigrants' ideological cohesion. He refused his followers' request, turning the dispute into a crisis of his leadership. Salman and other activists in Whitechapel viewed Choudary's reliance on Bakri's teachings as too narrow and uncompromising. They expressed their dismay to him in several meetings. When Choudary continued to rebuff them, they tried to remove him as network leader. After his attempted "coup" failed, Salman left al-Muhajiroun with twenty-five other activists. They formed a separate group in Poplar, East London, where Salman and his colleagues studied closely with Abu Bashir al-Tartusi, until he returned to his homeland in 2012 to lead a group of fighters in Syria's civil war.[138]

The Emigrants' insularity not only weakened it internally. It also prevented the activist network from building stronger relationships with outside groups that would have strengthened its standing in local Muslim communities at a time when authorities were cracking down. "They don't really have any links with the wider community," explains the research director of a think tank specializing in violent extremism. "They're sort of self-contained." This go-it-alone approach may have allowed activists to maintain their ideological cohesion, but it did not endear them to other British Muslims. "They've got no institutional support in the Muslim community," the research director adds. "There's

---

[137] See Scott Shane, *Objective Troy: A Terrorist, a President, and the Rise of the Drone* (New York: Tim Duggan, 2015).

[138] Interviews with Salman, Poplar, East London, July 24, 2015, and leading activist, Ilford, East London, December 12, 2014; field notes, Whitechapel, East London, July 16, 2012 and December 11, 2014. Also, see Duncan Gardham, "The Poplar preacher leading an armed gang of jihadis in Syria," *Daily Telegraph* (October 19, 2012), www.telegraph.co.uk/news/worldnews/middleeast/syria/9621352/The-Poplar-preacher-leading-an-armed-gang-of-jihadis-in-Syria.html [Accessed December 12, 2014].

not a single mosque in the country that would let them hold an event in their community, and no one will stand up for their right to do so either."[139]

It wasn't always this way. During al-Muhajiroun's early years, activists regularly held talks and other events at mosques and Islamic centers around Great Britain. Having access to these local venues facilitated their preaching, allowing them to spread their ideology to young people across the country. However, after 9/11, when they began to lose access, and after 7/7, when this trend accelerated, activists showed no interest in moderating their ideological stance or strategy to increase their legitimacy with local Muslims or maintain their access to mainstream organizations. "That's one thing they really haven't adapted to," says the research director of the London think tank. "Instead of just denouncing everyone who isn't in the group, if they adapted and developed alliances with some people, they would be in a lot stronger position in places like Tower Hamlets."[140]

The reason activists have not worked harder to build relationships with local communities is that they don't see their isolation as a problem. "They see it as a strength, to be honest," continues the research director. "Only they've got eyes on the 'true path.'"[141] Activists agree. "Of course we are the minority," confirms a respondent at a da'wah stall in Stratford, where most people walk around him without taking one of his leaflets. "You can look at how the Prophet [PBUH] used to teach. He would say it is the minority that gets the truth."[142] "Everybody claims to be on the right path," adds another activist, while giving da'wah at the same location, months earlier. "But the one on the true path never compromises his religion for anything, even if you kill him. Yet you see other people who will compromise their religion."[143] No matter how unwelcoming their environment becomes, activists have no desire to "compromise" their activism or to collaborate with anyone who threatens their ideological cohesion. If anything, they view their "persecution" by the authorities and their isolation from Muslim communities as proof they are on the "right path," a path that will end in their salvation, regardless of any real world success their activism achieves.

There is a cost to such conceit. As much as activists relish their claims to the moral high ground, their marginalization has made it harder for them to call Britain to Islam and respond to an increasingly hostile environment. When government authorities cracked down against the activist network in recent years, activists found it harder to secure the venues they needed to hold large public

---

[139] Interview with research director, think tank, Bloomsbury, Central London, December 14, 2010.
[140] Interview with research director, think tank, Bloomsbury, Central London, December 14, 2010.
[141] Interview with research director, think tank, Bloomsbury, Central London, December 14, 2010.
[142] Interview with rank-and-file activist, Stratford, East London, June 27, 2011; field notes, Stratford, East London, June 27, 2011.
[143] Interview with rank-and-file activist, Stratford, East London, November 29, 2010; field notes, Stratford, East London, November 29, 2010.

events. I witnessed an example of this early in my field work. In November 2010 activists planned to hold an "International Islamic Revival Conference" featuring speeches by Omar Bakri (who was to be piped in from Lebanon), Anjem Choudary, Abu Izzadeen Brooks, and other leading activists.[144] Given the Emigrants' isolation from local communities, hosting the conference in one of London's mosques or Islamic cultural centers was out of the question. This narrowed their options in finding a venue that was big enough to accommodate the audience they hoped to attract, at a price they could afford. Despite the challenge, conference organizers identified two halls in East London, booked one of them, and held the other as a "backup," in case they ran into problems with the first.[145]

Sure enough, after activists publicized the name and location of the hall in their advertisements for the conference, the managers of the venue received a visit from the authorities. Soon afterwards, the managers cancelled the booking. Activists then announced that the conference would move to a "secondary venue," the name and location of which they kept secret until two days before the conference. However, once this venue was publicized, the authorities swooped in again, contacting the proprietors and asking them to shut down the event, due to security concerns. They complied, forcing activists to cancel their conference at the last minute.[146] Activists then decided to hold a press conference the next morning to "expose the treachery of the British government." Yet almost as quickly as the press conference was announced, activists were again forced to cancel when the police intervened and stopped them from proceeding.[147]

In this case at least, the Emigrants were outfoxed by the police. With few venues to choose from initially, due to their marginalization from local communities, activists had limited options to convene their conference. When the authorities blocked the two remaining locations, they had no choice but to cancel and wait for a more opportune time to hold their event. But if activists had maintained stronger ties to local communities, they might have been able to stage their conference in one of London's numerous Islamic centers, as they did in the past. In follow-up interviews, respondents did their best to spin the cancellation of their conference as a "victory" for their activism, while also vowing "the struggle to express our ideas will continue."[148] But their anger and

---

[144] The International Islamic Revival Conference 2010, www.islamicrevival2010.com [Accessed various dates in November 2010], and *The International Islamic Revival Conference 2010 Official Booklet* (London: n.d.).

[145] Telephone interviews with three different activists, November 27, 2010; interview with another activist, Stratford, East London, November 29, 2010.

[146] Interview with business manager, Mile End, East London, December 1, 2010. Also, see Ted Jeory, "Islamic revival conference bluff," (November 26, 2010), http://trialbyjeory.wordpress.com/2010/11/26/islamic-revival-conference-bluff/ [Accessed November 29, 2012].

[147] Telephone interviews with four different activists, November 27, 2010.

[148] Telephone interviews with different leading and veteran activists, November 27, 2010.

disappointment was palpable. One leading activist put it bluntly: the authorities "embarrassed us all."[149]

Activists' dogmatism hampers their activism in another way. Like followers from a variety of religious traditions, the Emigrants believe that whatever they do, their actions and outcomes are already predetermined by God. "Whatever God has decided," notes one respondent, "our destiny is our destiny."[150] "Regardless of the consequences," confirms another activist, "we believe that good and bad, life and death is in the hands of the creator God, and on that basis we believe in destiny."[151] Yet activists also believe that as part of the "saved sect" of believers they enjoy special status in God's master plan. Their status may not save them from physical suffering in this life, it may in fact make them more likely to receive it, but it will lead to eternal salvation in the next. As long as they maintain their ideological cohesion and their activism remains "Islamically correct," activists believe they will receive their just reward in the afterlife, regardless of whether they adapt their activism to meet the worldly demands of the moment.

A leading activist highlights an important implication of al-Muhajiroun's belief in destiny and its saved status: "We don't need to adapt and change that much because we believe Allah's will is there to protect us." This does not mean that activists do not change their practices in response to external pressure. They do – and in the next chapter I show how. However, activists do believe that no changes they make will allow them to escape their fate, which is already predetermined. "We believe in taking precautions," continues the leading activist. "We don't believe that any amount of precaution is going to save you from the test that Allah has destined upon you." Drawing oblique reference to changes he has presided over, he continues: "So in our case, going underground, changing the policy, changing the structure, we do not need to change that much."[152] "The way we do our meetings and our stalls may change," confirms another respondent. "But our aim's always the same. We have to continue our da'wah and we have to continue calling for jihad in Muslim lands." This remains true, he adds, "Whether we get imprisoned or whether we get killed."[153]

In other words, activists' willingness to adapt to external pressure is both motivated and constrained by their conviction in their cause and the perceived virtue of their struggle. They view themselves as ideological warriors in a global struggle whose winners are determined by God, not men. Seen from this perspective, it may not matter whether Anjem Choudary missed an opportunity to

---

[149] Telephone interview with leading activist, November 27, 2010.

[150] Interview with rank-and-file activist, Stratford, East London, June 27, 2011. Also, interview with rank-and-file activist, Tottenham, North London, December 4, 2010.

[151] Interview with veteran activist, Islington, North London, July 21, 2012.

[152] Interview with leading activist, Woolwich, South London, September 22, 2007.

[153] Interview with rank-and-file activist, Stratford, East London, June 27, 2011.

strengthen his network by inviting Anwar al-Awlaki or Abu Bashir al-Tartusi to lecture to his students. It may not matter that he and other network leaders refused to enhance al-Muhajiroun's standing by building alliances with local groups and community centers. As far as activists are concerned, whether they avoid jail, whether they get killed, or whether they establish the Islamic state has less to do with the mistakes they fix and the improvements they make than with God's fate for them. "We continue as usual," confirms the leading activist. "Obviously, we change a thing here and there, individuals... organizations... But the propagation of Islam will never change, will never stop."[154]

CONCLUSION

Al-Muhajiroun is not just an activist network dedicated to establishing an Islamic caliphate. It is a community of practice whose participants learn by sharing their knowledge and performing their activism together. At the heart of al-Muhajiroun's community of practice are the relationships among activists, particularly the interactions between newcomers and veterans. Novices engage in lots of face-to-face interaction with more experienced activists. Da'wah stalls, demonstrations and halaqah circles all provide opportunities for engagement, as do activists' social gatherings. Activists engage in suhba or companionship with their teachers, following them around as they deliver talks and watching how they practice their activism and live their lives. Beyond these talks and travels, much of activists' culturing occurs in neighborhood-based halaqahs, where they meet each week to study with small groups of peers. Novices build friendships with other activists through these interactions, deepening their ties to the network. They also internalize the norms and beliefs that make up the network's ideology and culture. This not only strengthens their intellectual affiliation, it maintains the network's cohesion, even as al-Muhajiroun becomes more marginalized in British society.

Newcomers' learning does not stop there. Reflecting the Emigrants' core conviction that intellectual affiliates must not simply acquire knowledge but act on it, newly minted activists begin to practice what they learn almost immediately. While some halaqah discussions include tips on how to engage in da'wah, novices receive little formal training on how to perform their activism. Instead they learn by doing, calling society to Islam at da'wah stalls and commanding good and forbidding evil at demonstrations. The more they preach and the more they protest, the better they become at performing the network's trademark activism – and the deeper they slide into its community of practice. Some novices-turned-practitioners eventually become leading activists, attracting

---

[154] Interview with leading activist, Woolwich, South London, September 22, 2007. Also see Michael Kenney, "'Dumb' Yet Deadly: Local Knowledge and Poor Tradecraft among Islamist Militants in Britain and Spain," *Studies in Conflict and Terrorism* 33, no. 10 (October 2010), pp. 924–5.

followers and organizing events under the banner of their own spin-off groups and platforms. These emergent leaders allow al-Muhajiroun's community of practice to persevere by transforming successive generations of newcomers into committed insiders who embrace the network's culture and activism.

Activists not only improve their da'wah and hisbah through repeated performance, but by gathering together to review their activism. In these formal meetings and informal discussions, they identify problems and prospects, share ideas for how to improve, and brainstorm solutions to pressing dilemmas. Their discussions are often frank, with activists disagreeing over different matters. But these disagreements are limited to everyday tactics. Activists do not question Omar Bakri's vision. To the extent that they troubleshoot and learn, they do so by exploiting the styles and means of their activism, not by changing their strategy or reevaluating their ideology. Engaging in such exploratory learning would require them to question the underlying premises of their ideology and activism, something they are loath to do.[155]

The unwillingness to question the foundations of their activism reflects activists' conviction that they are the only Muslims in Britain, and the West more broadly, who are following the true path of Islam. Staying on this path, and out of the "hell fire," means their ideological cohesion must be maintained, even at the cost of losing members and marginalizing themselves from Britain's diverse Muslim communities. Far from being an elixir of learning that allows the Emigrants to adapt seamlessly to all challenges, the network's insular, dogmatic community creates its own challenges. In becoming true believers, activists limit their learning by refusing to question, let alone change, their beliefs, and by refusing to compromise, even when doing so would help them.

This exposes a deep tension between al-Muhajiroun's small-world-like structure, which facilitates its ability to survive an increasingly hostile environment, and its insularity and dogmatism, which do not. Even with redundant bridge nodes to replace decapitated leaders and decentralized halaqahs empowered to act locally, activists only learn the lessons that fit their narrow vision. In the next chapter, I discuss how activists manage this tension, by modifying their activism, rather than questioning the ideology on which it is based. Then, in the chapter after that, I explore why this tension ultimately becomes unsustainable for some, contributing to their decision to leave the Emigrants and its community of practice.

---

[155] James G. March, "Exploration and Exploitation in Organizational Learning." *Organization Science* 2, no. 1 (February 1991), pp. 71–87.

4

Resilient Activism

> We are adapting to the circumstances we've been put in.
>
> Ahmed, veteran activist

A week before the opening of the London Olympic Games in July 2012, I watched dozens of al-Muhajiroun activists as they performed a large public da'wah stall, or what they called an "Islamic roadshow," in the affluent north London borough of Islington. Activists set up tables along both sides of the main shopping road, and around forty brothers and twenty *niqab*-wearing sisters stood around the tables, handing out glossy leaflets and calling passersby to Islam. The leaflets, printed in the name of a network platform called the Khilafah (Caliphate) Movement, bore titles like "Shariah Law: Mercy for Mankind" and "The Need for Khilafah." Tables were festooned with banners, some inviting pedestrians to "Learn about Islam here," others declaring that "Sovereignty belongs to none but Allah." A loudspeaker played *nasheeds*, melodic *a cappella* songs or scriptural chants popular among activists. Small children ran about, playing as their parents talked with other activists and the occasional pedestrian who stopped to engage them. Several male and female activists held babies in their arms. After speaking with some activists I knew, I went over to one of the network leaders and asked him how it was going. He looked at me, shrugged, and said, "It's business as usual, Michael... We're still doing our da'wah."[1]

What made this apparently unremarkable scene all the more remarkable was that in the weeks and months leading up to the Olympics, British authorities, who were under enormous pressure to stage a peaceful Games, detained numerous activists. Several were arrested for their participation in two alleged terrorist plots. The first involved a planned attack on the Wiltshire town of

[1] Field notes, Islington, North London, July 21, 2012.

Royal Wootton Bassett; the second involved activists suspected of targeting the Olympics' canoeing venue.[2] During the same period, according to my respondents, other activists were arrested for fraud and other alleged crimes. These arrests did not capture the media attention of the "terrorism" plots, but activists believed the pressure was part of the government's strategy to keep them quiet and off-balance during the Olympics through "preemptive raids."[3] Police raided the home of one leading activist several months earlier. The respondent, who is no stranger to law enforcement pressure, said the raid "was a bit more enlightening this time because the police actually said, 'You're quite a high-profile figure, therefore you can expect to be raided every so often.'"[4]

Despite the raids and arrests here stood the high-profile figure and his fellow activists at the roadshow six days before the Olympic opening ceremonies, carrying on with business as usual. When asked about their plans for the Games, Ahmed demurred: "It's very difficult because the police, the British government, are really worried about the Olympics. They are worried about being embarrassed over any kind of controversy. In terms of doing demonstrations, in this atmosphere you need to be more creative."[5]

Days later it became clear what Ahmed had in mind when he and other activists announced a new campaign and website called "The Evil Olympics." The campaign was devoted to "exposing" the London Games' perceived evils, including its celebration of nationalism among countries that compete against each other not only through sports, but to "suppress Islam."[6] As part of their campaign activists vowed to engage in da'wah and hisbah during the Olympics. After one protest, planned for the opening ceremonies, was cancelled by the authorities, activists remained undeterred. They announced they would continue with "special surprises" in the coming days that would "create worldwide impact."[7] In addition to holding talks and da'wah stalls at different

---

[2] The two activists who were reportedly acting suspiciously near the canoeing venue in Waltham Abbey, Hertfordshire were released without charge after forty-eight hours of questioning. Two other activists pled guilty for their involvement in the Royal Wootton Bassett plot, which I discussed in the introductory chapter. Interview with Rohan, leading activist, Whitechapel, East London, July 16, 2012. Also, see Muslim Prisoners.com, "UK War on Islam and the Muslims," www.muslimprisoners.com/ [Accessed July 9, 2012]; Duncan Gardham, "London 2012: Two Muslim converts arrested over Olympic terror plot," *Daily Telegraph* (June 28, 2012), www .telegraph.co.uk/news/uknews/terrorism-in-the-uk/9362738/London-2012-Two-Muslim-converts-arrested-over-Olympic-terror-plot.html [Accessed July 27, 2012]; and Sean O'Neill, Rhoda Buchanan, and Fiona Hamilton, "Brothers arrested by anti-terror police in dawn raid on a house near Olympic Park," *The Times* (London) (July 6, 2012), p. 4.

[3] Email from veteran activist, July 12, 2012; field notes, London, July 14, 2012, and Islington, North London, July 21, 2012.

[4] Interview with leading activist, Leyton, East London, July 17, 2012.

[5] Interview with Ahmed, veteran activist, Islington, North London, July 21, 2012.

[6] The Evil Olympics, www.evilolympics.com/ [Accessed July 27, 2012].

[7] The Evil Olympics, press release, "Demonstration Exposing the Evil of the Olympics," www.evilolympics.com/ [Accessed July 27, 2012]; The Evil Olympics, press release, "British

locations around Britain, on the night of the closing ceremonies activists staged a demonstration near the Olympic Park in Stratford. With police officers and tourists looking on, they chanted slogans, handed out leaflets entitled "Exposing Teams of Terror," and waved signs announcing "War Criminals USA UK Russia" and "Shariah the Only Solution."[8] Afterwards, the leading activist declared himself satisfied with the event: "We were pleased to be able to address some of the atrocities being committed against Muslims around the world."[9]

Evil or not, the Olympics campaign can be read as a microcosm of al-Muhajiroun's activism in recent years. As authorities increased the pressure against the outlawed network, activists did not stop calling society to Islam and commanding good and forbidding evil. Instead, they tried "to be more creative" by adjusting their activism in response to the pressure. These changes included creating new spin-off groups and platforms, making their da'wah stalls less confrontational, and shifting their activism to the Internet. Activists made these and other adaptations in response to setbacks, as exemplified in the British government's crackdown in the run-up to the London Olympics. In the process, they demonstrated their ingenuity and resilience.

Resilience refers to the capacity of individuals, organizations, and communities to bounce back from setbacks to continue their activities.[10] Over the years the Emigrants have shown their capacity to recover from adversity by changing their structure and tactics. Chapter 1 focuses on one key structural change: al-Muhajiroun's transformation from a centralized, "scale-free-like" network built around a charismatic leader to a more decentralized, "small-world-like" network with multiple leaders connecting different clusters of activists organized into local halaqahs. This small-world structure was essential to the

---

Government Ban Peaceful Demonstration by Muslims," www.evilolympics.com/ [Accessed July 27, 2012]; Michael Holden, "Radical Muslims plan opening ceremony protest outside park," *Chicago Tribune* (July 27, 2012), www.chicagotribune.com/sports/olympics/sns-rt-us-oly-ceremony-protest-day0bre86q0zt-20120727,0,3246587.story [Accessed July 27, 2012].

[8] Associated Press, "Police: Small group of Islamist protesters near Olympic Park ahead of closing ceremony," *Washington Post* (August 12, 2012), www.washingtonpost.com/world/europe/police-small-group-of-islamist-protesters-near-olympic-park-ahead-of-closing-ceremony/2012/08/12/ce4a7ed4-e4b2-11e1-9739-eef99c5fb285_story.html [Accessed August 17, 2012]; Faye De Gannes, "Islamist Muslims protest against Olympics games in the last hours," *Demotix* (August 12, 2012), www.demotix.com/news/1385485/islamist-muslims-protest-against-olympics-games-last-hours/all-media [Accessed August 13, 2015]; and email from Douglas Weeks, researcher on al-Muhajiroun, August 12, 2012.

[9] Email from leading activist, August 17, 2012.

[10] Kathleen M. Sutcliffe and Timothy J. Vogus, "Organizing for Resilience," in *Positive Organizational Scholarship: Foundations of a New Discipline*, edited by Kim S. Cameron, Jane E. Dutton, and Robert E. Quinn (San Francisco, CA: Berrett-Koehler Publishers, 2003), p. 96; Norman Garmezy, "Resilience in Children's Adaptation to Negative Life Events and Stressed Environments," *Pediatric Annals* 20 (1991), pp. 459–66; and Stevan Weine, "Building Community Resilience to Violent Extremism," *Georgetown Journal of International Affairs* 14 (Summer/Fall 2013), pp. 81–9.

Emigrants' ability to absorb external pressure and continue their activism after being outlawed by the British government.[11]

In this chapter, I draw on interviews with activists and my observations of their activism over four-and-a-half years to discuss a number of tactical (rather than structural or strategic) adaptations that enhanced their resilience. Many of these changes were made in direct response to law enforcers' efforts to disrupt their da'wah and hisbah. These simple but effective adaptations were well-suited to activists' organizational and technological capabilities. But they represented only modest improvements to activists' practices, rather than major changes to their ideology or strategy. Similar to al-Muhajiroun's shift to a more decentralized, small-world-like structure, the adaptations described in this chapter allowed activists to continue their call to establish the caliphate in the face of significant adversity.

PROLIFERATING PLATFORMS

One way the Emigrants have demonstrated their resilience is by creating dozens of spin-off groups and platforms to coordinate and publicize their high-risk activism. On four occasions – July 2006, January 2010, November 2011, and June 2014 – different British Home Secretaries exercised their authority under the Terrorism Act (2006) to outlaw eleven al-Muhajiroun groups for glorifying terrorism.[12] Each time activists responded by laying low for a while before re-launching their activism under the banner of a newly-named group, such as Islam4UK, Muslims Against Crusades, or Need4Khilafah. These were not competing groups. Nor did their emergence suggest the network was "splintering" or losing its ideological coherence. Supporters of the "new" groups not only belonged to the proscribed one, they followed the same teachings and ideology of the larger network and they remained loyal to leaders like Omar Bakri and Anjem Choudary. Yet by identifying themselves as part of a "separate" group, network supporters felt emboldened to continue their activism. They then used the new banner to organize inflammatory events to attract attention from the media and British society and recruit new supporters. Inevitably, one or more of these rallies would provoke a firestorm of controversy in the United Kingdom, and political pressure would build for the authorities to crack down and outlaw the "new" platform. When this happened the cycle would begin

---

[11] For analysis of resilience by other dark networks, see René M. Bakker, Jörg Raab, and H. Brinton Milward, "A Preliminary Theory of Dark Network Resilience," *Journal of Policy Analysis and Management* 31, no. 1 (2012), p. 35, and Nathan P. Jones, *Mexico's Illicit Drug Networks and the State Reaction* (Washington, DC: Georgetown University Press, 2016), pp. 31–2.

[12] Home Office, *Proscribed Terrorist Organisations*, May 3, 2017, p. 6; Legislation.gov.uk, "Terrorism Act 2000 c. 11, Part II, Procedure, Section 3, Proscription," www.legislation.gov.uk/ukpga/2000/11/section/3.

again with supporters creating new spin-offs or reviving old platforms that had not been banned.

Since the Emigrants' earliest days in the late 1990s, these platforms have been essential to activists' ability to spread their message, attract new followers, and call Great Britain to the caliphate. However, after Omar Bakri issued a press release in October 2004 formally announcing al-Muhajiroun's termination, the spin-off groups became even more important.[13] While Bakri's announcement caught observers by surprise, in reality activists simply continued their da'wah and hisbah under new names. One leading activist who was present at the meeting that "dissolved" al-Muhajiroun explains that Bakri and his followers never intended to stop their activism. Instead, they sought to recast their ideological struggle in broader terms: "There was a massive conference in a friend's house and we got rid of al-Muhajiroun because we realized at that point that there's a bigger jama'ah, a bigger organization that links those things together, which is called Ahlus Sunnah wal Jama'ah. So forget al-Muhajiroun. We're part of a global movement."[14]

The new "platform" included many of the Emigrants' leaders and rank-and-file activists and followed the same Salafi-Islamist ideology described in the last chapter. Several weeks after Bakri's press release a journalist discovered some of these activists handing out flyers marked "Al-Muhajiroun, Followers of Ahlus Sunnah wal Jama'ah." One activist acknowledged the obvious, telling the reporter, "Al-Muhajiroun has been disbanded but we are still operating under different guises. The message is all the same... We all want to create a separate pure Islamic state."[15]

Al-Ghurabaa and the Saved Sect

Among the different guises through which network activists continued to organize were two closely related groups, al-Ghurabaa (Arabic for "the Strangers") and the Saved Sect. Both names have deep meaning in Islamic history and culture. They reflect activists' conviction that they are among the few believers on the right path, and therefore destined to be considered "strange" by their less zealous contemporaries – yet "saved" on the Day of Judgment. Both groups followed the network's strategy of activism and were led by prominent activists, including Omar "Abu Izzadeen" Brooks, Simon "Sulaymon" Keeler, and Sajid "Abu Uzair" Sharif. While activists continued to use the

---

[13] Omar Bakri Mohammed, press release, "An Official Declaration Dissolving Al-Muhajiroun," (October 8, 2004); Quintan Wiktorowicz, *Radical Islam Rising: Muslim Extremism in the West* (Lanham, MD: Rowman & Littlefield, 2005), pp. 126–7, 213.

[14] Interview with leading activist, Walthamstow, East London, December 2, 2010. Also, interview with leading activist, Ilford, East London, December 12, 2014.

[15] Dominik Lemanski, "Hate 'disbanded' Islam group still preaches on streets of UK," *Daily Star* (November 21, 2004), p. 9.

Ahlus Sunnah wal Jama'ah name to identify themselves and communicate with their supporters, they channeled much of their public activism through al-Ghurabaa and the Saved Sect. Activists from these platforms used websites and interviews with the media to promote their ideological views. They also organized high-profile demonstrations.[16] After the Danish newspaper *Jyllands-Posten* sparked a global debate by publishing cartoons depicting the Prophet Mohammed, the two platforms organized a march of several hundred protestors from the Regent's Park Mosque in Central London to the Danish embassy, where they waved signs declaring "annihilate those who insult Islam" and screamed violent slogans, including "Bomb, bomb Denmark! Bomb, bomb USA!"[17]

The Danish embassy protest received extensive media coverage and created a firestorm of controversy in Britain, increasing pressure on the authorities to crack down on the network. Law enforcers began an investigation that led to the conviction of several leading activists, including Mizanur Rahman, Abdul Muhid, and Abdul Rahman Saleem, for soliciting murder and inciting racial hatred based on their actions at the protest. The authorities also outlawed both groups. This was the first time a British Home Secretary took advantage of new powers in the Terrorism Act, as amended in 2006, to proscribe groups for "glorifying" terrorism, as opposed to committing it or supporting it materially.[18] This cut to the heart of the Emigrants' activism and made it a crime for people to belong to or support any group banned under this authority.[19] The law included a provision, also aimed at al-Muhajiroun,

---

[16] The al-Ghurabaa website contained the same registration address and contact number that had been used for al-Muhajiroun. Richard Ford, "Militant Islamist groups banned under terror law," *The Times* (July 18, 2006), p. 26; Mark Honigsbaum, "Terror measures: Radical cleric leaves, but his legacy remains," *The Guardian* (August 10, 2005), p. 8; and Amar Singh, "100 protest at police raid in the East End," *The Evening Standard* (June 9, 2006), p. 10.

[17] Interviews with Rohan, Whitechapel, East London, December 7, 2010, and another leading activist involved in this protest, Stratford, East London, June 20, 2011. Also, see Robin Simcox, Hannah Stuart, and Houriya Ahmed, *Islamist Terrorism: The British Connections* (London: The Centre for Social Cohesion, 2010), pp. 95–100; and Jyette Klausen, *The Cartoons that Shook the World* (New Haven, CT: Yale University Press, 2009), p. 118.

[18] For other contributions to the small, but growing, body of academic research on proscription, see Tim Legrand and Lee Jarvis, "Enemies of the State: Proscription Powers and their Use in the United Kingdom," *British Politics* 9, no. 4 (2014), pp. 450–71; Jenny Hocking, "Counter-Terrorism and the Criminalisation of Politics: Australia's New Security Powers of Detention, Proscription, and Control," *Australian Journal of Politics & History* 49, no. 3 (2003), pp. 355–71; and Julie B. Shapiro, "The Politicization of the Designation of Foreign Terrorist Organizations: The Effect on the Separation of Powers," *Cardozo Public Law, Policy and Ethics Journal* 6, no. 1 (Spring 2008), pp. 547–600.

[19] United Kingdom, Home Office, press release, "Terror Organisation Proscribed," (November 9, 2011), www.homeoffice.gov.uk/media-centre/news/mac-proscription [Accessed November 26, 2011]; United Kingdom, Home Office, "Proscribed Terrorist Organizations (July 6, 2012), www.homeoffice.gov.uk/publications/counter-terrorism/proscribed-terror-groups/proscribed-groups [Accessed August 4, 2012]; Legrand and Jarvis, "Enemies of the State," p. 453.

authorizing the Home Secretary to identify different platforms when banning an organization. Home Secretary John Reid did so by naming both al-Ghurabaa and the Saved Sect for proscription. In announcing the ban, Reid declared that he was "determined to act against those who, while not directly involved in committing acts of terrorism, provide support for and make statements that glorify, celebrate and exalt the atrocities of terrorist groups." "I am also committed," he added, referring to the Emigrants' spin-offs, "to ensuring that those organisations that change their name do not avoid the consequences of proscription."[20]

Some activist groups would have disbanded after such legislation, aimed squarely at them, was enacted. Not al-Muhajiroun. Instead, activists insisted that outlawing the glorification of terrorism and banning al-Ghurabaa and the Saved Sect would not stop them from practicing their da'wah and hisbah. A year after the banning of both groups, during a rebuilding period in which activists continued to call society to Islam and recruit new members to their community of practice, a leading activist explained, "We fully expect to be banned and for individuals to be arrested. We expect much more than that, in fact. It is not going to make you cower and think, 'It's finished.' No. The struggle has just begun. This is the next stage."[21]

Islam4UK

In the next stage activists used a variety of platforms to engage in contentious politics. In January 2007 Anjem Choudary and other network leaders were discovered propagating their views through an online discussion board called Followers of Ahlus Sunnah wal Jama'ah Muntada. Activists reportedly used the password-protected forum to upload videos and promote the "divine call of jihad" in Somalia and elsewhere.[22] In September 2008, activists organized a conference on the seventh anniversary of the 9/11 attacks under the name of a generic-sounding platform, the Association for Islamic Research. Entitled "Have the Lessons from 9/11 Been Learnt?," the conference featured speakers from several network platforms. Anjem Choudary represented the Shari'ah Court of the UK, while veteran activist "Abu Saalihah" represented the London School of Shari'ah, and "Saiful Islam" represented the Salafi Youth

---

[20] Andrew Woodcock, "Reid bans Islamist groups for glorifying terrorism," *Western Mail* (July 18, 2006), p. 9; Ford, "Militant Islamist groups banned under terror law," p. 26; and Martin Bentham, "Two groups outlawed for supporting terror," *The Evening Standard* (July 17, 2006), p. 4.

[21] Interview with leading activist, Woolwich, South London, September 22, 2007.

[22] Abul Taher, "UK preacher in secret web call for jihad," *The Sunday Times* (January 14, 2007), p. 7.

for Islamic Propagation. Omar Bakri participated as well, addressing the conference remotely from Lebanon.[23]

A week later, activists used a new platform and website, Islam4uk.com, to promote a separate conference aimed at Muslim youth. The conference was held in Walthamstow, East London, and featured speeches by veteran activists "Abu Uzair" and "Abu Waleed," identified by their Arabic nicknames or *kunyas*. In November 2008, activists organized another conference under the Islam4UK banner, this one held in Tower Hamlets, featuring Anjem Choudary, listed as head of the London School of Shari'ah, "Abu Muaz," leader of the UK Salafi Youth Movement, "Abu Yahya," spokesman for the Followers of Ahlus Sunnah Wal Jama'ah, "Abu Rumaysah," a student at the London School of Shari'ah, and Omar Bakri, who again addressed the audience by telephone from his home in Lebanon.[24] In June 2009, activists used Islam4UK to promote a public debate, "Shari'ah Law vs British Law," organized by another network platform, the Global Issues Society. The debate featured Anjem Choudary squaring off against Douglas Murray, director of the conservative think tank Centre for Social Cohesion, and doubled as the public relaunch of al-Muhajiroun, whose revival had been announced in a press release on the Islam4UK website two weeks earlier.[25] In addition to organizing public conferences and debates, activists used Islam4UK to promote "Islamic roadshows" in different areas of London, including Brixton, Edgware Road, Green Street, Lewisham, Wood Green, and in other cities, like Birmingham.[26]

---

[23] Robert Mendick, "Islamist sect banned as security threat 'is recruiting teenagers'," *The Evening Standard* (September 19, 2008); Duncan Gardham, "Radical Muslims warn of another 9/11," *Daily Telegraph* (September 13, 2008).

[24] Mendick, "Islamist sect banned as security threat 'is recruiting teenagers'"; Robert Mendick, "Banned militant Islamist sect 'is recruiting young Muslims'," *Daily Mail* (September 19, 2008), www.dailymail.co.uk/news/article-1058357/Banned-militant-Islamist-sect-recruiting-young-Muslims.html [Accessed December 2, 2010]; and David Cohen, "Islamic radicals make mockery of hate laws," *The Evening Standard* (November 10, 2008), p. 18.

[25] Catherine Zara Raymond, "Al Muhajiroun and Islam4UK: The Group Behind the Ban," (London: International Centre for the Study of Radicalisation and Political Violence, King's College, 2010), pp. 5–6; *Daily Telegraph*, "Police called to maintain order at Al Muhajiroun meeting," (June 18, 2009), www.telegraph.co.uk/news/uknews/5563508/Police-called-to-maintain-order-at-Al-Muhajiroun-meeting.html [Accessed August 20, 2015]; and Islam4UK, press release, "Al Muhajiroun: To be Re-launched!," (no date), www.islam4uk.com/current-affairs/uk-news/46-uk/298-newsflash-al-muhajiroun-to-be-re-launched [Accessed June 1, 2009].

[26] Interviews with activist, Lewisham, South London, December 11, 2010, and Brixton Salafi, Brixton, South London, November 5, 2010; Raymond, "Al Muhajiroun and Islam4UK," p. 15; Andrew Malone, "The jihad fanatic peddling a message of hate to 11-year-old Londoners (funded by the taxpayer)," *Daily Mail* (July 24, 2009), www.dailymail.co.uk/news/article-1200442/The-Jihad-fanatic-peddling-message-hate-11-year-old-Londoners-funded-taxpayer.html [Accessed June 16, 2011]; Ben Goldby, "Inside Islam4UK: How Birmingham boys turn to terror," *Sunday Mercury* (January 17, 2010), www.sundaymercury.net/news/midlands-news/2010/01/17/inside-islam4uk-how-birmingham-boys-turn-to-terror-66331-25617375/ [Accessed June 18, 2011]; Islam 4UK, "A Review of Lewisham Roadshow," (no date), www.islam4uk.com/current-affairs/uk-news/46-uk/327-review-of-lewisham-roadshow [Accessed August 5, 2009]; Islam4UK,

While these conferences and roadshows received some attention from the media, Islam4UK achieved much of its notoriety by staging provocative, high-profile demonstrations, many of them against British soldiers fighting in Iraq and Afghanistan. In March 2009, Islam4UK activists protested a homecoming parade for British troops in Luton, twenty miles north of London. Luton was an al-Muhajiroun stronghold for years, with one of the network's most active, and radical, halaqahs based in the industrial working-class city. During the parade, Islam4UK protestors shouted "terrorists" at the soldiers and waved signs denouncing them as "cowards," "killers," and the "Butchers of Basra." This provocative protest received substantial coverage from the British media.[27] It also led to the formation of the English Defence League, a British nationalist group that sought to counter al-Muhajiroun demonstrations over the next several years.[28]

Islam4UK sparked a national outcry several months later when activists announced in early January 2010 that they would march against British troops in Wootton Bassett, the market town in Wiltshire where soldiers killed in Iraq and Afghanistan were repatriated. Activists later cancelled the march, but not before the public uproar increased pressure on the government to crack down on the network. Shortly after the cancellation, British authorities formally banned Islam4UK and al-Muhajiroun, along with several other network platforms, including Call to Submission, Islamic Path, and the London School of Shari'ah.[29] Rather than stopping their activism, however, activists remained defiant and swore to continue. In response to the ban, they declared,

"A Review of Islamic Roadshows in Green Street & Wood Green," (no date), www.islam4uk .com/current-affairs/uk-news/325-a-review-of-islamic-roadshows-in-green-street-a-wood-green- [Accessed December 30, 2009].

[27] Thomas Harding and Richard Edwards, "Calls for crackdown on parade Muslim extremists," *Daily Telegraph* (March 11, 2009), www.telegraph.co.uk/news/uknews/4974031/Calls-for-crackdown-on-parade-Muslim-extremists.html [Accessed August 19, 2015]; *Daily Telegraph*, "Luton parade protesters 'were members of extremist group'," (March 12, 2009), www.telegraph.co.uk/news/uknews/4976105/Luton-parade-protesters-were-members-of-extremist-group.html [Accessed August 19, 2015]; Jenny Percival, "Two arrested after protest at soldiers' homecoming parade in Luton," *The Guardian* (March 10, 2009), www .theguardian.com/uk/2009/mar/10/two-arrested-army-protest-luton [Accessed October 20, 2017]; and Andrew Levy and Paul Harris, "Now an insult to the war dead," *Daily Mail* (March 12, 2009).

[28] For more on the English Defence League (EDL), see Juris Pupcenoks and Ryan McCabe, "The Rise of the Fringe: Right Wing Populists, Islamists and Politics in the UK," *Journal of Muslim Minority Affairs* 33, no. 2 (2013), pp. 171–84; James Treadwell and Jon Garland, "Masculinity, Marginalization, and Violence: A Case Study of the English Defence League," *British Journal of Criminology* 51, no. 4 (2011), pp. 621–34; and George Kassimeris and Leonie Jackson, "The Ideology and Discourse of the English Defence League: 'Not Racist, Not Violent, Just No Longer Silent'," *British Journal of Politics and International Relations* 17, no. 1 (2015), pp. 171–88.

[29] Raymond, "Al Muhajiroun and Islam4UK," pp. 3–4, 21–2; Legrand and Jarvis, "Enemies of the State," pp. 452, 459.

"we never called for Islam because either Blair or Brown liked it or allowed it but rather because it is a divine obligation upon Muslims." In the same press release, they promised that "another platform with a new name will arise to continue to fulfil these divine obligations until the Shari'ah has been implemented."[30]

Muslims Against Crusades

Several months later it became clear what the new platform would be. In June 2010, a little over a year after the Islam4UK demonstration against returning soldiers in Luton, a new group calling itself Muslims Against Crusades staged a similar protest in Barking at a parade honoring troops from the same infantry regiment. Protestors screamed "butchers" and "baby killers" at the parading soldiers, and waved black flags and signs saying "What are you dying for? £18k," and "Return of the 21st Century Crusaders."[31]

Mindful of the British government's recent banning of Islam4UK and al-Muhajiroun, activists in the new platform insisted their group was separate. "This isn't Islam4UK," a leading member of the group explained. "We're independent. We've got new members who were not members of Islam4UK or al-Muhajiroun."[32] However, he and other respondents admitted they studied with Anjem Choudary and participated in Islam4UK before it was banned.[33] Years later, after returning to Britain from Syria, he acknowledged that Muslims Against Crusades was closely affiliated with al-Muhajiroun.[34]

The new platform connected to the old ones through pre-existing social networks. When Muslims Against Crusades formed, activists who had

---

[30] Islam4UK, press release, "Declaration on Wootton Bassett Procession" (January 10, 2010), www.anjemchoudary.com/index.php?option=com_k2&view=item&id=15:declaration-on-wootton-bassett-procession&Itemid=7 [Accessed October 25, 2010].

[31] Like many of the Emigrants' most outrageous events, the protest in Barking was covered by Britain's tabloid media. See, for example, Andrew Levy, "Into the jaws of hate: Soldiers' parade marred by Muslim extremists and far-right," *Daily Mail* (June 16, 2010), www.dailymail.co.uk/news/article-1286784/Muslim-protesters-brand-war-heroes-murderers-homecoming-parade-turns-violent.html [Accessed October 11, 2010]; and Lynsey Haywood, "Extremists' insult to troops," *The Sun* (June 15, 2010), www.thesun.co.uk/sol/homepage/news/3015394/Extremists-insult-to-troops.html [Accessed October 12, 2010].

[32] Interview Muslims Against Crusades activist, Whitechapel, East London, November 9, 2010.

[33] Interviews with two different activists, Whitechapel, November 9, 2010, and interviews with other activists, Leyton, East London, November 14, 2010 and December 9, 2010, and Lewisham, South London, December 11, 2010.

[34] This respondent's subsequent admission of MAC's affiliation to al-Muhajiroun was reported in the media. I do not cite this report because doing so would violate his anonymity. For an earlier report that also notes the similarities between Muslims Against Crusades and al-Muhajiroun, see Duncan Gardham, "Muslims Against Crusaders protest group bares al-Muhajiroun hallmarks," *Daily Telegraph* (November 11, 2010), www.telegraph.co.uk/news/uknews/terrorism-in-the-uk/8126869/Muslims-Against-Crusaders-protest-group-bares-al-Muhajiroun-hallmarks.html [November 12, 2010].

participated in Islam4UK and al-Muhajiroun simply continued their activism in the new spin-off, joining new recruits who had not been involved in the earlier platforms but who received the same Salafi-Islamist culturing in in the network's halaqahs.[35]

Like earlier spin-off groups, Muslims Against Crusades, or MAC (pronounced "mack") as activists often referred to it, created a website to announce upcoming events, communicate with supporters, and spread the network's ideology. In response to Islam4UK's ban, however, which made any street preaching organized under its name illegal, activists in the new spin-off did not organize da'wah stalls and roadshows under the MAC name. They used other platforms for this, including Call2Tawhid, Convert2Islam, and Supporters of Sunnah.[36] "My part of the movement is Call2Tawhid," explains Salman, who helped create this da'wah platform, while also participating in MAC protests. "We have a website, Call2Tawhid, and you can look at our leaflet. We work to propagate the message because al-Muhajiroun was dismantled, but we didn't want to stop our obligation to call for Islam."[37]

If Call2Tawhid and other platforms allowed activists to satisfy their duty to perform da'wah, Muslims Against Crusades satisfied their obligation to perform hisbah by organizing protests. MAC adopted the same protest repertoire as al-Muhajiroun, demonstrating against British and American foreign policy by staging provocative rallies against high-profile targets. "Muslims Against Crusades has been set up to call people to the awareness of what's happening under their name," explained a leading activist in the group. "In this country people are blissfully unaware of what's happening inside Iraq and Afghanistan."[38] In addition to organizing the protest against returning British troops in Barking, Muslims Against Crusades organized demonstrations outside 10 Downing Street and the American embassy in Grosvenor Square. At the Downing Street protest, timed to coincide with Barack Obama's state visit to Britain in May 2011, male and female activists held signs denouncing the American president as the world's "most wanted terrorist" and promising that

---

[35] Interviews with two different activists, Whitechapel, November 9, 2010, and interviews with other activists, Leyton, East London, November 14, 2010 and December 9, 2010, and Lewisham, South London, December 11, 2010; field notes, November 17, 2010.

[36] Supporters of Sunnah should not be confused with Abu Hamza al-Masri's London-based extremist group, Supporters of Shariah. Interviews with activists, Bethnal Green, East London, November 28, 2010, and Ilford, East London, November 13, 2010. Field notes from Call2Tawhid da'wah stalls in Bethnal Green, East London, November 28, 2010 and December 5, 2010, Convert2Islam da'wah stall in Lewisham, South London, June 18, 2011, and Supporters of Sunnah da'wah stalls in Ilford, East London, November 13, 2010, Stratford, East London, November 29, 2010, and Tottenham, North London, December 4, 2010.

[37] Interview with Salman, Bethnal Green, East London, November 28, 2010. Salman, who I also interviewed after he left the network, was still active in al-Muhajiroun at the time of this interview.

[38] Interview with veteran activist, Whitechapel, East London, November 9, 2010.

"Muslims will conquer the White House."[39] Several weeks earlier, MAC staged a "funeral prayer" outside the American embassy to protest "Sheikh" Osama bin Laden's killing by Special Forces. After Anjem Choudary led the protestors in prayer, activists waved signs saying "Islam will dominate the world," while chanting "USA you will pay" and "down, down Obama."[40]

A signature feature of many Muslims Against Crusades protests was the burning of American and British flags and other symbols. On the ninth anniversary of the 9/11 attacks, protestors, led by Anjem Choudary, gathered outside the US embassy and burned replicas of the Stars and Stripes and the Union Jack while chanting "burn, burn USA" and "down, down democracy."[41] The following year, MAC demonstrators, again led by Choudary, returned to the embassy to celebrate the tenth anniversary of 9/11 by burning a replica of the American flag and shouting "burn, burn USA" during a moment of silence to remember when the first hijacked airplane crashed into the World Trade Center.[42] Two months later, MAC activists staged their most notorious protest when they gathered outside the Royal Albert Hall on the anniversary of Armistice Day, waved black jihadi flags and burned replicas of the poppy plant while shouting "British soldiers burn in hell" and "burn, burn murderers" as the rest of the country observed two minutes of silence (see Figure 4.1).[43]

---

[39] *Daily Mail*, "The bin Laden backlash: Angry Muslims demonstrate outside Downing Street as Obama visits Britain," (May 24, 2011), www.dailymail.co.uk/news/article-1390428/Anjem-Choudary-Obama-legitimate-target-extremists.html [Accessed May 25, 2011].

[40] Muslims Against Crusades, press release, "Demonstration + Funeral Prayer for Sheikh Usamah Bin Laden," (May 6, 2011); YouTube, "Osama's Funeral Party," (May 19, 2011), www.youtube.com/watch?v=9dE_6Kch0ag&feature=player_detailpage [Accessed July 27, 2012]; Nick Vinocur and Michael Holden, "Europe's Muslims voice doubt, anger on bin Laden," *Reuters* (May 6, 2011), www.reuters.com/article/2011/05/06/us-binladen-europe-muslims-idUSTRE7454UT20110506 [Accessed May 6, 2011].

[41] Peter Marshall, "Muslims burn US flag at London Embassy," *Demotix* (September 11, 2010), www.demotix.com/news/437093/muslims-burn-us-flag-london-embassy [Accessed October 1, 2010]; Muslims Against Crusaders, "Muslims Burn American Flag on 9/11 – US Embassy in London," *YouTube* (September 11, 2010), www.youtube.com/watch?v=0840bYQf1p8 [Accessed August 26, 2015].

[42] Andy Bloxham, "9/11 anniversary: Muslim protesters burn US flag outside embassy in London," *Daily Telegraph* (September 11, 2011), www.telegraph.co.uk/news/worldnews/september-11-attacks/8755834/911-anniversary-Muslim-protesters-burn-US-flag-outside-embassy-in-London.html [Accessed September 19, 2011]; *Daily Mail*, "100 protesters burn American flag outside US embassy in London during minute's silence for 9/11," (September 11, 2011), www.dailymail.co.uk/news/article-2036172/9-11-memorial-events-London-protesters-burn-American-flag-outside-US-embassy.html [Accessed August 26, 2015].

[43] The poppy flower is a central symbol in Armistice Day ceremonies. Many people in Britain wear the small red flower on their lapel in the days and weeks leading up to the anniversary. Field notes, Kensington, Central London, November 11, 2010; Caroline Davies, "Armistice Day silence falls overs Britain as millions honour the dead," *The Guardian* (November 11, 2010), www.guardian.co.uk/uk/2010/nov/11/armistice-day-silence-britain-remembrance [Accessed November 11, 2010]; Andy Bloxham, "Muslims clash with police after burning poppy in anti-Armistice Day protest," *The Daily Telegraph* (November 11, 2010), www.telegraph.co.uk/news/uknews/law-and-order/8126357/Muslims-clash-with-police-after-burning-poppy-in-anti-Armistice-Day-protest.html

FIGURE 4.1 Muslims Against Crusades activists at 2010 Armistice Day protest near Royal Albert Hall.
Photograph by Michael Kenney.

These and other MAC demonstrations, including a protest against Pope Benedict during the papacy's first state visit to the United Kingdom, nearly 500 years after the country split from Rome, earned the platform a great deal of notoriety and media attention.[44] Like their predecessors in the larger network, activists from the spin-off group learned that provocation works. By calling the Pope a "paedophile" or British troops "murderers," and by burning powerful symbols, MAC ensured that its message reached large numbers of people within and outside Britain through extensive media coverage, even though their demonstrations were quite small, with typically no more than

[Accessed November 11, 2010]; Muslims Against Crusades, press release, "Emergency Demonstration: Breaking the Silence: Muslims Against Remembrance Day," (no date), www .muslimsagainstcrusades.com/ [Accessed November 10, 2010].
[44] Interviews with activists, Whitechapel, East London, November 9, 2010; Muslims Against Crusaders, "Muslims Confront Pope Benedict XVI – Saturday 18 September Demonstration in London," (September 18, 2010), www.youtube.com/watch?v=awSd-Pno1rY [Accessed August 25, 2015]; Alex Milan Tracy, "MAC demonstrate against the Pope in London," *Demotix* (September 18, 2010), www.demotix.com/news/446775/mac-demonstrate-against-pope-london#media-448598 [Accessed August 25, 2015]; and Douglas Weeks, *Radicals and Reactionaries: The Polarisation of Community and Government in the Name of Public Safety and Security*, unpublished doctoral dissertation, University of St. Andrews, November 15, 2012, pp. 239–41.

thirty to fifty protestors.[45] "The poppy demonstration was very successful because it reached millions of people," emphasized Ahmed, several weeks after the protest, which he helped organize. "You couldn't dream of creating more public awareness than to get on the front page of a newspaper that is circulated into the millions," he continued. "That's free publicity. A few words and a ten-pound website and you can get into the public arena very easily." [46]

For all MAC's success in getting its message into the public arena, its activism increasingly drew the attention of the police and Muslim and non-Muslim counter-demonstrators. Prominent among the anti-MAC demonstrators was the English Defence League, a motley assortment of British nationalists who routinely showed up at MAC rallies to insult and threaten activists, adding to the public order challenges facing the London Metropolitan Police.[47] At the Armistice Day protest in 2010, fighting broke out when the leader of the EDL, Stephen Lennon, more commonly known by his pseudonym, "Tommy Robinson," breached the police barricade set up for MAC protestors. Several activists traded punches with Lennon, while others hit him with their flag poles. When riot police moved in to stop the melée, activists started punching the police officers, sending one of them to the hospital with a head wound.[48]

Like the Danish embassy protest organized by al-Ghurabaa and the Saved Sect in 2006 and the planned march through Wootton Bassett publicized by Islam4UK in 2010, MAC's poppy-burning protest caused a public uproar,

---

[45] During my observation of the 2010 Armistice Day protest, for example, I performed two separate counts of MAC activists in attendance, one near the beginning of the rally and one at the height of the demonstration, just before the poppy burning. Each time I counted thirty MAC activists. The English Defence League staged a counter-demonstration at this protest, which grew from around ten supporters at the beginning to well over one hundred at the height of the demonstration. The number of MAC activists at this protest is consistent with other MAC and al-Muhajiroun protests and Islamic roadshows I observed during my field work. I never observed more than fifty activists at an al-Muhajiroun event. Of course, there may have been more activists at other protests I did not attend. Field notes, Kensington, Central London, November 11, 2010.

[46] Interview with Ahmed, Tottenham, North London, December 4, 2010. Also, interview with another activist, Leyton, East London, November 14, 2010.

[47] Interviews with activists, Kensington, Central London, November 11, 2010, Leyton, East London, November 14, 2010, Lewisham, South London, December 11, 2010, and Mile End, East London, June 26, 2011, and two London Metropolitan Police officers, Westminster, Central London, June 29, 2011. Also see *BBC News*, "Is far-right extremism a threat?," (September 22, 2009), http://news.bbc.co.uk/2/hi/uk_news/8266933.stm [Accessed August 27, 2015].

[48] Field notes, Kensington, Central London, November 11, 2010 and Stratford, East London, November 29, 2010; and interview with rank-and-file activist, Stratford, East London, November 29, 2010. *BBC News*, "Man guilty of burning poppies at Armistice Day protest," (March 7, 2011), www.bbc.co.uk/news/uk-england-london-12664346 [Accessed March 10, 2011]; and Bloxham, "Muslims clash with police after burning poppy in anti-Armistice Day protest." Douglas Weeks describes similar scenes of mayhem between al-Muhajiroun activists and English Defence League counter-demonstrators at other protests he observed during his field work. See Weeks, *Radicals and Reactionaries*, pp. 241–3.

increasing pressure on the authorities to ban the platform. Shortly after MAC announced its intention to disrupt the 2011 anniversary of Armistice Day, British Home Secretary Theresa May officially banned the group.[49] In announcing the ban, May emphasized that "Muslims Against Crusades is simply another name for an organisation already proscribed under a number of names including Al Ghurabaa, The Saved Sect, Al Muhajiroun and Islam4UK... it should not be able to continue these activities by simply changing its name."[50]

Hours later, police officers raided three properties in East London associated with the activist network. These included the Centre for Islamic Services, the network's indoctrination center in Whitechapel where MAC activists listened to talks by Anjem Choudary and other leaders; Master Printers, a digital printing company above the Centre owned by Choudary's older brother, Yazdani; and Anjem Choudary's private residence. The police officers seized electronic devices, books and other documents. However, no activists were arrested or prosecuted for criminal offenses, leading Anjem Choudary to denounce the raids as a "fishing expedition." "[T]hey've got nothing on me," he told a reporter. "I haven't done anything illegal. Obviously it's inconvenient, but that doesn't stop me propagating what I believe."[51]

Predictably, Muslims Against Crusades responded to the ban by issuing a press release, declaring "we are hereby dissolved" and cancelling their planned "Hell for Heroes" protest on Armistice Day. Rather than ceasing their activism, however, they vowed to continue: "the call for Islam will never be silenced by any ban or proscription... we pledge that our call and activities will see added momentum and zeal and that we will never rest until the flag of Islam flys [sic] high over Downing Street!"[52] When asked how activists would respond, a

---

[49] Muslims Against Crusades, "Demonstration: Hell for Heroes," (October 31, 2011), www .muslimsagainstcrusades.com/press-releases/demonstration-hell-for-heroes [Accessed November 3, 2011]; Dominic Casciani, "Muslims Against Crusades banned by Theresa May," *BBC News* (November 10, 2011), www.bbc.co.uk/news/uk-15678275 [Accessed November 14, 2011].

[50] United Kingdom, Home Office, press release, "Terror Organisation Proscribed," (November 9, 2011), www.homeoffice.gov.uk/media-centre/news/mac-proscription [Accessed November 26, 2011].

[51] *The Daily Telegraph*, "170 members of English Defence League arrested near Cenotaph in London," (November 11, 2011), www.telegraph.co.uk/news/uknews/crime/8884583/170-members-of-English-Defence-League-arrested-near-Cenotaph-in-London.html   [Accessed November 14, 2011]; Ted Jeory, "Victory as hate group is raided," *Sunday Express* (November 13, 2011), www.express.co.uk/posts/view/283386/Victory-as-hate-group-is-raided [Accessed November 14, 2011]; Anjem Choudary, press release, "Police Raid Anjem Choudary Following MAC Ban," (November 11, 2011), www.anjemchoudary.com/ [Accessed November 12, 2011]. Also, interviews with Rohan, Whitechapel, East London, July 16, 2012, and another leading activist, Leyton, East London, July 17, 2012.

[52] Muslims Against Crusades, press release, "A Ban Will Never Silence Islam and Muslims!," (November 10, 2011), www.muslimsagainstcrusades.com/press-releases/muslims-against-crusades-official-statement-regarding-ban [Accessed November 10, 2011]. Anjem Choudary issued the same press release in an email, which he signed "Press Spokesman for MAC," and

leading network activist replied, "We'll form a different platform. The names don't bother us. It's just a name, what's most important is the call."[53]

United Ummah

Despite Theresa May's demand that the Emigrants not be able to continue their activism by simply changing their name, this is exactly what they did. Less than a month after the MAC ban, al-Muhajiroun activists held another demonstration – this one against American drone strikes and the killing of Anwar al-Awlaki – at their favorite protest site, the US embassy in Grosvenor Square.[54] In the days leading up to the protest, activists publicized it on Twitter, YouTube, and various online forums using the name of a new platform, United Ummah.[55] Sticking to their separate group story, activists insisted United Ummah was independent, with no connection to Muslims Against Crusades or other outlawed platforms.[56] However, numerous participants at the United Ummah protest had studied with Omar Bakri and Anjem Choudary and were deeply involved with MAC and al-Muhajiroun. Police officers monitoring the protest apparently agreed, arresting twenty demonstrators on suspicion of belonging to a banned organization, Muslims Against Crusades, and two more for violent disorder and obstruction.[57] One MAC activist who was arrested at the demonstration recalled being singled out by police, placed in the back

listed his private cell phone number. Anjem Choudary, email, "Press Release: A Ban Will Never Silence Islam or the Muslims," (November 10, 2011).

[53] Interview with leading activist, Ilford, East London, November 13, 2010. This interview took place a year before Muslims Against Crusades was actually banned, underscoring how activists fully expected their platform to be outlawed.

[54] *Demotix*, "More than 20 arrests at US Embassy during United Ummah protest – London," (December 2, 2011), www.demotix.com/news/951608/more-20-arrest-us-embassy-during-united-ummah-protest-london [Accessed December 8, 2011]; Katy Blottr, "Arrests made as drones demonstration turns violent at US Embassy," (December 2, 2011), www.blottr.com/london/breaking-news/arrests-made-drones-demonstration-turns-violent-us-embassy [Accessed December 8, 2011].

[55] unitedummahHD, www.youtube.com/user/unitedummahHD and www.youtube.com/watch?v=lA-EIsIKzwI [Both URLs accessed September 1, 2015]; Anjem Choudary, https://twitter.com/anjemchoudary [Accessed December 2, 2011].

[56] Interview with leading activist, Leyton, East London, July 17, 2012; Anjem Choudary, "Police Brutality Targets Innocent Muslims!," (Friday, December 2, 2011), www.anjemchoudary.com/press-releases/police-brutality-targets-innocent-muslims [Accessed December 8, 2011].

[57] Interview with leading activist, Leyton, East London, July 17, 2012; Anjem Choudary, "Police Brutality Targets Innocent Muslims!," (December 2, 2011), www.anjemchoudary.com/press-releases/police-brutality-targets-innocent-muslims [Accessed December 8, 2011]; Weeks, *Radicals and Reactionaries*, p. 244; *BBC News*, "London's US Embassy demo: 22 arrests made," (December 2, 2011), www.bbc.com/news/uk-england-16006035 [Accessed September 1, 2015]; *Daily Mail*, "Police arrest 20 protesters 'from banned group Muslims Against Crusades' outside US embassy in London," (December 2, 2011), www.dailymail.co.uk/news/article-2069190/Muslims-Against-Crusades-protesters-arrested-outside-U-S-embassy-London.html?ITO=1490 [Accessed December 8, 2011].

of a police van with other protestors and taken to Paddington Green Police Station, where he was put in a cell, given a change of clothes and allowed to wait for his solicitor. He was briefly interrogated by the police before being released from custody. However, like other activists arrested that day he was not charged with any crime and the police soon dropped their criminal investigation against him.[58]

The authorities' failure to prosecute activists at the United Ummah protest for belonging to a banned organization underscores the difficulties they faced in enforcing proscription. While activists were barred from belonging to Muslims Against Crusades and other proscribed spin-offs, they were not prevented from engaging in peaceful protests outside these groups. Even though some of the platforms they used to organize their contentious politics were outlawed, activists' street da'wah and hisbah were still protected in Britain's democracy, as long as they were not coordinated by any banned groups. Government authorities were forced to work within these constraints when proscribing groups that "glorify" terrorism through legal activism. Meanwhile, activists merely had to create "new" groups to organize and publicize their activism when old ones were outlawed. This forced the police to play "catch up" with the new platforms, spending time and resources collecting evidence proving that they were essentially the same outlawed network. They did so with no guarantee that the offense for glorifying terrorism would hold up to the evidentiary standards demanded in British courts because no such cases had been successfully prosecuted.

Two British officials I met with described the December 2011 United Ummah arrests as a "test case" for the government's proscription policy. According to these officials, the London Metropolitan Police prepared carefully for the protest and meticulously documented their arrests, to make sure they performed their duties legally and above reproach. After all the evidence gathering and police work, however, the Crown Prosecution Service, which has final say on whether criminal cases are prosecuted, was reluctant to pursue charges against activists who appeared to be exercising their democratic rights to free speech and protest.[59] Consequently, the government dropped all the proscription cases from the protest. Only one of the MAC activists arrested at the protest, Afsor Ali, was convicted of a crime, and this was because the police found a copy of al-Qaeda in the Arabian Peninsula's *Inspire* magazine on an MP3 player he was carrying in his pocket. For this Ali was convicted of possessing materials that could be used in a terrorist attack.[60]

---

[58] Interview with veteran activist, Islington, North London, July 21, 2012. Also, interviews with two leading activists, Whitechapel, East London, July 16, 2012, and Leyton, East London, July 17, 2012.
[59] Interview with two London Metropolitan Police officers, Westminster, Central London, July 19, 2012.
[60] *BBC News*, "Afsor Ali found guilty of terror information offences," (August 8, 2014), www.bbc .com/news/uk-england-london-28713336 [Accessed August 9, 2014]; Julian Robinson,

The British government's failure to prosecute any Emigrants for belonging to a banned organization meant that they were free to continue their activism. Months after the United Ummah protest, activists insisted they were carrying on as before, irrespective of the authorities' latest crackdown. "Nothing's changed at all," explained Rohan, who was arrested at the protest. "I mean no matter who you ban, or who you don't ban, every Muslim still has the same duty, so they're going to come out." He continued with an example: "Many people who worked with MAC, they're still giving da'wah, they're still coming out, they're still doing other new activities, like this campaign against prostitution."[61] He was referring to activists' "No To Prostitution" campaign which included a website and nightly foot patrols targeting "kerb crawlers" in East London.[62] "I still have a lot of platforms under which I can function, which have been going on for years," added another leading activist. "The ban's not going to have an impact at all. It's like if somebody said, 'We proscribe the Shariah Court in the UK.' Okay, proscribe it. We will still have many other platforms under which I can function."[63]

The Shariah Project and Need4Khilafah

This was not empty boasting. In the following months and years network activists used a number of different platforms to continue their activism. Two months after the United Ummah protest a small number of activists returned to the American embassy to stage another demonstration against US foreign policy, this one organized under a platform called, innocently enough, the Islamic Observatory Centre.[64] Later that year, another al-Muhajiroun platform with a safe name, the Syria Action Committee, organized a public conference in West Acton and a march for the "children of Syria" to the Syrian embassy near Buckingham Palace.[65]

"'Muslim extremist kept terror tutorials on his MP3 player and made YouTube video warning of attack on William and Kate's wedding'," *Daily Mail* (August 6, 2014), www.dailymail .co.uk/news/article-2717950/Muslim-extremist-kept-terror-tutorials-MP3-player-YouTube-video-warning-attack-William-Kate-s-wedding.html?ITO=1490&ns_mchannel=rss&ns_ campaign=1490 [Accessed August 6, 2014].

[61] Interview with Rohan, Whitechapel, East London, July 16, 2012.

[62] Interviews with leading and rank-and-file activists, Leyton, East London, July 17, 2012, and Islington, North London, July 21, 2012. No To Prostitution, www.notoprostitution.blogspot .co.uk/ [Accessed July 20, 2012]; Daniel Binns, "Campaigners to 'shame' kerb crawlers," *Waltham Forest Guardian* (June 19, 2012), www.guardian-series.co.uk/news/9768051.WALTHAM_ FOREST__Campaigners_to__shame__kerb_crawlers/?ref=mr [Accessed June 25, 2012].

[63] Interview with leading activist, Leyton, East London, July 17, 2012.

[64] Emails from activists, January 18, 2012 and January 20, 2012; Anjem Choudary, Twitter, (January 19, 2012), http://twitter.com/#!/anjemchoudary/statuses/159939818883784704 [Accessed January 20, 2012]; and Weeks, *Radicals and Reactionaries*, p. 245. Also, field notes, Mayfair, Central London, June 17, 2011.

[65] Emails from activists, April 24, 2012 and June 1, 2012; Syria Action Committee, "Syria in Crisis Conference," electronic copy of leaflet (April 24, 2012); Syria Action Committee, "March For

Activists also created a new platform they called The Shariah Project. This grew out of the No To Prostitution campaign, which they considered a success. The Shariah Project focused on, as one leading member put it, "forbidding the evil of man-made law," including alcohol consumption, gambling and prostitution.[66] As part of their anti-alcohol campaign, Anjem Choudary, Siddhartha Dhar, and other activists from The Shariah Project organized a march and rally against liquor sales in Brick Lane, a popular restaurant quarter located in the heart of London's Bangladeshi community in Tower Hamlets.[67] Another well-publicized feature of The Shariah Project was the Muslim Patrols, also called the Shariah Patrols. In this campaign, activists patrolled Walthamstow and Whitechapel at night, distributing leaflets, engaging in da'wah, and, on several occasions, confronting pedestrians whose behavior they judged immoral and un-Islamic.[68]

A leading activist in Muslim Patrols, Abdul Muhid, created another platform he called Muslim Prisoners. The platform's main purpose was to organize letter writing campaigns in support of incarcerated activists and other prisoners convicted of terrorism-related offenses. Muhid, who served a prison sentence for soliciting murder and terrorism fundraising, sometimes used his website to publicize network protests, including one outside Paddington Green Police Station. He and other activists organized this demonstration to protest the "increasing number of Muslim youth being arrested and imprisoned for

Children of Syria," (May 29, 2012), www.youtube.com/watch?v=15TizU8kcNg&feature=plcp [Accessed June 1, 2012].

[66] Interview with leading activist, Ilford, East London, December 9, 2014. Also interviews with leading and rank-and-file activists, Whitechapel, July 16, 2012, and Westminster, Central London, September 6, 2013. The Shariah Project, "Don't Let Alcohol Make You Earn the Curse of Allah!," (September 9, 2013), www.theshariahproject.com/1/post/2013/09/dont-let-alcohol-make-you-earn-the-curse-of-allah.html [Accessed September 17, 2013]; Anjem Choudary, Twitter, September 21, 2013, https://twitter.com/anjemchoudary/status/381457003047948288/photo/1 [Accessed September 4, 2015]; No To Prostitution, www.notoprostitution.blogspot.co.uk/ [Accessed July 20, 2012].

[67] The Shariah Project, press release, "Rally Against Alcohol," (December 13, 2013), www.theshariahproject.com/ [Accessed December 13, 2013]; Adam Barnett, "'Fear Allah', hate preacher Anjem Choudary tells shopkeepers at anti-alcohol march," *East London Advertiser* (December 13, 2013), www.eastlondonadvertiser.co.uk/news/court-crime/video_fear_allah_hate_preacher_anjem_choudary_tells_shopkeepers_at_anti_alcohol_march_1_3111141 [Accessed December 16, 2013]; Trevor Grundy, "British shop owners threatened with 40 lashes for selling alcohol," *Washington Post* (December 16, 2013), www.washingtonpost.com/national/religion/british-shop-owners-threatened-with-40-lashes-for-selling-alcohol--resend/2013/12/16/7b950054-668b-11e3-997b-9213b17dac97_story.html [December 17, 2013].

[68] Interviews with leading activist, Leyton, East London, July 17, 2012, and Ilford, East London, December 9, 2014, the Shariah Project spokesperson, Islington, North London, July 21, 2012 and Skype, June 26, 2013, and another activist, Stratford, East London, December 13, 2014. Also, see Ben Quinn, "'Muslim Patrol' vigilante pleads guilty to assault and threats," *The Guardian* (October 18, 2013), www.theguardian.com/uk-news/2013/oct/18/muslim-patrol-vigilante-guilty-assault [Accessed November 26, 2013].

merely traveling to Syria."[69] The protest was held in January 2014, several months before Abu Bakr al-Baghdadi declared the establishment of the Islamic caliphate in Iraq and Syria, when British authorities were already struggling to stem the flow of young citizens emigrating to the region.

Leading activists also created another platform, Need4Khilafah, which, like Islam4UK and Muslims Against Crusades, specialized in organizing high-profile demonstrations and roadshows.[70] Finally, in response to several violent incidents against British Muslims after the gruesome murder of Lee Rigby by Michael Adebowale and Michael Adebolajo, activists from The Shariah Project created another platform they called Islamic Emergency Defence to protect local Muslims and their property from attacks.[71] Activists often referred to this new platform by its provocative acronym, IED, intended to mimic the abbreviation for "improvised explosive device," which caused so many deaths of British and American troops in Iraq and Afghanistan.

As active as many of these platforms were in the years after the MAC ban, only two – The Shariah Project and Need4Khilafah – were eventually outlawed by the authorities, along with a third spin-off in Cardiff, Wales called the Islamic Da'wah Association. The low number of banned groups reinforced the challenges facing authorities in outlawing specific platforms that organize lawful protest politics. With the addition of these three platforms to the British government's list of proscribed terrorist organizations in June 2014, the network was outlawed under eleven different names.[72] However, as shown in the list of platforms in Table 4.1, many al-Muhajiroun spin-offs have never been banned. In response to the British government's proscription policy, the number of platforms used by activists has grown steadily over the years. In *Radical Islam Rising*, published in 2005, Quintan Wiktorowicz identified fifty former and current al-Muhajiroun

[69] Muslim Prisoners, press release, "Demonstration Against the British Oppression of Muslims!," (January 30, 2014), www.muslimprisoners.com/demostration.html [Accessed February 2, 2014]; email from leading activist, January 31, 2014.

[70] Need4Khilafah, press release, "Demonstration Outside Lebanese Embassy!," (March 31, 2014), www.need4khilafah.com/?p=795 [Accessed March 31, 2014]; Need4Khilafah, press release, "Rally Against British Crusade," (April 17, 2014), www.need4khilafah.com [Accessed April 17, 2014]; Need4Khilafah, press release, "Rally Against the Kufr Saudi Regime," (April 24, 2014), www.need4khilafah.com [Accessed April 24, 2014].

[71] Interview with spokesperson for The Shariah Project, Skype, June 26, 2013. Also, Islamic Emergency Defence, press release, "Islamic Response to Walsall Terror Bomb Plot," www.islamicemergencydefence.com [Accessed June 27, 2013]; Islamic Emergency Defence, IED Official Twitter profile, https://twitter.com/iedefence [Accessed February 23, 2018]; Martin Robinson, "Muslim group backed by hate preacher Anjem Choudary called IED 'mocks Britain's war dead' with its name," *Daily Mail* (June 25, 2013), www.dailymail.co.uk/news/article-2347987/Muslim-group-backed-hate-preacher-Anjem-Choudary-called-IED-mocks-Britain-s-war-dead.html [Accessed June 25, 2013].

[72] James Brokenshire, Immigration and Security Minister, Home Office, "Alternative Names for Proscribed Organisation Al Muhajiroun," (June 26, 2014), www.gov.uk/government/speeches/alternative-names-for-proscribed-organisation-al-muhajiroun [Accessed September 4, 2014]; Home Office, *Proscribed Terrorist Organisations* (March 27, 2015), pp. 5–6.

TABLE 4.1 *Al-Muhajiroun Platforms and Spin-Off Groups*

#No2Democracy Yes2Islam	Defenders of the Prophet	Islamic Verdict Newspaper	Project Dawah
#StayMuslimDontVote	Evil Olympics	Islamic Viewpoint Magazine	Prophet's Ummah (Norway)
1984 Society	Global Issues Society	Islamic World League	Reflect Project
Action Committee against British Terrorism	Global Shariah	Izharudeen	Revolution Muslim (USA)
Ahlus Sunnah wal Jama'ah	Global Tawheed	Jamaat al-Nusra	Sakina Security Services
Al-Ansaa Society	Global Truth	Jama'at al-Tawheed (France)	Salafi Media
Al-Ghurabaa	Greenwich Dawah	Jihad in Manchester	Salafi Youth Movement
Al-Khilafah Movement (also called Khilafah Movement)	Hizb ut Tawhid	Kaldet til Islam (Call to Islam) (Denmark)	**Saved Sect** (also called **Saviour Sect**)
Al-Khilafah Newsletter	Human Society	Kosovo Support Council	**... School of Shariah** groups (5): Derby, **London**, Luton, Sheffield, Walthamstow
Al-Mansoora Youth Organisation	Ilm Centre Studios	Lewisham Islamic Centre	Shariah Court of the UK
Al-Muhajiroun	Info 2000 Software Ltd	London Da'wah	Shari'ah Court, Tripoli, Lebanon
Al-Muhajiroun Community Centre in Luton	Intellectual Society	Luton Islamic Education Centre	Shariah4... groups (20): Andalus (also Spain), America (also USA), Australia, Bangladesh, Belgium, Denmark, Egypt, Finland, France, Germany, Hind (India), Holland, Indonesia, Maldives, Norway, Pakistan, Poland, South Africa, UK, World
Al-Muhajiroun Publications (also called ALM Publications)	Intellectual Thinkers	Maddad (also called al-Maddad Society)	**The Shariah Project**

TABLE 4.1 *(cont.)*

As-Sahwa Magazine	International Islamic Front	Mansoor Media	Slough Islamic Forum
Association for Islamic Research	International Shariah Court	Mujahid Distribution Network	Society of... groups (10): Converts to Islam, Converts to Islamic Freemasons, Juristic Scholars, Muslim Doctors, Muslim Lawyers, Muslim Parents, Muslim Scholars, Muslim Teachers, Muslim Women, Muslim Youth
Association of London Muslims	International Shariah Movement	Muslim Committee	Submit2Allah
Association of Muslim Students	Iqaamah	Muslim Cultural Society	Supporters of... groups (4): Hamas, Sunnah, Taliban, Tawheed
Bureau of Islamic Resources	**Islam4** groups (4): Belgium, Denmark, Ireland, **UK**	Muslim Entrepreneur Foundation	Syria Action Committee
Caliphate Movement	Islamic Advise Bureau	Muslim Media Forum	Syria Against Torture
Call to Submission	Islamic Awareness Society	Muslim Patrols (also called Shariah Patrols)	Tawheed Movement
Call2Islam	Islamic Council of Britain	Muslim Youth Forum	Tayfatul Mansoorah
Call2Tawhid (also called Call2Tawheed)	Islamic Cultural Society	Muslims in the UK	Truth Commission
Captive Support	**Islamic Da'wah Association**	Muslim Prisoners	UKgovexposed
Central London Muslim Association	Islamic Da'wah Foundation	**Muslims Against Crusades**	United Ummah
Centre of Islamic Services	Islamic Emergency Defence	N17 Studios	Voting is Shirk
Chechnya Support Council	Islamic Heritage Society	**Need4Khilafah**	Waltham Forest Muslims
Concerned Muslim Citizens for Justice	Islamic Observatory Centre	One Muslim Ummah	Way for Unity
Convert2Islam	**Islamic Path**	One-to-One Society	West London Islamic Cultural Society
Dawah2Tawheed	Islamic Revolution	Party of the Future	West London Muslim Forum

(continued)

TABLE 4.1 (*cont.*)

Da wah4Sharia	Islamic Society of... groups (18): Birmingham, Bolton & Preston, Bradford & Halifax, Crawley, Derby, Greenwich, Hounslow, Kent, Leeds, Leicester, Luton, Maidenhead, Manchester, Nottingham, Rochdale, Sheffield, Slough, Stoke-on-Trent	Path to Tawheed	Wood Green Dawah
Dawah4Sharia4Women	Islamic Tahreek for Pakistan	Peaceful Society	Woolwich Dawah Network (also called Woolwich Dawah Forum)
Defenders of the Faith	Islamic Thinkers Society (USA)		

Note: Sources for this list include news reports, interviews and field observations, along with Wiktorowicz, *Radical Islam Rising*, p. 121, and Raymond, "Al Muhajiroun and Islam4UK," p. 13. This table includes 181 separate platforms, some of which exist in name only. The eleven platforms that have been outlawed by British authorities are highlighted in **bold**.

platforms and fronts.[73] Table 4.1, based on research extending another decade, lists 181 spin-off groups and platforms network supporters have used to facilitate their activism, within and outside Britain.

As this list demonstrates, the Emigrants are more than capable of creating new spin-off groups and platforms. In coming up with new names, activists are limited only by their imagination, which is to say, not much at all. They also organize protests and da'wah stalls without using names. "We can still carry on and propagate Islam without a name," explains one respondent. "We don't necessarily have to have a name."[74] This has become more common in recent years, as activists face more pressure from law enforcers. They now frequently engage in da'wah without using banners that publicize their platforms. In a separate interview, several months after the latest ban – and ten years to the day after Omar Bakri announced the end of al-Muhajiroun, a leading network activist remarked, "They keep banning us and proscribing us and

---

[73] Wiktorowicz, *Radical Islam Rising*, p. 121.
[74] Interview with veteran activist, Whitechapel, November 9, 2010.

we pop up again."[75] Creating new spin-off groups and platforms has allowed the Emigrants to pop up again and again, demonstrating their resilience and resourcefulness.

GOING GLOBAL: THE SHARIAH4 PHENOMENON

The majority of al-Muhajiroun's activism takes place within Britain, but over the years numerous spin-off groups have appeared in different countries, adding a transnational dimension to the network's activism. Activists have tried to connect with supporters in other countries, both as a response to law enforcement pressure in Britain and as part of their strategy to establish the Emigrants as a leader of the Salafi-jihadi movement in Europe. "You can't just work in the UK," explains a leading activist. "You need to establish a fifth column in Europe. The Muslims in Europe need to be one unified body putting pressure on European governments to say 'you cannot mess with the Muslims.'"[76] Some respondents insist that repression from the authorities in Britain, including proscription, has enhanced their standing among young Muslims in Europe and elsewhere. This helped them create spin-off groups in these countries. In making this point, a veteran activist unintentionally echoes a larger critique of the government's proscription policy, that it increases the profile and legitimacy of banned organizations.[77] "One of the best things the British government did was to ban al-Muhajiroun, Islam4UK, and all of those other organizations," he explains. "Because now we're more prominent and our message is brighter in the eyes of the Muslim youth. It gives us more credibility."[78]

Activists have leveraged their credibility to inspire supporters from other countries to model their activism after the Emigrants. The main vehicle for this expansion was the "Shariah4" movement through which activists in different countries formed their own groups modeled on al-Muhajiroun's Shariah4UK platform. The same veteran activist discusses several of these groups, highlighting their connection to the government's proscription policy: "Since the banning of Islam4UK you've got Shariah4UK, Shariah4Belgium, Shariah4Australia. That never would have happened without proscription."[79] In a separate interview he adds, "They're banning organizations but it's very counter-productive. Many organizations have popped up. Shariah4Belgium, Shariah4France,

---

[75] Interview with leading activist, Skype, October 8, 2014.

[76] Interview with leading activist, Ilford, East London, November 13, 2010. Also, interviews with veteran activist, Leyton, East London, November 6, 2010, and think tank researcher, Islington, North London, December 6, 2010.

[77] Legrand and Jarvis, "Enemies of the State," p. 465.

[78] Interview with veteran activist, Southall, West London, June 28, 2011.

[79] Interview with veteran activist, Southall, West London, June 28, 2011. Also, interview with leading activist, Whitechapel, East London, September 4, 2013.

Shariah4Holland, Shariah4Australia. Where are they being inspired from? The da'wah of Londonistan."[80]

Among the Shariah4 platforms in Europe, none was as inspired by al-Muhajiroun as Shariah4Belgium. In March 2010, several weeks after Islam4UK was banned by British authorities, a petty criminal-turned-militant preacher named Fouad Belkacem visited Choudary in London to ask for his help in starting an activist group. "I went through the history of al-Muhajiroun, how we set it up," Choudary later told a journalist.[81] Belkacem acknowledged that he and his followers saw themselves as following in Islam4UK's footsteps: "We were inspired by this type of movement which seemed to work well in the UK. Our acts of provocation were meant to raise awareness of certain problems ingrained in our society."[82] Choudary was soon lecturing the group on PalTalk, an online chatroom network activists have used for years. He and Belkacem also set up an informal exchange program. Choudary sent several of his followers to Belgium to advise Belkacem and his supporters, while Belkacem sent some of his students to Britain to study with Choudary.[83]

Belkacem and his followers proved to be fast learners. Shariah4Belgium modeled its inflammatory activism after the Emigrants, organizing da'wah stalls and protests in Antwerp, Brussels, and smaller Belgian towns. Also like their British counterparts, they posted videos online showcasing their activism and lectures, many of them delivered by Belkacem. In one demonstration to mark the anniversary of 9/11, the Belgian spin-off borrowed a page from al-Muhajiroun's repertoire of contentious activism by burning a replica of the American flag. At another protest, Shariah4Belgium activists scuffled with the police after a woman was reportedly manhandled by local authorities who were trying to arrest her for wearing a veil in public. They also collaborated with Choudary and Dutch activists to form another al-Muhajiroun spin-off, Shariah4Holland.[84]

---

[80] Interview with veteran activist, Wembley Central, West London, June 25, 2011.

[81] Ben Taub, "Journey to Jihad: Why are teen-agers joining ISIS?," *The New Yorker* (June 1, 2015), www.newyorker.com/magazine/2015/06/01/journey-to-jihad [Accessed May 26, 2015]; Andrew Higgins, "Head of Belgian group said to recruit fighters for Syria gets 12-year term," *New York Times* (February 11, 2015), www.nytimes.com/2015/02/12/world/europe/fouad-belkacem-sharia4belgium-verdict-trial-belgium.html [Accessed September 22, 2015]; Lorenzo Vidino, "Sharia4: From Confrontational Activism to Militancy," *Perspectives on Terrorism* 9, no. 2 (April 2015), pp. 2–16; and Assaf Moghadam, *Nexus of Global Jihad: Understanding Cooperation among Terrorist Actors* (New York: Columbia University Press, 2017).

[82] *The Brussels Times*, "Sharia4Belgium–'I do not run an agency dispatching fighters to Syria'," (October 14, 2015), http://brusselstimes.com/rss-feed/4279/sharia4belgium-i-do-not-run-an-agency-dispatching-fighters-to-syria [Accessed October 16, 2015].

[83] Taub, "Journey to Jihad."

[84] Taub, "Journey to Jihad"; Marco Hochgemuth, "Shariah4Holland: Kids' gang or terror threat?," *Radio Netherlands Worldwide* (May 24, 2012), www.rnw.nl/english/article/shariah4holland-kids-gang-or-terror-threat [Accessed May 24, 2012]; and Vidino, "Sharia4," p. 6.

After Belgian authorities cracked down on the group and jailed Fouad Belkacem for inciting hatred against non-Muslims in 2012, Shariah4Belgium activists began making their way to Syria. The first to go were several core activists who connected with local fighters in Syria. Once they were established in Syria, these Shariah4Belgium activists recruited their friends and supporters, who, in turn, recruited their own contacts. In this way, activists exploited their social networks to mobilize a growing number of Belgians to fight in Syria. By October 2012, Shariah4Belgium was officially dissolved, and the pipeline to Syria, grounded in activists' social ties, was firmly established. The Shariah4 pipeline contributed to Belgium's unwelcome status as the highest per capita contributor of Western European fighters to the conflict.[85] Over the next eighteen months approximately fifty activists and affiliates from the group traveled to the war-torn country, where most of them joined ISIS or al-Qaeda's Syrian franchise, Jabhat al-Nusra. When a Belgian court convicted forty-five members of Shariah4Belgium of belonging to a terrorist group in February 2015, only seven defendants, including Belkacem, were still in Belgium. The others, found guilty in absentia, were believed to be fighting for the Islamic State and other militant groups – or to have died while doing so.[86]

Not all of al-Muhajiroun's international spin-offs were as "successful" as Shariah4Belgium. Some platforms, such as Shariah4America, Shariah4Hind, and Shariah4Pakistan, had little substance beyond flashy websites that spread the Emigrants' Salafi-Islamist ideology. Other groups, including Shariah4Andalus, Shariah4Bangladesh, Shariah4Egypt, Shariah4Finland, Shariah4Hind, and Shariah4Pakistan, were actually created by network activists in London. Others, such as Shariah4America, Shariah4Australia, Shariah4Holland, Shariah4Italy, Jama'at al-Tawheed (France), Kaldet til Islam (Denmark), and Prophet's Ummah (Norway), and Revolution Muslim (United States) were run by local activists.[87] Irrespective of whether they were directed by al-Muhajiroun activists or simply inspired by them, none of these platforms

---

[85] Peter R. Neumann, "Foreign fighter total in Syria/Iraq now exceeds 20,000; surpasses Afghanistan conflict in the 1980s," *ICSR Insight* (January 26, 2015), http://icsr.info/2015/01/foreign-fighter-total-syriairaq-now-exceeds-20000-surpasses-afghanistan-conflict-1980s/ [Accessed June 18, 2015].

[86] Vidino, "Sharia4," p. 10; Taub, "Journey to Jihad"; *BBC News*, "Sharia4Belgium trial: Belgian court jails members," (February 11, 2015), www.bbc.com/news/world-europe-31378724 [Accessed April 6, 2015]; and Higgins, "Head of Belgian group said to recruit fighters for Syria gets 12-year term."

[87] Interviews with activists, Whitechapel, East London, November 9, 2010, September 4, 2013, and December 14, 2014, and Southall, West London, June 28, 2011; interview with London Metropolitan Police officer, Westminster, Central London, June 29, 2011. Also, see Nick Lowles and Joe Mulhall, *Gateway to Terror: Anjem Choudary and the al-Muhajiroun Network* (London: Hope not hate, 2013), pp. 36–7; R. Green, "Shari'a Movement Struggles to Globalize Campaign for Islamizing Western World," Middle East Media Research Institute, *Inquiry &*

received significant support from Muslims in their home countries, nor, beyond hosting a provocative demonstration or two, were they capable of sustained activism. Many of the platforms disbanded well before the Emigrants succeeded in establishing their desired fifth column in Europe. But the transnational scope of Anjem Choudary's influence was brought into sharp relief after several spin-off groups, Shariah4Belgium, Shariah4Holland, Jama'at al-Tawheed, Kaldet til Islam, and Prophet's Ummah, were implicated in sending fighters to Syria and other conflict zones.[88]

The Emigrants were eager to take credit for their foreign colleagues' escalation from jihad of the tongue to jihad of the sword, at least before their own support of the Islamic State in Iraq and Syria in 2014 led to another British government crackdown. "By the grace of Allah, our own effort has produced results which have ricocheted around the world," crowed a leading activist, eight months before Abu Bakr al-Baghdadi declared the caliphate. "There are many people, from Bangladesh, from Belgium, from Denmark, who have more or less disappeared into Syria. All of the people that we used to be associated with, they're all now fighting on the front-line in those places."[89] Highlighting al-Muhajiroun's influence on their radicalization into political violence, he continues: "These people started off secular, integrated into Belgian and Holland societies. But they came across us and they became mature in their understanding of the shariah and Islam and the sunnah, and they decided that what we were calling for here, the domination of Islam within Europe, they're going to go and actually fight for in Syria, Afghanistan, and many other places. They decided to do the ultimate sacrifice, to give their lives for their beliefs."[90]

Analysis Series Report No. 723 (August 2011), www.memri.org/report/en/print5565.htm [Accessed November 9, 2011]; and Jesse Morton and Mitchell Silber, "NYPD vs. Revolution Muslim: The Inside Story of the Defeat of a Local Radicalization Hub," *CTC Sentinel* (April 2018), pp. 1–7.

88 Karla Adams, "Britain's anti-terror strategy tested by move against prominent preacher," *Washington Post* (August 5, 2015), www.washingtonpost.com/world/europe/britains-new-anti-terror-policy-tested-by-move-against-prominent-preacher/2015/08/05/fba962e0-3b72-11e5-b34f-4e0a1e3a3bf9_story.html [Accessed August 6, 2015]; Gordon Corera, "Is preacher Anjem Choudary a radicalising force?," *BBC News* (May 14, 2015), www.bbc.com/news/uk-32732124 [Accessed September 24, 2015]; Lisa Lundquist, "Danish Salafist leader said to have been killed in Syria," *Long War Journal* (October 4, 2013), www.longwarjournal.org/archives/2013/10/_shiraz_tariq_left_a.php [Accessed August 1, 2014]; Dominik Lemanski and Neil Doyle, "New links found between ISIS fighters and preacher Anjem Choudary," *Daily Star* (June 15, 2014), www.dailystar.co.uk/news/latest-news/383905/New-links-found-between-Isis-fighters-and-preacher-Anjem-Choudary [Accessed June 20, 2014].

89 Interview with leading activist, Whitechapel, East London, September 4, 2013.

90 Interview with leading activist, Whitechapel, East London, September 4, 2013. Also, interviews with two other activists, Whitechapel, East London, November 9, 2010.

If creating new spin-off groups within and beyond Britain is one of al-Muhajiroun's most consequential adaptations, it is not the only one. Another way activists have demonstrated their resilience is by adapting their da'wah stalls, moving them to avoid police pressure and making them less provocative and political over time.

ADAPTABLE DA'WAH

Street preaching has been a cornerstone of the Emigrants' activism since the network was first formed in 1996. "Da'wah is their bread and butter," explains an officer from the London Metropolitan Police.[91] Calling people to Islam allows activists to spread their interpretation of the faith. They consider this an essential duty, one that is commanded by God and rewarded in the afterlife. As I discussed in Chapter 2, da'wah stalls also provide activists the opportunity to recruit new members and build their network. Activists reach out to potential recruits by holding stalls and larger roadshows in different neighborhoods within and outside London.

Given the importance of public preaching for their activism, it is not surprising that network activists have adapted their da'wah in response to pressure. In *Radical Islam Rising*, based on field work he carried out in 2002, Quintan Wiktorowicz describes the typical al-Muhajiroun stall as a "miniprotest" in which activists shout offensive language at passersby and show gruesome photos of mutilated bodies they claim are Muslim victims of Western and Israeli aggression.[92] Similarly, Ali, one of the former activists I interviewed, remembers how during the British and American airstrikes against Iraq in December 1998 he and his colleagues displayed provocative photos at their stalls showing bombing victims, including "pictures of innocent people and babies, brothers and sisters getting bombed every day." "It's like publicity, or a selling point," he adds. "To attract attention."[93] Abdul, another former activist, recalls how network leaders encouraged him and other rank-and-file activists to act out on the stalls. "They used to preach being aggressive," he explains. "We used to shout and be very aggressive. There were always arguments. It was just adrenaline all the time."[94]

As Ali and Abdul suggest, the purpose of these aggressive displays was to call attention to their activism by provoking "moral shock" and outrage among pedestrians and sympathy from potential supporters.[95] But the displays

---

[91] Interview with London Metropolitan Police officer, Westminster, Central London, June 29, 2011.

[92] Wiktorowicz, *Radical Islam Rising*, p. 68.

[93] Interview with Ali, Hounslow, West London, December 13, 2010.

[94] Interview with Abdul, Whitechapel, East London, June 18, 2011.

[95] Interviews with Ali, Hounslow, West London, December 13, 2010, and Abdul, Whitechapel, East London, June 18, 2011. Also, see Wiktorowicz, *Radical Islam Rising*, p. 68. For more on using moral shock to stimulate participation in high-risk activism, see James M. Jasper

also led to frequent confrontations with law enforcers who were policing the stalls, or who arrived after receiving disturbing the peace complaints. Activists typically responded by arguing with the police, insisting that they were merely expressing their "free speech" and showing how Muslims were mistreated throughout the world. Sometimes these arguments escalated into fights and arrests, especially when activists refused to comply with police demands to remove their most grisly images. Ali reminisces about one such incident he saw first-hand, "Outside the Southall roadway, in midday. They had a proper fist fight with the police."[96]

The da'wah stalls and roadshows I observed during my own field work around London between 2010 and 2015 were different. To be sure, on more than one occasion I saw activists push and shout at passersby they felt were disrespecting them. In general, however, the public preaching I witnessed in Hounslow, Ilford, Islington, Lewisham, Stratford, Tottenham, and Wembley was low-key, at least in comparison to the earlier scenes described by Wiktorowicz and my respondents. At stalls I attended, activists typically stood around one or more tables handing out leaflets and interacting with the few people who stopped to talk with them. These discussions typically centered on existential questions and religious issues rather than politics. Some da'wah stalls had banners bearing the name of the spin-off group running the stall, such as Supporters of Sunnah. Other banners displayed provocative slogans, like "Jesus was a Muslim." Posters, if they were displayed at all, addressed matters of religious doctrine ("Islam: the Way of God") or politics ("6 Reasons Why the Rulers are Kuffar").[97] In all the stalls and roadshows I visited, I never saw photos of atrocities and other appalling images designed to shock pedestrians.

When I asked them about the lack of atrocity photos and political banners at their da'wah stalls, several respondents admitted that this was a tactical change in their activism. They also conceded that this change was a direct result of police pressure. After recalling his arrest at a stall in 2003 for holding a placard calling Israel and the United States "The Nazis of Today," the veteran activist Ahmed, who later left Britain to join the Islamic State in Iraq and Syria, agreed that recent stalls were less provocative: "That's a very good point. The government clamped down very, very hard on us."[98] Rather than risking

and Jane Poulsen, "Recruiting Strangers and Friends: Moral Shocks and Social Networks in Animal Rights and Antinuclear Protest" *Social Problems* 42 (November 1995), pp. 493–512; and Quintan Wiktorowicz and Karl Kaltenthaler, "The Rationality of Radical Islam," *Political Science Quarterly* 121, no. 2 (2006), pp. 295–319.

[96] Interview with Ali, Hounslow, West London, June 21, 2011, and interviews with Abdul, Whitechapel, East London, June 18, 2011, and Maryam, former female activist, Hounslow, West London, June 21, 2011. Also, see Wiktorowicz, *Radical Islam Rising*, pp. 68–69, and Wiktorowicz and Kaltenthaler, "The Rationality of Radical Islam," pp. 308–9.

[97] Field notes and photos, al-Muhajiroun da'wah stalls, Wembley Central, West London, June 25, 2011, and Islington, North London, July 21, 2012.

[98] Interview with Ahmed, Tottenham, North London, December 4, 2010.

confrontations with the police and ending their da'wah stalls before they could communicate their message, activists decided they were better off removing the images that led to so many public disorder complaints.

"It's true da'wah stalls have changed," admits another respondent, "not significantly but marginally." Like Ahmed, he is clear on the cause: "The reason why it has changed is because there's so much law enforcement out there regulating what's being said. For us to shout out against the foreign policies of this land, for us to shout out against the culture and system of this land, they just don't like it."[99] "The reason why all the graphic pictures stopped at the stalls is because the government came down hard on the Muslims for doing stuff like that," adds a third activist, who was running a Supporters of Sunnah stall in Stratford while we talked. Emphasizing the connection between this change and police pressure, he adds, "People were stopped and searched just for having the pictures of babies being killed in Palestine."[100]

Activists refuse to be intimidated by such pressure. Rather than stopping their da'wah, they respond to it by making tactical changes. These adaptations are small and simple, but they allow them to avoid the brunt of law enforcement pressure, while continuing their activism. Activists are highly motivated to adapt their da'wah, as long as it remains true to their understanding of God's commands. As intellectual affiliates in al-Muhajiroun's community of practice they feel divinely obligated to call society to Islam, irrespective of any hardship they might experience. "You accommodate your call to fit your environment," explains a leading activist, who served several years in prison for an inflammatory speech he made at one protest, only to continue his activism once he was released. "Now that doesn't mean compromising your call, but it can be tailored to fit your environment. You need to really tailor your message. We can pass our message within the boundary of the law without a problem."[101]

"Our approach has become a little... I wouldn't say compromised, just different," adds Ahmed, explaining his group's activism at a da'wah stall I observed in Tottenham, North London. "We are adapting to the circumstances we've been put in."[102] Adapting to the circumstances they've been put in has meant avoiding the use of violent imagery at stalls and coming up with innovative ways to capture the attention of busy pedestrians. These include putting a protestor on top of a makeshift scaffold near the Israeli embassy, as I discussed

---

[99] Interview with rank-and-file activist, Bethnal Green, East London, December 5, 2010.
[100] Interview with veteran activist, Stratford, East London, December 6, 2010.
[101] Interview with leading activist, Leyton, East London, November 8, 2010. Other respondents made this point as well. Interviews with leading, veteran and rank-and-file activists: Leyton, East London, November 6, 2010, Walthamstow, East London, December 2, 2010, Tottenham, North London, December 4, 2010, Lewisham, South London, December 11, 2010 and June 18, 2011, Stratford, East London, June 25, 2011, and Hounslow, West London, June 28, 2011.
[102] Interview with Ahmed, Tottenham, North London, December 4, 2010.

FIGURE 4.2 Al-Muhajiroun activists drive rental van with loudspeakers tied down on roof during Islamic roadshow in Wembley Central.
Photograph by Michael Kenney.

in the last chapter, or strapping loudspeakers to the roof of a rental van and driving it up and down the High Road in Wembley, calling people to their interpretation of Islam (see Figure 4.2).[103]

Activists have also adapted to police pressure by moving their da'wah stalls to different locations within and outside London. When the police make them feel unwelcome in certain areas, such as the high streets in Ilford, Whitechapel or Walthamstow, activists simply move their stalls to other areas with less pressure. "We used to have a da'wah stall right there," explains a leading activist, pointing to the main square in Walthamstow. "They banned us in this area, but the UK is big enough for us. If they don't allow us here, we go further down the road. We won't stop. They ban us from here, we move to another area."[104] Another leading activist describes the police pressure that compelled his halaqah to move their regular da'wah stall from Ilford: "We're dealing with local authorities here. A week after you came, they said, 'We're going to question you under the terrorism law, blah, blah, blah,' that kind of thing. They said to us, 'Don't come back here again.'"[105] After moving their stall to

[103] Field notes and photos from Islamic roadshow in Wembley Central, West London, June 25, 2011.
[104] Interview with leading activist, Walthamstow, East London, June 22, 2011. Also, email from Douglas Weeks, researcher on al-Muhajiroun, June 26, 2012.
[105] Interview with leading activist, Ilford, East London, November 29, 2010.

other locations around London for a few weeks, the leading activist and his colleagues returned to their old spot in Ilford, which they liked because of the steady stream of Saturday afternoon shoppers.

In addition to rotating their stalls among different London neighborhoods, including Hounslow, Ilford, Lewisham, Oxford Street, Shepherd's Bush, Stratford, Walthamstow, and Whitechapel, activists have set up da'wah stalls outside the capital. "The whole world is like a big da'wah stall for us to spread and propagate Islam," explains one activist. Describing how he and his colleagues moved their da'wah beyond London to Oxford, Brighton, and Weymouth, he continues: "We don't necessarily just stick to one location. It's good to spread around. You meet new people and your message is spread as far."[106]

Activists have also responded to police pressure by making their stalls less provocative, while emphasizing the religious nature of their da'wah. Rather than buttonholing pedestrians over political issues, they focus their initial da'wah on existential questions, such as the origin of life, and spiritual matters, like the meaning of tawheed or monotheism in Islam. At some stalls, activists have even taken to handing out free copies of the Qur'an, a common practice among quietist groups that perform da'wah in London.[107] This was not something Quintan Wiktorowicz described in his field work in 2002, nor did I see it myself during the first years of my field work, between 2010 and 2012. When I asked respondents back then why activists did not hand out Qur'ans, they jeered at the idea, saying it wasn't how they propagated Islam. "No, we don't give copies of the Qur'an," scoffed Ali, the former activist. "We don't and we never did. Our objective was not to give copies of the Qur'an. It was to establish the khilafah [caliphate]. Our da'wah stall was different from other Islamic groups, where they give you a copy of the Qur'an."[108]

By the fall of 2013 these dismissive attitudes had given way to a practical desire for al-Muhajiroun's stalls to resemble those organized by quietist groups. Such stalls can be found throughout London and often feature apolitical proselytizers or da'is handing out free copies of the Qur'an. These stalls attract far less attention from bystanders and the police, allowing dai's to engage in da'wah relatively unmolested.

One network stall I visited in Stratford in December 2014 epitomized the shift in the Emigrants' public preaching. The timing of the stall was significant. It occurred several months after counter-terrorism police rounded up the

---

[106] Interview with rank-and-file activist at da'wah stall, Tottenham, North London, December 4, 2010.

[107] Field notes, da'wah stalls in Hounslow, West London, September 4, 2013, and Wembley Central, West London, September 5, 2013; interview with rank-and-file activist, Hounslow, West London, September 4, 2013. Also, Muslim Prisoners, "Innocent man was attacked by cops..." (September 24, 2013), https://twitter.com/MuslimPrisoners/status/382424487146180608/photo/1 [Accessed October 26, 2017].

[108] Interview with Ali, Hounslow, West London, December 13, 2010.

leaders of al-Muhajiroun for allegedly supporting the Islamic State in Iraq and Syria. Many of these activists remained under restrictive bail conditions at the time and the network faced intense pressure as the authorities continued their investigation into several leading activists.[109] As hundreds of pedestrians and Christmas shoppers entered and exited a nearby shopping mall, nine activists handed out flyers bearing the title, "Jesus (Peace Be Upon Him) The Prophet of Allah." Unlike some stalls I attended, activists did not set up a table with literature, but they did display a sign announcing, "Islam The Way of God." They also set up a loudspeaker, which a leading activist used to invite people to Islam and explain the reasons for their preaching, rather than shout offensive slogans at passersby. They did not show any atrocity photos, nor was there any political edge to their da'wah. The vast majority of shoppers walked by, politely ignoring activists' outstretched hands holding the flyers. When pedestrians did stop to talk, activists asked them about their religious beliefs. Pedestrians' responses shaped the flow of the conversations, which focused on spiritual matters rather than world politics or the West's perceived oppression of Muslims. It was a decidedly low-key affair, one that was largely identical to other da'wah stalls carried out by quietist groups throughout Britain that afternoon.[110]

In making their stalls less distinctive and more discreet, al-Muhajiroun activists were motivated by their desire to respond to law enforcement pressure, rather than by competition with quietist Muslims. The main threat to their activism came from the police, not other proselytizing groups. The Emigrants were trying to continue their da'wah and recruit new supporters even as the authorities outlawed their spin-off groups and arrested their leaders for different offenses. The shift to lower profile stalls did not represent any change in al-Muhajiroun's ideology or strategy of activism. Activists continued to follow Omar Bakri's Salafi-Islamist worldview and they continued to engage in hisbah, organizing political demonstrations where they chanted angry slogans and waved offensive signs. However, they also understood the difference between commanding good and forbidding evil, which calls for agitation, and calling people to Islam, which does not. The da'wah stalls that I visited from September 2013 onward consistently emphasized religious themes over political ones, demonstrating activists' flexibility and resilience.

---

[109] Field notes, Stratford, East London, December 13, 2014. Also see Vikram Dodd and Josh Halliday, "Anjem Choudary among nine arrested in London anti-terrorism raid," *The Guardian* (September 25, 2014), www.theguardian.com/uk-news/2014/sep/25/nine-arrested-london-anti-terrorism [Accessed September 25, 2014]; Dominic Casciani, "Anjem Choudary held in London Terror Raids," *BBC News* (September 25, 2014), www.bbc.com/news/uk-england-29358758 [Accessed September 25, 2014]; and David Barrett and Nicola Harley, "Anjem Choudary among nine men arrested by counter-terror police," *Daily Telegraph* (September 25, 2014), www.telegraph.co.uk/news/uknews/terrorism-in-the-uk/11120438/Anjem-Choudary-among-nine-men-arrested-by-counter-terror-police.html [Accessed September 25, 2014].

[110] Field notes, Stratford, East London, December 13, 2014.

CHANGING VENUES AND MIGRATING TO THE INTERNET

Daʿwah stalls are not the only thing al-Muhajiroun has changed in response to state pressure. In recent years activists have found it harder to book halls for their public talks and conferences, forcing them to seek alternative venues. "It is very difficult to book venues now, community centers, mosques, local authority venues," said Anjem Choudary as early as 2002, in an interview with Quintan Wiktorowicz. "They know that you are from al-Muhajiroun coming to book a venue. They are not going to have you there."[111] Choudary was referring to the period immediately after 9/11, but securing venues for public talks has continued to be a challenge for activists since then. I discussed one example in the last chapter, when activists were forced to cancel their "International Islamic Revival Conference" in November 2010, after losing access to different venues they reserved in East London. "They've had a real problem booking event halls," confirms the research director of a British think tank, contrasting the network's current difficulties with its pre-9/11 years, when Choudary and Omar Bakri regularly delivered talks at mosques within and outside London.[112] "Al-Muhajiroun's ability to book venues is very limited now," adds an American official based in London. "This hampers their ability to communicate their message and recruit new followers."[113]

Activists agree. When asked if booking venues remained a problem after the government banned Muslims Against Crusades, Rohan replied curtly, "it's still a problem."[114] Another leading activist complained of the difficulties he and his colleagues faced when trying to reserve venues for their talks. "They would start asking me *so* many questions, 'Who are you? What's it for? Is it an Islamic organization? Is the talk Islamic?' Everything is focused towards the Islamic side of things."[115]

As mentioned in the last chapter, government authorities sometimes pressure the people who run local venues to avoid renting space to individuals and groups that are affiliated with al-Muhajiroun. I interviewed two London businessmen who hosted network events at their halls to learn more about this. Both respondents acknowledged that government officials spoke with them about their halls being used by activists. "The local authority and the police sat down with us and said, 'Look, don't let them use the premises,'" recalls one respondent, who ran a hall in the northeast London borough

[111] Wiktorowicz, *Radical Islam Rising*, p. 120.
[112] Interview with research director, think tank, Bloomsbury, Central London, December 14, 2010.
[113] Interview with US government official, Mayfair, Central London, December 3, 2010.
[114] Interview with Rohan, Whitechapel, East London, July 16, 2012. Also, interview with veteran activist, Southall, West London, June 28, 2011.
[115] Interview with leading activist, Walthamstow, East London, June 22, 2011.

of Waltham Forest. "And we agreed. They stopped them from using other venues as well."[116]

Activists have adapted to this in a number of ways. When reserving halls, they mislead proprietors by using the names of lesser known spin-off groups or innocuous-sounding platforms. To guard against the possibility of a last-minute cancellation by venue managers who face pressure from the authorities, they reserve a second hall as a backup location for the event. When activists fear their primary and secondary bookings may be cancelled, they publicize the talk or conference but not its location, waiting until the day of the event to tell the general public, and even their own followers, where to go. When planning to hold their event at a private venue, they ask their supporters to gather at one location, such as a restaurant or the entrance to a London Underground station, before proceeding together to the location.[117]

When these precautions prove insufficient, as they sometimes do, activists move their talks to public parks, the private homes of their supporters, or smaller venues they control. The latter include space in office buildings activists have leased through separate companies, some of which were owned by Anjem Choudary's older brother, Yazdani, a prominent local businessman.[118] At these venues, including the Centre for Islamic Services and the Ilm Centre, both in Whitechapel, and the Bureau of Islamic Resources, in Lewisham, activists gathered in small groups to hang out and hear talks by network preachers.[119]

Moving their talks into private homes and centers has allowed activists to gather and indoctrinate each other in small group settings, but these venues do not have the seating capacity to host large groups of people. This has

---

[116] Interview with businessman and community activist, Walthamstow, East London, December 16, 2010. Also, interviews with businessman, Whitechapel, East London, December 1, 2010, and leading activist, Ilford, East London, November 29, 2010.

[117] Interviews with Salman, Bethnal Green, East London, November 28, 2010, veteran activist, Southall, West London, June 28, 2011, and Rohan, Whitechapel, East London, July 16, 2012, research director, think tank, Bloomsbury, Central London, December 14, 2010, and two London Metropolitan Police officers, Westminster, Central London, June 29, 2011. Also, see Wiktorowicz, *Radical Islam Rising*, p. 120.

[118] Interviews with Salman, Bethnal Green, East London, November 28, 2010, leading activist, Walthamstow, East London, June 22, 2011, and London Metropolitan Police officer, Westminster, Central London, June 29, 2011. Also, see Ted Jeory, "Islamic preacher Choudary peddles hatred from a sweet shop," *Sunday Express* (May 26, 2013), www.express.co.uk/news/uk/402663/Islamic-preacher-Choudary-peddles-hatred-from-a-sweet-shop [Accessed June 10, 2013]; and Yazdani Choudary, *LinkedIn* profile page, www.linkedin.com/pub/yazdani-choudary/33/271/440 [Accessed August 1, 2014].

[119] Field notes, Whitechapel, East London, December 16, 2010, June 16, 2011, June 23, 2011, and July 24, 2015; Lewisham, South London, June 23, 2011, and July 18, 2012; interviews with leading and rank-and-file activists, Ilford, East London, November 13, 2010, Lewisham, South London, June 18, 2011, Walthamstow, East London, June 22, 2011, Haroon, former contact, Westminster, Central London, June 14, 2011, and two London Metropolitan Police officers, Westminster, Central London, June 29, 2011. Also, see Ted Jeory, "Muslim hate cleric targets

made it harder for them to attract new supporters through public conferences, making their street da'wah even more important for recruitment. Activists have responded to the loss of large halls by recording their lectures and private conferences and uploading them to different websites, where they are shared with the wider public. A veteran activist with considerable experience recording lectures and posting them online highlights the popularity of these sites: "Our websites, such as Salafi Media and Izharudeen, are receiving many hits each day, and that's globally. So we don't get upset because we lost one community hall. We go to the park and we have a little conference there with about ten brothers and after uploading the conference video we reach all the way to Australia the next morning."[120] Of course, it is harder to attract potential recruits from Australia or Bangladesh when they can't attend next week's halaqah in Hounslow or Whitechapel.

Al-Muhajiroun was an early adopter of online communication and activists have been using the Internet for years. Many of the more prominent spin-offs, including al-Ghurabaa, the Saved Sect, Islam4UK, Muslims Against Crusades, Need4Khilafah, and The Shariah Project, had their own websites. Activists used these sites to issue press releases addressing current events, post videos of recent talks and da'wah stalls, and announce upcoming conferences and demonstrations. When British authorities outlawed individual spin-off groups, activists shut down their accompanying websites and replaced them with different sites affiliated with new platforms. Other sites that were independent of banned spin-off groups lasted longer, but were not immune to disruption, including from private hackers who targeted them for cyber-attacks. One private hacker, who went by the online pseudonym, "Jester," took down Anjem Choudary's website shortly after he admitted to reporters that Lee Rigby's killer, Michael Adebolajo, had participated in network events.[121]

By the summer of 2013, many al-Muhajiroun websites I visited regularly during the first years of my field work, including salafimedia.com, izharudeen.com, and anjemchoudary.com were no longer running. When I asked a leading activist about this, he acknowledged that the websites' disappearance was largely due to external pressure. But he also suggested that new sites were being created to replace the old ones. "You have a different website. You have

Kate Middleton's and Prince Williams's big day," *Daily Express* (April 17, 2011), www.express.co.uk/posts/view/241205/Muslim-hate-cleric-targets-Kate-Middleton-s-and-Prince-Williams-big-day [Accessed April 17, 2011]; and Jeory, "Victory as hate group is raided," *Sunday Express* (November 13, 2011), p. 12.

120 Interview with veteran activist, Southall, West London, June 28, 2011. Interview with same activist, Wembley, West London, June 25, 2011.

121 Michael Moynihan, "Hackers are everywhere," *Newsweek* and *The Daily Beast* (May 29, 2013), www.thedailybeast.com/newsweek/2013/05/29/hackers-are-spying-on-you-inside-the-world-of-digital-espionage.html [Accessed June 27, 2013].

a different name. Sometimes you just need to stay one step ahead of the law. It could be that they've been taken down and changed to new sites."[122]

In fact, new sites affiliated with network activists continued to appear, including muslimprisoners.com, iqaamah.co.uk, and ilm-centre.co.uk. But in recent years activists have shifted away from static websites, which are vulnerable to hacking and disruption, and embraced social media. Sounding like a Silicon Valley entrepreneur, one leading activist who maintained a popular website described his own turn to social media: "With the arrival of Twitter, the website has become a bit redundant because when you are on Twitter you get fresh information faster than being uploaded on the website."[123] He and other activists have essentially abandoned their old websites to focus their online da'wah on social media, which allows for more interaction with their followers. Until recently, numerous activists had their own Twitter accounts, Facebook pages, and YouTube channels.[124] Activists used these platforms the same way they used their websites: to announce upcoming events, post their latest videos, and communicate with their followers. In 2016 many of these social media accounts were deleted by their host companies following the convictions of activists for supporting the Islamic State in Iraq and Syria and other criminal offenses. However new sites featuring different activists continued to pop up, even as I made the final revisions to this book.[125]

Another important online tool for network activists was PalTalk. In the last chapter I described how a number of Omar Bakri's students replaced him as the day-to-day leaders of al-Muhajiroun after he left Britain. Also easing the pain of Bakri's departure was PalTalk, an online chatroom utility popular among activists.[126] From his new home in Tripoli, Lebanon, Bakri regularly logged onto PalTalk to lecture his British students and answer their questions. Activists also used Skype and other online tools to communicate with "Sheikh Omar" and pipe

[122] Interview with leading activist, Skype, June 26, 2013.

[123] Interview with leading activist, Wembley, West London, September 5, 2013.

[124] Examples include, but are not limited to: twitter.com/anjemchoudary, twitter.com/Abu_Baraa1, twitter.com/MuslimPrisoners/, facebook.com/AbuBaraa2015, youtube.com/user/anjemchoudary, youtube.com/user/abubarauk, and youtube.com/user/abuizzudeenuk. As this list illustrates, leading activists often maintained a presence on multiple social media platforms simultaneously. Some activists also use *Tumblr*, another micro-blogging platform, *WhatsApp*, the mobile messaging service, and other encrypted applications. Separate interviews with two leading activists, Wembley, West London, September 5, 2013. For more on al-Muhajiroun's social media presence, with emphasis on the network's virtual connections to foreign fighters in Iraq and Syria, see Jytte Klausen, "Tweeting the Jihad: Social Media Networks of Western Foreign Fighters in Syria and Iraq," *Studies in Conflict & Terrorism* 38, no. 1 (2015), pp. 1–22.

[125] See, for example, the YouTube channels for "Anthony Small boxer" and "Izharudeen Media," respectively: www.youtube.com/user/anthonysmallspeaking, www.youtube.com/channel/UCMsOcpbwINQaz712jCoX0eQ [Both accessed January 2, 2018].

[126] Interviews with leading and rank-and-file activists, Leyton, East London, November 4 and 6, 2010, Walthamstow, November 16, 2010, Whitechapel, East London, June 17, 2011, Mile End, East London, June 26, 2011, Ilford, East London, December 9, 2014, and US government official, Mayfair, Central London, December 3, 2010.

him into their public conferences. "We were listening to more of his talks on PalTalk then we did when he was here," claims a leading activist, with some exaggeration. "He was doing a PalTalk almost every night. It was almost as if you were in the same room as him. You could hear him clearly, ask questions. You could laugh and smile. You could use emoticons. You could be in the same room without him being in the room. The world is that small nowadays." While Bakri did interact with his students on PalTalk, it was not every night, or even every week. Reflecting on some of the other online tools activists used to keep in touch with Bakri, the respondent continues: "With the Internet and especially social media and things like Skype, there's no need for someone to be with you for you to get the information. We missed him dearly, but we still had access to him."[127]

After it was reported in the press that Bakri was making a mockery of British authorities by communicating with his followers on PalTalk, the company that runs the software came under pressure to block his profile, which it reportedly did.[128] This solution proved to be short-lived, however. Bakri was soon back on PalTalk lecturing his followers, but not as frequently as before, especially after he ran into legal problems in Lebanon. Between November 2010 and July 2015, Bakri faced several criminal cases, which resulted in his conviction on numerous charges, including belonging to a terrorist group and recruiting people to fight in Iraq and Syria.[129] Even before he was sentenced to prison, the legal challenges disrupted Bakri's ability to engage with his followers. By then, however, several of his closest students had their own followers on PalTalk and social media, allowing them to communicate the Emigrants' message to activists in Britain – and globally. "When I do my PalTalk sessions I have people from Egypt and Australia listening to my lectures," explains one leading activist. "I couldn't do that were it not for the fact that they've heard about me via social media and via the mainstream media. I think this is very important. It's not about the number of people who are with you. It's not about the names of the organizations. It's about how effective you are at passing your message. This is the important thing."[130]

---

[127] Interview with leading activist, Ilford, East London, December 9, 2014.

[128] Mark White, "Banned cleric preaching to Brits," *Sky News* (December 13, 2008); Tom Rayner, "Web chat room bans radical cleric," *Sky News* (January 6, 2009).

[129] Ian Johnston, "Banned radical cleric Sheikh Omar Bakri Mohamed arrested in Lebanon over 'links to terrorism'," *The Independent* (May 26, 2014), www.independent.co.uk/news/world/middle-east/banned-radical-cleric-sheikh-omar-bakri-mohamed-arrested-in-lebanon-over-links-to-terrorism-9434213.html [Accessed July 7, 2014]; *Daily Star*, "Lebanon sentences 5 over terror charges," (April 20, 2015), www.dailystar.com.lb/News/Lebanon-News/2015/Apr-20/295139-lebanon-sentences-5-over-terror-charges.ashx [Accessed June 26, 2015]; *Daily Star*, "Military court sentences Salafist sheikh to 3 years in fresh case," (July 1, 2015), www.dailystar.com.lb/News/Lebanon-News/2015/Jul-01/304683-military-court-sentences-salafist-sheikh-to-3-years-in-fresh-case.ashx [Accessed July 3, 2015].

[130] Interview with leading activist, Ilford, East London, December 9, 2014. Also, interview with London Metropolitan Police officer, Westminster, Central London, June 29, 2011.

CONCLUSION

The adaptations described in this chapter allowed the Emigrants to continue their activism despite persistent efforts by the British government to stop them. Activists bounced back from government pressure by changing their activities in a number of simple, but effective ways. They created dozens of new spin-off groups and revived old ones when the authorities outlawed their most prominent platforms. They moved their da'wah stalls to new areas, made them less provocative, and stressed the religious side of their preaching when officials tried to prevent them from calling people to Islam. They used deception to reserve venues, moved their conferences to smaller halls, and posted their talks online when officials restricted their access to brick-and-mortar venues. And they re-established contact with their original emir through PalTalk and other online tools when authorities tried to decapitate the network by effectively banishing Omar Bakri from Great Britain.

In making these tactical changes, activists overcame setbacks and continued their proselytizing in an increasingly hostile environment. Al-Muhajiroun's adaptability, reinforced by the commitment of its activists, made for a resilient network. The Emigrants' malleability also allowed them to remain relevant in the global jihadi movement, even as their network weakened and became increasingly marginalized in Britain. The diffusion of al-Muhajiroun's brand of provocative, high-risk activism to countries like Belgium ensured that its influence expanded. And the persistence of its activism enhanced the network's credibility among vulnerable young Britons who saw government efforts to stop activists as proof they were on the right path.

I do not wish to overstate the effectiveness of these adaptations. Al-Muhajiroun was hurt by counter-terrorism policies and local communities' rejection of its mission. The network has not generated the same level of enthusiasm among British youth in recent years, nor drawn the same number of supporters to its protests and conferences as it did during the heyday of its activism in the late 1990s and early 2000s, when Omar Bakri and his acolytes thrived in a more permissive environment. The Emigrants remained intact, however, surviving more than a decade of government efforts to destroy them.

Al-Muhajiroun's resilience raises difficult questions for policy makers and the public. The network's relentless ability to absorb and recover from setbacks suggests that the British government's proscription policy and efforts to eliminate it did not produce the intended result. Yet many observers believe the authorities turned the corner on the activist network in 2016 after convicting Anjem Choudary and Mizanur Rahman of supporting the Islamic State in Iraq and Syria. With these convictions, and additional government controls against other leading and veteran activists, has the network finally reached the limit of its endurance? Or will the Emigrants rise once more, rebounding from these latest setbacks to continue their call? I return to these questions in the final chapter of this study. But first I examine why many activists leave al-Muhajiroun on their own, long before they face the threat of criminal prosecution.

5

Leaving al-Muhajiroun

I just didn't have that kind of mentality anymore. Basically, I was growing up. That's what actually happened. Towards the end of my stay with the group I was thinking, 'I don't want to do this for the rest of my life.' I grew up and I realized this wasn't for me.

Abdul, former activist

You have to understand something. When you corner people sometimes they have no choice but to go there. I'm sure if they didn't corner him, he wouldn't have gone over there. It was because he was cornered and he probably thought, 'I've got nowhere else to go apart from over there.'

Salman, former activist

After interviewing Rohan on a brisk winter day in 2014, I decided to stop by the network's educational center nearby. During previous trips to London, I visited the center and the candy store above it, both of which were leased by Anjem Choudary's brother, Yazdani, a local businessman. In my visits to the center I listened to talks by Anjem and other speakers and hung out with activists as they explained their beliefs and preached to me. Recently I had heard that activists were no longer using the center after it had been raided in the British government's latest crackdown. I wanted to see if the reports were true, so after saying goodbye to Rohan I walked several blocks to New Road, near the Royal London Hospital in Whitechapel. When I arrived I was surprised to see someone carrying a stack of chairs from the basement and putting them into a rental truck parked on the street. Another man, who looked familiar to me, was standing on a ladder in front of the candy store removing the sign on top of the store's entrance. I approached him and asked if the store was open. He climbed down the ladder, turned to me and said, "No." We looked at each other for a moment and I tried to remember why he seemed so familiar. Apparently, he was thinking the same thing because as soon as I recognized him as the respondent I am calling Salman, he said, "I think I know you." "You do," I replied. "I'm Michael Kenney and you're [activist's name withheld]." He laughed and said "that was my nickname back then."

He then told me his real name, which I also remembered from our first encounters, years before. Seeking to jog his memory, I reminded Salman of our first meeting in 2007, when I interviewed him and two other activists, along with one of the leaders of al-Muhajiroun. I added that we also met on several occasions in the fall and winter of 2010, during some of the busiest months of my field research. Salman's face brightened as he recalled our meetings. But after a moment he grew quiet and looked at me warily. "I've left them," he said quickly, almost sheepishly. "I'm no longer with Anjem and those guys." He went on to explain that shortly after my field work in 2010, he and other "brothers" in the Whitechapel halaqah became increasingly disillusioned with their activism, which they saw as too provocative and counter-productive. When Anjem Choudary refused their request to moderate their activism and invite outside preachers to deliver halaqah talks, they left, bringing numerous activists with them. While this internal dispute was the immediate catalyst for his departure from al-Muhajiroun, in our discussion Salman elaborated on why he left. "I grew up," he said, sounding like other former activists I interviewed. "I grew up and got more responsibilities, to my family and my kids."[1]

Over the years I interviewed a number of former activists, many of whom shared similar insights, even as they left the Emigrants at different times, under different circumstances. In this chapter, I draw on these interviews, and my field work more broadly, to trace the processes by which activists leave the network and its community of practice, and the different outcomes they experience afterwards. Like entering al-Muhajiroun, exiting it is a dynamic process involving multiple "push" and "pull" factors. These factors interact in different ways for different people.[2] Notwithstanding this variation certain patterns do emerge. Many activists gradually mature out of the Emigrants as they age beyond adolescence and accept the responsibilities of adulthood. They also burn out from the network's demanding activism, particularly as they face competing demands on their time and biographical availability, like parenthood. Some become disillusioned with al-Muhajiroun, finding contradictions or problems in its ideology and activism. As their frustration mounts, they reduce their involvement and pursue other activities, including education and employment. But leaving the Emigrants is

---

[1] Field notes, Whitechapel, East London, December 11, 2014.
[2] Mary Beth Altier, Christian N. Thoroughgood and John G. Horgan, "Turning Away from Terrorism: Lessons from Psychology, Sociology, and Criminology," *Journal of Peace Research* 51, no. 5 (2014), p. 648; Bert Klandermans, *The Social Psychology of Protest* (Cambridge, MA: Blackwell Publishers, 1997), p. 97.

hard, especially for those who have invested substantial time and social capital in the network's community of practice. Recognizing this, leaders and rank-and-file activists make it harder to leave by putting pressure on those who consider quitting.

Activists who manage to leave al-Muhajiroun follow multiple pathways. Some demobilize from the network without necessarily "deradicalizing" in the sense of moderating their attitudes and beliefs. Others leave and change their ideological views in profound ways. This includes several respondents who now devote their careers to countering the extremist "narratives" promoted by the Emigrants and other militant groups in Britain. Tragically, some activists leave only to radicalize further into political violence. In recent years, numerous respondents in my sample became implicated in terrorist plots in Britain or left the country to fight for the Islamic State in Iraq and Syria.

Studies on leaving social movements and extremist groups are not as developed as the literature on joining. A growing number of researchers have sought to address this imbalance by explaining how and why participants turn away from political violence, extremism, and social activism.[3] A separate body of scholarship seeks to understand how terrorist organizations decline and die.[4] This chapter is more concerned with individual defection than organizational death. To be sure, al-Muhajiroun has declined in recent years and remains marginalized in Britain. However, the network has not rejected its goal of establishing a global caliphate, nor has it abandoned its activism. As I explored in the last chapter, al-Muhajiroun has endured setbacks and remains resilient, with activists continuing to engage in da'wah and hisbah. Yet defection can

---

[3] Researchers who examine why people disengage from political extremism and violence include James Aho, "Out of Hate: A Sociology of Defection from Neo-Nazism," *Current Research on Peace and Violence* 11, no. 4 (1988), pp. 159–68; John Horgan, *Walking Away From Terrorism: Accounts of Disengagement from Radical and Extremist Movements* (New York: Routledge, 2009); Fernando Reinares, "Exit from Terrorism: A Qualitative Empirical Study on Disengagement and Deradicalization among Members of ETA," *Terrorism and Political Violence* 23, no. 5 (2011), pp. 780–803; and Julie Chernov Hwang, *Why Terrorists Quit: The Disengagement of Indonesian Jihadists* (Ithaca, NY: Cornell University Press, 2018), among others. Researchers who discuss why activists leave social movements include Sharon Erickson Nepstad, "Persistent Resistance: Commitment and Community in the Plowshares Movement," *Social Problems* 51, no. 1 (2004), pp. 43–60; James Downton Jr. and Paul Wehr, *The Persistent Activist: How Peace Commitment Develops and Survives* (Boulder, CO: Westview Press, 1997); and Klandermans, *The Social Psychology of Protest*.

[4] See, for example, Jeffrey Ian Ross and Ted Robert Gurr, "Why Terrorism Subsides: A Comparative Study of Canada and the United States," *Comparative Politics* 21, no. 4 (July 1989), pp. 405–26; Martha Crenshaw, "How Terrorism Declines," *Terrorism and Political Violence* 3, no. 1 (1991), pp. 69–87; and Audrey Kurth Cronin, *How Terrorism Ends: Understanding the Decline and Demise of Terrorist Campaigns* (Princeton, NJ: Princeton University Press, 2009). Examples of both the disengagement and termination literatures are found in Tore Bjørgo's and John Horgan's edited volume, *Leaving Terrorism Behind: Individual and Collective Disengagement* (New York: Routledge, 2009).

be an important source of organizational decline, particularly when networks and organizations fail to recruit new supporters to replace the departed. The Emigrants are not immune to this. Many activists have left in recent years, including respondents I interviewed during the early years of my field work. In this chapter, I tell their stories to explore how and why activists leave – and the different paths they take after their departure.

TURNOVER AND "PERSISTENT ACTIVISTS"

Participation in al-Muhajiroun is largely a youth phenomenon. Young men and women typically become involved in the Emigrants during their middle to late teenage years and early twenties. Once engaged, they participate enthusiastically for several months to a few years before eventually turning away. This suggests that turnover is high in al-Muhajiroun, a point conceded by current and former activists. "The vast majority of them drop out, after two, three or four years," observes Haroon, the former administrative affiliate who spent two years in the network.[5] "People were coming in and out," explains Rashid, a former activist who became heavily involved in the network. "There was lots of turnover."[6] Indeed, turnover is so common among rank-and-file activists that network leaders have resigned themselves to it. "People come and go," explains Rohan. "It's not anything strange and we are not really keeping count of who's with us and who's not."[7]

Leaders like Rohan accept that just as individuals become intellectually affiliated with al-Muhajiroun's community of practice by embracing its ideology and culture, so they remove themselves from the community when they cease to follow these beliefs. "The more someone disassociates themselves from us, the more they change their understanding, the less they are affiliated," explains another leader. "As soon as he stops believing in the same ideas, then he's no longer considered to be a member of the organization."[8]

The principal exception to al-Muhajiroun's high turnover is a group of long-time activists who have been involved in the network for many years. These are what social movement scholars call "persistent activists," devoted followers who parlay their passion for a cause into a career.[9] Persistent activists in al-Muhajiroun include people like Anjem Choudary, Abu Izzadeen Brooks,

---

[5] Interview with Haroon, Westminster, Central London, June 14, 2011. Of course, turnover is high in many activist groups. For more on this, with reference to peace and labor activists in the Netherlands, see Klandermans, *The Social Psychology of Protest*, p. 97.

[6] Interview with Rashid, Whitechapel, East London, June 26, 2011.

[7] Interview with Rohan, Whitechapel, East London, December 7, 2010.

[8] Interview with leading activist, Leyton, East London, November 4, 2010.

[9] See Klandermans, *The Social Psychology of Protest*; Downton and Wehr, *The Persistent Activist*; and Donatella della Porta, "Leaving Underground Organizations: A Sociological Analysis of the Italian Case," in *Leaving Terrorism Behind: Individual and Collective Disengagement*, edited by Tore Bjørgo and John Horgan (New York: Routledge, 2009), pp. 66–87.

Mizanur Rahman, Abdul Muhid, Mohammed Alamgir, and Mohammed Shamsuddin. Reflecting their centrality in the network, all six individuals rank among the top ten nodes for degree or betweenness centrality during at least one of the three time periods in the social network analysis in Chapter 1. They were among al-Muhajiroun's leading and most committed activists, as I came to appreciate during my field work. They organized its da'wah stalls and protests, formed its spin-off groups, indoctrinated activists in its ideology, and represented the network to the news media.

Consistent with Downton's and Wehr's definition of "persisters," all six veterans had been active in al-Muhajiroun for at least five years at the time of my field work, usually much longer.[10] They joined the Emigrants at a relatively young age and studied closely with Omar Bakri Mohammed. Their commitment to Bakri and his blend of Salafi-Islamism knows few bounds. They have been arrested and had their homes raided repeatedly. Most have been imprisoned for crimes related to their activism and several are currently incarcerated or under some form of government control. They are frequently vilified in the news media and by mainstream Islamic groups in the United Kingdom. Despite the pressure, most of these persistent activists have continued to participate in the network's high-risk activism well into their thirties and, in some cases, forties. One expert on al-Muhajiroun from the London Metropolitan Police contrasts the reliability of these core supporters with the high levels of turnover among rank-and-file activists. The latter, he points out, "come and go, but the core remains the same. We call them the old school. They stay through thick and thin."[11]

This is consistent with what I observed during my repeated research trips to London. Each year I saw new faces among the activists calling society to Islam at da'wah stalls, waving signs at demonstrations, and attending talks at the network's indoctrination centers.[12] But among the changing newcomers there was always a core of "old school" activists who delivered the talks, organized the stalls, and led the protests. Even during lean years, when the number of rank-and-file activists was down and the Emigrants struggled to put together a decent showing at their events, the persistent activists remained remarkably stable. What distinguished them from rank-and-file supporters was their extraordinary commitment to the network and its ideology.[13] Al-Muhajiroun owed much of its resilience to their tenacity.

---

[10] Downton and Wehr, *The Persistent Activist*, p. 13.
[11] Interview with London Metropolitan Police officer, Westminster, Central London, June 29, 2011.
[12] Field notes, various dates and locations in London, November 2010, December 2010, June 2011, July 2012, September 2013, December 2014, July 2015.
[13] Similarly, Downton's and Wehr's study of peace activists in Colorado and Klandermans' study of peace activists in the Netherlands find that persistent activists had higher levels of commitment to the cause than those who left. See Downton and Wehr, *The Persistent Activist*, p. 133; Klandermans, *The Social Psychology of Protest*, p. 29; and Nepstad, "Persistent Resistance," p. 45.

GETTING PUSHED OUT

With so much turnover among rank-and-file activists, network leaders try to avoid kicking people out of al-Muhajiroun. But it does happen. So essential is the notion of intellectual affiliation to the network that one of the few ways activists are forced out is when they fail to commit themselves to a halaqah. As discussed in previous chapters, these small, neighborhood-based study circles are the Emigrants' main organizational unit and the primary vehicle for activists' indoctrination. Participation in these discussion groups is mandatory. When activists repeatedly fail to attend their halaqah meetings, without permission from their masoul or providing an acceptable excuse for their absence, they may be temporarily suspended, or even expelled. "You had to attend your weekly halaqah," explains Rashid, who served as a masoul during his years in the network. "If people didn't attend, they would be warned and if they still didn't attend, they would be kicked out."[14]

Reflecting the importance of ideological cohesion in al-Muhajiroun, another way that activists, even leading ones, can get kicked out is by promoting the teachings of external preachers. Leading activists zealously seek to limit the influence of outside ideologues. This includes prominent Salafi-jihadi preachers like Anwar al-Awlaki and Abu Bashir al-Tartusi who shared similar views. When these preachers were still lecturing in Britain, individual activists sometimes attended their talks, but they were not allowed to study their teachings in al-Muhajiroun halaqahs, nor distribute recordings of their lectures at da'wah stalls and conferences.[15]

Activists who failed to follow approved preachers exclusively were driven out of the Emigrants. After some insisted on distributing lectures by other scholars at network events and on their websites, they were "pushed away from certain roles and stopped from talking," explains Salman. "They wouldn't give any lectures" on behalf of the network. When I asked him if he was talking about someone who lectured prolifically on behalf of al-Muhajiroun but also maintained a website that distributed audios and videos of talks by a number of external preachers, Salman confirmed my suspicion: "It happened to Abu Waleed. It happened to a few brothers I know. It even happened to Abdul Rahman Saleem."[16]

For many years Abdul Rahman Saleem was one of the Emigrants' most persistent activists. His central position in the network is shown in Chapter 1,

---

[14] Interview with Rashid, Whitechapel, East London, June 26, 2011. Also, interview with Ali, former activist, Hounslow, West London, December 13, 2010, and Quintan Wiktorowicz, *Radical Islam Rising: Muslim Extremism in the West* (Lanham, MD: Rowman & Littlefield, 2005), pp. 50–1.

[15] Interviews with Salman, Poplar, East London, July 24, 2015, and Rashid, Whitechapel, East London, June 26, 2011.

[16] Interview with Salman, Poplar, East London, July 24, 2015.

where he ranks third and fifth in node-level degree centrality among all activists during Time Periods 2 and 3. Saleem's brokerage rankings are even higher. He ranks tenth in betweenness centrality in Time Period 1 and third during Time Periods 2 and 3. His rankings reflect the prominent roles he performed for the network and his willingness to address the media. Saleem served as a spokesperson for al-Muhajiroun in Britain and Pakistan, where he spent time trying to establish a local presence for the network, which was ultimately unsuccessful. Later, he followed Omar Bakri to Lebanon when the network founder was banned from returning to Britain in the wake of the 7/7 bombings.[17] After he was deported back to Britain by Lebanese authorities, Saleem continued his activism on behalf of the Emigrants, organizing high-profile protests in London that received substantial media coverage. His participation in two separate demonstrations, one outside the Regent's Park Mosque protesting the war in Iraq, and another at the Danish embassy protesting the publication of cartoons depicting the Prophet Mohammed, led to his conviction for inciting racial hatred and murder for terrorist purposes.[18] He served several years in prison for these crimes, after which he returned to his activism, preaching on behalf of the network and participating in other al-Muhajiroun events, including a protest near the Lebanese embassy after Omar Bakri's arrest in Lebanon.[19]

Despite his long, extensive involvement with the Emigrants, Abdul Rahman Saleem lost his leadership role after he began to study with scholars outside the network. "He was pushed out because of his opinion change after he came out of prison," explains Salman, who was deeply involved in the network at the time. "He was not allowed to give any lectures." When asked why Abdul Rahman changed his opinion, Salman replied, "He started going to other people's lectures and talks. Al-Muhajiroun didn't like that he was attending lectures by a sheikh who they classified as kafir [non-believer]." Saleem, who had been one of the network's most outspoken and persistent activists, was disgraced. This contributed to his humiliation and departure from the network: "Everyone saw it, them pushing him out." Generalizing beyond this to other examples, Salman adds, "As soon as they realize that you're going a little bit astray, they stop you from talking and lecturing."[20] So rigid is the network's ideology that even leading activists who have sacrificed a lot for the cause are removed if they fail to meet the narrow standards of its community of practice.

[17] Interviews with three leading activists, Ilford, East London, November 29, 2010 and December 9, 2014, and Walthamstow, East London, December 2, 2010.

[18] Robin Simcox, Hannah Stuart, and Houriya Ahmed, *Islamist Terrorism: The British Connections* (London: The Centre for Social Cohesion, 2010), pp. 95–6.

[19] Field notes, network protest near Lebanese embassy, Kensington, Central London, November 15, 2010. Also, see the YouTube video documenting this protest produced by the al-Muhajiroun platforms, Tawheed Movement and Salafi Media: "Free Sheikh Omar Bakri Muhammad part 3," www.youtube.com/watch?v=T5sn5FQXQWc [Accessed September 11, 2017].

[20] Interview with Salman, Poplar, East London, July 24, 2015.

BURNING OUT AND GROWING UP

Unlike Abdul Rahman Saleem, most activists leave al-Muhajiroun on their own terms and for their own reasons. The process of leaving is as complex as the process of joining, and respondents cite a number of reasons for their departure. Some once committed participants eventually "burn out" from the constant demands of their activism, not unlike members of social movements and workers in stressful occupations, such as nursing and social work.[21] The pace of activism in al-Muhajiroun is, as Quintan Wiktorowicz first observed years ago, "fast-paced, demanding, and relentless."[22] In any given week activists spend countless hours studying in halaqah circles, preaching at da'wah stalls, agitating at protests, and performing other tasks related to their activism. Some of these activities, such as halaqah sessions, can stretch deep into the night, causing activists to miss leisure time with their families. "I used to attend lectures until three, four o'clock, six o'clock in the morning," explains Salman, who was working full-time, in addition to performing his activism.[23] Ali describes the challenges he and his halaqah brothers faced in balancing their activism with work and family obligations: "In the evening, we would stay all night – and you've got a day job. All of us work guys had kids. I had to start my shift at six in the morning. They used to drop me off at my work at five. I'd have a shower there and start work. All of us were like this!"[24]

Like participants in other communities of practice, intellectual affiliates can feel overwhelmed by the constant demands on their time and the frantic pace of their activism. Many activists eventually grow weary and frustrated, causing them to reconsider their commitment. "I was getting tired of constantly having to turn up and repeating the same things, again and again," explains one

---

[21] Numerous researchers argue that burn out contributes to voluntary disengagement from different militant and terrorist groups, including the Italian Red Brigades, Basque Country and Freedom (ETA), the Quebec Liberation Front (FLQ), American Neo-Nazis, and American anarchists. See, respectively, della Porta, "Leaving Underground Organizations," Reinares, "Exit from Terrorism," Ross and Gurr, "Why Terrorism Subsides," Aho, "Out of Hate," and Erika Summers Effler, *Laughing Saints and Righteous Heroes: Emotional Rhythms in Social Movement Groups* (Chicago: University of Chicago Press, 2010), p. 98. For more on burn out in social movements, see Downton and Wehr, *The Persistent Activist*, pp. 107–8; and Klandermans, *The Social Psychology of Protest*, pp. 103–4. For burn out's impact on highly stressful occupations, see Paula McFadden, Anne Campbell, and Brian Taylor, "Resilience and Burnout in Child Protection Social Work: Individual and Organisational Themes from a Systematic Literature Review," *British Journal of Social Work* 45, no. 5 (2015), pp. 1546–63; Jenny S. Lee and Syed Akhtar, "Effects of the Workplace Social Context and Job Content on Nurse Burnout," *Human Resource Management* 50, no. 2 (2011), pp. 227–45; and Don L. Kurtz, "Controlled Burn: The Gendering of Stress and Burnout in Modern Policing," *Feminist Criminology* 3, no. 3 (July 2008), pp. 216–38.

[22] Wiktorowicz, *Radical Islam Rising*, p. 47.

[23] Interview with Salman, Poplar, East London, July 24, 2015. Also interview with Abdul, another former activist, Whitechapel, East London, June 18, 2011.

[24] Interview with Ali, Hounslow, West London, June 21, 2011.

former activist.[25] Fatigue was not the only factor that turned him and other respondents away from al-Muhajiroun, but it was part of the process that led to their departure from the activist network.

Individuals also burn out from the emotional stress and family problems caused by their activism. Many activists live at home with parents who do not support their involvement in al-Muhajiroun. Parents often reject the network's revivalist ideology and revolutionary objectives, which are fundamentally opposed to their understanding of Islam. "Many see us as radical," explains a young activist in a lecture delivered to more than thirty listeners at the network's center in Whitechapel. "And our families are concerned that we are putting ourselves in harm's way. I know many brothers that have been kicked out their houses for their beliefs."[26] This is not surprising given that the Emigrants' vision of creating the Islamic caliphate in Britain would destroy the land of their parents and grandparents, who came to the country as economic migrants seeking a better life. In addition to worrying about the beliefs their sons and daughters are learning in al-Muhajiroun, parents fear the harm their children's activism is having on their education and future job prospects. "Many brothers I knew didn't have a good relationship with their parents," explains Rashid, "because their parents were pushing them to get an education," while they were more interested in pursuing their activism.[27]

Activists often fight with their parents and other relatives, especially when they preach the Emigrants' interpretation of Islam at home. "I was forever fighting with my family," recalls Maryam, the former female activist. "I broke up with my mom. I didn't speak to my dad."[28] "I used to have fights with my parents," recalls Abdul, another activist, who, like most of my respondents, grew up in a Muslim household. "'Why are you stopping me? It's Islam I'm doing it for.'"[29] Salman recalls how he pressured his father, who was then active in local politics, not to vote: "I told my father, 'If you vote you're going to leave the fold of Islam and I will never come and visit you.'" On another occasion, he told his father to stop smoking and join him on the *hajj*, the mandatory pilgrimage to Mecca, "otherwise I'm going to disown you."[30]

Such conflicts and emotional blackmail take their toll on some activists, contributing to their decision to leave al-Muhajiroun. "I thought, 'This is not me and I need to step out of it now,'" explains Maryam. "I just had enough."[31]

[25] Interview with former activist, Walthamstow, East London, July 17, 2012.
[26] Field notes, Whitechapel, East London, June 16, 2011.
[27] Interview with Rashid, Whitechapel, East London, June 26, 2011. Also, interview with Ali, Hounslow, West London, June 21, 2011.
[28] Interview with Maryam, Hounslow, West London, December 13, 2010.
[29] Interview with Abdul, former activist, Whitechapel, East London, June 18, 2011.
[30] Interview with Salman, Poplar, East London, July 24, 2015.
[31] Interview with Maryam, Hounslow, West London, December 13, 2010. Also, separate interview with Maryam, Skype, November 20, 2012.

"There was family tension with my mom and dad," recalls Abdul. "I was being rude, aggressive to them, always disrespecting them. And I realized, 'These are the people who are providing for me.'"[32] Even after leaving the network, some respondents feel guilty about the way they treated their parents during their activism. "Look at all the problems I caused in my house," laments Salman. "My heart hurts and I feel guilty."[33]

In addition to the family quarrels, some activists tire from their lack of progress in achieving the Emigrants' lofty objectives. Despite their best efforts to call Britain to Islam and establish a global caliphate, these respondents see few tangible, real-world results. "I didn't see any progress or anything productive with the so-called da'wah," observes Rashid.[34] In their halaqahs, activists learn they are preparing society for the caliphate, but before Abu Bakr al-Baghdadi's declaration of the Islamic State they had no indication as to when or where it would appear. The uncertainty frustrated some. "It's not progressing," explains Maryam, who was active years before al-Baghdadi's bold announcement in June 2014. "We are doing all the donkey's work, when are we going to see the khilafah?"[35] "I got tired of asking the same questions for four or five years," adds a third former activist. "When is the Islamic state going to come and where is it going to come? I would never get an answer. Here we were chanting 'shariah, khilafah, shariah, khilafah,' and the answers were not coming. That was quite annoying."[36]

Another annoyance that contributes to activists' exit are the personal sacrifices they make on behalf of their activism. "People get burnt out," notes Rashid, "because they've been so active in it and they haven't thought of sorting their own lives out."[37] As their involvement in al-Muhajiroun deepens, activists watch old friends and acquaintances who never joined finish their degrees, advance their careers, and make money. Meanwhile, explains Abdul, who belonged to the network for four years, "I was working in low-paying, menial jobs and I wasn't going anywhere. My life was going nowhere. I wanted to do something with myself."[38] Activists are taught that their worldly sacrifices will lead to a much greater reward in the afterlife, but such promises eventually wear thin for many. "That's why they leave," notes Haroon, speaking of activist friends from his days with al-Muhajiroun: "After three or four years, they realize 'I can't manage, I need to go to university.' They realize that kind of lifestyle isn't really conducive to having a good job, earning a bit of money, getting married, enjoying life."[39]

---

[32] Interview with Abdul, Whitechapel, East London, June 18, 2011.
[33] Interview with Salman, Poplar, East London, July 24, 2015.
[34] Interview with Rashid, Whitechapel, East London, June 26, 2011.
[35] Interview with Maryam, Skype, November 20, 2012.
[36] Interview with former activist, Walthamstow, East London, July 17, 2012.
[37] Interview with Rashid, Whitechapel, East London, June 26, 2011.
[38] Interview with Abdul, Whitechapel, East London, June 18, 2011.
[39] Interview with Haroon, Westminster, Central London, June 14, 2011.

Such realizations are part of a broader process experienced by many activists: "maturing out" of al-Muhajiroun. As they grow older and acquire more responsibilities, activists' enthusiasm for the cause begins to wane. Referring to the Emigrants' radical vision, which he initially found so inspiring, Rashid explains, "We had a call, which was very revolutionary sounding. 'We're gonna change the world.' As a young person, that's really attractive." His youthful enthusiasm, however, eventually gave way to a more sober assessment: "As you grow and you mature, you realize that it's not so simple like that."[40] "I just didn't have that kind of mentality anymore," adds Abdul. "Basically, I was growing up. That's what actually happened. Towards the end of my stay with the group I was thinking, 'I don't want to do this for the rest of my life.' I grew up and I realized this wasn't for me."[41]

For many people part of growing up is embracing the responsibilities of adulthood, including marriage and children. Consistent with research on militant and social movement groups, Emigrants who get married and have children often struggle to manage competing demands on their time, leading some to question their involvement.[42] These activists lose their "biographical availability" to engage in high-risk activism as they mature into adulthood.[43] Asked to explain why he left al-Muhajiroun, Salman recalls, "Back then I was younger and I had more free time to engage in activism, but now I have more responsibilities to my family and my kids and I have less time."[44] "When my second child was born, I had to leave her with my wife," adds Ali. "I hauled myself to the halaqah and I had to go fly posting at night."[45] Compared to the birth of his child, putting stickers on billboards and traffic lights seemed trivial, even un-Islamic, causing him to reconsider his activism: "I started questioning."[46] Of course, some persistent activists have children without seriously questioning their involvement. These old school activists bring their kids to da'wah stalls and demonstrations, socializing them into the network's community of practice from an early age.[47] For less committed respondents in my sample, however, having kids reduced their enthusiasm and their biographical availability for high-risk activism and contributed to their disengagement from the network.

[40] Interview with Rashid, Whitechapel, East London, June 26, 2011.
[41] Interview with Abdul, Whitechapel, East London, June 18, 2011.
[42] Downton and Wehr, *The Persistent Activist*, pp. 99–103; della Porta, "Leaving Underground Organizations," p. 79; Reinares, "Exit from Terrorism," p. 798.
[43] Nepstad, "Persistent Resistance," p. 56; Doug McAdam, "Recruitment to High-Risk Activism: The Case of the Freedom Summer," *American Journal of Sociology* 92, no. 1 (July 1986), pp. 64–90, and McAdam, *Freedom Summer* (New York: Oxford University Press, 1988).
[44] Field notes, Whitechapel, East London, December 11, 2014.
[45] Interview with Ali, Hounslow, West London, December 13, 2010.
[46] Interview with Ali, Hounslow, West London, December 13, 2010. Also, interview with Maryam, Skype, November 20, 2012.
[47] Field notes, Ilford, East London, November 13, 2010, Wembley Central, North London, June 25, 2011, Islington, North London, July 21, 2012, and Westminster, Central London, September 6, 2013.

"FROM SOMETHING SMALL TO SOMETHING BIG"

In the process of leaving al-Muhajiroun, activists become disillusioned with the network, and their own role within it. Their growing frustration unfolds over many weeks, months, even years. During this period they increasingly question the nature and direction of the Emigrants' activism, and the strategy and knowledge of the leaders behind it. A single dispute rarely leads to departure. Leaving is a process, not an event, and activists' grievances tend to accumulate over time. As Ali explains, grievances can "start with something very small, but lead to something very big," departure from the network.[48] Sometimes activists express their discontent, risking censure and conflict with fellow activists and network leaders. For this reason, and because they may doubt their ability to question leaders on matters of strategy and doctrine, many avoid open confrontation. They keep quiet and let their grievances "pile up." This continues until one frustration too many becomes the catalyst for their departure.[49]

One area of disagreement regards al-Muhajiroun's confrontational protest tactics. As highlighted in previous chapters, network activists stage provocative demonstrations that include burning flags and other symbols, and shouting offensive slogans at passersby. The purpose of these inflammatory displays is to capture the attention of the media and public through moral shock. This is an important part of al-Muhajiroun's strategy of activism, but it can become a sore spot for some supporters. "My argument with Anjem and with Omar Bakri," explains Rashid, "was that we're focusing too much on creating controversy to get a reaction, to get on the front pages of the papers, whereas our aim should be to present what Islam really is to the people so that they don't see us as a threat." Rashid was active during the network's early years, when it was less marginalized among local communities than it later became. But even he grew tired of constantly having to defend the Emigrants' tactics to other Muslims in London: "It came to a point that whenever I was going to a meeting in mosques, community centers, or at stalls I was defending something which I didn't agree with in my heart... So eventually I just left."[50] Rashid's story suggests that when activists continue to interact with fellow Muslims outside the network, it can sow the seeds for their eventual departure. This has practical implications for countering the Emigrants, and I return to this theme in the next chapter.

Other respondents who left al-Muhajiroun also identified the network's provocative tactics as one of the factors that pushed them away. Salman participated in symbolic burnings, including activists' torching of replica poppies at the 2010 Armistice Day demonstration. But his frustration with such tactics

---

[48] Interview with Ali, Hounslow, West London, December 13, 2010.
[49] Separate interviews with Ali and Maryam, Hounslow, West London, December 13, 2010, and Rashid, Whitechapel, East London, June 26, 2011.
[50] Interview with Rashid, Whitechapel, East London, June 26, 2011.

eventually contributed to his departure. "When you go out and burn the poppy," he later explained, "all you're doing is causing animosity because the poppy is something which is sacred to the non-Muslims." In Salman's view, these actions not only distorted the meaning of hisbah, or commanding good and forbidding evil, but produced a backlash against local Muslims. "When you insult something like that, they're going to insult you the same way," he argued. "Even the Messenger Muhammad [PBUH] said, 'Do not insult their gods, because they will insult yours.'" "And that's what happened," he continued, recalling his own participation at one of the flag-burning protests, which drew the ire of counter-protestors from the English Defence League: "I was at a demonstration myself at the American embassy. I participated in burning the American flag and I remember seeing the EDL burning the Qur'an."[51] Salman's participation in this and other fiery protests did not trigger his immediate departure from al-Muhajiroun, but it did lead him to question his involvement and begin the gradual process of turning away from the network.

Another source of discontent for some respondents was their role in al-Muhajiroun, and the contributions they were asked to make in support of their activism. As I discussed in the Introduction, the Emigrants rely heavily on the voluntary labor and financial contributions of their supporters. While activists are taught they will be rewarded in the afterlife for these contributions, the constant requests for money and time aggravates some. Abdul was frequently asked to transport his colleagues to different events because he had a car and a "low-paying job" in a local warehouse to pay for gasoline. The role began to grate on him after a while. "I was fed up with driving people around, taxi driving," he recalls. "I only had a little bit of money a week and a lot of that money was spent on petrol and driving people around. It wasn't fair. I never used to have any money for myself." He also complained about his other financial contributions to the network, including "putting money in for printing leaflets and stuff. I didn't want to do that anymore."[52] Dissatisfaction with his role and the costs of his activism were not the only factors that pushed Abdul away from al-Muhajiroun, but they contributed to the process by which he eventually decided to leave.

Other activists who worked made their regular financial contributions to the network without complaint, but objected when they were asked to contribute additional funds for special events. After network leaders developed a grandiose plan to stage a "massive conference" at a prestigious venue in London, they asked working activists to donate "one month's wages" to support it. Ali, who was involved in al-Muhajiroun at the time, balked. "I said, 'Look, why are we paying so much money? I've got so many bills, debts.'" Ali expressed support for donating to save people "who are going through a disaster," but "we shouldn't waste money on a big hall like this to get publicity for

---

[51] Interview with Salman, Poplar, East London, July 24, 2015.
[52] Interview with Abdul, Whitechapel, East London, June 18, 2011.

the group. That's why I disagreed."[53] He did not leave al-Muhajiroun over this dispute, but it did add to his growing list of "little" grievances.

Among Ali's other grievances were controls placed on his activism by leading activists. Network leaders have a clear sense of what they want rank-and-file activists studying in the halaqahs. This is to protect the Emigrants' ideological cohesion. When activists stray from these sources, leaders are quick to direct them back to what they want them doing. After leaders discovered that Ali spent time teaching his halaqah brothers the Qur'an, they ordered him to stop. "I was told by the head that I should not be doing this," he recalls. "'This is not your job. There are better things for you to do. You need to go and start doing some fly posting, you need to get the leaflets ready.'" When he resisted, Ali was summoned to a meeting, where he was reprimanded by his masoul: "I was told, 'Don't do this again. We want to know what you're doing. If you've got nothing to do, we will give you something to do.'" Ali objected to his halaqah leader's attempt to discipline him. "I said, 'No.' I disagreed with the idea of fly posting on the street, covering all the signs." When his masoul pushed back, Ali remained defiant. "I was told, 'You don't question, you just obey.' I said, 'No, I am not obeying. When things are wrong, we correct them.'" Ali was not kicked out of al-Muhajiroun for his insubordination, nor was he yet ready to leave on his own. But he was "labeled a trouble maker," which contributed to his growing dissatisfaction with the network.[54]

More consequential than these "small" grievances, however, were Ali's concerns about changes in Omar Bakri's aqeedah or theological beliefs. When Ali joined the Emigrants, Bakri did not subscribe to Salafism, which follows a "literalist" – as opposed to a "rationalist" – theology. In fundamentalist creeds like Salafism, each word of scripture is interpreted literally, rather than symbolically or figuratively, as permitted in more conventional rationalist understandings. "At the time," according to Ali, Bakri identified himself as "part of the Maturidi sect."[55] This refers to a non-fundamentalist strain of Sunni Islam that follows a rationalist theology. Later Bakri announced that "he changed his views on the aqeedah issue," Ali explained. "He became a Salafi." Bakri's embrace of the Salafi creed, along with its literalist understanding of scripture, was a major theological change and led Ali to question his leader's religious credibility. "I thought, 'Hang on a minute, all these years we've been listening to you, studying with you, we were all in the wrong?'"

After the 9/11 attacks, Bakri shifted his theological stance again, changing from what Ali called a "normal," non-violent Salafi to "a deep Salafi," a Salafi-jihadi who expressed his admiration and support for "Osama bin Laden,

[53] Interview with Ali, Hounslow, West London, December 13, 2010. Also, interview with Rashid, Whitechapel, East London, June 26, 2011.

[54] Interview with Ali, Hounslow, West London, December 13, 2010.

[55] Interview with Ali, Hounslow, West London, December 13, 2010. Also, see Wiktorowicz, *Radical Islam Rising*, p. 184.

[Ayman] al-Zawahiri, and the Taliban."[56] Persistent activists who remained with al-Muhajiroun altered their views to accommodate Bakri's shifting beliefs.[57] However, the changes proved too much for Ali, who was not a fundamentalist and had no desire to become one. Bakri's repeated changes caused Ali to lose faith in him. "I thought, 'If you change your aqeedah, your creed, twice what's next? How can we trust you?'"[58] In addition to all the "little things" that had been "piling up over many months," this was a "major thing," the final grievance that pushed him out the door.

Other respondents were also turned off by Bakri's embrace of Salafi-jihadism, which they saw as an opportunistic gambit to position al-Muhajiroun as al-Qaeda's standard bearer in Europe, while the United States and other Western powers waged war on the Salafi-jihadi network in Afghanistan. "I think it was more of a political thing," observes Rashid. "Because you had more Salafi-jihadis involved in their fight with the States and others and to be accepted by them, he had to change his tune. Before, he would attack the Salafis."[59]

Even before his turn to Salafi-jihadism, Bakri's perceived opportunism undermined his credibility among some followers. In 1997, he allowed Jon Ronson, a writer and documentary filmmaker, to accompany him while he and his supporters performed their activism around London.[60] In his film, *Tottenham Ayatollah*, Ronson portrays Bakri as a fool. The portrayal did not sit well with his followers. "Looking at Bakri's depiction in that documentary shocked me to my very foundations," recalls one former activist: "Because we called him 'Sheikh' and we got religious rulings from him, yet he was made to look like a clown. And we had never seen that side of him. We knew he made errors in his talks. He didn't speak English properly and he made a silly job of it sometimes, but not like that. *Tottenham Ayatollah* was a real watershed for me."[61] Consistent with other respondents, this one incident did not cause him to leave al-Muhajiroun. However, it did contribute to his departure by leading him to question his involvement in the network.

Other respondents who left al-Muhajiroun also came to doubt Omar Bakri's interpretation of Islam and questioned whether he had the credentials to be a legitimate scholar. In recent years local Salafis and non-fundamentalist

---

[56] Interview with Ali, Hounslow, West London, December 13, 2010.

[57] Interviews with leading and veteran activists, Ilford, East London, November 13, 2010, Stratford, East London, November 29, 2010, and Whitechapel, East London, June 22, 2011.

[58] Interview with Ali, Hounslow, West London, December 13, 2010.

[59] Interview with Rashid, Whitechapel, East London, June 26, 2011. Also, interviews with Maryam, Hounslow, West London, December 13, 2010, and Abdul, Whitechapel, East London, June 18, 2011.

[60] Jon Ronson, "Tottenham Ayatollah," *Channel Four*, RDF Media, April 8, 1997, http://video.google.com/videoplay?docid=-2560493866437684563# [Accessed from Britain, June 19, 2011]. Also, see Jon Ronson, *Them: Adventures with Extremists* (London: Picador, 2001), especially "Chapter 1: A Semi-Detached Ayatollah."

[61] Interview with former activist, Walthamstow, East London, July 17, 2012.

Muslims have challenged Bakri's religious education and credentials.[62] Maryam, the former activist, was influenced by these critiques. In one interview, after alluding to hadith stories highlighting the Prophet Mohammed's compassion towards Jews and other non-Muslims, she complains that "these were stories that were concealed from us" by Omar Bakri and other network leaders. "Then," she adds, referring to questions that local Salafis raised about Bakri's religious training, "we found out that he wasn't actually a scholar and we were just being deceived."[63] "In the beginning, I thought of him as a real good Muslim scholar who I wanted to follow," explains Rashid, another former activist, "but eventually I thought of his understanding" of the religion "as simply *his* understanding."[64]

What troubled Rashid and other respondents was that the Emigrants relied solely on Bakri's interpretation of the Qur'an and the hadiths, to the exclusion of other Islamic scholars. As I emphasized in Chapter 3, one downside of al-Muhajiroun's ideological cohesion and "cultish" community of practice is that it is insular and dogmatic. This is reflected in activists' utter dependence on Bakri's teachings. "He was our only source of information," explains Rashid. "People treated his words like they would treat the Qur'an. If you say that to them, they will deny it. They will say, 'No, no, no. He's a sheikh, we take his understanding.' But in reality, they will not take from anyone who disagrees with their sheikh. They have a blind allegiance to him. This is the biggest danger."[65]

One incident, which I mentioned in Chapter 3, underscores another problem that can arise from activists' uncompromising allegiance to Bakri's teachings. After he left Britain, Bakri's senior followers, led by Anjem Choudary, continued to lecture on his behalf, working from their notes of his old talks. Although some of these speakers were engaging, they were not fluent in Arabic, nor were they as skilled in deriving their interpretation of Islamic thought and action from scripture. In response, activists from the network's halaqah in Whitechapel asked Choudary if they could invite other preachers, including Anwar al-Awlaki and Abu Bashir al-Tartusi, to lecture to them. Choudary refused, seeing this as a threat to the Emigrants' cohesion. This led

---

[62] For an extended theological attack on Bakri's teachings by two Salafi quietists, see Abu Ameenah AbdurRahman as-Salafi and Abdul Haq al-Ashanti, *A Critical Study of the Multiple Identities and Disguises of "Al-Muhajiroun"* (London: Jamiah Media, 2009). Of course, Bakri is not the only Salafi-jihadi preacher to be challenged by his co-religionists. Salafi quietists often criticize Salafi activists and jihadis and question the religious credentials of the clerics they follow. For more on this, see Quintan Wiktorowicz, "The Salafi Movement: Violence and the Fragmentation of Community," in *Muslim Networks: From Hajj to Hip Hop*, edited by Miriam Cooke and Bruce B. Lawrence (Chapel Hill, NC: University of North Carolina Press, 2005), p. 215.

[63] Interview with Maryam, Skype, November 20, 2012.

[64] Interview with Rashid, Whitechapel, East London, June 26, 2011.

[65] Interview with Rashid, Whitechapel, East London, June 26, 2011. Also, interview with Maryam, Skype, November 20, 2012.

the Whitechapel activists to become increasingly frustrated with his leadership. "They're not willing to ask other scholars for the knowledge," recalls Salman, who belonged to this halaqah. "Omar Bakri says it, that's it. Anjem Choudary says it, that's it. I found that hard to take."[66]

He was not the only one. Along with two other prominent activists from his halaqah, Salman met with Choudary on several occasions to complain. "We would tell him, 'Look, the way you're doing da'wah needs to change. And there's ways around 'forbidding evil.' You need to change that and allow other lecturers to get involved. There's no harm in compromising on certain things.' But he said he won't compromise." Choudary's loyalty to Bakri's teachings and his refusal to compromise led the three activists to try to remove him as emir. They held meetings with other activists from their halaqah and "senior members" from the network, to convince them that Choudary should step down. According to the respondent, a number of senior and rank-and-file activists took their side in the dispute. "When we got the go-ahead from some of the senior members," he recalls, "we thought, 'Let's go for it.' Basically, we tried to do a coup. We said we'll come back into the group if Anjem Choudary comes down."

Faced with stiff resistance, Choudary convinced the mutineers to return, at least temporarily. "But a lot of politics happened," Salman continues. "He didn't step down and we thought, 'Let's go.'" Salman left, along with "twenty-five brothers," splitting the Whitechapel halaqah in two. The departing activists formed a splinter group and opened their own center in Poplar, where they received lectures and private talks from non-al-Muhajiroun speakers. Under the guidance of their new spiritual leader, Abu Bashir al-Tartusi, the splinter group dropped their confrontational hisbah, which they no longer followed.[67] Meanwhile those who remained with al-Muhajiroun, in Whitechapel, Luton, Cardiff, and elsewhere, continued to "command good, forbid evil" and work towards establishing the caliphate. Although the coup did not succeed in overthrowing Choudary, it did underscore the extent to which some activists were willing to challenge his dogmatism, and their willingness to leave the network over this.

Such splits were rare in al-Muhajiroun, unlike other Salafi-jihadi networks and terrorist groups, which frequently splinter over ideological and practical disputes.[68] Individuals have always come and gone from the Emigrants, but this

---

[66] Interview with Salman, Poplar, East London, July 24, 2015.

[67] Interview with Salman, Poplar, East London, July 24, 2015. Salman provided the details of this episode, but I was able to confirm his account from an independent source in Whitechapel. Field notes, Whitechapel, East London, July 16, 2012.

[68] On fractionalization among Salafi-jihadi and radical Islamist groups, see Fawaz A. Gerges, "The Decline of Revolutionary Islam in Algeria and Egypt," *Survival*, 41, no. 1 (1999), pp. 113–25; and Jérôme Drevon, *Institutionalising Violence: Strategies of Jihad*, unpublished book manuscript. For more on splintering among terrorist groups, see Cronin, *How Terrorism Ends*, pp. 67–8; Martha Crenshaw, "Theories of Terrorism: Instrumental and Organisational Approaches," *Inside Terrorist Organisations*, edited by David C. Rapoport (London: Frank

was the only group-level split I observed during my years of field work. More often than splintering, the network formed spin-offs of like-minded activists to avoid law enforcement pressure, as I showed in the previous chapter. These spin-off groups continued to follow Bakri's ideas and the network's contentious politics.

The relative absence of splintering in al-Muhajiroun is due to its ideological cohesion and close-knit community of practice. While the community's dogmatism and insularity kept activists from studying with external preachers like Abu Bashir al-Tartusi, it also ensured they received the same "culturing" through the indoctrination provided by their halaqahs and their suhba or companionship with network leaders. By participating in the network's community of practice intellectual affiliates were socialized into a coherent set of beliefs and practices based exclusively on the teachings of Omar Bakri and his closest students. This minimized their exposure to potentially disruptive ideas and influences of outside ideologues, like Abu Hamza and Abu Qatadah.

Despite its cohesion, the Emigrants' community of practice does not prevent disputes among activists. Another conflict that has caused activists to leave al-Muhajiroun revolves around the contentious issue of whether it is permissible to carry out violent attacks within Britain. Network leaders, including Anjem Choudary and Omar Bakri, have repeatedly declared that Muslims in Britain, and the West more broadly, are bound by a "covenant of security" that prohibits them from attacking their home countries as long as their lives and property are protected. "If they ask about doing jihad in this country," Choudary told a reporter in 2009, "I tell them they live here under a covenant of security and that they are not allowed to kill people or target their wealth."[69] In interviews for this research, network activists consistently voiced their support for this covenant.[70] However, respondents also emphasized that the decision to follow this agreement is a personal one, to be made by individual activists, not network leaders. Moreover, activists stressed that the covenant does not apply to conflicts overseas, particularly where Western armies have "invaded" Muslim countries, like Iraq and Afghanistan.[71]

Over the years, a number of activists have disagreed with al-Muhajiroun's contention that violent attacks are not allowed in Britain and other Western

Cass, 2001), pp. 13–31; and John F. Morrison, "Splitting to Survive: Understanding Terrorist Group Fragmentation," *Journal of Criminological Research, Policy and Practice* 3, no. 3 (2017), pp. 222–32.

[69] David Cohen, "'Britain's most reviled man? I wear that badge with pride'," *Evening Standard* (March 13, 2009).

[70] Interviews with leading, veteran, and rank-and-file activists: Walthamstow, East London, November 16, 2010, Ilford, East London, November 13, 2010, Whitechapel, East London, December 7, 2010, Stratford, East London, June 27, 2011, Islington, North London, July 21, 2012, and Skype, June 26, 2013 and August 28, 2014.

[71] Interviews with activists, Whitechapel, East London, November 6, 2010, and Skype, October 8, 2014 and March 23, 2011. Also, field notes, Whitechapel, East London, June 16, 2011.

countries. Some have even left over this issue. I witnessed an example of this discord during a talk on the covenant of security by Rohan, one of the network's leading ideologues. Rohan delivered his talk online using PalTalk, the chatroom utility popular among activists. After completing his prepared remarks, he solicited questions and comments from his audience. Several participants asked him tough questions, essentially challenging his interpretation of the covenant. At one point, a forum member who went by the handle "Victory or Martyrdom" asked whether it was true that "several brothers" had recently left the network because they felt that the covenant of security "no longer holds in Britain." Rohan confirmed this and said that each person may interpret the covenant differently and that he was only sharing his interpretation, which was grounded in "Sheikh Omar Bakri Mohammed's" teachings.[72]

Several days later, I asked Rohan to elaborate in a follow-up interview. "I believe that I have security in Britain and I can't betray that," he explained. "There are other people who disagree with me on that and obviously they have strong arguments as well." The source of the PalTalk disagreement was the recent stabbing of a British Minister of Parliament by Roshonara Choudhry, a former university student who was reportedly influenced by Anwar al-Awlaki's call for Muslims to carry out violent attacks in the West.[73] When I asked Rohan whether activists left the network over this issue, he conceded the point: "Yes, you can have people leaving. People leave over many issues."[74] Referring to the same PalTalk exchange I witnessed, another leading activist agreed: "There are certain people in the UK who don't aspire to this notion of the covenant of security, even a few people who formerly used to be with us but no longer are."[75] As if to underscore the limits of the Emigrants' ideological coherence, and the divisive influence of external preachers, some activists felt that with Awlaki's call, the covenant of security no longer applied in Britain. These individuals were inspired by Roshonara Choudhry's attack and some of them left al-Muhajiroun as a result. But "these arguments have been going on for years, since before 7/7," Rohan emphasized. "We've always had these kinds of debates. It's nothing new at all."[76]

---

[72] Field notes, PalTalk chatroom, "Read In the Name of your Lord IQRA," November 27, 2010.

[73] Vikram Dodd, "Roshonara Choudhry: Police interview extracts," *The Guardian* (November 3, 2010), www.guardian.co.uk/uk/2010/nov/03/roshonara-choudhry-police-interview [Accessed January 10, 2011]; Katherine Faulkner, "Extremist website inspired stabbing of Stephen Timms urges Muslims to 'raise the knife of jihad' to other MPs," *Daily Mail* (November 5, 2010), www.dailymail.co.uk/news/article-1326842/Extremist-website-inspired-Stephen-Timms-stabbing-urges-raise-knife-jihad.html [Accessed November 6, 2010].

[74] Interview with Rohan, Whitechapel, East London, December 7, 2010.

[75] Interview with leading activist, Ilford, East London, November 29, 2010.

[76] Interview with Rohan, Whitechapel, East London, December 7, 2010. Also, interviews with another leading activist, Ilford, East London, November 29, 2010 and Wembley Central, West London, September 5, 2013, interviews with two different activists in Leyton, East London, November 6, 2010, and interview with a third activist in Bethnal Green, East London, November 28, 2010. Other researchers have noted earlier conflicts within al-Muhajiroun over

"A VERY HARD DECISION"

Leaving al-Muhajiroun is difficult. As they move towards full participation in the network's community of practice, activists develop strong relationships with their "brothers" and enjoy the community's fellowship first hand. They also internalize a set of religious beliefs that make clear they will face scorching consequences in the afterlife for leaving. Activists deepen their beliefs and friendships by spending lots of time with each other, studying in halaqahs, hanging out at da'wah stalls and demonstrations, eating in cafes and restaurants, playing sports and exercising, going on picnics and other trips, even completing the hajj to Mecca. Exiting the Emigrants means leaving all this, which presents a real obstacle for some. "It was a very, very hard decision for me to leave," explains Ali. "I was heartbroken because I detached myself from the brotherhood. The brotherhood was so strong." Asked what he missed most, Ali does not hesitate to answer: "The friendship with the boys and with Omar Bakri, with my masoul, with the mushrif [local area leader], with everybody."[77] "It was emotionally distressing," adds his wife, Maryam, discussing her own experience in a separate interview. "I had to break up with a lot of friends."[78]

Activists find it even harder to leave al-Muhajiroun when their family members remain involved. Abdul recalls the conflict in his immediate family when he decided to quit. His parents, who never supported his activism, were "overjoyed" by his decision, but his younger sister, who joined the Emigrants a year earlier, was equally dismayed. "Towards the latter stage of my experience with al-Muhajiroun, I was getting torn apart," he explains. "One of my family members got heavily involved with al-Muhajiroun and didn't appreciate that I had left. This caused some resentment." In addition to upsetting his sister, Abdul's decision to leave angered his closest friend, a veteran activist who recruited him and "was like an older brother to me." Abdul's departure challenged his sister's and his friend's identities and they both pressured him to stay. "It was difficult to leave because my family member was saying to me, 'Why are you leaving?' And [friend's name deleted] was saying, 'Why are you leaving? What's the point of leaving? What are you going to do with yourself?'" When his sister and friend realized he wasn't returning, it "caused a rift," a termination of two close relationships that continued to the time of our interview, a decade later.[79]

---

the legitimacy of political violence. See Wiktorowicz, *Radical Islam Rising*, pp. 213–14; Horgan, *Walking Away From Terrorism*, pp. 133–4; and Catherine Zara Raymond, "Al Muhajiroun and Islam4UK: The Group Behind the Ban," (London: International Centre for the Study of Radicalisation and Political Violence, King's College, 2010), pp. 6–7.

[77] Interview with Ali, Hounslow, West London, December 13, 2010.

[78] Interview with Maryam, Skype, November 20, 2012.

[79] Interview with Abdul, Whitechapel, East London, June 18, 2011.

Abdul was not the only respondent to suffer the emotional costs of leaving al-Muhajiroun. As his experience suggests, committed activists do not take their colleagues' departure lightly because it threatens their identities and the meaning of their activism. It is harder for activists to maintain they are engaged in a worthy cause when their closest colleagues reject the same cause and leave. Consistent with Albert Hirschman's analysis of business firms and political associations, and other researchers' discussions of religious sects, the Emigrants seek to make exit "costly" by exerting psychological pressure on members who are thinking of leaving.[80]

When activists realize their friends are in the process of leaving, they pressure them in an increasingly desperate bid to get them to stay. They call, email, and pester their departing colleagues, reminding them of their "obligation" to continue the call and warning them of the "hellish" consequences for quitting. "When I left, I had phone calls coming left, right and center from the sisters saying, 'How could you do that?,'" recalls Maryam. "They were intimidating, calling me and saying, 'You are sinful!'"[81] When her halaqah sisters failed to convince Maryam to return, her mushrif began to call her and her husband, Ali. "The brother who was leading the group in West London kept calling my husband, kept calling myself, saying 'Sister, why have you left?,'" she recalls.[82] After Maryam "cut off" her phone number in response to the calls, her former colleagues increased the pressure: "Two or three times I had sisters following me [in the street], saying, 'You are sinful. It is an obligation. Why have you given up this obligation which was placed upon you?'" Despite the pressure, Maryam denied ever feeling physically threatened. "It was more of a psychological pressure," she said. Her former sisters tried to exploit her "sense of isolation" for leaving the Emigrants, reinforcing "that psychological fear."[83]

In some cases, the psychological intimidation goes further. "They hold a grudge" when you leave, explains Haroon. "They try to smear your name in the community. 'He's an alcoholic, he does drugs, he's strayed off the platform, he has girlfriends.'"[84] Activists held a big grudge against his friend, Abdul, after he left. In an indication of how highly he was valued in al-Muhajiroun, Abdul received calls from Omar Bakri himself, asking him to return. Referring to Bakri by his initials, Abdul admits, without any hint of pride or pleasure, "I had OBM call me and say [mimics Bakri's voice], 'Brother, why are you leaving the group?'" When he told Bakri that he was frustrated with his personal life and

---

[80] Albert O. Hirschman, *Exit, Voice, and Loyalty: Response to Decline in Firms, Organizations, and States* (Cambridge, MA: Harvard University Press, 1970), p. 96; James T. Richardson, Jan van der Lans, and Frans Derks, "Leaving and Labeling: Voluntary and Coerced Disaffiliation from Religious Social Movements," *Research in Social Movements, Conflicts and Change* 9 (1986), pp. 97–126; and Thomas Robbins, *Cults, Converts and Charisma* (London: Sage, 1988).

[81] Interview with Maryam, Hounslow, West London, December 13, 2010.

[82] Interview with Maryam, Skype, November 20, 2012.

[83] Interview with Maryam, Skype, November 20, 2012.

[84] Interview with Haroon, Westminster, Central London, June 14, 2011.

"needed to study and try and get a family and stuff," the leader replied, "'we can provide you with women, no problem.'" But Abdul was no longer interested in anything Bakri or the Emigrants could offer. After he left, his former best friend in the network, who "was very angry" at him, and some other brothers helped arrange a marriage between his sister and another activist. The marriage had long-standing ramifications for Abdul and his family. Ten years later he still viewed it as his old friend's way of "getting back at me":

They purposefully set up a marriage between somebody and my sister and it caused a rift. Because I'd left they held a grudge against me and they got my sibling to marry somebody who wasn't appropriate, who wasn't worthy. He wasn't working, he wasn't doing anything. He's an active member of the group. It was not nice the way they treated me with all the stuff that I did for them... OBM phoned me up and said, 'Brother, this brother wants to marry your sister,' and stuff like that. I was like, 'Why are you phoning me? Why are you getting involved?' On the day of their marriage I was at university... My mom and my dad and I don't see my sister so much now. They caused a massive rift in my family.[85]

Despite the emotional price he paid, Abdul has few, if any, regrets about leaving. "Thank God I did leave because I'm fairly successful in what I do now," he explains. "After I got out of there, I furthered my career and got married. I have kids and stuff. Life is a lot more interesting now."[86] Other respondents share similar stories. "I am so grateful to God that I am out of al-Muhajiroun," notes Maryam. "I am in my second year of going to university. I am studying criminology, with a minor in sociology... I am myself now. I wear the jeans, I wear the *hijab* [veil that covers the head and chest but not the face]. I love my music as well."[87] "My life now is pretty good," adds Salman. "Since I've left al-Muhajiroun, I've done well for myself, my kids go to private school. All my mates who left with me, their children go to private schools. They're all business owners, investors. We're all pretty well off now."[88] These examples suggest that there is life after al-Muhajiroun, even for activists who were involved for years and found it difficult to leave.

DISENGAGEMENT VERSUS DERADICALIZATION

People who leave al-Muhajiroun experience a range of outcomes. Some activists "disengage" from the network without necessarily "deradicalizing" in the sense of changing their ideological beliefs. Others leave and gradually alter their political and religious attitudes in basic and profound ways. Still others depart only to escalate further into political violence.[89] The stories below draw

---

85 Interview with Abdul, Whitechapel, East London, June 18, 2011.
86 Interview with Abdul, Whitechapel, East London, June 18, 2011.
87 Interview with Maryam, Skype, November 20, 2012.
88 Interview with Salman, Poplar, East London, July 24, 2015.
89 The distinction between "disengagement" and "deradicalization" comes from the work of John Horgan and others. See Horgan, *Walking Away From Terrorism*; Altier, Thoroughgood, and

TABLE 5.1 *Status of al-Muhajiroun Respondents, circa 2017*

Estimated status of respondent at end of data collection	Number of al-Muhajiroun respondents	Percentage of al-Muhajiroun respondent sample (n = 48)
Left al-Muhajiroun	7	15%
Status unknown	18	38%
Still intellectually affiliated with al-Muhajiroun	13	27%
In prison custody serving sentences for crimes related to their activism	10	21%
Implicated in terrorist plot in the UK or left Britain to join ISIS or another militant group in Iraq and Syria	9	19%

Note: Readers should interpret these numbers with caution. The percentages refer only to my sample of respondents and cannot be generalized to larger populations, within or outside al-Muhajiroun. Also, eighteen "status unknowns" in a sample of forty-eight is a lot of missing data. I share these figures to illustrate the different trajectories of my respondents, rather than to suggest that I have complete information about their outcomes. Finally, the respondent count in the table's middle column is higher than forty-eight because I coded several respondents as being imprisoned yet still intellectually affiliated with al-Muhajiroun. These individuals continued to follow the network's ideology despite their incarceration.

on my respondents' experiences to illustrate these different outcomes. One insight that emerges from their experiences is that thinking of radicalization and deradicalization in binary "either/or" terms is not particularly helpful when tracing specific cases of departure.

Variation in exit outcomes is reflected in my respondent sample. Out of forty-eight respondents who were actively involved in al-Muhajiroun at the time of their interviews at least seven left the activist network in the years afterwards without radicalizing further into violent extremism. This represents 15 percent of my interview sample of al-Muhajiroun activists (but see my note in Table 5.1). The real number of activists who left without radicalizing further is probably higher because I do not know what happened to eighteen respondents who were active in the network when I interviewed them. While several of these "status unknown" respondents were devoted insiders in the network's community of practice, many were administrative affiliates who I saw only once or twice at da'wah stalls and other events. At least some of these eighteen individuals likely discontinued their activism without radical-izing further.

Other respondents, many of them persistent activists, continued their involvement in the Emigrants. At least thirteen of my forty-eight al-Muhajiroun respondents were still involved in the network at the conclusion of my field work. This represents 27 percent of my activist sample. I am more confident in this estimate because I could see for myself that these activists remained involved. However, the real number is again probably higher given that I don't know what happened to eighteen of my respondents. Also, not all respondents coded in Table 5.1 as being "intellectually affiliated" are still involved in day-to-day activism. Several of them are serving prison sentences for crimes related to their activism and others are under some form of government control, including Anti-Social Behaviour Orders (ASBOs) and Terror Prevention and Investigation Measures (TPIMs), which prevent them from interacting with other activists.

The seven activists in the table who left al-Muhajiroun do not include seven more respondents who had already left the network by the time I interviewed them, between 2010 and 2016. In other words, I interviewed at least fourteen people who left al-Muhajiroun, half before they left and half after. While these people no longer participate in the network's preaching and protests, not all of them have left its ideology behind. Rather than simply rejecting their old beliefs, some "formers" remain true to their intellectual affiliation long after the demands of parenthood, the desire to advance their careers, and other respon-sibilities pull them away. Some still believe in the network's culture even if they are no longer biographically available for activism. They demobilized from al-Muhajiroun, but they did not deradicalize. "Even if they aren't involved with it anymore, they still believe in it," explains Haroon.[90] In a separate interview several days later, he adds, "there are people who did not necessarily break off completely, but just kind of drifted out. They are very sympathetic to the cause."[91]

Some disengaged activists move away from al-Muhajiroun not because they disagree with the cause but because they object to how the network tries to bring it about. As I noted earlier in my discussion of the Emigrants' protest tac-tics, these respondents disagree with the network's strategy of calling attention to their activism through moral shock and provocation. While they still sympa-thize with the ideals they acquired through the network's community of prac-tice, they also believe that this strategy, and the incendiary tactics behind it, are counter-productive and bring great harm to Muslim communities. Abdul explains: "I agree with what they are trying to do, but I don't agree with how

---

[90] Interview with Haroon, Westminster, Central London, June 14, 2011.
[91] Interview with Haroon, Whitechapel, East London, June 18, 2011. Also, interview with leading activist, Ilford, East London, November 29, 2010.

they are doing it. They are fighting for a good cause. But do it the right way. Don't be aggressive about it."[92]

Other respondents no longer believe in many of the ideas they followed as activists. Some of these former supporters are more accepting, in their beliefs and actions, of Britain's secular democracy than they were as activists. Salman provides a remarkable example. I met with him several times during my field work, both when he was still active in al-Muhajiroun and after he left. This allowed me to observe changes in his beliefs and behaviors over time, in a sort of "natural experiment."

When I knew Salman from his activist days he was all in. He accepted the Emigrants' cause and culture without reservation. He studied exclusively with Omar Bakri Mohammed and other network ideologues. Like other activists Salman considered himself a "takfiri," someone who denounces other Muslims as non-believers, meaning that violence against them is justified. He believed that all forms of "man-made" law, including democracy, were irretrievably corrupt and that he had a divine obligation to help establish an Islamic state in Britain based on shariah law. Salman implemented his beliefs through his activism, participating regularly in da'wah stalls and demonstrations and forming a spin-off group that focused on street preaching. He was arrested on at least one occasion, after violently disrupting a campaign event for a local politician. In our interviews when he was still active, Salman emphasized that it was forbidden for him to integrate in British society and he downplayed his citizenship, identifying himself first and last as a Muslim.[93]

In the years since he left the Emigrants, Salman has altered his beliefs in basic and profound ways. "I have changed a lot of opinions," he acknowledges. "I no longer agree with Anjem Choudary or Omar Bakri." He rebukes al-Muhajiroun's insularity and insists that his days of studying exclusively with network ideologues, or any single cleric, are over: "I've opened my horizon. I study with many scholars now." Perhaps as a consequence of expanding his intellectual horizon, Salman no longer considers himself a takfiri: "I used to call the imam and scholar of the East London Mosque kafir because he believed in voting. I've taken that back. I don't believe he's kafir." He also cites the well-known American scholar, Yassir Qadhi, in this context: "I've listened to his lectures. I think he's okay. I might not believe everything he believes, but I do believe that you should take the good and leave the bad. If I turn and say, 'he's a kafir,' all I'm doing is making his blood *halal* [permissible]."[94]

Far removed from his days of disrupting campaign events, Salman now rejects the Emigrants' provocative hisbah, including the street demonstrations and flag

---

[92] Interview with Abdul, Whitechapel, East London, June 18, 2011. Also, interview with Rashid, Whitechapel, East London, June 26, 2011.

[93] Interviews with Salman, Bethnal Green, East London, November 28, 2010, and Leyton, East London, December 9, 2010.

[94] Interview with Salman, Poplar, East London, July 24, 2015.

burnings he used to enjoy. "I disagree with their approach," he explained after
I ran into him in Whitechapel, years after our first interviews. "It's too confrontational and it causes a lot of damage to the Muslim community."[95] In a follow-
up interview seven months later, Salman went so far as to express his support for
a recent government crackdown against the activist network. "They've got too
many restrictions against them," he said, referring to pressure against halaqahs
in Luton and Cardiff, two network strongholds. "I'm sorry for smiling, but
I think it's good that the authorities have done that because they [activists]
caused more harm, even though I love them and they're my brothers."[96]

Salman views individual activists with sympathy, but he sees their ideas
and activism as misguided: "I think some things they say is good, and some
things they say is bad, and I think sometimes it's ignorance why they do certain things." He no longer advocates for Islamic law in Britain: "I'm not here
to implement shariah." Nor does he support the Islamic State in Iraq and Syria
and the people who have joined it, including some of his old colleagues: "They
are going over there because of ignorance." Salman has even changed the way
he engages in da'wah, rejecting al-Muhajiroun's aggressive street preaching
in favor of a more traditional quietist approach. "I distribute the Qur'an and
I joined a group" that provides food to the homeless in London, Muslim and
non-Muslim alike.[97]

Salman's views on politics in Britain are particularly interesting – and complex. He still denounces national-level politicians as corrupt, but he no longer
rejects the political system out of hand: "I don't believe in Tony Blair, but I do
believe there are good people you can put in power." Paradoxically, he adds, "I
still don't believe in democracy, but as Muslims living here, you can participate
in a certain way," by which he means supporting local government: "the local
councils and community work, even mayors." Salman shows his passion for his
home country in rejecting the Emigrants' belief that Muslims are not allowed
to integrate in British society: "There's nothing wrong with it. Forget what they
say, I was *born* here. I might be Muslim by name and Islamic by religion, but
this is my country. I am going to interact and integrate with society." As part of
this integration, he defends his right to express his political views. "It doesn't
mean I can't speak against the government. I don't agree with David Cameron.
But I love this country, man."[98]

Salman still holds beliefs that many of his fellow citizens would find objectionable. He may have disengaged from al-Muhajiroun, but at the time of
our last interview it would be a mistake to characterize him as completely
"deradicalized." Yet part of what makes him so compelling is that his evolving
beliefs and actions underscore the futility in thinking of radicalization/

---

[95] Field notes, Whitechapel, East London, December 11, 2014.
[96] Interview with Salman, Poplar, East London, July 24, 2015.
[97] Interview with Salman, Poplar, East London, July 24, 2015.
[98] Interview with Salman, Poplar, East London, July 24, 2015.

deradicalization as an either/or proposition, akin to a metaphorical switch that can be turned on or off once certain attitudinal or behavioral thresholds are reached. Instead it is more helpful to think of him as engaged in an ongoing intellectual (and spiritual) journey away from al-Muhajiroun. This process unfolds along a "radicalization-deradicalization" spectrum, with many possible resting places on the continuum. Viewed from this perspective, Salman has made significant strides towards the "deradicalization" end of the continuum since leaving al-Muhajiroun. He rejects the activist network, along with its goal of bringing the Islamic State to Britain. Like other politically engaged citizens, he takes issue with certain government policies and denounces elite politicians, but he believes the country's political system is legitimate and deserving of his support. He sees Britain as his home and expresses no desire to raise his young family elsewhere. While there are no guarantees about where Salman's journey will take him in the future, I suspect he will continue to move closer towards the deradicalization end of the continuum as he matures into early middle age.

Other former activists have moved even closer to the deradicalization end of the spectrum. Four respondents who were involved in al-Muhajiroun for years not only disengaged from the activist network, they changed their attitudes and behaviors so profoundly that they ended up working in the new field of countering violent extremism. Maryam explains how "my whole perception of Islam has changed" since leaving al-Muhajiroun. Asked whether she retained any beliefs or values from her activist days, she replies, "my personal belief that God is ever-loving. Nothing else, to be honest. I have totally removed myself from them." After leaving the network, Maryam completed a bachelor's degree and worked as a counselor and project manager in one of the many deradicalization and community engagement programs that emerged in Britain after the 7/7 bombings.[99] Her husband, Ali, who left al-Muhajiroun shortly after her own departure, also works on countering violent extremism by counseling at-risk individuals.[100]

A third former activist who counsels at-risk youth draws on the expertise he developed as an al-Muhajiroun recruiter to steer his clients away from violent beliefs. "I always try to understand where the young person is coming from first," he explains. "If there are tell-tale physical signs of extremism, I will approach it in a soft way. If I see someone is ready for debate, I debate. There is never one way I can intervene with someone." Similar to his recruitment days with the Emigrants, he meets regularly with these youth, to engage them in discussion and build rapport. In his meetings, which can be one-on-one or in small groups of several youth, "I address them from my understanding of jihad and terrorism." Describing his own journey towards the deradicalization end of the spectrum, he recalls that after "two years of doubt and questioning, I just started to dislike *takfiri* ideology quite seriously. When you are fed up

---

[99] Interview with Maryam, Skype, November 20, 2012.
[100] Interview with Ali, Hounslow, West London, June 21, 2011.

with the ideology, the skin starts to shed." It took several more years for his al-Muhajiroun skin to shed completely and to find his calling in countering violent extremism (CVE): "It was not until 7/7, not until the 8th of July 2005 that I woke up and realized who I was. And as a result of realizing who I was, I realized what I must do next."[101]

EXITING AND RADICALIZING FURTHER INTO VIOLENCE

Not everyone who leaves al-Muhajiroun rejects political violence. Like a number of activists from different social movements, some Emigrants disengage because they become frustrated with peaceful activism and believe violence is necessary to achieve their political goals.[102] They wish to wield the sword of jihad, either in the United Kingdom or overseas. One respondent describes the fate of two young friends who introduced him to al-Muhajiroun. After studying for a period in one of the network's halaqahs and participating in da'wah stalls, both of his companions rejected the Emigrants' focus on da'wah, along with the covenant of security. "For those two brothers, it was all about jihad," he recalls. "They left with that mentality, only jihad, no da'wah."[103] The respondent does not know what happened to his friends, but numerous activists who left the network were later implicated in terrorist plots in Britain and elsewhere, while others emigrated to Iraq and Syria to join one of the militant groups fighting there or were caught trying.

Among the forty-eight individuals who were involved in al-Muhajiroun at the time of their interviews, nine were later implicated in terrorist plots in the United Kingdom or left Britain to fight on behalf of the Islamic State in Iraq and Syria. This represents 19 percent of my sample of al-Muhajiroun activists

---

[101] Interview with former activist, Walthamstow, East London, July 17, 2012.

[102] Political activists from a variety of groups and countries have escalated to violence. A classic example is the Weather Underground in the United States, which was created by several former leaders of the non-violent civil rights organization, Students for a Democratic Society. One hundred years earlier, in Tsarist Russia, disenchanted student activists formed the People's Will, which specialized in terrorist bombings and assassinations. In Italy and Germany, small networks of formerly non-violent activists created the Italian Red Brigades and the West German Red Army Faction, and in the Netherlands frustrated peace activists joined violent protest groups, including the anti-fascist movement. For more on the Weather Underground, see Ehud Sprinzak, "The Psychopolitical Formation of Extreme Left Terrorism in a Democracy: The Case of the Weathermen," in *Origins of Terrorism: Psychologies, Ideologies, Theologies, States of Mind*, edited by Walter Reich (Washington, DC: Woodrow Wilson Center Press, 1998), pp. 65–85. For discussion of the People's Will, see Marc Sageman, *Turning to Political Violence: The Emergence of Terrorism* (Philadelphia, PA: University of Pennsylvania Press, 2017), especially Chapter 4. For more on the Red Brigades and Red Army Faction, see Donatella della Porta, *Social Movements, Political Violence, and the State* (New York: Cambridge University Press, 1995). And for discussion of the Dutch peace and anti-fascist movements, see Klandermans, *The Social Psychology of Protest*, pp. 107–8.

[103] Interview with rank-and-file activist, Lewisham, South London, December 11, 2010.

(see Table 5.1, including my methodological note). Three of these nine activists were later reported in the media as being killed while fighting in Iraq or Syria. At least one has returned to the United Kingdom. Five more respondents tried to leave Britain for Iraq and Syria but were caught before they made it and sent home by the authorities. When added to the list of those who made it to ISIS' "caliphate" or who were implicated in recent terrorist plots in the United Kingdom, this suggests that at least fourteen activists in my sample, representing 29 percent, radicalized into political violence. Like the other outcomes I discussed earlier, the real number may be higher given that I don't know what happened to eighteen of my respondents. Either way, this confirms that for network activists movement along the radicalization-deradicalization continuum occurs in both directions.

Other activists I did not interview were also implicated in violent attacks after they left al-Muhajiroun. For example, in May 2013 Michael Adebowale and Michael Adebolajo shocked Britain by running over Lee Rigby, an off-duty British soldier, with a car and then hacking him to death with butcher knives and a meat cleaver. Adebowale attended al-Muhajiroun demonstrations outside the US embassy and St Paul's Cathedral months before the killing.[104] Adebolajo, the lead attacker, had been involved with the Emigrants, on and off, from approximately 2004 to 2010. During these years Adebolajo occasionally participated in a halaqah circle based in Woolwich and listened to talks by Omar Bakri and Anjem Choudary. He also handed out leaflets at da'wah stalls and attended demonstrations around London. While respondents, and Adebolajo himself, deny that he was ever a fully committed insider, his religious and political views were shaped by his activism. "He was on our ideological wavelength," Choudary acknowledged to one reporter.[105]

At some point in his development, Adebolajo became increasingly violent. He rejected al-Muhajiroun's stance on the covenant of security in favor of wielding the sword of jihad. Perhaps self-servingly, activists believe this change did not occur during Adebolajo's time with them, but after he was reportedly assaulted by Kenyan security forces during an ill-fated attempt to emigrate to Somalia by way of Kenya, in hopes of joining al-Shabaab. These respondents

---

[104] Sean O'Neill, "Cameron confronts 'extremist narrative'," *The Times* (London) (December 20, 2013), p. 9; BBC One, "From jail to jihad?," *Panorama* (May 12, 2014 at 20:30 BST), www.youtube.com/watch?v=_-GJtgGywWc#t=52 [Accessed August 2, 2014].

[105] Andrew Gilligan, "Woolwich attack: 'Lone wolves' who run with the pack," *Sunday Telegraph* (May 25, 2013), www.telegraph.co.uk/news/uknews/terrorism-in-the-uk/10080864/Woolwich-attack-Lone-wolves-who-run-with-the-pack.html [Accessed June 10, 2013]; and Esther Addley and Josh Halliday, "Lee Rigby murder: Adebolajo tells court soldier killed in 'military attack'," *The Guardian* (December 9, 2013), www.theguardian.com/uk-news/2013/dec/09/lee-rigby-murder-accused-adebolajo-religion-is-everything [Accessed December 16, 2013]. Also, interviews with activists, Skype, June 26, 2013, Whitechapel, East London, September 4, 2013, and Wembley Central, West London, September 5, 2013.

also cite pressure from British intelligence officers to make Adebolajo an informant after he was deported to the United Kingdom. "I believe he was tortured in Kenya and it may well have been that the British forced him to work for them in some form or another," explains a leading activist. "So maybe he did not believe there was a covenant anymore and he believed he was in a state of war with the non-Muslims."[106]

During his murder trial, Adebolajo acknowledged he participated in network protests and other events.[107] At one demonstration, he was arrested for assaulting two police officers. While being held by the police after his arrest, Adebolajo said he began to view peaceful protests as a form of "impotent rage." "It allows you to let off steam," he told the Old Bailey criminal court, but "[t]he reality is no demonstration will make a difference. Even the 1 million people [who] marched against the Iraq war… did not change a single thing."[108] In addition to becoming disillusioned with the Emigrants' protests, Adebolajo disagreed with Anjem Choudary's interpretation of jihad and the covenant of security. "If he would speak about jihad I would find it very difficult to accept what he had to say because I never knew him to fight jihad," Adebolajo testified, adding, "I think he is a good man, however he encourages his followers that jihad in this country is not allowed. He said we have a covenant of security."[109] Stymied in his attempt to wage jihad in Somalia and sent back to Britain, where he viewed non-violent protests as futile and possibly faced pressure from the authorities, Adebolajo may have concluded that the time had come for him to carry out an attack.

Michael Adebolajo was detained before he could fight on behalf of al-Shabaab, but other activists who left al-Muhajiroun succeeded in joining terrorist groups overseas. In recent years, a number of former activists have migrated to Iraq and Syria to join ISIS and other militant groups, or been caught trying. Contributing to these activists' willingness to leave Britain was not only the worsening of the Syrian conflict and Abu Bakr al-Baghdadi's declaration of the Islamic State, but legal problems related to their activism

---

[106] Interview with leading activist, Skype, June 26, 2013. Also interviews with another leading activist, Whitechapel, East London, September 4, 2013, and veteran activist, Wembley Central, West London, September 5, 2013.

[107] Sean O'Neill, "Radical clerics who shaped mind of Woolwich murderer," *The Times* (of London) (December 19, 2013), www.thetimes.co.uk/tto/news/uk/article3953568 [Accessed December 19, 2013]; Natalie Evans and Peter Stubley, "Lee Rigby trial: Recap updates as defence case for Woolwich murder suspect Michael Adebolajo begins," *Daily Mirror* (December 9, 2013), www.mirror.co.uk/news/uk-news/lee-rigby-trial-recap-updates-2907783 [Accessed September 29, 2014].

[108] Addley and Halliday, "Lee Rigby murder."

[109] Evans and Stubley, "Lee Rigby trial"; and Laura Smith-Spark and Kellie Morgan, "What led Michael Adebolajo and Michael Adebowale to murder Rigby?," *CNN* (December 19, 2013), www.cnn.com/2013/12/19/world/europe/uk-soldier-killing-profiles/ [Accessed September 29, 2014].

back home. As the authorities turned up the heat against them in Britain, the attraction of waging jihad and building the caliphate intensified. Government pressure, in other words, helped push these activists towards political violence.[110]

In March 2014, one of al-Muhajiroun's most outspoken activists, Abu Rahin Aziz, fled to Syria while on bail for beating up a bystander at a da'wah stall in London's West End.[111] As a leading activist explained, Aziz likely "found it expedient not to be around when his criminal case was going on, so he found himself abroad. Who wants to sit in prison for a few years when they can avoid it?"[112] Salman, who served with Aziz in al-Muhajiroun, agrees: "He went to Syria because he was going to get charged for GBH [grievous bodily harm, a British legal term for violent assault], so he thought the only way forward was to run off over there, rather than serve five years in prison here."[113]

In Syria, Aziz joined the Islamic State, becoming, as he told one journalist, part of its "regular fighting force."[114] He also applied propaganda skills he developed as an activist on behalf of his new organization. He made himself available to Western journalists, who reported on his latest exploits in Syria. In one interview he boasted of his desire to "behead an American or British soldier," while predicting that a terrorist attack in Britain was "inevitable."[115] In another, which featured a dramatic photo showing him shooting a heavy caliber assault rifle, he claimed to have "participated in many battles," including those "in which we liberated towns and villages... [and] where we were attacked and we managed to repel the enemies."[116] When not fighting, the former al-Muhajiroun activist continued his ideological struggle through Twitter, posting links to the latest ISIS propaganda videos and repeatedly calling for terrorist

---

[110] Other scholars who observe this dynamic in different militant groups include Donatella della Porta, *Clandestine Political Violence* (New York: Cambridge University Press, 2013); Cronin, *How Terrorism Ends*; Sageman, *Turning to Political Violence*; and Stefan Malthener, *Mobilizing the Faithful: Militant Islamist Groups and their Constituencies* (Frankfurt: Campus Verlag, 2001).

[111] Steve Swann and Secunder Kermani, "Pair under police investigation skip bail 'to fight in Syria'," *BBC News* (June 18, 2014), www.bbc.com/news/uk-27911081 [Accessed June 23, 2014]; *Luton On Sunday*, "Luton radical Abu Aziz has joined ISIS in Syria," (January 20, 2015), www.luton-dunstable.co.uk/Luton-radical-Abu-Aziz-joined-ISIS-Syria/story-25892785-detail/story.html [Accessed May 15, 2015].

[112] Interview with leading activist, Skype, August 28, 2014.

[113] Interview with Salman, Poplar, East London, July 24, 2015.

[114] David Churchill, "Jihadis who skipped bail to fight with IS: 'Extremists are waiting to attack UK'," *The Evening Standard* (February 11, 2015), www.standard.co.uk/news/london/jihadis-who-skipped-bail-to-fight-with-is-extremists-are-waiting-to-attack-uk-10038273.html [Accessed February 12, 2015].

[115] Churchill, "Jihadis who skipped bail to fight with IS."

[116] *PI Magazine*, "'West Can't Defeat Islamic State' British IS Fighter," *PassionIslam News and Sport* (February 2015), http://issuu.com/passionislam/docs/pi_magazine_february_2015/0 [Accessed June 10, 2015].

attacks in Britain.[117] In one especially provocative set of tweets, he posted photos of a "TNT explosive belt" filled with shrapnel and suggested possible targets around London, urging his followers to "Let the reality hit home," so that Londoners may experience "the taste of chaos, carnage and bloodshed."[118] A day after tweeting another threat, vowing that the 2015 anniversary of the 4th of July would be a "day to remember," Aziz himself was killed in a series of US airstrikes targeting ISIS fighters in Raqqa.[119]

Another activist, Siddhartha "Abu Rumaysah" Dhar, fled to Syria with his young family after being released on bail following his arrest in the September 2014 roundup of network leaders. Describing Dhar's motivations for leaving Britain, a leading activist recalled his former student's enthusiasm for the Islamic State: "He wanted to bring up his children there, he was extolling the virtues of it. So it's to fulfill a dream, that's the reason."[120] Salman, who knew Dhar well from their days together in the Whitechapel halaqah, highlighted the legal pressure his friend faced in Britain: "You have to understand something. When you corner people sometimes they have no choice but to go there. I'm sure if they didn't corner him, he wouldn't have gone over there. It was because he was cornered and he probably thought, 'I've got nowhere else to go apart from over there.'"[121] The leading activist agrees, adding that British authorities gave his student the opportunity when they released him from custody without securing his passport, which they failed to confiscate during their raid on his home: "I think he thought, 'I won't get another chance, they're going to take my passport,' so let's take the chance and just go."[122]

[117] Abu Abdullah Britani@dugma4uk (various tweets from April 18 to April 25, 2015), https:// twitter.com/dugma4uk [Accessed April 25, 2015]; Abu Abdullah Britani ɣ@dugma4europe (tweet from April 30, 2015), https://twitter.com/dugma4europe/status/593846101477826560 [Accessed April 30, 2015]; Abu Abdullah Britani@Time4Dugma (various tweets from May 3–4, 2015), https://twitter.com/Time4Dugma [Accessed May 4, 2015].

[118] Rita Katz, "IS fighters continue tweeting threats after Texas attack and Twitter won't stop them," *Insite Blog on Terrorism and Extremism* (May 19, 2015), https://news.siteintelgroup .com/blog/index.php/entry/384-is-fighters-continue-to-openly-tweet-threats-after-texas-attack-and-twitter-won%E2%80%99t-stop-them [Accessed May 20, 2015].

[119] Brian Ross, Megan Churchmach, and Cho Park, "Turnabout: ISIS fighter makes July 4 threat, reportedly killed that day," *ABC News* (July 6, 2015), http://abcnews.go.com/International/ turnabout-isis-fighter-makes-july-threat-reportedly-killed/story?id=32259819 [Accessed July 8, 2015]; James Dunn and Corey Charlton, "British jihadi who fled to Syria to join ISIS after stabbing football fan in the head 'among ten killed' following Coalition airstrikes on group's capital of Raqqa," *Daily Mail* (July 5, 2015), www.dailymail.co.uk/news/article-3150149/ Coalition-hits-ISIS-s-capital-16-airstrikes-terror-group-s-propaganda-arm-releases-images-people-say-dead.html [Accessed July 8, 2015].

[120] Interview with leading activist, Ilford, East London, December 9, 2014.

[121] Interview with Salman, Poplar, East London, July 24, 2015.

[122] Interview with leading activist, Ilford, East London, December 9, 2014. Also interview with another leading activist, Stratford, East London, December 13, 2014.

Just go Dhar did, ending up in Syria soon afterward, where, like Aziz, he put his propaganda talents to work for the Islamic State. In a series of tweets he ridiculed Britain's "shoddy security system" for allowing him "to breeze through Europe to the Islamic State" and he called on his fellow "emigrants" in Britain to "make hijrah" to the fledging caliphate.[123] He also wrote and posted reports that justified ISIS' use of violence against civilians and romanticized life in Syria under the "just shade" of the khilafah.[124]

As his time in Syria lengthened and he experienced the ravages of the country's devastating war first hand, Siddhartha Dhar's radicalization progressed. In *A Brief Guide to the Islamic State*, posted online after he'd been in Syria for more than six months, Dhar described "feeling angry – very angry" after witnessing what he identifies as an American airstrike against "a regular police station" that killed "forty civilians." He concludes his report with a message to his Western readers, promising that the Islamic State will "spill your blood," "destroy your statues," "erase your history," and "most painfully, convert your children."[125] While the world continues to wait for ISIS to descend, as Dhar promised, on "Damascus and Baghdad," let alone "London, Paris and Washington," his terrorist career advanced. In early January 2016, the former al-Muhajiroun activist was identified as the likely narrator in a new propaganda video. The video reportedly shows him and another former activist, Mohammed Haque, along with three other masked gunmen, shooting, execution style, five "spies" in the backs of their heads as they kneel in front of them.[126] Two years later, in January 2018, Dhar was placed on the US State Department's list of Specially

[123] Abu Rumaysah tweets (November 24 and 25, 2014), https://twitter.com/aburumaysah1435 [Accessed November 25, 2014]; Lizzie Dearden, "War against ISIS: British radical Abu Rumaysah taunts police and heralds new 'generation' of terrorist as he parades 'newborn son' in Syria," *The Independent* (November 26, 2014), www.independent.co.uk/news/uk/home-news/british-isis-supporter-abu-rumaysah-parades-newborn-son-in-syria-9884255.html [Accessed November 26, 2014].

[124] Abu Rumaysah al Britani, "Jihadi John & the Right to be Violent," (March 2, 2015), http://justpaste.it/right2violence [Accessed March 5, 2015]; and Abu Rumaysah al Britani, *A Brief Guide to the Islamic State [2015]*, (May 19, 2015), http://justpaste.it/l81f [Accessed May 19, 2015].

[125] Abu Rumaysah al Britani, *A Brief Guide to the Islamic State [2015]*, p. 46.

[126] BBC News, "Islamic State video suspect thought to be Briton Siddhartha Dhar," (January 5, 2016), www.bbc.com/news/uk-35228558 [Accessed June 5, 2016]; Martin Evans, "New Jihadi John suspect 'skipped bail over terror offences' and declared ISIL support on the BBC," *Daily Telegraph* (January 5, 2016), www.telegraph.co.uk/news/worldnews/islamic-state/12081552/new-jihadi-john-Siddhartha-Dhar-isil-terrorist.html [Accessed June 3, 2016]; Duncan Gardham, "Former hate preacher bodyguard nicknamed the 'Giant' feared to be the second British killer filmed shooting dead 'spies' in latest sick ISIS video," *Sunday Mail* (January 16, 2016), www.dailymail.co.uk/news/article-3403037/Former-hate-preacher-bodyguard-nicknamed-Giant-feared-SECOND-British-killer-filmed-shooting-dead-spies-latest-sick-ISIS-video.html [Accessed October 27, 2016].

Designated Global Terrorists, suggesting he was still alive even as the caliphate to which he sacrificed so much lay largely in ruins.[127]

CONCLUSION

For every activist who becomes an executioner for the Islamic State, many others disengage from al-Muhajiroun and go on to lead lives of ordinary industriousness in Great Britain. Participation in the activist network for these individuals is a passionate, and ultimately passing, fancy of adolescence. While no single cause or path leads activists away from the Emigrants, certain patterns are apparent. As they mature into adulthood many lose their desire and biographical availability to engage in high-risk activism. After watching old friends and acquaintances from outside the network move on with their careers and personal lives, the weight of activists' sacrifices appears heavier. The rewards of the afterlife remain desirable, but earthly concerns – to complete the education they interrupted for their activism, to get married and start a family, to earn money and establish themselves in a satisfying career – begin to outweigh their desire to call society to Islam and command good and forbid evil. Activists start to burn out from the relentless pace of their activism, of constantly having to participate in yet another da'wah stall or demonstration. They grow tired of repeating the same lessons in their weekly halaqahs and listening to the same speakers, often working from their notes of Omar Bakri's old lectures. They become frustrated with the network's demands on their time and other resources, including the frequent requests for money. They grow weary of fighting with their parents, of having to justify their activism to Muslim relatives who dispute their understanding of the religion.

In the midst of all this growing up and burning out, activists' commitment to the Emigrants weakens. They begin to question how shouting inflammatory slogans at passersby, covering street signs and traffic lights with stickers, and burning replicas of British and American flags will actually lead to the caliphate. They see that the network's strategy of activism has produced few tangible results, beyond landing some activists in jail and building up their leaders' public profiles as some of the most reviled men in Great Britain. They realize that their incendiary hisbah causes more harm than good to local Muslims who are stigmatized with the network's extremist beliefs and belligerent activism. And they become disillusioned with al-Muhajiroun's understanding of Islam, which they see is grounded in one man's interpretation of scripture, a man who lacks the educational pedigree of more established scholars and who has changed his theological beliefs more than once.

---

[127] US Department of State, press release, "State Department Terrorist Designations of Siddhartha Dhar and Abdelatif Gaini," (January 23, 2018), www.state.gov/r/pa/prs/ps/2018/01/277594 .htm [Accessed February 2, 2018].

Somewhere along the way, in this process of questioning and reevaluating their commitment, many activists reach a point of no return. As much as they hate to leave their friendships and al-Muhajiroun's fellowship behind, they become convinced that exiting is the only solution to their discontent. Before they go, some give voice to their disillusionment, explaining to fellow activists why they are leaving and where they think the network has gone wrong. Their claims are met with counter-arguments and psychological pressure, as those who remain scold them for their lack of commitment and warn them of the blazing consequences for their betrayal. When repeated phone calls, emails, and visits prove insufficient to turn them around, the psychological coercion may escalate to retribution. Activists who feel threatened by their departure may slander them and look for other ways of "getting back" at them. But such desperate efforts to increase the costs of exit rarely work. Individuals who have advanced this far in leaving al-Muhajiroun generally complete the process, moving beyond their youthful dalliance in the network to enter the next chapter of their still young lives.

Life beyond the Emigrants takes many forms. Some activists leave and become productive members of British society by completing their education, embarking on new careers, and raising young families. Some of these individuals remain sympathetic to their ideals. They disengage from the network but do not fully deradicalize from its culture. Others truly leave al-Muhajiroun behind, rejecting its core beliefs and confrontational activism, accepting that Britain's "sovereignty of man" has much to offer her Muslim citizens. But demobilizing from the Emigrants is neither simple nor easy. It involves moving along a spectrum of attitudinal and behavioral changes rather than merely flipping a metaphorical switch. Some activists move farther along this continuum than others, transforming their old activist passion into a new-found vocation to counter al-Muhajiroun's narrative among those most vulnerable to it. Sadly, others move in the opposite direction, radicalizing further into political violence. Some of these individuals become involved in terrorism or emigrate to join ISIS and other militant groups that wield the sword of jihad. Their paths display certain patterns, such as the influence of state pressure in nudging them towards violence. But the exceptions to every observation challenge my ability to make general statements or hard-and-fast predictions. After all, some activists left Britain to pick up the sword of jihad without being under any legal pressure for their activism, while others faced arrest and imprisonment in Britain without deciding it was time to flee the country – or wage war within it.

Whether they left al-Muhajiroun to pursue jihad or to combat it, the departure of so many supporters in recent years has further weakened the network. Replacing the likes of Abu Rahin Aziz and Siddhartha Dhar is not easy, particularly for an already marginalized network that faces growing resistance from local communities and intense pressure from government authorities. What has kept the network going in the face of such hostility are its "persistent activists," the highly committed insiders who have dedicated their lives to their activism. These old-school veterans continue their mission, recruiting a diminished flow of new supporters and indoctrinating them in the Emigrants' revolutionary vision. In doing so, they provide the weakened network with a measure of resilience, along with the hope that it might someday recapture the notoriety it once enjoyed.

Conclusion: Ending the Emigrants

> If I see any of their members, I debate them. I talk to them and say, "This is the wrong way. This is not the way of the sunnah and of the Qur'an."
>
> Salman, former activist

On July 28, 2016, almost two years after British authorities raided their homes and arrested them, Anjem Choudary and Mizanur Rahman were found guilty of encouraging support for the Islamic State in Iraq and Syria. A jury of six men and six women reached the verdict following a five-week trial in which prosecutors presented evidence of an online pledge, issued in their names and declaring their support for the "Islamic Caliphate State." Other key pieces of evidence included YouTube lectures by both men discussing why they believed Abu Bakr al-Baghdadi's caliphate was authentic and why Muslims should support it.[1] Choudary's conviction was celebrated in the media as a turning point in Britain's struggle against violent extremism. With the United Kingdom's most famous hate preacher finally in jail, many hoped the country would finally be rid of his activist network.

A careful reading of this book suggests otherwise. To be sure the outlawed activist network today is smaller and weaker than it has been in many years.

---

[1] London Metropolitan Police, "Two men guilty of encouraging support for terrorist organisation," (August 16, 2016), http://news.met.police.uk/news/two-men-guilty-of-encouraging-support-for-terrorist-organisation-179432 [Accessed October 28, 2016]; Martin Evans, Nicola Harley, Ben Farmer, and Ben Riley-Smith, "Radical preacher Anjem Choudary behind bars as police reveal his links to 500 ISIL jihadists," *Daily Telegraph* (August 16, 2016), www.telegraph.co.uk/news/2016/08/16/radical-preacher-anjem-choudary-behind-bars-after-drumming-up-su/ [Accessed August 17, 2016]; Fiona Hamilton and Duncan Gardham, "Jail at last for hate cleric after terror links exposed," *The Times* (London) (August 17, 2016), www.thetimes.co.uk/article/jail-at-last-for-hate-cleric-after-terror-links-exposed-kr8lb7bfl [Accessed August 22, 2016].

Leaders like Choudary and Rahman are in jail or under government control orders. Choudary himself was placed on the US State Department's list of international terrorists.[2] Rank-and-file supporters no longer have access to him and other leading activists who bridged different halaqahs. Activists have stopped commanding good and forbidding evil in public rallies. The vast majority of British Muslims, who already rejected the network's quixotic attempt to establish the Islamic state in their home country, have been dismayed by al-Muhajiroun's embrace of ISIS and its avid brutality.

Given the Emigrants' current weakness and marginalization, government authorities may be forgiven for concluding they have eliminated the activist network. Yet residues of al-Muhajiroun remain, radicalized and resilient. Supporters continue to perform da'wah, calling others to their extreme vision of Islam. Local halaqahs meet and indoctrinate activists, while carefully avoiding the public limelight. Even more troubling for security officials, some former activists have concluded that the covenant of security no longer applies in Britain, allowing them to engage in political violence against their fellow citizens. This includes the devastating rampage by Khuram Butt who, along with two accomplices, killed eight people and wounded dozens more at the London Bridge and Borough Market in June 2017.[3]

We may not have seen the last of al-Muhajiroun or its persistent activists. In this final chapter I draw on my findings to explain why. I also consider some of the larger implications of my research, as they relate to ongoing debates about radicalization and whether the Emigrants are a "conveyor belt" to political violence or a "safety valve" for alienated youngsters.

THE EMIGRANTS: DEAD OR DORMANT?

Previous chapters describe the British government's various crackdowns against al-Muhajiroun, along with the activist network's simple yet sundry adaptations to these setbacks. The latest crackdown bears some similarities to one of the authorities' earliest and most effective offensives, ten years before

---

[2] US Department of State, press release, "State Department Terrorist Designations of El Shafee Elsheikh, Anjem Choudary, Sami Bouras, Shane Dominic Crawford, and Mark John Taylor," (March 30, 2017), www.state.gov/r/pa/prs/ps/2017/03/269306.htm [Accessed March 5, 2018].

[3] Lizzie Dearden, "London attack linked to hate preacher Anjem Choudary's extremist network," *The Independent* (June 6, 2017), www.independent.co.uk/news/uk/home-news/london-attack-bridge-borough-isis-perpetrators-khuram-butt-links-anjem-choudary-documentary-jihadis-a7776101.html [Accessed June 6, 2017]; Rukmini Callimachi and Katrin Bennhold, "London Attackers Slipped By Despite an Avalanche of Warnings," *New York Times* (June 6, 2017), www.nytimes.com/2017/06/06/world/europe/london-assailants-terrorism-warning-signs-fbi.html [Accessed June 7, 2017]; Robert Booth, Ian Cobain, Vikram Dodd, Matthew Taylor, and Lisa O'Carroll, "London Bridge attacker named as Khuram Butt," *The Guardian* (June 6, 2017), www.theguardian.com/uk-news/2017/jun/05/london-bridge-attacker-named-as-khuram-butt [Accessed June 6, 2017].

the recent convictions. This first crackdown occurred after activists from al-Ghurabaa and the Saved Sect organized a large march of several hundred protestors to the Danish embassy in London in 2006, where they were filmed calling for violence in response to the publication of cartoons lampooning the Prophet Mohammed in a Danish newspaper. Following a public outcry over the demonstration, Home Secretary John Reid used new powers from the amended Terrorism Act to outlaw both spin-off groups for glorifying terrorism. Meanwhile Reid's colleagues in the British government began criminal investigations that led to the imprisonment of several leading activists for their actions at the protest and an earlier demonstration against the Iraq war at the Regent's Park Mosque in 2004.

While Anjem Choudary avoided prosecution in this early crackdown, Mizanur Rahman did not. In two separate trials, he was found guilty of inciting racial hatred and solicitation to commit murder. Originally sentenced to serve nine years for his crimes, Rahman later had his sentence reduced on appeal. Similar to other persistent activists like Abdul Muhid, Sulaymon Keeler, and Abu Izzadeen Brooks, who were also convicted of crimes related to the protests, Rahman ended up serving a four-year sentence. This included two years of custodial imprisonment followed by two years of supervised release in the community. He spent most of his prison time at Belmarsh, the same maximum security facility where he and Anjem Choudary were sent a decade later to begin their five-and-a-half year sentences for supporting ISIS.

By April 2008, Rahman and other persistent activists who organized al-Muhajiroun's biggest events were incarcerated and the network's primary spin-off groups were officially outlawed. The Emigrants went dormant, but their network did not collapse. Then something remarkable happened. Instead of abandoning their activism, activists set about quietly rebuilding their network. Under Anjem Choudary's leadership, over the next couple of years they recruited new supporters and indoctrinated them in al-Muhajiroun's blend of Salafi theology and Islamist ideology. As they revitalized their network, activists minimized their public profile, focusing more on da'wah than attention-grabbing hisbah. Meanwhile, Rahman, Muhid, Keeler, and Brooks used their time in jail to deepen their study of Arabic and Islamic scripture, becoming even more dogmatic in their religious and political beliefs. When these and other incarcerated veterans were released from prison, they were often met at the prison gates by activists eager to reconnect them to the network. They did not disappoint. Virtually all of them re-engaged with the Emigrants. Following Brook's release from Pentonville prison for speeches he made at the 2004 Iraq war protest, he was greeted by over a dozen delighted activists. Moments after embracing his supporters, he resumed his activism quite literally where he left off, climbing on top of the prison wall and making an impromptu speech denouncing British soldiers in Iraq and Afghanistan as rapists and murderers.[4]

---

[4] Duncan Gardham, "Terrorist whips up crowd minutes after release from jail," *Daily Telegraph*

Referring to Abu Izzadeen and other colleagues who were imprisoned for their roles in the Danish embassy and Iraq war protests, one leading activist, who was present at Brook's release, confirmed, "Every single one of those people that have come out of prison have come back into the da'wah – and they're stronger on the da'wah."[5] Rather than turning these persistent activists away from al-Muhajiroun, arrest and incarceration strengthened their commitment, prolonged their activism, and increased their status in the network. I saw this myself at da'wah stalls and demonstrations. At one demonstration, in support of Omar Bakri following his 2010 arrest in Lebanon, I saw five different activists who had served prison time for crimes related to their activism. Several were identified at the protest as leading students of Bakri and gave speeches in support of their mentor.[6]

These and other persistent activists sparked a revival in al-Muhajiroun by working closely with their young colleagues, many of whom joined during this rebuilding period. Leaders like Mizanur Rahman and Abu Izzadeen Brooks were highly regarded among the new recruits because they had demonstrated their commitment to the cause by serving time for their activism and returning to it following their release. Working closely with the new activists, these resilient veterans helped create spin-off groups like Islam4UK and Muslims Against Crusades, which breathed new life into the network's activism. Under the loose guidance of Brooks, Rahman, Anjem Choudary, and others, these platforms organized highly provocative demonstrations that brought the network unprecedented press coverage and a steady stream of new recruits. By the fall of 2010, when I began my field work, the activist network was back, better than ever.

The Emigrants were not the only ones who refused to give up. Scotland Yard continued to target the activist network, monitoring their events, arresting activists, and raiding their homes whenever possible. Choudary's and Rahman's decision to pledge loyalty to the Islamic State may have been understandable, even predictable, given their long-standing commitment to the caliphate, but it also gave law enforcers the opportunity they needed. Both men were imprisoned for supporting the Islamic State, and several activists from Luton, including long-time veteran Mohammed Alamgir, were convicted of similar charges after their halaqah was infiltrated by an undercover officer.[7] After being detained in Hungary while reportedly attempting to travel to Turkey, Brooks and Keeler

(October 28, 2010), www.telegraph.co.uk/news/uknews/terrorism-in-the-uk/8094429/Terrorist-whips-up-crowd-minutes-after-release-from-jail.html [Accessed October 28, 2010]; *Daily Mail*, "Hate preacher is freed from jail and immediately tells Britons not to wear Remembrance Day Poppies," (October 28, 2010), www.dailymail.co.uk/news/article-1324603/Hate-preacher-says-Remembrance-Day-Poppies-shunned-released-jail.html# [Accessed October 28, 2010].
[5] Interview with leading activist, Walthamstow, East London, June 22, 2011.
[6] Field notes, protest against Omar Bakri's arrest in Lebanon, Kensington, Central London, November 15, 2010.
[7] The Crown Prosecution Service, "Men jailed for supporting terrorism," (February 2, 2017), www.cps.gov.uk/news/latest_news/men_jailed_for_supporting_terrorism/ [Accessed June 23, 2017].

were sent back to Britain and jailed for violating the Counter-Terrorism Act (2008) by leaving the country illegally.[8] Other leading and veteran activists, including Abdul Muhid, Mohammed Shamsuddin, and Afsor Ali, were placed on restrictive government controls such as the Terror Prevention and Investigation Measures (TPIMs), Anti-Social Behaviour Orders (ASBOs), and Multi-Agency Public Protection Arrangements (MAPPA). Meanwhile, Omar Bakri Mohammed languished under hard labor in a Lebanese prison, where he was serving a lengthy sentence for promoting extremism and encouraging violence.

Throughout this book, especially in Chapter 1, I have argued that al-Muhajiroun's small-world-like network, with its tight local clusters and the redundant nodes bridging them, was more resistant to leadership decapitation than the scale-free network built around Omar Bakri during the Emigrants' early years. But the recent pressure against so many leading and veteran activists raises an important question. Have British authorities finally succeeded in removing enough nodes that bridge different clusters to fragment its small-world network into isolated halaqahs?

There is evidence to support this. Many activists who connected the different halaqahs are no longer active in al-Muhajiroun. All seven of the top-ranked activists for node-level degree centrality in the final period of the network analysis in Chapter 1 – Anjem Choudary, Omar Bakri, Abu Izzadeen Brooks, Abdul Rahman Saleem, Abdul Muhid, Ibrahim Hassan, and Mizanur Rahman – are either in prison, under some administrative control, or have left the network. The same holds true for the top seven ranked activists in the final period for the more relevant measure of betweenness centrality, which measures brokerage, the ability to connect otherwise unconnected nodes. These incapacitated brokers include Choudary, Bakri, Saleem, Brooks, Muhid, Afsor Ali, and Mohammed Shamsuddin.[9] Other veteran activists not captured

---

[8] The Crown Prosecution Service, "The Counter-Terrorism Division of the Crown Prosecution Service (CPS) – cases concluded in 2015," www.cps.gov.uk/publications/prosecution/ctd_2015 .html#a30 [Accessed June 23, 2017]; *BBC News*, "Two jailed for breaching terror laws after Hungary deportation," (January 8, 2016), www.bbc.com/news/uk-england-london-35262460 [Accessed October 27, 2016].

[9] The reason I discuss seven activists for each measure, and not the ten shown in the tables in Chapter 1 is because both measures contain three false positives. The three false positives for node-level degree centrality (Table 1.5) are Abu Hamza, Ali Beheshti, and Afzal Munir. The three false positives for betweenness centrality (Table 1.6) are Abu Hamza, Omar Khyam, and Afzal Munir. Some of these individuals belonged to the Emigrants, but none of them acted as prominent brokers in the network by bridging different halaqahs. Consistent with my analysis, none of these four individuals are currently active in al-Muhajiroun. Abu Hamza is currently serving a lifetime prison sentence without parole in the United States after being convicted of eleven terrorism offenses. Omar Khyam is serving a twenty-year prison sentence in the United Kingdom for his role in the fertilizer bomb plot. Afzal Munir was killed by a US missile attack in Afghanistan in 2001 while reportedly fighting for the Taliban. Ali Beheshti, the lone success story of the bunch, has reportedly deradicalized and turned his life around since completing a prison sentence for firebombing the home of a British publisher in 2008. For more on Beheshti's

in these rankings but who brokered connections to different halaqahs before being imprisoned recently include Anthony Small, Ricardo MacFarlane, and Sulaymon Keeler. Local halaqahs continue to function, but they are led by persistent activists who can only mobilize a few supporters.[10] Connections between clusters have diminished greatly. The network has lost its former cohesiveness and is now highly fragmented.

The apparent loss of their small-world structure has further weakened the Emigrants. Many supporters have left and the network is smaller and less capable of performing public da'wah and hisbah than it was during its heyday. The network no longer organizes large demonstrations, public conferences, or even "Islamic roadshows." The da'wah stalls activists do manage to hold are small and low-key, with a focus on the religious side of their preaching. After years of bad press in Britain's tabloids and widespread opposition towards ISIS, al-Muhajiroun is even more marginalized from the country's Muslim communities. This can be seen in the complete lack of public support for Choudary and Rahman during their trial and following their convictions for what are essentially speech crimes. If nothing else, the Islamic State's repressive theocracy in Iraq and Syria has tarnished once romantic notions of the caliphate's triumphant return, the abiding goal of the Emigrants' twenty years of activism. The vast majority of Muslims living in Great Britain, and the West more broadly, have little desire to see the Islamic State's brutal system of governance implemented where they live. And they have little sympathy for al-Muhajiroun and other extremists who, appallingly in their view, see the "Islamic Caliphate State" as the embodiment of God's rule on Earth. British Muslims' anger and exasperation towards fringe extremists has only intensified in the wake of several deadly incidents in 2017, including a motor vehicle and stabbing attack near the Houses of Parliament in March, a suicide bombing at a music concert in Manchester in May, and the London Bridge and Borough Market rampage by Khuram Butt and his accomplices in June.

Given the Emigrants' current weakness and marginalization, it is understandable that the activist network has been largely written off. But whether al-Muhajiroun is truly dead, or merely dormant, remains to be seen. Will surviving activists abandon their activism, giving up on what they see as something God commands them to do, or will they seek to rebuild their network, as they did in the years after British authorities' first crackdown? Much will depend on the fate of its persistent activists, the leaders and veterans who have weathered previous counter-terrorism storms, only to emerge more committed to their activism and the Emigrants' community of practice.

---

turn from violent extremism, including the role played by Usman Raja and his charity, the Unity Initiative, see Chris Vallance, "How one extremist rejected violence," *BBC Radio 4*, PM Programme (July 2, 2013), www.bbc.com/news/uk-23131706 [Accessed January 7, 2018].

[10] Email from Douglas Weeks, researcher on al-Muhajiroun, October 15, 2017.

One such figure is Mizanur Rahman. He has been here before. He knows what to expect and he knows how to use his prison time to his benefit. Many observers have expressed concern over the possibility that he and Anjem Choudary will radicalize other prisoners, but Rahman is more likely to use his time to quietly study Arabic and Islamic scripture. Even if he is largely isolated from other prisoners, he is unlikely to crack under the stress of being locked up or to experience a jailhouse "conversion" away from his Salafi-Islamist ideology. Rahman emerged from his earlier incarceration in Belmarsh prison even more dedicated to his cause, despite having received, like other activists, "deradicalization" programming. Rather than fundamentally questioning his beliefs, he seems more likely to recommit to them, drawing inspiration from his imprisonment by comparing the "repression" he and his fellow activists face in Britain with the sufferings of the Prophet Muhammad and his followers when they were persecuted in Mecca during the early years of Islam.

Anjem Choudary follows the same convictions, but his path is less certain simply because he has not been in this situation before. While he has been arrested and had his home raided on numerous occasions, this is his first extended imprisonment. Like other jailed activists, he views his incarceration as an opportunity to engage in da'wah with other prisoners. In July 2017 Choudary became one of the first inmates in a special new isolation unit at Frankland prison in north-east Britain. He was sent to the unit, which is designed to limit prison radicalization, after reportedly refusing to stop proselytizing to other inmates at Belmarsh. It is not clear whether Choudary's placement in the Frankland unit will prevent him from indoctrinating other prisoners given that it contains other extremists considered too dangerous to be housed with regular inmates. He is no religious scholar, but Choudary's knowledge of Islamic scripture and history is considerable, at least compared to other extremists such as Michael Adebolajo, Lee Rigby's murderer, who until recently was also housed at Frankland.[11]

Despite Choudary's public persona as a rabid ideologue, he is sociable and charming when he wants to be. He enjoys engaging Muslims and non-Muslims in da'wah and intellectual debate. His enforced isolation may be hard on him. If nothing else, prison gives people time to think. It is certainly possible that he, along with Mizanur Rahman, may use his prison time to "account" himself and review his beliefs and behavior. Also like Rahman, Choudary will likely receive some form of deradicalization programming while in prison and afterwards, while on conditional release. Such programming should not try

---

[11] Richard Kerbaj, "Hate preacher sent to jail isolation unit," *Sunday (London) Times* (July 23, 2017), www.thetimes.co.uk/article/hate-preacher-sent-to-jail-isolation-unit-jbwx92snv [Accessed November 22, 2017]; Alan Travis, "Extremist prisoners to be held in 'separation centres' inside jails," *The Guardian* (April 20, 2017), www.theguardian.com/uk-news/2017/apr/21/extremist-inmates-to-be-held-in-separation-centres-inside-prisons [Accessed November 22, 2017].

to persuade these men that their interpretation of Islam is "wrong." Instead, they should be encouraged to explore the work of other scholars beyond their mentor, Omar Bakri. Given Choudary's and Rahman's identification as Salafis, these scholars could include knowledgeable Salafi clerics who reject ISIS and other violent jihadis based on their close reading of scripture and deep understanding of Islamic history. If Choudary or Rahman were to recant their beliefs and embrace a less militant interpretation of Islam, they could emerge as powerful voices for moderation among remaining activists, not unlike Sayyid Imam al-Sharif's influence among Egyptian Islamic Group members who abandoned violence.[12]

This may be wishful thinking. Anjem Choudary and Mizanur Rahman are not likely to experience jailhouse "conversions" and radically change their beliefs. They have been professional activists for many years. Their immersion in Omar Bakri's teachings and al-Muhajiroun's ideology is complete, and barring their emir's own jailhouse conversion in Lebanon, they are not likely to renounce their beliefs. Religious activism forms the core of the identities of all three men, and they are not likely to abandon it, even as they pay a high price for their commitment. Nor are they likely to believe their ideology has failed them, even with the collapse of ISIS' territorial caliphate. Instead, like true believers in many religious cults, Bakri, Choudary, and Rahman are more likely to view their earthly struggles as confirmation they are on the "right" path, a path that will lead to their salvation, as long as they remain committed to their beliefs.[13]

Another factor that probably strengthens Choudary's and Rahman's resolve is the realization that they will serve only half of their five-and-a-half year sentences in prison custody, with their remaining sentences to be finished outside prison under a form of supervised parole known in the British legal system as being "on license." Barring unforeseen developments, both men could be released from prison as early as fall 2018.[14] While they are certain to receive

---

[12] Sayyid Imam al-Sharif was a leading ideologue for the Egyptian Islamic Group and al-Qaeda for many years. He wrote two booklets that formed the doctrinal foundation for jihad of the sword, *The Faithful Guide for Preparation* and *The Compendium in Pursuit of Noble Knowledge*. Al-Sharif eventually retracted his most extreme views and published an influential "revision," *Rationalizing Jihad in Egypt and the World*, that moderated his judgments on the permissibility of jihad. For more on how al-Sharif's changing views impacted the Egyptian Islamic Group, see Lawrence Wright, "The rebellion within: An al Qaeda mastermind questions terrorism," *The New Yorker* (June 2, 2008); Diaa Rashwan, "The Renunciation of Violence by Egyptian Jihadi Organizations," in *Leaving Terrorism Behind*, edited by Tore Bjørgo and John Horgan (New York: Routledge, 2009), pp. 113–31; and Jérôme Drevon, *Institutionalising Violence*, p. 101.

[13] Leon Festinger, Henry W. Riecken, and Stanley Schacter, *When Prophecy Fails: A Social and Psychological Study of a Modern Group that Predicted the Destruction of the World* (New York: Harper & Row, 1964); and John Lofland, *Doomsday Cult: A Study of Conversion, Proselytization, and Maintenance of Faith* (Englewood Cliffs, NJ: Prentice-Hall, 1966).

[14] Vikram Dodd, "Anjem Choudary jailed for five-and-a-half years for urging support of ISIS," *The Guardian* (September 6, 2016), www.theguardian.com/uk-news/2016/sep/06/anjem-choudary-jailed-for-five-years-and-six-months-for-urging-support-of-isis [Accessed September 6, 2016];

additional MAPPA restrictions and conditions, both activists will likely return home to be reunited with loved ones who support their activism.[15]

In the meantime, activists who have not left al-Muhajiroun, been imprisoned, or placed under ASBOs, TPIMs, and other administrative controls, continue to engage in da'wah. Their numbers have fallen and their network has fragmented, but their missionary zeal has not abated. These persistent activists continue to propagate the Emigrants' ideology and try to recruit new supporters for different halaqahs in London and other cities. These tightly-knit groups form the social basis of the Emigrants' activism. They remain the vehicle through which activists socialize each other and coordinate their diminished efforts to establish the Islamic state. In the face of government "persecution," halaqah leaders and other persistent activists call on their supporters to remain steadfast and to share what they have learned from Anjem Choudary and Mizanur Rahman with others.[16] Their activism continues at the "grassroots" level, where they are more discreet and no longer enjoy the resources of a larger, cohesive network to unite them. In pursuing this ad hoc strategy, persistent activists seek to ride out the current storm, as they did in the wake of the British government's crackdown against them ten years earlier. It is far from certain whether the Emigrants can rebound as robustly as they did when activists created Islam4UK and Muslims Against Crusades. But they seem determined to try, buoyed by the hope that their jailed leaders may soon rejoin them in the ideological struggle to establish God's rule on Earth.

WHAT AL-MUHAJIROUN TEACHES US ABOUT RADICALIZATION

Over the past decade the concept of violent radicalization has received a lot of attention from terrorism scholars and counter-terrorism practitioners.[17]

Richard Kerbaj, "Police prepare for Muslim extremist clashes on Anjem Choudary's release," *Sunday Times* (May 27, 2018), www.thetimes.co.uk/edition/news/police-prepare-for-extremist-clashes-on-preacher-s-release-xlj923s9c [Accessed May 27, 2018].

[15] Hannah Duguid, "We want to change the world," *The Guardian* (June 29, 2003), www.guardian.co.uk/world/2003/jun/30/gender.uk [Accessed September 5, 2012]; Martin Evans, "Anjem Choudary's wife now faces police investigation," *Daily Telegraph* (August 17, 2016), www.telegraph.co.uk/news/2016/08/17/anjem-choudarys-wife-now-faces-police-probe/ [Accessed December 21, 2016].

[16] Al-Muhajiroun press release, "The Truth Behind Anjem Choudary's Conviction," (September 6, 2016), courtesy of Douglas Weeks; Sam Christie, "Jailed duo Anjem Choudary and Mizanur Rahman's supporters are using their twisted pals' convictions to recruit more hate preachers," *The Sun* (August 29, 2016), www.thesun.co.uk/news/1691415/jailed-duo-anjem-choudary-and-mizanur-rahmans-supporters-are-using-their-twisted-pals-convictions-to-recruit-more-hate-preachers/ [Accessed September 22, 2016].

[17] Select examples from the academic literature include John Horgan, *The Psychology of Terrorism* (New York: Routledge, 2005); Clark McCauley and Sophia Moskalenko, *Friction: How Radicalization Happens to Them and US* (New York: Oxford University Press, 2011); Peter R. Neumann, "The Trouble with Radicalization," *International Affairs* 89, no. 4 (2013),

Recent studies have contributed to our understanding, but researchers continue to debate a number of issues, including the importance of religious doctrine and online interactions in the radicalization process. What, if anything, does this book have to tell us about radicalization? A number of things, it turns out.

One of the most important, if not necessarily surprising, findings is that al-Muhajiroun is largely a youth phenomenon. While the network relies on older, deeply committed activists to convey its ideology and coordinate its activism, many rank-and-file supporters join as teenagers and young adults. Consistent with research in terrorism studies, many of the respondents in my sample are disarmingly normal, but disillusioned and rebellious. A few are new converts to Islam, another factor that has received considerable attention from terrorism scholars. However, most of my respondents grew up in Muslim households that were not particularly religious, at least by fundamentalist standards. In fact, none of them were raised in homes that practiced the conservative form of Islam known as Salafism, which observers often associate with radicalization. Instead, they were raised as Sufis, Barelwis, Deobandis, even "cultural Muslims" who observed few religious practices at home. This lack of religiosity bothers some activists, as does the pressure to reconcile their family's ethnic and cultural heritage with growing up in predominately "white and secular" Britain. Some of these youth experience identity crises. They rebel against their parents' plan for their future. They question their role in British society. The Emigrants provide an opportunity for them to establish their own identity and reinvent themselves by joining something that is bigger than themselves and stands apart from their parents.

Of course, many young people go through rebellious periods, identity crises and personal turning points without joining an outlawed network that seeks to transform their country into an Islamic state. What explains why the identity-seeking youth in my sample turned to al-Muhajiroun, rather than other religious and non-religious groups based in London? Consistent with decades-old research on social movements, religious cults, and terrorist networks, an important part of the answer lies in social relationships. Developing friendships with recruits is often essential in getting them to join. This is why activists recruit from their own social networks, reaching out to their friends, siblings, spouses, coworkers, and even neighborhood acquaintances. Activists leverage their personal connections to draw people in. Once connected, they build relationships with recruits by hanging out with them, sharing meals, participating in social activities, and studying together in halaqah circles. Through these interactions and small group settings, activists build fellowship with recruits and establish themselves as trusted sources of information, priming recruits to absorb Omar Bakri's ideology.

pp. 873–93; and Marc Sageman, *Misunderstanding Terrorism* (Philadelphia, PA: University of Pennsylvania Press, 2017).

As important as social networks and small groups are to the Emigrants, personal relationships alone are insufficient to pull in some people. The convictions championed by network activists must resonate with these seekers' religious and political beliefs. Relationships may be key, but doctrine and ideology still matter – at least for some recruits. Much of the literature on radicalization in terrorism studies downplays doctrinal influences. There are good reasons for this. For one thing, many terrorists, including those who identify with different Islamic traditions, are not particularly devout and have a poor understanding of the scriptures they claim to follow. Moreover, believing in radical religious and political ideas is not the same as engaging in violent action on behalf of those beliefs.[18] Salafism, the Islamic tradition most closely associated with the current "religious wave" of international terrorism, illustrates this point.[19] Millions of Salafis throughout the world subscribe to religious beliefs that would dramatically change Western society if these beliefs were converted into policy, but most Salafis are not political activists or terrorists. In fact, Salafism is a quietist form of Islam that focuses on individual purification and indoctrinating believers in its fundamentalist view of the religion.

This helps explain why numerous Salafis I interviewed in London between 2007 and 2012 were aghast at al-Muhajiroun's appropriation of their creed. These respondents included leaders and rank-and-file congregants from a well-known Salafi mosque in Brixton that quarreled with the Emigrants whenever they brought their da'wah stalls to this South London neighborhood. The "Brixton Salafis" saw the Emigrants' embrace of their creed as a cynical ploy by Omar Bakri and his followers to enhance their religious credentials by wrapping themselves in the cloak of the Prophet Mohammed. According to these respondents, network activists were not Salafis, as they liked to claim, but "khawarij," akin to an early sect that caused conflict within the Muslim community, and "takfiris," Muslims who recklessly excommunicate their co-religionists and call for violence against them.[20]

Whether one considers the Emigrants to be Salafis, takfiris, khawarij, or something else, one thing is certain: ideology and theology matter to the activist network. Individuals do not progress to intellectual affiliation without internalizing a series of religious beliefs that are typically associated with the Salafi creed. Reflecting al-Muhajiroun's intellectual lineage, activists also absorb political beliefs from Hizb ut-Tahrir on governance, activism, and warfare. Mashed to form a "syncretic" Salafi-Islamist whole, these ideas include the

---

[18] McCauley and Moskalenko, *Friction*, p. 5.

[19] For more on the four waves of international terrorism since the late nineteenth century, see David C. Rapoport, "The Four Waves of Modern Terrorism," in *Attacking Terrorism: Elements of a Grand Strategy* edited by Audrey Kurth Cronin and James M. Ludes (Washington, DC: Georgetown University Press, 2004), pp. 46–73.

[20] Five interviews with four different Salafi respondents, Brixton, South London, October 23, 2007, and November 5 and 12, 2010.

conviction that Islam is a perfect political, economic, and judicial system that must be overseen by a caliph who applies a strict reading of shariah. A crucial corollary, also drummed into recruits through suhba and halaqah sessions, is that activists are divinely obligated to strive for the caliphate in Britain, and globally, through three modes of activism: da'wah, hisbah, and – under certain conditions – jihad.

Respondents repeatedly emphasize their attraction to these ideas when choosing to become intellectually affiliated with al-Muhajiroun rather than one of its Salafi and Islamist competitors in London. Of course, these accounts should be interpreted with caution, given the tendency of some respondents to shape their memories to fit their current dedication to the activist network.[21] Conversely, administrative affiliates who spent time hanging out with their friends in the activist network without internalizing these beliefs emphasize the eccentricity of its views as one reason for keeping their distance. And several respondents who once belonged to the Emigrants but later left highlight their growing aversion to Omar Bakri's religious and political teachings, especially his opportunistic embrace of Salafi-jihadism after 9/11.

Indeed, a defining feature of al-Muhajiroun's canon, and hence activists' indoctrination, is its exclusive reliance on one man's interpretation of scripture and its application to contemporary society. Whether they admit it or not, intellectual affiliates accept Sheikh Omar's teachings without reservation, along with those of a few select students who mimic his views. Learning from preachers outside the network and expressing alternative views on doctrinal matters is forbidden and can lead to expulsion. While this enhances the Emigrants' ideological cohesion, some respondents eventually question Bakri's reading of scripture and his legitimacy as an Islamic scholar. Other activists chafe under the insularity and rigidity of the leaders who replaced Bakri following his departure to Lebanon in 2005.

As they mature and learn more about their religion, activists often realize that Bakri, Choudary, and other ideologues base their arguments on select verses of the Qu'ran and the hadiths. Bakri and his students cherry pick these verses from the much larger, more robust scriptural tree of Islam. They cite these verses approvingly and repeatedly in talks and halaqah discussions, while ignoring many other verses and stories that undermine their reading of scripture. Network ideologues largely ignore the historical contexts surrounding their preferred passages, nor do they think hard about whether the circumstances the verses refer to are relevant for British Muslims today. Once they realize that Omar Bakri and his fellow ideologues are promoting their own interpretation of Islam, rather than presenting what they understand

---

[21] For more on this tendency in other extremist groups and cults, see Kathleen M. Blee, *Inside Organized Racism: Women in the Hate Movement* (Berkeley, CA: University of California Press, 2002), and Eileen Barker, *The Making of a Moonie: Choice or Brainwashing?* (Oxford: Basil Blackwell, 1984).

to be the religion's immutable truth, these individuals begin to break free from the ideological bonds their teachers have wrapped around them.

Al-Muhajiroun's ideological bonds are woven in real and virtual spaces. The Internet's role in the radicalization of activists is another important finding from this research. Preceding chapters illustrate how network activists have used the Internet and other communications technologies over the years to spread their ideology and facilitate their activism. Operating under the banner of different platforms like Need4Khilafah and Muslims Against Crusades, activists have created a number of websites to issue press releases, post videos, and announce upcoming protests. When their websites were disrupted, activists moved to social media, using Twitter, YouTube, and Facebook to engage in online da'wah and hisbah, while exploiting other tools, like Skype and PalTalk, to interact with their supporters in real time. At the same time that government pressure made it difficult for activists to coordinate and pass their message through brick-and-mortar venues in Britain, their online communications increased the transnational scope of their activism, allowing them to reach supporters in Australia, Bangladesh, and other countries. In some of these places, the impact of al-Muhajiroun's online da'wah was minimal; in others it encouraged the creation of viable spin-off groups, including Shariah4Belgium, Kaldet til Islam (Denmark), and Prophet's Ummah (Norway). These spin-offs pursued the same mission as their parent organization, and some of them, such as Shariah4Belgium, developed into recruitment pipelines, through which dozens of fighters flowed to the Islamic State. The upshot is that al-Muhajiroun's online proselytizing allowed it to remain relevant in the global Salafi-jihadi movement at the same time activists were becoming increasingly marginalized in their own country. In this manner, the Emigrants were early, if less sophisticated adopters of the same tools ISIS later made famous with its online recruitment and propaganda videos.

The ethnographic research in this study also provides an important correction to overblown accounts of the alleged power of "online radicalization," where vulnerable youth are portrayed as near-mindless zombies who radicalize quickly and simply following their exposure to violent videos or interacting with recruiters through social media and encrypted messaging applications. While some disenfranchised young men and women in the West have proven vulnerable to the Islamic State's online grooming, the picture that emerges among the Emigrants is different. Of course, network recruits go online and listen to lectures by leading activists and watch videos of da'wah stalls and demonstrations. They also communicate with more experienced activists through text, email, PalTalk, Skype, Facebook, Twitter, WhatsApp, and other social media.

Yet as numerous respondents emphasized in their interviews, real-world connections between activists are necessary to develop the knowledge and identity recruits need to become fully committed insiders in al-Muhajiroun's community of practice. "The Internet is not the main way of radicalizing someone," explains the former activist Maryam, who belonged to the network for several years. "It's the actual sitting down and meeting... You sit down and talk to them about your problem and that person will play on your vulnerability and bring you in."[22] In a separate interview, a leading activist who knows a thing or two about radicalization elaborates: "I don't think people are going to be cultured on the Internet, really. It's rare that people sit and listen to hours of lectures. They want shorter, ten-minute clips and the news, but deep culturing must come from the halaqahs and by face-to-face interaction ... This is the only way that the knowledge will really pass. It will never pass *just* via the Internet."[23] Through endless discussions in halaqahs, restaurants, and other small group settings, participants indoctrinate each other and learn to become activists. They also develop the trust, fellowship, and shared identity that solidifies their community of practice. This process unfolds over time through frequent face-to-face communication and real-world companionship, not by simply watching a few YouTube videos or participating in some encrypted chats.

NOT A CONVEYOR BELT TO TERRORISM

In recent years, a growing number of Emigrants have been implicated in terrorist plots and attacks in the United Kingdom and fighting on behalf of the Islamic State and other militant groups in Iraq and Syria. The involvement of so many activists in political violence within and outside Britain has led many observers to conclude that al-Muhajiroun is a "gateway" or "conveyor belt" to terrorism. The network drives people to violence, so the argument goes, by indoctrinating them in ideological beliefs that legitimize bloodshed by waging "jihad." This study highlights the importance of indoctrination for network activists, but it also argues that radicalization into political violence is not as clear-cut as mechanistic analogies like gateways and conveyor belts suggest. Participation in al-Muhajiroun is neither a necessary nor a sufficient condition for mobilization to violence.

Few have made the conveyor belt argument more forcefully than HOPE not hate, an anti-fascist advocacy organization based in London that published a report on the activist network titled simply, *Gateway to Terror*.[24] Compiling a wide array of individual cases from media reports, the report's authors, Nick Lowles and Joe Mulhall, claim that at least seventy people connected to al-Muhajiroun have been convicted of terrorism or terrorism-related offenses in the United Kingdom or died overseas since 1998. Lowles and Mulhall correctly identify several activists implicated in political violence, examples I have also

---

[22] Interview with Maryam, former activist, Hounslow, West London, June 21, 2011.
[23] Interview with leading activist, Skype, June 26, 2013.
[24] Nick Lowles and Joe Mulhall, *Gateway to Terror: Anjem Choudary and the al-Muhajiroun Network* (London: HOPE not hate, 2013).

discussed in this book. If updated to include suicide bombings and other violent attacks attributed to network activists in Iraq and Syria since the report was published in 2013, their list would grow even longer.

Unfortunately, HOPE not hate's expansive list of "terror connections" contains numerous individuals whose links to al-Muhajiroun are, at best, tenuous. These include the so-called "Aden Ten" who planned to carry out a series of attacks in Yemen in 1998 before they were arrested by local authorities, the 2001 shoe bomber Richard Reid, Mohammed Siddique Khan, and the other perpetrators behind the London bombings in 2005, and Abdullah Ali and two more conspirators from the transatlantic liquid-bomb plot in 2007.[25] Some of these individuals may have attended one or more talks by Omar Bakri or Anjem Choudary, but this likely represented the extent of their involvement in the activist network.

The HOPE not hate report also identifies seven al-Muhajiroun activists who were convicted of "terrorism-related" offenses for their participation in the 2006 Danish embassy protest and speeches they made against British and American troops at the Regent's Park Mosque in London during the first Battle of Fallujah in 2004. These activists, along with an eighth person not named in the report, were found guilty of various crimes, including inciting racial hatred, terrorist fundraising, and inciting murder for terrorist purposes. However reprehensible their actions may have been, these individuals were essentially convicted of speech-acts more closely associated with provocation and moral shock than political violence. By classifying these crimes as "terrorism-related," and by linking violent perpetrators who were only loosely connected, if at all, to the activist network, HOPE not hate inflates the number of activists who supposedly engaged in political violence. This weakens its argument that al-Muhajiroun is a conveyor belt to terrorism.

Similarly, in a statistical analysis of 124 individuals who carried out terrorist attacks or were convicted of what they loosely call "Islamism-related offenses" in the United Kingdom between 1999 and 2009, the Centre for Social Cohesion, a conservative think tank in London that later became part of the Henry Jackson Society, found that nineteen, representing 15 percent of their sample, were connected to al-Muhajiroun.[26] Similar to the HOPE not hate report, the Centre for Social Cohesion's estimate overstates al-Muhajiroun's involvement in political violence by conflating violent terrorist incidents with non-violent crimes. Of the nineteen activists identified by the Centre for "Islamism-related" convictions, nine were found guilty of crimes related to their high-risk activism rather than their involvement in violent acts or terrorist plots. These include the speakers at the Regent's Park Mosque protest in 2004, the leaders of the Danish Embassy demonstration in 2006, and another activist who was

[25] Lowles and Mulhall, *Gateway to Terror*, pp. 26–7.
[26] Robin Simcox, Hannah Stuart, and Houriya Ahmed, *Islamist Terrorism: The British Connections* (London: The Centre for Social Cohesion, 2010), pp. viii–ix.

convicted of inciting racial hatred for handing out al-Muhajiroun leaflets in 2000 that called on Muslims to fight and kill Jews.[27] When these individuals are removed, only ten people remain who were associated with al-Muhajiroun and who engaged in or planned acts of political violence in Britain or abroad between 1999 and 2009.

Of course, the number of activists implicated in political violence has increased since the Centre for Social Cohesion's report was first published. In my own sample of forty-eight al-Muhajiroun activists I interviewed between 2010 and 2015, nine were later implicated in terrorist plots in the United Kingdom or left Britain to fight for the Islamic State in Iraq and Syria. When added to the Centre for Social Cohesion's figures for activists involved in planning or carrying out terrorist plots, this suggests that at least nineteen individuals escalated to political violence following their exposure to the network's ideology. The real number is higher because several more respondents in my sample tried to flee Britain and join ISIS but did not make it, nor did I interview every activist from this period who later engaged in political violence. However disturbing these figures are – and even one activist who engages in political violence is too many – they do not prove that al-Muhajiroun is a conveyor belt that leads inevitably to terrorism and insurgency.

There are two reasons for this. First, network activists who escalated to political violence were exposed to many other influences besides al-Muhajiroun. How can we separate the network's causal impact on their radicalization to violence from these other factors? The short answer is we can't. Because the sample of violent activists is too small to perform reliable statistical tests and because the causes of terrorism are so numerous and complex, I cannot identify and control for any single influence, even one that appears in numerous examples, as having a decisive impact on a specific individual. To recall one example discussed in this book, Michael Adebolajo listened to numerous lectures by Omar Bakri and Anjem Choudary. He attended a network halaqah and participated in da'wah stalls and demonstrations. Adebolajo was undoubtedly involved in al-Muhajiroun, but did his activism cause him to brutally murder Lee Rigby on the streets of London years after he'd left the network? Or was it his exposure to other experiences, such as his reported abuse at the hands of Kenyan security forces and alleged efforts by British intelligence officers to recruit him as a confidential source? Was it some combination of factors, with the Emigrants serving as a preconditioning influence and his abuse by Kenyan authorities, harassment by British officials, and other events serving as accelerants and triggers?[28]

---

[27] Simcox, Stuart, and Ahmed, *Islamist Terrorism*, pp. 95–100, 174–7; Centre for Social Cohesion, "One in Seven UK Terror-related Convictions Linked to Islamist Group Now Threatening to Relaunch," press briefing (June 1, 2009).

[28] For discussion of the preconditions and precipitants that may lead to terrorist violence, see Martha Crenshaw, "The Causes of Terrorism" *Comparative Politics* 13, no. 4 (July 1981), pp. 379–99.

In Adebolajo's case, along with a few respondents from my sample I came to know through repeated interactions, al-Muhajiroun likely served as a preconditioning influence on their personal pathways to violent radicalization. In each case, however, their journeys were influenced by other factors as well. These influences include British and American foreign policy in the Middle East and the legal pressures activists like Siddhartha Dhar and Abu Rahin Aziz faced in Britain. If the West's apparent "war on Islam" and the early success of ISIS' caliphate pulled Dhar and Aziz towards Syria, their arrests and releases on bail provided the final push. Having determined they were no longer free to pursue jihad of the tongue in Britain, and having been told by network leaders that ISIS met the conditions of a legitimate caliphate, they apparently decided it was time to engage in jihad of the sword in Iraq and Syria. In these few cases at least, government counter-terrorism pressure likely accelerated their escalation into political violence. A leading activist made essentially the same point early on in my field work, years before Dhar and Aziz became heroes to network activists: "the only purpose that Muslims have in the UK is to propagate Islam. If the government stops Muslims from propagating Islam, their only option is jihad."[29]

Of course, without access to Adebolajo and the ability to conduct follow-up interviews with my respondents who joined ISIS, the answers to such questions are ultimately unknowable. What I can say with some degree of confidence is that al-Muhajiroun gave them the ideology to frame and justify their acts of violence long after they left the activist network. A short speech Michael Adebolajo made just after attacking Lee Rigby – when he told a video-recording eyewitness, "We must fight them as they fight us" – could have been made by any number of activists. One network leader admitted as much in a follow-up interview a month after the assassination, when he praised his former student for being "very clear" in "the message he passed to the world."[30]

Maintaining that al-Muhajiroun is a preconditioning influence on the violent radicalization of Michael Adebolajo, Siddhartha Dhar, and a few others does not mean that the activist network is a necessary condition or conveyor belt for terrorism. The second reason why even the most egregious cases like Adebolajo's and Dhar's do not demonstrate this is because so few activists who step on the belt carry out violent attacks. Since the Emigrants' creation in 1996, thousands of people have been exposed to their message, delivered by activists at da'wah stalls, demonstrations, halaqah circles, and the Internet. The vast majority of these individuals did not radicalize by becoming intellectually affiliated with al-Muhajiroun, and far fewer participated in acts of political violence in Great Britain or elsewhere. When advocacy organizations like HOPE not hate and the Centre for Social Cohesion focus exclusively on the few, but still too many, individuals who engage in violence, they create the

---

[29] Interview with leading activist, Leyton, East London, November 6, 2010.
[30] Interview with leading activist, Skype, June 26, 2013.

misimpression that exposure to al-Muhajiroun inevitably pushes people down the path to radicalization and violence.

What these reports miss are the many people who have been exposed to the Emigrants' high-risk activism without becoming involved in terrorism and insurgency. Unlike the HOPE not hate and the Centre for Social Cohesion reports and other studies on violent radicalization, this book provides variation on the dependent variable by including individuals who did not radicalize, let alone become involved in political violence. One of the most important findings from this study is that not everyone who hears al-Muhajiroun's siren song steers his or her ship towards its rocky shores. Consistent with the literature on social movements, many people are exposed to the activist network but never actually join or internalize its ideology. Much of activists' hectoring and cajoling about the need for the caliphate, and the fiery consequences facing those who do not heed their call, fall on metaphorical deaf ears.

Countless Muslims and non-Muslims who encounter activists in the street and on the Internet are not interested in what they have to say. This was something I saw again and again during my field work, each time I visited one of their da'wah stalls or roadshows. Activists struggled to get passersby to take one of their leaflets, let alone stop and engage them for a few minutes. It was not uncommon for a da'wah stall with several activists handing out flyers over the course of two or more hours to have conversations with less than a handful of the hundreds of people passing them on the street. At a typical stall, activists spent more time talking with each other than indoctrinating others. By the end of any given stall, many unwanted leaflets would be found nearby, dropped on the ground or thrown into nearby trash bins.

Even people with strong ties to al-Muhajiroun do not automatically accept its ideology and become involved in its high-risk activism. Some of my respondents, including Haroon, had good friends who were activists. Haroon and other administrative affiliates were coached in the network's ideology for years as they hung out with their friends. But even they refused to join. Relationships and the structure of social networks does not eliminate the influence of agency. Haroon was thoroughly exposed to the activist network during its zenith, when it was expanding rapidly into a scale-free-like network centered on Omar Bakri. He got on the conveyor belt, at least administratively, attending da'wah stalls, protests, even halaqah sessions with "Sheikh Omar" himself. Despite his activism, and despite being surrounded by friends urging him to join, Haroon's commitment to his education and a professional career outweighed his interest in the Emigrants' ideology, which he later dismissed as "actually quite crazy."[31] Unlike most intellectual affiliates I interviewed, Haroon was not disillusioned with British society, or his place within it. Nor was he seeking to give his life meaning through religious activism. He knew

---

[31] Interview with Haroon, Westminster, Central London, June 14, 2011.

what he wanted and calling Britain to the Islamic state was not it. He rejected al-Muhajiroun's ideology, eventually turning away from the activist network. After completing his education, he established himself in his chosen field and became a productive member of British society. Our first interview, years after he left the network, took place one summer afternoon in an upscale pub in Westminster. Over a couple of pints, interrupted by occasional smoking breaks outside the bar, he told me his story. "I drink more than most Muslims," he deadpanned at one point.[32]

If the Emigrants are a conveyor belt to violent radicalization and terrorism, how do we explain the experiences of Haroon and other respondents? According to the metaphor's logic, they should have escalated from network contact to committed activist to religious insurgent and terrorist. But they never made it past the contact stage. Nor are they the only respondents who became involved in the network only to depart a few years later without radicalizing further. Out of the forty-eight activists I interviewed in al-Muhajiroun, at least seven, representing 15 percent of my activist sample, eventually left the network without progressing into political violence. As I mentioned in the last chapter, the actual number is likely higher, given that I don't know what happened to eighteen activists in my activist sample. I also interviewed seven other respondents who left al-Muhajiroun before my field work began. Unlike Haroon, all fourteen of these former activists not only stepped on the conveyor belt, they rode it for a while, radicalizing into intellectual affiliation in the network's community of practice. In fact, while these respondents eventually disengaged from their activism, they did not necessarily "deradicalize" by discarding all of their previous beliefs.

Some readers may wonder whether these activists really stepped off the belt. Maybe it's just a matter of time before they re-engage and radicalize further into violence. I cannot discount this entirely. However, like Salman, the former activist who tried to overthrow Anjem Choudary, many of these respondents are engaged in ongoing intellectual journeys away from the network. They no longer support al-Muhajiroun's strategy of activism, which they see as harmful to British Muslims given the backlash from the network's confrontational hisbah. Since leaving the Emigrants they have established themselves as ordinary Britons, getting jobs, raising families, and accepting the legitimacy of the country's political and economic system.

Of course, I do not know how their personal journeys will end, and re-engaging is always a possibility. But it is unlikely that these former activists will carry out political violence in Britain or overseas. Based on my analysis of their interviews and my interactions with them, I expect they will continue to integrate themselves in British society and move even closer to the deradicalization end of the radicalization-deradicalization spectrum. Several

---

[32] Field notes, Westminster, Central London, June 14, 2011.

of the former activists in my sample who have been out of al-Muhajiroun for many years, have deradicalized even further. Four of these respondents have so thoroughly left the network behind that they now work to counter its narrative. These outcomes contradict the conveyor belt metaphor, which mechanistically suggests that all fourteen former activists in my sample, seven of whom were active at the time of my interviews and seven of whom were not, should have radicalized further into political violence.

"A RELEASE FOR ANGRY YOUNG MEN"

In contrast to anxious metaphors of gateways and conveyor belts, some observers believe that extremist groups like al-Muhajiroun and Hizb ut-Tahrir act as "safety valves" against violence by directing their participants' anger towards non-violent activism. Not surprisingly, such arguments are popular among activists. Responding to allegations that he was responsible for radicalizing the activists who plotted to bomb the London Stock Exchange in 2010, Anjem Choudary countered that he and Omar Bakri worked "to channel the energies of the youth into the ideological struggle in Britain as opposed to the military one."[33] Numerous respondents echo the network leader. Omar Bakri "controlled the youth," explains one veteran activist, several years after his teacher fled to Lebanon. "He channeled their emotions towards peaceful demonstrations, to posting stickers, to leafleting."[34] "Organizations like MAC [Muslims Against Crusades] and al-Muhajiroun are beneficial," adds another respondent, "because they channel the youths' emotions in a more correct way," meaning towards non-violent activism. "We believe in the covenant of security," he continues, alluding to the network's belief that activists must not attack the people with whom they live. "Other people don't."[35] Indeed, some activists argue that without Omar Bakri and Anjem Choudary around to reinforce the covenant of security and steer young people into non-violent activism, Britain is likely to experience more terrorist attacks.[36] Khuram Butt's London Bridge and Borough Market rampage is seen in this light. Like other former intellectual affiliates who escalated to violence, Butt apparently decided that the covenant no longer applied to him, freeing him to attack his fellow citizens.

Such sentiments might be expected from network activists, who are eager for their leaders to rejoin them in the ideological struggle for the caliphate.

[33] Anjem Choudary, press release, "The Nine Muslims Accused of Terrorism are Innocent!," (February 9, 2012), www.anjemchoudary.com/press-releases/the-nine-muslims-are-innocent [Accessed August 9, 2012].

[34] Interview with veteran activist, Leyton, East London, November 14, 2010.

[35] Interview with veteran activist, Whitechapel, East London, November 9, 2010.

[36] Interviews with activists, Leyton, East London, November 14, 2010, Islington, North London, July 21, 2012, Wembley Central, West London, September 5, 2013.

But other observers, including researchers and government officials, have made similar arguments. In a broad discussion referring to al-Muhajiroun and Hizb ut-Tahrir, Clark McCauley and Sophia Moskalenko suggest that "legal activism can serve as a safety valve for the expression of grievances that might otherwise lead to terrorism."[37] Referring specifically to the Emigrants, Douglas Weeks, who has engaged in extensive research on the activist network, argues that the "the threat [of violence] has increased" with the removal of Choudary, Rahman, and other leaders "because now people have no purpose or direction."[38]

Even British authorities concede that groups like al-Muhajiroun may act as more of a safety valve than a conveyor belt to violence. One counter-terrorism officer I interviewed describes the Emigrants' confrontational hisbah as "a release for angry young men." Their protests, he adds, "provide them with opportunities to get out and shout and wave placards and act on their anger in support of a cause."[39] Other government officials have expressed similar views. In a classified memorandum that was leaked to the press, a senior official for Britain's Department for Communities and Local Government wrote that groups like al-Muhajiroun and Hizb ut-Tahrir "provide a legal 'safety valve' for extreme views."[40] Another memorandum, entitled "Government strategy towards extremism," declared "[w]e do not believe that it is accurate to regard radicalisation in this country as a linear 'conveyor belt' moving from grievance, through radicalisation, to violence," adding that such characterizations "misread" how radicalization occurs and "give undue weight to ideological factors."[41] Yet, we can recognize that ideology is important to al-Muhajiroun and acknowledge that some activists have engaged in political violence, while also understanding that hundreds of people have been exposed to the network's ideology over the years without escalating to violence

Although most activists leave the Emigrants without radicalizing into terrorism or insurgency, enough of them have engaged in violence to raise legitimate concerns among public officials charged with protecting the United Kingdom. The tragedy of al-Muhajiroun is that despite its focus on confrontational but mostly peaceful activism, it has contributed to violence, if only marginally, by encouraging activists to follow the same Salafi-jihadi beliefs as al-Qaeda and ISIS and by convincing them that they have a divine obligation to support Abu Bakr al-Baghdadi and his caliphate.

---

[37] McCauley and Moskalenko, *Friction*, p. 219.

[38] Email from Douglas Weeks, researcher on al-Muhajiroun, October 15, 2017.

[39] Interview with London Metropolitan Police officer, Vauxhall, South London, June 15, 2011.

[40] Andrew Gilligan, "Hizb ut Tahrir is not a gateway to terrorism, claims Whitehall report," *Sunday Telegraph* (July 25, 2010), www.telegraph.co.uk/journalists/andrew-gilligan/7908262/Hizb-ut-Tahrir-is-not-a-gateway-to-terrorism-claims-Whitehall-report.html [Accessed November 28, 2010].

[41] Gilligan, "Hizb ut Tahrir is not a gateway to terrorism, claims Whitehall report."

Paradoxically, the Emigrants have also dampened violence within the United Kingdom, again only marginally, by convincing their supporters they live under a covenant of security that prevents them from attacking people in Britain. Throughout my field research, activists have consistently voiced their support for the covenant. During my first interview with one leading activist, in September 2007, he told me clearly and emphatically, "We believe in the covenant of security... we will not betray people with whom we live."[42] Seven years later, after enduring considerable pressure from the authorities, he continued to accept the covenant in Britain, even when ISIS called on its supporters to carry out attacks in the West. "We have a covenant of security, an individual one," he declared, adding, "as long as we live here and our life and wealth are protected, we do not target the life and the wealth of the people with whom we live."[43]

Other respondents go even further, suggesting that they would try to stop someone from carrying out a terrorist attack in Britain if they knew about it beforehand. When asked what he would have told Roshonara Choudhry, the former King's College London student who stabbed the government minister Stephen Timms several times for his support of the Iraq war, another leading activist remarked, "I would have said you're not allowed to do that. It's not allowed, you're living under the covenant of security." Generalizing beyond this hypothetical example to real-world ones, he adds, "We're trying to prevent that kind of situation."[44]

For activists who are committed to the covenant of security, participation in al-Muhajiroun can act as a safety valve, allowing them to express their dissatisfaction with British and American foreign policy and channel their anger into non-violent dissent. Many of these young men and women are unlikely to leave Britain or engage in violence against their fellow citizens, yet they support replacing the country's political and economic system with a religious theocracy. Their activism is a form of political participation in a democratic country that allows its citizens, including dissidents, to express their views peacefully, however unpopular those views may be. Activists "exploit" their freedom to blow off steam and build themselves up emotionally, giving their lives a sense of purpose that does not involve violence.

From the perspective of British security services, this safety valve is fraught with risk. Law enforcers have monitored the network for years and pursued investigations against many individuals who came across their radar through their involvement in al-Muhajiroun. But they have not been able to stop some activists from escalating to terrorism and others from joining the caliphate in Iraq and Syria. Nor can they count on activists telling them if one of their fellow Emigrants turns to violence. A valid safety concern for officials is that

---

[42] Interview with leading activist, Woolwich, South London, September 22, 2007.

[43] Interview with leading activist, Skype, October 8, 2014.

[44] But he also said he would not report this person to the police, which is consistent with what other respondents have told me. Interview with leading activist, Ilford, East London, November 29, 2010.

some activists who remain free in Britain after the removal of network leaders – and the collapse of the Islamic State – may believe the covenant of security no longer applies. Khuram Butt, who died in the London Bridge and Borough Market attack, illustrates this danger. With the Islamic State "being driven out of Syria and Iraq," explains Douglas Weeks, these activists "may decide that violence is acceptable in response to government intervention here and abroad. Essentially, the Khuram Butt syndrome."[45]

Of course, for every Khuram Butt there are other Emigrants who decide that the covenant remains valid, preventing them from carrying out attacks in Britain. But this may be of little consolation to security officials charged with the difficult task of monitoring these potential terrorists. In a rare public speech, Andrew Parker, the head of Britain's domestic intelligence agency, the MI5, acknowledged the country experienced "a dramatic upshift in the threat" from Islamist terrorism in 2017. "It's at the highest tempo I have seen in my 34-year career," he added. "Today there is more terrorist activity, coming at us more quickly, and it can be harder to detect."[46] This threat extends well beyond the Emigrants, but many of the perpetrators in the recent attacks and disrupted plots in Britain follow a similar ideology.

British officials face another challenge: What to do about the potential threat from returned foreign fighters.[47] As I have shown in this book, numerous activists left the United Kingdom to join ISIS and other militant groups in Iraq and Syria. Like the larger number of approximately 850 people from Great Britain who traveled to the Islamic caliphate, most of these individuals have not returned home, in part because so many of them were killed overseas. However, at least one respondent in my sample who moved to Syria has since returned to Britain. Will he pick up the sword of jihad in his home country? I suspect not. In many interactions with him during my field work,

---

[45] Email from Douglas Weeks, researcher on al-Muhajiroun, October 15, 2017.

[46] Vikram Dodd, "UK facing most severe terror threat ever, warns MI5 chief," *The Guardian* (October 17, 2017), www.theguardian.com/uk-news/2017/oct/17/uk-most-severe-terror-threat-ever-mi5-islamist [Accessed October 22, 2017]. Also, see Arj Singh, "Britain faces higher threat as ISIS loses fight in Syria and Iraq, security minister says: The collapse of ISIS territory is encouraging homegrown terrorism in Europe," *The Independent* (August 19, 2017), www.independent.co.uk/news/uk/politics/is-threat-britain-syria-iraq-isis-islamic-state-ben-wallace-a7901616.html [Accessed September 15, 2017]; and Lizzie Dearden, "UK terror arrests rise almost 70% in a year to reach record high, new figures show," *The Independent* (September 14, 2017), www.independent.co.uk/news/uk/crime/uk-terror-arrests-70-per-cent-2016-figures-london-attacks-manchester-arena-plots-isis-police-mi5-a7945996.html [Accessed September 15, 2017].

[47] The threat of Western foreign fighters in the Middle East returning home to carry out violent attacks has received considerable attention from scholars and security officials in recent years. Examples of the academic literature include Thomas Hegghammer, "Should I Stay or Should I Go? Explaining Variation in Western Jihadists' Choice between Domestic and Foreign Fighting," *American Political Science Review* 107, no. 1 (February 2013), pp. 1–15; David Malet, *Foreign Fighters: Transnational Identity in Civil Conflicts* (New York: Oxford University Press, 2013); and Daniel Byman, "The Jihadist Returnee Threat: Just How Dangerous?," *Political Science Quarterly* 131, no. 1 (Spring 2016), pp. 69–99.

he consistently expressed his commitment to the network's ideology, including the covenant of security, which he followed. While insisting in our discussions that fighting against foreign invaders of Muslim lands overseas was allowed, he made a sharp distinction between such "defensive" jihad and engaging in violence in Britain, where he enjoyed the protection of the British government.[48] Of course, he may have changed his mind in the years since I last met him. Did his experience in Syria radicalize him further or did it cause him to burn out and curb his militancy? I do not know and can only hope Her Majesty's security officials do.

BEYOND NETWORKS

Building on the convictions of Anjem Choudary, Mizanur Rahman and other activists, British authorities are likely to continue their efforts to disrupt the activist network. Evidence of these efforts can be seen in the recent convictions of Anthony Small and Richardo MacFarlane, and the renewal of administrative controls against other leading activists, like Abdul Muhid and Mohammed Shamsuddin. As I conclude this book, it remains unclear whether al-Muhajiroun will absorb and bounce back from these setbacks, as it did following previous crackdowns, or whether the Emigrants' end is truly at hand. The social basis for a resurgence – small group halaqahs and social ties among activists – remains in place. Some supporters continue to meet and indoctrinate each other through discussion and companionship. What is largely missing, at least for now, are the hubs and brokers who could rebuild the network's small-world-like structure if given the chance. For this reason, government authorities are likely to continue to target persistent activists like Choudary, Muhid, and MacFarlane by using the legal and administrative tools at their disposal to prevent them from indoctrinating recruits and meeting with activists, whether they are in prison or outside it.

From a counter-terrorism perspective, the authorities' disruption of al-Muhajiroun may be considered a success. Today, the Emigrants are smaller, more fragmented, and less capable than they have been since the earliest days of their activism. They have declined from hundreds of intellectual and administrative affiliates who followed Bakri and Choudary during the network's scale-free-like heyday to, at most, a few dozen supporters. Rank-and-file activists are largely isolated from network leaders. Without the ongoing interactions necessary to strengthen ties and build camaraderie across halaqahs, the network's community of practice is wilting. Apart from the occasional da'wah stall organized by local halaqahs, the Emigrants' public activism has essentially collapsed. The network survives, but just barely.

---

[48] Interviews with veteran activist, Whitechapel, East London, November 9, 2010, June 16, 2011, and Leyton, East London, November 14, 2010, December 9, 2010. Also, field notes, Centre for Islamic Services, Whitechapel, East London, June 16, 2011.

Rather than blowing the horn of victory, however, we may be wiser to acknowledge an unintended consequence of the government's strategy. British authorities' efforts to destroy one security threat has created another: a diffuse collection of disgruntled individuals who follow the same subversive beliefs, and at least some of whom have concluded that the covenant of security no longer holds in Great Britain. This suggests that we may have reached the limits of the government's "kinetic" approach to combatting al-Muhajiroun. Unless British officials are prepared to target surviving activists by preventing them from meeting in small groups and preaching on the streets of London and other cities, a questionable undertaking that would likely violate the political rights and civil liberties of these British citizens, its current strategy may not destroy what remains of the activist network.

One reason for this is the resilience not of the Emigrants overall network, which law enforcement officials have effectively disrupted, but the persistence of its halaqahs. These small, tightly-knit groups remain essential to al-Muhajiroun. They allow activists to indoctrinate each other in the network's ideology and coordinate their activism despite intense counter-terrorism pressure. Even as the network's overall small-world structure has fragmented, the halaqahs continue to provide a social base for what remains of the Emigrants' activism. This small group structure gives activists the ability to meet and interact on a regular basis, strengthening their in-group ties and fellowship. Halaqah sessions also allow activists to discuss challenges to their activism and brainstorm potential solutions. These discussions help supporters make sense of setbacks, including the recent incarcerations of network leaders, and fortify their commitment to a cause that, from the outside, seems increasingly implausible.

A second reason the Emigrants appear likely to persist, at least in some diminished form, has to do with the ideology that inspires its supporters. This ideology is bigger than Omar Bakri, Anjem Choudary, and al-Muhajiroun. It encompasses al-Qaeda, ISIS, and many other groups and networks, even "lone wolves" who subscribe to its Salafi-jihadi leanings. This malleable belief system, steeped in a selective, highly bellicose reading of Islamic scripture and history, has survived decades of repression and civil war in numerous countries, and the US-led "war on terror," only to become stronger.[49] As exploited by al-Muhajiroun and other practitioners, the ideology provides its believers with a simple, yet sweeping narrative that explains the West's "war on Islam" and their own role in this cosmic conflict. It provides a rationale for even the most extreme acts of violence: Our religion is under attack and must be defended at all costs. Traditionally, most Emigrants in Britain have understood their role in this struggle to be primarily ideological. This is precisely what Omar Bakri, Anjem Choudary and other network leaders taught them. Under the influence of their mentors, activists readily engaged in the battle of ideas

---

[49] Shiraz Maher, *Salafi-Jihadism: The History of an Idea* (New York: Oxford University Press, 2016), pp. 21 and 211.

through da'wah, hisbah, and jihad of the tongue. They were also taught that participating in this struggle is a divine obligation, righteous activism for which they will be rewarded on the Day of Judgment.

For many persistent activists, no amount of counter-terrorism pressure, including isolation in special prison units and the extension of administrative controls like the ASBOs and TPIMs, is likely to change these beliefs. Paradoxically, such pressure tends to reinforce them, reminding activists they must be on the right path because, in accordance with their reading of scripture, the "hypocrites" and "non-believers" hate them. Supporters who self-identify as part of the broader Salafi-jihadi movement that encompasses what remains of both al-Qaeda and ISIS follow the same logic.[50] Nor will the fall of ISIS' territorial caliphate likely delegitimize this ideology, at least in the eyes of its true believers. As the war on terror, at risk of being widened and recast as the "war on radical Islam," unfolds in the months and years ahead, scholars and practitioners should remember not just the persistence of al-Muhajiroun's small group structure, but the resilience of its ideology.

COUNTERING THE NARRATIVE AND CREATING NEW NETWORKS

If the British government's kinetic approach to combatting al-Muhajiroun has reached the point of diminishing returns, there are other options available to public officials and communities who wish to keep activists from reforming into a cohesive small-world network. One of the key findings from this study is that individuals often leave the Emigrants following a period of youthful experimentation in its high-risk activism. There are many reasons for this. They burn out from the constant demands of their activism. They grow tired of arguing with family members who question their understanding of Islam and their blind devotion to the teachings of a single cleric. And they grow up, maturing into the responsibilities and opportunities of adulthood, which become increasingly attractive as they watch old friends and acquaintances become successful members of British society.

Participating in formal deradicalization programs may not be as important to this process as is commonly thought. For all the attention "countering violent extremism" (CVE) has received in the United States and Great Britain, all but one of the fourteen former activists in my sample left the Emigrants without participating in a CVE program. And of the one that did, it is not clear what impact the program had on his decision to leave the activist network rather than other influences, like simply maturing out. Even the four "formers" who left al-Muhajiroun and later worked in countering violent extremism did

---

[50] Maher, *Salafi-Jihadism*; William McCants, *The ISIS Apocalypse: The History, Strategy, and Doomsday Vision of the Islamic State* (New York: St. Martin's Press, 2015); and Barak Mendelsohn, *The Al-Qaeda Franchise: The Expansion of al-Qaeda and Its Consequences* (New York: Oxford University Press, 2016).

not participate in deradicalization programs. They all left the activist network on their own. This does not mean that British prevention and intervention programs like Channel and Project Safe Space do not help turn individuals away from violent extremism. They do. Some former activists I did not interview have reportedly been helped by intervention programs like Centri, the Unity Initiative, and West London Impact. These and other CVE programs, including Fida Management, STREET, and the Active Change Foundation, have also helped youngsters who did not find their way to al-Muhajiroun, but were exposed to other extremist influences, online and off.

However, the collective experience of my respondents does suggest that participation in a CVE program is not necessary for turning individuals away from violent extremism. Many activists eventually leave the Emigrants on their own terms, for their own reasons. Forcing these people into intervention programs, and prosecuting them for offenses related to their activism can have the unintended effect of confirming the network's narrative, rather than undermining it. It may also accelerate their radicalization, increasing their desire to convert themselves from metaphorical emigrants in Britain to real ones in Libya, Yemen, or elsewhere. One of the factors separating the few persistent activists who escalated to political violence from the many who did not is that some of the first faced criminal prosecution for their activism. With the prospect of jail looming for what they saw as obeying God's command, these activists decided they could no longer practice their faith in Great Britain. When the opportunity to emigrate to Iraq and Syria was given to them by officials who released them from custody without securing their passports, they took it. Government law enforcement pressure did not deter these activists from "making hijrah" to Iraq and Syria, it emboldened them.

The fact that so many Emigrants left the network and turned their lives around without participating in deradicalization programs shows that formal "deprogramming" was not necessary for them to mature into conscientious citizens. What is essential for many of these younger, less committed activists is creating networks of family members, friends and supporters who support their decision to leave and help them build new identities outside al-Muhajiroun. Maryam describes her personal struggle to replace the friendships and fellowship she enjoyed in the network with something else: "Coming out of al-Muhajiroun it got a bit worse. I wanted to belong to another group. Once it is in you, you want to be part of a group, you want to join another jama'ah."[51] In the months afterwards, Maryam tried to satisfy her need for identity and belonging by joining other activist groups. Yet she soon found that the ideas they championed no longer appealed to her. Eventually, through her work and education, Maryam formed friendships with Muslims and non-Muslims outside

---

[51] Interview with Maryam, Skype, November 20, 2012.

al-Muhajiroun and London's Islamist scene. These individuals became her new friends and support system. She gradually changed her beliefs by learning from them, rather than participating in a deradicalization program: "My friends, thank god, they helped me to deradicalize my thoughts."[52]

Maryam's experience, which is not unique among my respondents, highlights the need for initiatives to address activists' desire to establish healthy, self-affirming identities and to belong to something greater than themselves. Alternative social networks can support this. People leaving the Emigrants are more likely to deradicalize if they form trusted relationships with other people who support them and their new way of thinking. The families and old, pre-al-Muhajiroun friends of network activists can be vital in this process. Of course, family members and close friends may be troubled, even appalled, by their sons' and daughters' acceptance of al-Muhajiroun's ideology and their tiresome insistence on preaching to them at every opportunity. As much as they cherish their loved ones, they may be tempted to push them away, even to sever relationships with them. Such responses are understandable, but they can backfire by encouraging activists to retreat to the Emigrants, further isolating themselves in the network's insular community of practice.

Rather than pushing activists away, families and friends should engage them and challenge their extremist ideas. Such engagement forces activists to hear different views and maintain healthy relationships outside the activist network. These competing bonds and beliefs can help pull them out of the rabbit hole of al-Muhajiroun when they are ready to leave. Part of this engagement may include acknowledging the "merits" of their involvement, such as leading a less hedonistic lifestyle, while raising questions about the network's narrow interpretation of Islam. This will likely be more productive than demonizing the Emigrants and refusing to engage the loved one in debate. Rashid, the former activist, recalls a conversation he had with his father while he was still deeply involved. "He said, 'Take it easy. It's good you're not taking drugs, drinking alcohol, and having sex outside marriage, but calm down. Don't just take one person's view.' I remember having that conversation with my dad."[53] This single discussion did not cause Rashid to leave al-Muhajiroun, but it did make an impression on him, as did others he had with his Muslim parents during his activism. Rashid's continuing dialogue with his parents was one of the factors that pulled him out of the activist network. Meaningful relationships with friends and family members can help pull people away from the Emigrants.[54] Networks in, networks out.

---

[52] Interview with Maryam, Skype, November 20, 2012.
[53] Interview with Rashid, former activist, Whitechapel, East London, June 26, 2011.
[54] For a similar argument in her study of female white supremacists, see Blee, *Inside Organized Racism*, p. 191.

Engaging activists effectively requires knowledge of their views. Few people are better positioned to question the network's ideology than former activists. As prior affiliates in al-Muhajiroun's community of practice, they understand its religious doctrine and political ideology, and the personal pathways to – and from – the activist network. In carrying out my research I have interviewed a number of thoughtful, intellectually engaging former activists. This study is richer for their insights. But why should an American professor be the only one who benefits from their experience and expertise? Despite the growth in CVE programs in Great Britain over the past decade, there has been no organized attempt to channel deradicalized former activists into a coherent network or community of practice focused on countering al-Muhajiroun's narrative. A small number of formers, including respondents in my sample, work in different prevention programs, but these government-funded initiatives focus on an assortment of people who have been exposed to a range of extremist influences.

What I am proposing here is different: a small, community-led intervention composed of former Emigrants who come together on a volunteer basis to engage young people who are still involved in the activist network. These formers could seek out and interact with current activists where they are largely unchallenged, at their da'wah stalls and halaqah circles. They could draw on the knowledge they developed in al-Muhajiroun to talk with activists about their religious and political beliefs. They could recall aggravations from their own days in the network, such as the constant demands on their time and the frequent requests for money. They could share their stories of how they came to question the network's ideas and activism before eventually leaving. They could remind activists that virtually all of the Emigrants' teachings are based on the lectures and writings of a single person who is not even a classically trained scholar and a few of his hand-picked students. And they could encourage activists to expand their intellectual horizons by considering other Islamic scholars, within and outside the Salafi tradition.

Of course, activists cannot simply be told that their beliefs are erroneous and sent on their way. Individuals who are thinking of leaving must be supported with alternative networks and communities that understand what they are going through and can reinforce their intellectual journeys away from the network. For this reason, former activists would do well to engage them on a regular basis, while also encouraging them to reconnect with their loved ones outside the network. In this manner, current and former members could create their own community of practice, one that not only counters the Emigrants' narrative, but helps activists construct new identities and satisfies their need to belong to something bigger than themselves.

If this proposal sounds naïve, it is worth pointing out that some formers already engage activists, informally. "Every now and again I still preach to young brothers," explains Salman, who does not work in CVE, but talks to activists on his own: "If I see any of their members, I debate them. I talk to them and say, 'This is the wrong way. This is not the way of the sunnah and of the Qur'an."[55] Such ad hoc exchanges should be encouraged, but it might be more useful for former activists like Salman to pool their experience into a community of practice. This informal community would be composed of other formers who want to show activists they can practice their religion and build lives of meaning outside of al-Muhajiroun, without establishing the caliphate in Britain. This community would give former activists more opportunities to interact with old friends who have also left the network, something many of them enjoy. If these formers had the chance to meet with each other, to share a meal and a laugh, while engaging current activists, showing them that there is life after the Emigrants, many of them might accept the challenge.

The success of such an undertaking remains far from certain. If directed towards the most persistent activists, it is not likely to be effective. These deeply committed insiders will continue to accept Omar Bakri's teachings, irrespective of such interventions. However, if the initiative focused on youngsters who have been exposed to the Emigrants' ideology without becoming full-blown activists, it may help some of them turn away from extremism. Even without knowing the exact impact such a program might have, now seems a good time to try, while the network remains weak and activists lack access to their most knowledgeable and charismatic leaders.

Creating a community of practice to counter al-Muhajiroun's already diminished one may further weaken the activist network, but wiping it out completely may prove elusive. With its strong ideological orientation, and its notion of membership as intellectual affiliation, the Emigrants, along with the larger Salafi-jihadi movement, remain as much a state of mind as a specific collective. Thankfully, in the United Kingdom merely having a certain state of mind, even one that many find deeply offensive, is not illegal. Britain and other Western democracies can continue to deal with the threat of violent extremism without sacrificing the political rights and civil liberties that sustain their own identities as democratic societies. Part of the solution is to allow groups that engage in peaceful protest the room to express their grievances lawfully. This is part and parcel of what makes Britain great.

Finally, readers can take comfort in knowing that, as I have emphasized throughout this study, the Emigrants' state of mind is highly marginalized in Britain. Like other ethnographers, I draw big conclusions from small facts. But this remains a case study of a single activist network. I draw parallels between al-Muhajiroun and the Salafi-jihadi movement to which it belongs, but I do not claim the network resembles broader Muslim communities in Great Britain or the United States. I don't believe it does. If anything, the Emigrants have

---

[55] Interview with Salman, Poplar, East London, July 24, 2015.

become increasingly ostracized from Britain's diverse Muslim population, especially after allying themselves with ISIS. Even if Anjem Choudary and Mizanur Rahman rebound from their prison sentences, rising once more to continue their activism, they and their followers will not likely return the activist network to its former glory – let alone establish the Islamic state in Britain.

Appendix: The Method of Ethnographic Network Analysis

With Stephen Coulthart and Dominick Wright

This study combines "thin" quantitative analysis of network measures and structures with "thick" qualitative descriptions of network processes. This mixed method, which I call ethnographic network analysis, combines the precision and measurement validity of social network analysis with deep, contextual knowledge of a specific case. The disciplined configurative case presented in the preceding chapters draws on theories and concepts in a number of areas, including radicalization, resilience, adaptation, communities of practice, and de-radicalization, to explain how the Emigrants experience these processes and outcomes.[1] This appendix describes the research procedures used to collect and analyze the data for this case study. I begin with the methods and measures Stephen Coulthart, Dominick Wright and I use for the formal network analysis presented in Chapter 1 before describing the interviews and observational data I draw on throughout the book.

The data for our formal network analysis on al-Muhajiroun come from news reports. We purposively sampled these articles from Lexis Nexis Academic using a variety of search terms.[2] These search terms included various spellings of al-Muhajiroun and the names of different spin-off groups, including the

---

[1] For more on disciplined configurative case studies, see Alexander L. George and Andrew Bennett, *Case Studies and Theory Development in the Social Sciences* (Cambridge, MA: The MIT Press, 2005), p. 75; Alexander L. George, "Case Studies and Theory Development: The Method of Structured, Focused Comparisons," in *Diplomacy: New Approaches in History, Theory, and Policy* (New York: Free Press, 1979), ed. Paul Gordon Lauren, pp. 43–68; and Harry Eckstein, "Case Study and Theory in Political Science," in *Strategies of Inquiry*, Vol. 7 of *The Handbook of Political Science* (Reading, MA: Addison-Wesley Publishing Company, 1975), eds. Fred I. Greenstein and Nelson W. Polsby, pp. 79–138.

[2] Lexis Nexis is an electronic database that contains full-text articles from over 200 newspapers throughout the world beginning in 1980. Details from this and the following paragraphs are taken from Michael Kenney, John Horgan, Cale Horne, Peter Vining, Kathleen M. Carley, Michael W. Bigrigg, Mia Bloom, and Kurt Braddock, "Organisational Adaptation in an Activist

Saved Sect, Islam4UK, and Muslims Against Crusades. Using the search terms our assistants gathered over four thousand newspaper articles from Lexis Nexis. When reviewing this initial dataset, however, we discovered that it contained hundreds of duplicate articles and "false positives." The duplicate articles came from identical wire service reports that appeared in numerous publications in the Lexis Nexis database. False positives came from articles that appeared under one of our search terms, such as the Saved Sect, but whose content was not related to al-Muhajiroun. We cleaned the dataset by removing these duplicates and false positives. This produced a final dataset of 3,306 articles published in over sixty newspapers from 1996 through November 2012.

Reflecting al-Muhajiroun's substantive importance in the United Kingdom, most of these articles came from British publications. However, other countries with publications in the final dataset included Canada, China, Ireland (and Northern Ireland), Israel, Malaysia, New Zealand, Russia, Scotland, Singapore, and the United States. We made no attempt to sample or "balance" our selection of newspaper articles according to different publications' political leanings. If the non-duplicate article about al-Muhajiroun or its activists appeared in an English-language newspaper in Lexis Nexis during the years in our sampling frame we included it in our dataset. The dataset contained publications from across the political spectrum, including those that are often identified as "conservative" (*The Daily Mail, The Times, The Daily Telegraph*), "liberal" (*The Guardian, The Observer, The Independent*), and "moderate" (BBC Monitoring-International Reports). We did not include articles from non-English sources because our network mining tool, AutoMap, works only with English-language text.

After creating the dataset of newspaper articles for our social network analysis, we separated the articles into three time periods corresponding to major events in the Emigrants' history (see Table 1.1). The next step was to create a thesaurus or list of activists, people who participated in al-Muhajiroun or one of its successor groups, either as administrative or intellectual affiliates (Chapter 3 discusses the meaning of these terms). Because the results of our social network analysis would depend on the accuracy of our thesaurus, we devoted considerable effort to creating the cleanest list of activists or "agents" we could, based on our understanding of al-Muhajiroun. We revised the thesaurus by verifying that each person on our list was administratively or intellectually affiliated with the Emigrants based on their involvement in network activities. After removing false positives, our final thesaurus contained 364 unique nodes or agents.

We then processed the newspaper data in each time period with our refined thesaurus using AutoMap, a content analysis program that extracts networks

Network: Social Networks, Leadership, and Change in al-Muhajiroun," *Applied Ergonomics* 44, no. 5 (September 2013), pp. 739–47.

from texts.[3] AutoMap generates a network based upon the proximity of agents in the thesaurus that appears in the same text, depending on a user defined "window." The extraction settings we used connected individuals who were mentioned in the same news report, irrespective of the number of words between them. If two agents were mentioned in the same report, we coded them as being connected regardless of their location in the article.[4] This allowed us to create a bipartite proxy network of al-Muhajiroun activists for each time period based on their connections with each other in the news reports. We used news reports as the source of our relational data because a detailed account of associations among the Emigrants across all three periods was not available. We treat the networks that emerge from our newspaper data as proxies for al-Muhajiroun, but we recognize that they do not capture all the social relationships in the real network. We also recognize, as emphasized in Chapter 1, that the proxy networks are smaller than the real networks for each period because news reports about the Emigrants typically do not name rank-and-file activists.

Once we extracted proxy networks from the news reports for each of the three time periods, we uploaded each network into the Organizational Risk Analyzer (ORA) program to calculate the node and network-level measures. Like other international relations scholars, we use degree centrality at the node-level of analysis to measure access power and betweenness centrality to measure brokerage power. At the node-level, degree centrality refers to the sum of the value of ties between the node being measured and all other nodes in the network. Nodes that rank high on this measure have more connections to other nodes in the same network.[5] Node-level betweenness centrality measures the number of shortest paths that pass through a node in the network. It measures the extent to which a node is the most efficient path between other nodes in

---

[3] Kathleen M. Carley, Dave Columbus, Michael Bigrigg, and Frank Kunkel, *AutoMap User's Guide 2011*, Technical Report, CMU-ISR-11e108 (Pittsburgh, PA: Carnegie Mellon University, School of Computer Science, Institute for Software Research, 2011).

[4] We adopted this setting after experimenting with various window sizes that produced unrealistically sparse networks. Some might object that our approach is likely to produce false positives, connecting agents that should not be connected. We cannot discount this possibility entirely. However, we do not believe this is a significant source of error in our extraction process, given the "cleanliness" of our thesaurus, which contains few, if any, individuals who were not involved with the Emigrants at some point. The false positives that appear in Chapter 1, including Abu Hamza al-Masri, Afzal Munir, Aftab Manzoor, and Mohammed Omar, were affiliated with the activist network. Their high rankings for node-level degree and betweenness centrality reflect their appearance in many news reports, usually due to their involvement in political violence, rather than their prominence in the network. For more discussion on this and related issues, see Michael Kenney and Stephen Coulthart, "The Methodological Challenges of Extracting Dark Networks: Minimizing False Positives through Ethnography," in *Illuminating Dark Networks*, edited by Luke M. Gerdes (New York: Cambridge University Press, 2015), pp. 52–70.

[5] Each node's degree centrality is the normalized sum of its row and column degrees, as calculated on the network's node-by-node matrices. For more on node-level degree centrality and how it is interpreted in ORA, see Kathleen M. Carley, Jeffrey Reminga, Jon Storrick, and Dave

the network. Nodes that score high in betweenness centrality often serve as brokers, connecting otherwise poorly connected nodes.[6]

At the network-level of analysis we use degree centralization, betweenness centralization, average path length, and the clustering coefficient to measure centralization and clustering. Network-level degree centralization measures the extent to which all the network's connections are concentrated in one or several persons, while betweenness centralization calculates the extent to which the shortest paths between nodes are concentrated in one or more persons. The average path length of a network refers to the average number of nodes that must be crossed in the shortest path between any two nodes in the network.[7] A small path length means that the network is cohesive because, on average, it takes few steps to cross from one end of the network to the other. Conversely, the clustering coefficient measures "clumpiness" or bunching across the network by averaging the density of each node's ego network. Networks with high clustering coefficients contain numerous tightly-knit clusters.[8]

In addition to measuring centrality and clustering within al-Muhajiroun, we also seek to determine whether the activist network is scale-free, small-world, or something else. We use aggregate measures of network structure for this, including different algorithms that place the observed al-Muhajiroun networks on a continuum of possible values for node degree and clustering. Our first aggregate test determines whether the network is scale-free by examining its relative distribution of node degree. Node degree is a count of all connections the node shares with other nodes in the network. The relative frequency of node degree produces a distribution that can be analyzed to see how closely it follows a power law, a signature feature of scale-free networks.[9] According to Clauset, Shalizi, and Newman,[10] a value x follows a power law distribution if it is drawn from a probability distribution:

$$p(x) \propto x^{-\alpha} \tag{1}$$

Columbus, *ORA User's Guide 2011*, Carnegie Mellon University, School of Computer Science, Institute for Software Research, Technical Report, CMU-ISR-11e107 (2011).

[6] The betweenness centrality of a node is defined as: Across all node pairs that have a shortest path containing the node, the percentage that pass through that node. This is calculated on node-by-node matrices. For more on betweenness centrality and how it is measured in ORA, see Carley *et al.*, *ORA User's Guide 2011* (2011). For a broader discussion of betweenness centrality, see Linton C. Freeman, "Centrality in Social Networks: Conceptual Clarification," *Social Networks* 1, no. 3 (1979), pp. 215–39.

[7] Duncan J. Watts, "Networks, Dynamics, and the Small-World Phenomenon," *American Journal of Sociology* 105, no. 2 (September 1999), p. 498; Carley *et al.*, *ORA User's Guide 2011* (2011); and Thomas W. Valente, *Social Networks and Health: Models, Methods, and Application,* (New York: Oxford University Press, 2010).

[8] Valente, *Social Networks and Health.*

[9] Albert-László Barabási, *Linked: The New Science of Networks* (Cambridge, MA: Perseus Press, 2002).

[10] Aaron Clauset, Cosma Rohilla Shalizi, and M. E. J. Newman, "Power-Law Distributions in Empirical Data." *SIAM Review* 51, no. 4 (2009), p. 662.

The exponent, α, is a scaling parameter that shapes the distribution and tends to fall in the range 2 < α < 3, with some exceptions. Determining whether an observed distribution exhibits the properties of a power law involves estimating alpha using a maximum likelihood estimation (MLE) procedure. Clauset and his co-authors suggest a two-step procedure that we use.[11] The first step is to estimate a value for alpha that applies to the observed distribution. The next step is to compare the observed distribution of α against a simulated distribution for the same parameter. If the observed and simulated distributions are not different and the estimated alpha is within range, we consider the observed distribution to follow a power law and the network to be scale-free. If the observed and simulated distributions are not significantly different, but the estimated alpha falls outside the range 2 < α < 3, we consider the network to be "scale-free-like." We discuss this "likeness" category in Chapter 1.

Our second aggregate test measures whether an observed network exhibits small-world properties as described by Watts and Strogatz.[12] Small-world networks are characterized by shorter average path lengths and higher clustering than distributed networks of similar size. When two nodes have connections with one another and they share connections with a third node, a relational triangle forms between them. This is a form of clustering that can be measured. A high degree of clustering occurs when a node's connections in a network form more triangles than found in distributed networks.

In their seminal contribution, Watts and Strogatz show how the simple process of rewiring a ring lattice creates small-world networks characterized by high clustering coefficients and short path lengths, which can be expressed in a small-world quotient.[13] Their contribution has been valuable, but it also produced a broad class of networks that are considered small worlds. In response, Humphries and Gurney created a more nuanced measure, one that builds on Watts and Strogatz but proposes a continuous measure of small-world

---

[11] Few empirically observed distributions conform to a power law throughout their entire range of *x* values. This makes it necessary to inspect the observed frequency distribution (e.g., as a histogram) and to determine where to set the "floor" that defines the subset of *x* values that follow a power law. Fitting a power law to the distribution provides an estimate for alpha to use as a starting point for the maximum likelihood estimation procedure. In our case, we supply several measures to the "igraph" R package and its power.law.fit function, including *x*, *x* as a discrete value, the *x*-range floor, and the prior estimate of α. This produces an MLE for alpha in the form of $\hat{\alpha}$, along with an evaluation for statistical significance difference between the observed distribution and a power law distribution simulated according to $\hat{\alpha}$.

[12] Duncan J. Watts, and Steven H. Strogatz, "Collective Dynamics of 'Small-World' Networks," *Nature* 393, no. 6684 (1998), pp. 440–2.

[13] Also known as a "regular" network, a ring lattice is a structure with nodes arranged in a circle. Connections between nodes occur among immediate neighbors as well as neighbors that are one path length away. Beginning with a ring lattice and rewiring its connections with probability *p* progressively produces a random network as *p* nears one.

indicators.[14] Like Watts and Strogatz, Humphries and Gurney derive their measure of small-world properties by comparing an observed network, nw_g, to a random network with the same number of nodes and ties, nw_{rand}. This measure consists of three components. The first component is Humphries and Gurney's version of clustering, C^Δ. This is a ratio with three times the number of triangles in a network in the numerator and the total number of path lengths equal to a length of two in the denominator.[15]

$$C^\Delta = \frac{3 \times \text{number of triangles}}{\text{number of paths of length 2}} \tag{2}$$

The second component is a clustering ratio, which places the clustering value for nw_g in the numerator and the clustering value for nw_{rand} in the denominator.

$$\gamma_g^\Delta = \frac{C_g^\Delta}{C_{rand}^\Delta} \tag{3}$$

The third component begins with the mean value of the minimum path length between all node pairs in a network, L_g, and then combines them to form a ratio.

$$\lambda_g = \frac{L_g}{L_{rand}} \tag{4}$$

These three components are then combined to create a metric of "small-world-ness," essentially a ratio of ratios.

$$S^\Delta = \frac{\gamma_g^\Delta}{\lambda_g} \tag{5}$$

According to Humphries and Gurney, a network is small-world if $S^\Delta > 1$. We use this same definition while making a change to their procedures. Rather

---

[14] Mark D. Humphries and Kevin Gurney, "Network 'Small-World-Ness': A Quantitative Method for Determining Canonical Network Equivalence," *PLoSOne* 3, no. 4 (2008), pp. 1–10. Brian Uzzi and Jarret Spiro develop a similar continuous measure of small-world-ness, which they call "small world Q." See Brian Uzzi, and Jarrett Spiro, "Collaboration and Creativity: The Small World Problem," *American Journal of Sociology* 111, no. 2 (2005), p. 470.

[15] Watts and Strogatz use a slightly different measure for clustering:

$$c_i^{ws} = \frac{2E_i}{k_i(k_i - 1)}$$

Here, c_i^{ws} is the clustering value for node i, which is two times the number of connections shared among its neighbors divided by the degree of i times its degree minus one. The quantity produces marginally different behavior than the clustering measure defined by Humphries and Gurney.

than calculating a single score based upon comparison to only one random network, we calculate an average small-world score drawn from a comparison of 1,000 random simulations. This adds confidence to our final assessment of al-Muhajiroun's "small-world-ness." If a network's Humphries-Gurney score is less than but within one standard deviation of 1, we consider the network to be "small-world-like."

ETHNOGRAPHY AND PROCESS TRACING

The formal network analysis in this study allows us to measure, with some degree of precision, node and network-level centrality and clustering, and to see how network relationships and structures change over time. This, however, is only part of the book's explanation. The preceding chapters also explain why activists decide to join the network, how they learn its Salafi-Islamist ideology, how they become committed insiders in its community of practice, and why they eventually decide to leave.

Answering these questions requires an additional method of analysis, one that complements the "thin" method above to produce "thick," ethnographic network analysis. This approach, combined with process tracing, allows me to peer inside the outlawed network, to understand how activists acquire knowledge, how they make decisions, and how they change their activities in response to feedback. My attempt to understand the beliefs and behaviors of the members of this cultural group through thick description is what makes this ethnography.[16] But the ethnography remains deeply informed by network theory and analysis. Throughout this book, I draw on the measures of centrality and network structure to inform my interpretation of al-Muhajiroun. Finally, my effort to trace the complex processes through which individuals make decisions, and the network performs collective action, is what makes this study process tracing.[17] All this methodological scaffolding should not obscure an important point: My goal in interpreting the Emigrants and understanding the processes behind their activism is not to aid or empower them. Nor is it to give them a platform to propagate their views. Rather, taking my cue from Clifford Geertz, my goal is to understand them, to make them accessible to outsiders, to reveal their normality without sacrificing their particularity.[18]

[16] John W. Creswell, *Qualitative Inquiry & Research Design*, 2nd edition (Thousand Oaks, CA, 2007), p. 68; Michael Agar, *The Professional Stranger: An Informal Introduction to Ethnography* (New York: Academic Press, 1980).

[17] For more on process tracing, see Gary Goertz and James Mahoney, *A Tale of Two Cultures: Qualitative and Quantitative Research in the Social Sciences* (Princeton, NJ: Princeton University Press, 2012), pp. 106–9; George and Bennett, *Case Studies and Theory Development in the Social Sciences*, pp. 6–7, 205–32; and Andrew Bennett and Jeffrey T. Checkel, "Process Tracing: From Philosophical Roots to Best Practices," in *Process Tracing: From Metaphor to Analytic Tool*, edited by Bennett and Checkel (Cambridge: Cambridge University Press, 2015), pp. 1–37.

[18] Clifford Geertz, "Thick Description: Toward an Interpretive Theory of Culture," in *The Interpretation of Cultures: Selected Essays by Clifford Geertz* (New York: Basic Books, 1973), p. 14.

Gaining insight into cultural practices like da'wah and hisbah, and processes like radicalization and learning, requires access to cultural data that capture the beliefs and behaviors of those being studied, and the ability to trace the processes by which they acquire them. Knowledge of these cultural facts is not randomly distributed within a given population. It is shared among certain people, some of who know more about the beliefs and behaviors than others. As I emphasize in the introduction to this book, one of the biggest challenges in studying radicalization and political violence is accessing respondents who can discuss these phenomena, accurately and reliably. That chapter also tells the story of how I gained access to al-Muhajiroun.

Once they opened their world to me, these activists allowed me to make the most of my seven research trips to Britain, between November 2010 and July 2015. During these trips, and with the help of my initial "seeds," who served as both respondents and gatekeepers to other activists, I used snowball and convenience sampling to build a respondent pool of forty-eight activists, with whom I conducted ninety-seven interviews. These respondents represented a diverse cross-section of al-Muhajiroun activists, including eight leaders, eleven veterans with years of experience in the network, and twenty-nine rank-and-file "dai's" or proselytizers who carried out much of the Emigrants' day-to-day activism. In exchange for allowing them to engage in da'wah with me, many of these individuals took the time to answer my questions and tell me their stories.

Did these respondents always tell me the truth? After all, as members of an outlawed network, they had plenty of incentives to downplay their involvement in al-Muhajiroun. At times during my field work I encountered activists who did just that. However, given that I was usually interviewing them at their da'wah stalls and protests, or while we were hanging out with their fellow activists at restaurants and the network's centers, most of these respondents did not deny their association with the Emigrants or their participation in high-risk activism. Instead, most of the deceptions I confronted revolved around specific matters, such as one young activist who, rather curiously, lied about his age, only to be challenged by another activist. Another respondent, perhaps more understandably, denied he had been arrested at a certain protest, even though I had been at the demonstration myself and the media had already reported his arrest. Fortunately, these incidents were outliers. Some activists did try to deceive me, but most of them were honest with me most of the time.

There are several reasons for this. The first has to do with the context in which my interviews occurred. As I describe in Chapter 2, numerous interviews took place as activists fulfilled their divine obligation to engage in da'wah. They understood that intentionally lying about themselves during these conversations would be a sin for which they would be held accountable on the Day of Judgment. Under these circumstances, it was better for them not to lie, to avoid the wrath of Allah, and their fellow activists. A second factor that minimized deception had to do with how I conducted the interviews. Before each discussion, I asked my respondents to avoid talking about anything that made them uncomfortable. If they didn't want to answer a question, I encouraged them to move on to the next one. My strategy was to make it easier for them to skip over an unwelcome query than to fabricate a deceptive response. Some respondents exercised this option by refusing to answer certain questions, usually having to do with internal administrative matters. When faced with these refusals I did not press the point, but quickly moved on to the next question.

A third factor minimizing deliberate deception in interviews had to do with the relationships I built with my gatekeepers and many respondents. These were not one-off interviews. They were part of a larger data-gathering process, involving multiple trips to London. Potential respondents could see and verify for themselves my presence and the purpose of my visits. By the time I asked them for an interview, many respondents had already seen me hanging out with other activists, they had seen me observing and taking notes at their da'wah stalls and protests, and they had seen me engaging with gatekeepers who were often the leaders of their local halaqahs. To recall one story I told in the Introduction, respondents understood that it was okay to talk with me because, as one gatekeeper put it, "We have a relationship." [19]

Another important set of respondents for this book were the former activists who left al-Muhajiroun after being involved in its high-risk activism for years. These "formers" were among the most difficult respondents to access. Apart from a handful of individuals who now make their living countering the same narratives they once championed, formers activists are often reluctant to discuss their adolescent involvement in al-Muhajiroun. This makes it hard to track them down and even harder to get them to agree to an interview. Of course, difficult does not mean impossible. Through my research contacts within and outside al-Muhajiroun, I identified and located a number of former activists. When they agreed to be interviewed, and not all of them did, these respondents were full of rich insights about their own journeys to and from the Emigrants and how the network worked when they were still involved.

Unlike activists who were still in the network, no questions were off-limits to the formers. They provided details on internal administrative affairs I could not get from active supporters, such as the attempted overthrow of Anjem Choudary by leaders of the network's halaqah in Whitechapel. Salman, who told me about the coup attempt and whose journey I document throughout this book, is a case in point. When I first interviewed him he was deeply involved in the Whitechapel halaqah, leading da'wah stalls in Bethnal Green and even forming his own network platform, Call2Tawhid. When I ran into him years later, largely by chance, he had long since left al-Muhajiroun and its controversial hisbah, but he was reluctant to give me another interview. After following up with him through several phone calls, which unfolded over the course of

---

[19] Field notes, Whitechapel, East London, November 9, 2010.

two separate trips to Britain, I eventually persuaded him to give me another. My efforts were not in vain. Salman was as candid with me as a former as he had been as an activist, only now I had the benefit of interviewing him both at the height of his activism and afterwards, when his views had changed dramatically.

In addition to interviewing activists and former activists, I also interviewed forty-one people who were not personally involved in al-Muhajiroun, but who followed the network's activism, from different perspectives. These included United States and British law enforcers and security officials, academics and think tank researchers based in London, former Hizb ut-Tahrir activists now working on countering violent extremism, and fifteen quietist Salafis from a mosque in Brixton that clashed repeatedly with the Emigrants. In all, I conducted 148 interviews with ninety-seven people within and outside al-Muhajiroun.

All these interviews followed a semi-structured format. This allowed me to ask respondents standard questions focused on the major themes of my research, while giving me the flexibility to pursue different leads as they developed during the interviews. Most of my respondents, including all of the Emigrants, let me record their interviews on my audio recorder. When respondents, usually government officials, did not give me permission to tape their interviews, I took extensive hand-written notes. I converted these notes into electronic form on my computer as soon as possible after the interview, while the conversation was still fresh in my mind. When observing da'wah stalls, demonstrations, and other events, I recorded my impressions in a paper note pad and took photographs on my camera. I later expanded on these field note jottings when converting them into electronic form on my laptop, often at the end of a long day of field work.

When I returned home from periodic trips to London, I arranged for my audio files to be converted into verbatim texts by professional transcribers and graduate students. I carefully checked and corrected each transcript against the original audio files before uploading them to NVivo, the software program I used to code and analyze these data. Through a reiterative process of reading, coding, and reflecting on the interview transcripts, field notes, and hundreds of additional documents, I gradually created a coding index that contained two thousand themes and sub-themes. Some of these themes, including adaptation, leadership, and social networks, were based on research questions and hypotheses I had before entering the field. Others, like suhba, hisbah, and the covenant of security emerged from my respondents. Consistent with a "grounded theory" approach to field work and qualitative analysis, these concepts were generated by the people who experienced them. They were essential in helping me understand in their own terms how the Emigrants engaged in high-risk activism.[20]

---

[20] For more on grounded theory, see John W. Creswell, *Qualitative Inquiry & Research Design*, 2nd edition (Thousand Oaks, CA: Sage, 2007), pp. 62–8; and Barney G. Glaser and Anselm L. Strauss, *The Discovery of Grounded Theory: Strategies for Qualitative Research* (New Brunswick, NJ: Aldine, 1967). For more on qualitative coding, see Lyn Richards, *Handling Qualitative Data: A Practical Guide*, 3rd edition (London: Sage, 2015), pp. 109–15.

As important as the interviews were to my research, early on in my field work I realized that the best way to learn about the Emigrants was not just to talk with activists but to watch them perform their activism. Over the four-and-a-half year period of my field work, I spent hundreds of hours observing activists in their "natural setting" at twenty-four separate da'wah stalls, demonstrations and other events, and from hanging out with them at restaurants and two different indoctrination centers in East London. As I walked around their rallies I read their protest signs and asked them questions about their ideology and political grievances. At their da'wah stalls I encouraged them to preach to me and I engaged them in cheerful debates about the meaning of life. At their centers I bantered with them while we waited for private talks to begin and I talked with them some more when the talks were over. At local cafés and restaurants I commiserated with them about the weather and the Tube's latest service delays while sipping coffee or breaking bread.

Watching respondents in action helped me understand what they were telling me in their interviews. Numerous activists talked about hierarchy in our taped-recorded discussions, but first-hand observation showed me the network's hierarchy in action, allowing me to see how veterans directed the rank-and-file at demonstrations, and which leaders arrived late to deliver their speeches. During interviews respondents gamely answered my questions about learning, but direct observation showed me how activists actually learned their activism by doing it: handing out leaflets, waving protest signs, yelling chants at passersby. During their interviews, respondents highlighted the importance of face-to-face discussions with their peers, but hanging out with them let me view these interactions first-hand, to see for myself how they enhanced the network's fellowship and in-group radicalization. Observing activists in action allowed me to draw inferences from what they actually did and not just what they told me.[21]

Spending time with activists at da'wah stalls and sharing meals with them at kebab shops helped me build the trust and rapport that is so essential to ethnography. This resulted in richer interactions and more candid interviews. "Only by establishing long-term relationships based on trust can one begin to ask provocative personal questions, and expect thoughtful, serious answers," writes Philippe Bourgois, describing his own ethnography on crack dealers in East Harlem.[22] Unlike Bourgois, and Malinowski, I did not live in the

---

[21] For similar observations, see Richard F. Fenno, Jr., *Home Style: House Members in Their Districts* (New York: Pearson, 2002), p. 252; Edward Schatz, ed., *Political Ethnography: What Immersion Contributes to the Study of Power* (Chicago: University of Chicago Press, 2009); and Bronislaw Malinowski, *Argonauts of the Western Pacific: An Account of Native Enterprise and Adventure in the Archipelagoes of Melanesian New Guinea* (Prospect Heights, IL: Waveland Press, 1984 [1922]), pp. 17–22.

[22] Philippe Bourgois, *In Search of Respect: Selling Crack in El Barrio*, 2nd edition (New York: Cambridge University Press, 2003), p. 13.

community I studied, but I did establish "long-term, organic relationships" with many of the people I write about in this book. Some of these people did not know what to make of me at first. But they opened up after watching me visit their East London neighborhoods repeatedly. They knew that I was a white, American university professor, a bewhiskered, scruffily-clad student of Islamic activism whose research was funded by the US government.[23] My position of privilege, and my willingness to listen, observe, and interact, gave me access to their lives. Some of them hoped – rather wishfully in my view – that I had the ear of American officials and policy makers, to whom I would tell their stories. Others hoped, even more wishfully, that once I understood their beliefs the scales would fall from my eyes and I would embrace their call. In reality, I often disagreed with my respondents, especially during their initial interviews, when they quoted the same verses of scripture and repeated stock grievances against Western foreign policy. But I always avoided criticizing them or their views, even when they sought to provoke me with outrageous comments. I did my best to treat my respondents with dignity and respect. I listened closely to what they were telling me and I asked questions, seeking to engage them on their own terms. Once they saw that I was eager to discuss their ideas and experiences candidly and courteously, they often reciprocated my behavior.

While I learned something from every interaction, my most illuminating conversations were with activists and former activists who I interviewed on multiple occasions.[24] When I interviewed the same activist repeatedly, his sermonizing ceased and he became more willing to answer my questions directly, without rhetorical boilerplate or subterfuge. He became more open, in other words, to having a frank and meaningful conversation. Many of these respondents were the network's leading and veteran activists. Not only did they tend to be the most articulate activists, they were also the most knowledgeable, with the most cultural expertise to share. Some would tell me things about themselves and their activism during our second, third, and fourth conversations that they would never have shared during our first meeting. One leading activist I came to know over the course of several years was standoffish during our initial encounters. But after meeting with him a few times, he gradually opened up to me, sharing more insights into his activism with each succeeding conversation. During our fourth interview, several months after he

---

[23] For more on positionality and reflexivity, see Dvora Yanow, "Dear Author, Dear Reader: The Third Hermeneutic in Writing and Reviewing Ethnography," in *Political Ethnography: What Immersion Contributes to the Study of Power*, edited by Edward Schatz (Chicago, IL: University of Chicago Press, 2009), pp. 275–302.

[24] Similarly, when discussing her repeated interviews with El Salvadoran peasants directly affected by the country's civil war, Elisabeth Wood argues that returning to the same communities several times allowed her to gather high quality data from her respondents. See Elisabeth Jean Wood, "Ethical Challenges of Field Research in Conflict Zones," *Qualitative Sociology* 29, no. 3 (2006), pp. 375, 378.

had been arrested in the September 2014 round-up of network leaders, I asked him whether he trusted me. "Yes I do," he responded. "I trust you to the extent that I will sit with you, talk with you, engage with you. There's nothing more than that."[25]

His second point was as important as his first. In clarifying that "there's nothing more than that," this senior activist, who liked to refer to himself as a "convicted terrorist" because he had been jailed for crimes related to his activism, was marking the boundaries of his trust, and our relationship. We were friendly, but not friends. Steeped in my identity as an "objective" social scientist, I took comfort in such remarks, rather than being offended by them. I had no desire to fall victim to "ethnographic seduction" by letting my personal feelings towards him and other activists get in the way of my research.[26] Wary of engaging in deception, I often reminded respondents that I was there to study their activism rather than "convert" to their cause. They also sought to maintain their distance from me, even when, after multiple interactions, they grew comfortable teasing me about my wispy beard or whether I might be a spy for the CIA. Activists' acceptance of me was provisional, the sort of approval one grants a curious – and not completely trusted – outsider. "I trust you to the extent that I will... engage with you," the "convicted terrorist" said, exemplifying this attitude. All teasing and rapport-building aside, he and I both understood that I would always remain a stranger to the Emigrants – and they to me. Sometimes it is precisely a stranger, someone who, in Simmel's terms, is "in but not of" a cultural scene that can describe that scene with enough insight – and detachment – to create an interpretation that explains rather than sensationalizes such a highly politicized, poorly understood phenomenon as al-Muhajiroun.[27]

---

[25] Interview with leading activist, Stratford, East London, December 13, 2014.

[26] Antonius C. G. M. Robben, "Ethnographic Seduction, Transference, and Resistance in Dialogues about Terror and Violence in Argentina," *Ethos* 24, no. 1 (1996), pp. 71–106.

[27] Ann Mische, *Partisan Publics: Communication and Contention Across Brazilian Youth Activist Networks* (Princeton, NJ: Princeton University Press, 2008), p. 367; Georg Simmel, *The Sociology of Georg Simmel*, translated, edited, and introduced by Kurt H. Wolff (New York: Free Press, 1950); and Yanow, "Dear Author, Dear Reader," p. 286.

Appendix: Interviews

This appendix lists 148 interviews I conducted during my research on al-Muhajiroun. The interviews are presented in chronological order, proceeding from earliest to most recent. To protect my respondents' privacy and the confidentiality of what they told me, no real names appear below.

Person(s) Interviewed	Date	Location	Type of Interview
Two leading activists, one veteran activist, and "Salman," rank-and-file activist	9/22/2007	Woolwich, South London	Group
Brixton Salafi	10/23/2007	Brixton, South London	Individual
Leading activist	11/4/2010	Leyton, East London	Individual
Brixton Salafi	11/5/2010	Brixton, South London	Individual
Brixton Salafi	11/5/2010	Brixton, South London	Individual
Brixton Salafi	11/5/2010	Brixton, South London	Individual
Brixton Salafi	11/5/2010	Brixton, South London	Individual
Think tank researcher	11/5/2010	Westminster, Central London	Individual
Leading activist	11/6/2010	Leyton, East London	Individual
Veteran activist	11/6/2010	Leyton, East London	Individual
Leading activist	11/8/2010	Leyton, East London	Individual
Former Hizb ut-Tahrir activist	11/8/2010	Westminster, Central London	Individual
Veteran activist	11/9/2010	Whitechapel, East London	Individual
Veteran activist	11/9/2010	Whitechapel, East London	Individual
London Metropolitan Police officer	11/9/2010	Hertfordshire, United Kingdom	Individual

Person(s) Interviewed	Date	Location	Type of Interview
Veteran activist	11/11/2010	Kensington, Central London	Individual
Veteran activist	11/11/2010	Kensington, Central London	Individual
Rank-and-file activist	11/11/2010	Kensington, Central London	Individual
Two veteran activists	11/11/2010	Kensington, Central London	Group
One veteran, one rank-and-file activist	11/11/2010	Kensington, Central London	Group
Veteran activist	11/11/2010	Kensington, Central London	Individual
Rank-and-file activist	11/11/2010	Kensington, Central London	Individual
Brixton Salafi	11/12/2010	Brixton, South London	Individual
Brixton Salafi	11/12/2010	Brixton, South London	Individual
Rank-and-file activist	11/13/2010	Ilford, East London	Individual
Rank-and-file activist	11/13/2010	Ilford, East London	Individual
Rank-and-file activist	11/13/2010	Ilford, East London	Individual
Rank-and-file activist	11/13/2010	Ilford, East London	Individual
Leading activist	11/13/2010	Ilford, East London	Individual
Rank-and-file activist	11/14/2010	Leyton, East London	Individual
Rank-and-file activist	11/14/2010	Leyton, East London	Individual
Two veteran activists	11/14/2010	Leyton, East London	Group
Veteran activist	11/14/2010	Leyton, East London	Individual
Veteran activist	11/15/2010	Kensington, Central London	Individual
Veteran activist	11/15/2010	Kensington, Central London	Individual
Veteran activist	11/16/2010	Walthamstow, East London	Individual
Leading activist	11/27/2010	Phone interview, London	Individual
Leading activist	11/27/2010	Phone interview, London	Individual
Veteran activist	11/27/2010	Phone interview, London	Individual
"Salman," rank-and-file activist	11/28/2010	Bethnal Green, East London	Individual
Veteran activist	11/29/2010	Stratford, East London	Individual
Rank-and-file activist	11/29/2010	Stratford, East London	Individual
Leading activist	11/29/2010	Ilford, East London	Individual
Rank-and-file activist	11/29/2010	Stratford, East London	Individual
Veteran activist	11/29/2010	Stratford, East London	Individual
Local businessman	12/1/2010	Mile End, East London	Individual
Leading activist	12/2/2010	Walthamstow, East London	Individual
US government official	12/3/2010	Mayfair, Central London	Individual

(*continued*)

Person(s) Interviewed	Date	Location	Type of Interview
East London Mosque employee	12/3/2010	Whitechapel, East London	Individual
Rank-and-file activist	12/4/2010	Tottenham, North London	Individual
Rank-and-file activist	12/4/2010	Tottenham, North London	Individual
"Ahmed," veteran activist	12/4/2010	Tottenham, North London	Individual
Veteran activist	12/5/2010	Bethnal Green, East London	Individual
Rank-and-file activist	12/5/2010	Bethnal Green, East London	Individual
Veteran activist	12/6/2010	Stratford, East London	Individual
Think tank researcher	12/6/2010	Islington, North London	Individual
"Rohan," leading activist	12/7/2010	Whitechapel, East London	Individual
Former Hizb ut-Tahrir activist	12/7/2010	Westminster, Central London	Individual
"Salman," rank-and-file activist	12/9/2010	Leyton, East London	Individual
Veteran activist	12/9/2010	Leyton, East London	Individual
Two veteran activists	12/9/2010	Leyton, East London	Group
Brixton Salafi	12/9/2010	Birmingham, United Kingdom	Individual
Veteran activist	12/11/2010	Lewisham, South London	Individual
Rank-and-file activist	12/11/2010	Lewisham, South London	Individual
"Ali," former activist	12/13/2010	Hounslow, West London	Individual
"Maryam," former activist	12/13/2010	Hounslow, West London	Individual
Research director, think tank	12/14/2010	Bloomsbury, Central London	Individual
Leading activist	12/16/2010	Whitechapel, East London	Individual
Community activist	12/16/2010	Leyton, East London	Individual
Leading activist	3/23/2011	Skype, Online	Individual
Veteran activist	3/23/2011	Skype, Online	Individual
"Haroon," former contact	6/14/2011	Westminster, Central London	Individual
London Metropolitan Police officer	6/15/2011	Vauxhall, South London	Individual
London Metropolitan Police officer	6/15/2011	Vauxhall, South London	Individual
Veteran activist	6/16/2011	Whitechapel, East London	Individual
Veteran activist	6/17/2011	Whitechapel, East London	Individual
Veteran activist	6/17/2011	Whitechapel, East London	Individual
Veteran activist	6/17/2011	Mayfair, Central London	Individual

Person(s) Interviewed	Date	Location	Type of Interview
Rank-and-file activist	6/18/2011	Lewisham, South London	Individual
Academic researcher	6/18/2011	Lewisham, South London	Individual
"Abdul," former activist	6/18/2011	Whitechapel, East London	Individual
"Haroon," former contact	6/18/2011	Whitechapel, East London	Individual
Leading activist	6/20/2011	Stratford, East London	Individual
Rank-and-file activist	6/20/2011	Stratford, East London	Individual
"Maryam," former activist	6/21/2011	Hounslow, West London	Individual
"Ali," former activist	6/21/2011	Hounslow, West London	Individual
Leading activist	6/22/2011	Whitechapel, East London	Individual
Leading activist	6/22/2011	Walthamstow, East London	Individual
Think tank researcher	6/23/2011	Westminster, Central London	Individual
Veteran activist	6/25/2011	Wembley Central, West London	Individual
Veteran activist	6/25/2011	Wembley Central, West London	Individual
Leading activist	6/25/2011	Wembley Central, West London	Individual
Contact	6/25/2011	Wembley Central, West London	Individual
Contact	6/25/2011	Wembley Central, West London	Individual
Rank-and-file activist	6/26/2011	Mile End, East London	Individual
London Metropolitan Police officer	6/26/2011	Wood Green, North London	Individual
"Rashid," former activist	6/26/2011	Whitechapel, East London	Individual
Rank-and-file activist	6/27/2011	Stratford, East London	Individual
Research director, think tank	6/27/2011	Bloomsbury, Central London	Individual
Veteran activist	6/28/2011	Southall, West London	Individual
Rank-and-file activist	6/28/2011	Southall, West London	Individual
Rank-and-file activist	6/28/2011	Southall, West London	Individual
Academic researcher	6/28/2011	Central London	Individual
Two London Metropolitan Police officers	6/29/2011	Westminster, Central London	Group
Former London Metropolitan Police officer	7/14/2011	United States	Individual
Leading activist	11/8/2011	Skype, Online	Individual

(*continued*)

Person(s) Interviewed	Date	Location	Type of Interview
Brixton Salafi	7/12/2012	Brixton, South London	Individual
Brixton Salafi	7/12/2012	Brixton, South London	Individual
Brixton Salafi	7/13/2012	Brixton, South London	Individual
Brixton Salafi	7/13/2012	Brixton, South London	Individual
Brixton Salafi	7/14/2012	Brixton, South London	Individual
Brixton Salafi	7/14/2012	Brixton, South London	Individual
Brixton Salafi	7/14/2012	Brixton, South London	Individual
Brixton Salafi	7/14/2012	Brixton, South London	Individual
"Rohan," leading activist	7/16/2012	Whitechapel, East London	Individual
Brixton Salafi	7/16/2012	Brixton, South London	Individual
Leading activist	7/17/2012	Leyton, East London	Individual
Former activist	7/17/2012	Walthamstow, East London	Individual
Two London Metropolitan Police officers	7/19/2012	Westminster, Central London	Group
Veteran activist	7/21/2012	Islington, North London	Individual
Leading activist	7/21/2012	Islington, North London	Individual
"Ahmed," veteran activist	7/21/2012	Islington, North London	Individual
Rank-and-file activist	7/21/2012	Islington, North London	Individual
Rank-and-file activist	7/21/2012	Islington, North London	Individual
Rank-and-file activist	7/21/2012	Islington, North London	Individual
"Maryam," former activist	11/20/2012	Skype, Online	Individual
Leading activist	6/26/2013	Skype, Online	Individual
Rank-and-file activist	6/26/2013	Skype, Online	Individual
"Rohan," and two leading activists, one veteran activist	9/4/2013	Whitechapel, East London	Group
Leading activist	9/4/2013	Hounslow, West London	Individual
Rank-and-file activist	9/4/2013	Hounslow, West London	Individual
Leading activist	9/5/2013	Wembley Central, West London	Individual
Leading activist	9/5/2013	Wembley Central, West London	Individual
Veteran activist	9/6/2013	Westminster, Central London	Individual
Veteran activist	9/6/2013	Westminster, Central London	Individual
Rank-and-file activist	9/6/2013	Westminster, Central London	Individual
Leading activist	8/28/2014	Skype, Online	Individual
Leading activist	10/8/2014	Skype, Online	Individual

Person(s) Interviewed	Date	Location	Type of Interview
Leading activist	12/9/2014	Ilford, East London	Individual
Former Hizb ut-Tahrir activist	12/10/2014	Newham, East London	Individual
"Rohan," leading activist	12/11/2014	Whitechapel, East London	Individual
Leading activist	12/12/2014	Ilford, East London	Individual
Leading activist	12/13/2014	Stratford, East London	Individual
Leading activist	12/14/2014	Whitechapel, East London	Individual
Leading activist	7/23/2015	Ilford, East London	Individual
Leading activist	7/24/2015	Edgware Road, West London	Individual
"Salman," former activist	7/24/2015	Poplar, East London	Individual
Former activist	3/19/2016	United States	Individual

Appendix: Da'wah Stalls, Demonstrations, Road Shows, and Private Talks

This appendix lists, in chronological order, the twenty-four da'wah stalls, demonstrations, "Islamic road shows," and private talks organized by network activists that I observed during my field work. Activists used platform names to promote some, but not all, of these events.

Platform (if applicable)	Event	Location	Date
Muslims Against Crusades	Protest against Armistice Day anniversary	Kensington, Central London	November 11, 2010
Supporters of Sunnah	Da'wah stall	Ilford, East London	November 13, 2010
	Protest against Omar Bakri's arrest in Lebanon	Near Lebanese embassy, Kensington, Central London	November 15, 2010
Call2Tawhid	Da'wah stall	Bethnal Green, East London	November 28, 2010
Supporters of Sunnah	Da'wah stall	Stratford, East London	November 29, 2010
Supporters of Sunnah	Da'wah stall	Tottenham, North London	December 4, 2010
Call2Tawhid	Da'wah stall	Bethnal Green, East London	December 5, 2010
	Da'wah stall	Stratford, East London	December 6, 2010
	Da'wah stall	Lewisham, South London	December 11, 2010

Platform (if applicable)	Event	Location	Date
Centre for Islamic Services	Private talk	Whitechapel, East London	December 16, 2010
Centre for Islamic Services	Private talk	Whitechapel, East London	June 16, 2011
	Protest against Al-Saud monarchy	Outside Royal Embassy of Saudi Arabia, Mayfair, Central London	June 17, 2011
Convert2Islam	Da'wah stall	Lewisham, South London	June 18, 2011
	Da'wah stall	Stratford, East London	June 20, 2011
Centre for Islamic Services	Private talk	Whitechapel, East London	June 23, 2011
	Islamic roadshow	Wembley Central, West London	June 25, 2011
	Da'wah stall	Stratford, East London	June 27, 2011
	Da'wah stall	Hounslow, West London	June 28, 2011
	Islamic roadshow	Islington, North London	July 21, 2012
	Da'wah stall	Hounslow, West London	September 4, 2013
	Islamic roadshow	Wembley Central, West London	September 5, 2013
	Protest against proposed burka ban	Parliament, Westminster, Central London	September 6, 2013
	Da'wah stall	Stratford, East London	December 13, 2014
Ilm Centre	Private talk	Whitechapel, East London	July 24, 2015

Glossary of Arabic Terms

Ahlus Sunnah wal Jama'ah   The people of Sunna, those who follow the way of the Prophet Mohammed. One of al-Muhajiroun's spin-off groups adopted this name.

Aleyhi al-Salam   Literally translates to "may peace be upon him." It is typically said after the mentioning of a Prophet, especially the Prophet Mohammed. Al-Muhajiroun respondents often invoke this honorific when referring to Mohammed. In this book I shorten these references to the conventional English abbreviation, PBUH (Peace Be Upon Him).

Aqeedah (also spelled akeeda or aqīda)   An Islamic term meaning core doctrinal belief or "creed." This refers to any of several systems of Islamic theological beliefs.

Ayat (plural)   Verses of the Qur'an.

Bayat (plural)   An Islamic term meaning pledges or oaths of allegiance. These may be directed towards an Islamic leader or to the Prophet Mohammed.

Burka   Full body cloak worn by Muslim women.

Da'i also spelled da'ee   Refers to a propagator or preacher of Islam. Al-Muhajiroun activists refer to themselves as *da'is*.

Da'wah   Literally translates to "invitation." Within an Islamic context, da'wah means preaching, propagating, or calling people to the faith. This is a cornerstone of Al-Murajiroun's activism.

Dar al-Kuffar   Non-Muslim countries, enemy land, sometimes used as a synonym for dar al-harb (literally meaning "land of war").

Deen   Religion or faith.

Emir   Leader or ruler. This term can also refer to the leader of an organization, network, or group of activists.

Fatwa   An Islamic ruling based on a religious scholar's interpretation of law and scripture.

Al-Ghurabaa (plural)   The term *Ghurabaa* (from the singular *gharib*) literally means "strangers" or "foreigners." The name "al-Ghurabaa" – mentioned in one of the verses of the Hadith – was adopted by one of al-Muhajiroun's spin-off groups.

Al-Hadith   Collections of sayings, deeds, and habits of the Prophet Mohammed. Hadith collections contain information not found in the Qur'an; Mohammed's relatives and contemporaries are said to have provided these details.

Hajj   Literally means "pilgrimage." Within an Islamic context, *hajj* refers to the annual pilgrimage to Mecca, which each Muslim is to complete at least once in his or her lifetime. The *hajj* is one of the five pillars of Islam.

Halaqah   An Islamic study circle. The basic unit of indoctrination and organization in al-Muhajiroun.

Halal   That which is permissible according to Islam.

Haram   That which is forbidden according to Islam.

Hijab   A veil worn by Muslim women; covers the head and chest but not the face.

Hijrah (also spelled Hijra)   Literally means emigration. Within an Islamic context, this term refers to the emigration of Mohammed and his followers from Mecca to Medina. This event marks the beginning of the Islamic calendar.

Hisbah   "Commanding good and forbidding evil." This is a cornerstone of al-Muhajiroun's activism, typically expressed through public protests.

Iftar   The meal that breaks the fast each day during Ramadan following the Maghrib prayer, which is held just after sunset.

Iman   Faith; belief in Islam.

Inshallah   If God wills it; God willing.

Iqra (imperative form)   Translates to the command "read"; according to the Qur'an, the Angel Gabriel commanded Mohammed to read in the name of the Lord.

Jama'ah   Organization or group; activists use this term to refer to al-Muhajiroun.

Jihad   A spiritual or worldly struggle. In this book jihad refers to the physical struggle against perceived enemies of Islam. This is also called the "lesser jihad," in contrast to the "greater jihad" of individual self-improvement. For al-Muhajiroun this physical struggle takes the form of "jihad of the tongue" and "jihad of the sword."

Kafir (singular; also spelled kafr; pl. kuffar)   An unbeliever; someone who does not believe that the Qur'an is the word of God or that Mohammed is the final prophet.

Khawarij (plural)   Dissenters of Islam; an early sect that caused much chaos and conflict within the wider Muslim community.

Khalifah   Caliph; leader of the caliphate.

Khilafah   Islamic caliphate, transnational Islamic state ruled by the khalifah; a central goal in al-Muhajiroun's activism.

Manhaj   Literally means methodology. Within an Islamic context, this is the method of implementing the beliefs (aqeedah) of Islam.

Masjid   Mosque.

Masoul   Literally means "official" (i.e. religious or political official). In al-Muhajiroun, this refers to the halaqah group leader (one level above da'i).

Maturidi   One who follows Abu Mansur al-Maturidi's rationalist (as opposed to literalist) theology.

Al-Muhajiroun   Historically, the Emigrants who followed Mohammed to Medina in the *hijrah*. Al-Muhajiroun adopted this name for their network of activists.

Muntada   Forum, or meeting place for discussion.

Murtad   An apostate; one who leaves the Islamic faith.

Mushrif   Literally means "supervisor"; al-Muhajiroun uses it to mean the leader of a local area, the person one level above the masoul.

Niqab   Full face veil used by some female Muslims, including Salafis.

Sahabah (plural)   Literally means "companions." Within an Islamic context, refers to the companions and early followers of the Prophet Mohammed.

Salafi   Follower of a fundamentalist strain of Sunni Islam that adopts a literal interpretation of Islamic scripture; seek to emulate the first three generations of Muslims or "pious predecessors"; al-Muhajiroun activists self-identify as Salafis, an attribution that quietist Salafis dispute.

Shariah   Islamic law or legal system.

Sheikh (also spelled shaykh)   An honorific title; may be used to refer to tribal leader, religious cleric, teacher, or senior person worthy of respect. In al-Muhajiroun the title is reserved for senior activists who teach others, usually Omar Bakri Mohammed, but in some cases Anjem Choudary and Omar "Abu Izzadeen" Brooks.

Suhba   Literally means "companionship"; to accompany someone and learn from them by observing them as they carry out their activities.

Sunnah   Traditions and habits of the Prophet Mohammed transmitted through stories; serves as a model of perfect behavior for Muslims.

Takfiri   A Muslim who accuses other Muslims of apostasy, thereby excommunicating them and sanctioning violence against them.

Tawheed (also spelled tawhid)   Arabic term for monotheism. This is a core theological belief among Salafis.

Ummah   The global community of Muslims, tied together by a shared history and faith.

Usul al-Fiqh   Islamic jurisprudence. This is a major topic at al-Muhajiroun's private talks and public lectures.

Yawm al-Dīn   The Day of Judgment.

Selected Bibliography

Abedin, Mahan. "Al-Muhajiroun in the UK: An Interview with Sheikh Omar Bakri Mohammed." *Jamestown Monitor* (2004). Published electronically on March 23. www.jamestown.org/news_details.php?news_id=38.

Abun-Nasr, Jamil M. *Muslim Communities of Grace: The Sufi Brotherhoods in Islamic Religious Life.* New York: Columbia University Press, 2007.

Agar, Michael. *The Professional Stranger: An Informal Introduction to Ethnography.* New York: Academic Press, 1980.

Aho, James A. "Out of Hate: A Sociology of Defection from Neo-Nazism." *Current Research on Peace and Violence* 11, no. 4 (1988): 159–68.

The Politics of Righteousness: Idaho Christian Patriotism. Seattle, WA: University of Washington Press, 1990.

Altier, Mary Beth, Christian N. Thoroughgood, and John G. Horgan. "Turning Away from Terrorism: Lessons from Psychology, Sociology, and Criminology." *Journal of Peace Research* 51, no. 5 (2014): 647–61.

Amaral, Luis A. Nunes, Antonio Scala, Marc Barthelemy, and H. Eugene Stanley. "Classes of Small-World Networks." *Proceedings of the National Academy of Sciences of the United States of America* 97, no. 21 (2000): 11149–52.

Arquilla, John, and David Ronfeldt, eds. *Networks and Netwars: The Future of Terror, Crime, and Militancy.* Washington, DC: RAND Corporation, 2001.

as-Salafi, Abu Ameenah AbdurRahman, and Abdul Haq al-Ashanti. *A Critical Study of the Multiple Identities and Disguises of "Al-Muhajiroun."* London: Jamiah Media, 2009.

Avant, Deborah, and Oliver Westerwinter. "Introduction: Networks and Transnational Security Governance." In *The New Power Politics: Networks and Transnational Security Governance*, edited by Deborah Avant and Oliver Westerwinter, pp. 1–18. New York: Oxford University Press, 2016.

Awan, Imran. "Muslim Prisoners, Radicalization and Rehabilitation in British Prisons." *Journal of Muslim Minority Affairs* 33, no. 3 (2013): 371–84.

Ayoob, Mohammed. *The Many Faces of Political Islam: Religion and Politics in the Muslim World.* Ann Arbor, MI: University of Michigan Press, 2008.

Bail, Christopher. *Terrified: How Anti-Muslim Fringe Organizations Became Mainstream*. Princeton, NJ: Princeton University Press, 2015.

Bakker, René M., Jörg Raab, and H. Brinton Milward. "A Preliminary Theory of Dark Network Resilience." *Journal of Policy Analysis & Management* 31, no. 1 (Winter 2012): 33–62.

Barabási, Albert-László. *Linked: The New Science of Networks*. Cambridge, MA: Perseus Press, 2002.

Barabási, Albert-László, and Réka Albert. "Emergence of Scaling in Random Networks." *Science* 286, no. 5439 (1999): 509–12.

Barker, Eileen. *The Making of a Moonie: Choice or Brainwashing?* Oxford: Basil Blackwell, 1984.

Barkey, Karen, and Ronan Van Rossem. "Networks of Contention: Villages and Regional Structure in the Seventeenth-Century Ottoman Empire." *American Journal of Sociology* 102, no. 5 (1997): 1345–82.

Baxter, Kylie. *British Muslims and the Call to Global Jihad*. Clayton, Australia: Monash University Press, 2007.

Bennett, Andrew and Jeffrey T. Checkel. "Process Tracing: From Philosophical Roots to Best Practices." In *Process Tracing: From Metaphor to Analytic Tool*, edited by Bennett and Checkel, pp. 1–37. Cambridge: Cambridge University Press, 2015.

Berger, Peter. *A Rumor of Angels*. Garden City, NY: Doubleday, 1969.

Berkey, Jonathan Porter. *The Transmission of Knowledge in Medieval Cairo: A Social History of Islamic Education*. Princeton, NJ: Princeton University Press, 1992.

Bernard, H. Russell. *Research Methods in Anthropology: Qualitative and Quantitative Approaches*. 4th ed. Lanham, MD: Altamira, 2006.

Bjørgo, Tore, and John Horgan, eds. *Leaving Terrorism Behind: Individual and Collective Disengagement*. New York: Routledge, 2009.

Blee, Kathleen M. *Inside Organized Racism: Women in the Hate Movement*. Berkeley, CA: University of California Press, 2002.

Bloom, Mia. *Dying to Kill: The Allure of Suicide Terror*. New York: Columbia University Press, 2005.

Borum, Randy. "Radicalization into Violent Extremism II: A Review of Conceptual Models and Empirical Research." *Journal of Strategic Security* 4, no. 4 (2011): 37–62.

Bourgois, Philippe. *In Search of Respect: Selling Crack in El Barrio*. 2nd ed. New York: Cambridge University Press, 2003.

Brokenshire, James. "Written Statement to Parliament: Alternative Names for Proscribed Organisation Al Muhajiroun." Home Office, 2014.

Brown, John Seely, and Paul Duguid. "Organizational Learning and Communities-of-Practice: Toward a Unified View of Working, Learning, and Innovating." *Organization Science* 2, no. 1 (1991): 40–57.

Burke, Jason. *The New Threat: The Past, Present, and Future of Islamic Militancy*. New York: The New Press, 2015.

Byman, Daniel. "The Jihadist Returnee Threat: Just How Dangerous?" *Political Science Quarterly* 131, no. 1 (2016): 69–99.

Carley, Kathleen M., Dave Columbus, Michael Bigrigg, and Frank Kunkel. *AutoMap User's Guide 2011*. Technical Report, CMU-ISR-11e108. Pittsburgh, PA: Carnegie Mellon University, School of Computer Science, Institute for Software Research, 2011.

Carley, Kathleen M., Jeff Reminga, Jon Storrick, and Dave Columbus. *ORA User's Guide 2011*. Carnegie Mellon University, School of Computer Science, Institute for Software Research, Technical Report, 2011.

Carley, Kathleen M., Ju-Sung Lee, and David Krackhardt. "Destabilizing Networks." *Connections* 24, no. 3 (2002): 31–34.

Carpenter, Charli. "Governing the Global Agenda: 'Gatekeepers' and 'Issue Adoption'." In *Who Governs the Globe?*, edited by Deborah Avant, Martha Finnemore and Susan Sell, pp. 202–37. Cambridge: Cambridge University Press, 2010.

Carpenter, Charli. *"Lost" Causes: Agenda Vetting in Global Issue Networks and the Shaping of Human Security*. Ithaca, NY: Cornell University Press, 2014.

Centre for Social Cohesion. "One in Seven UK Terror-Related Convictions Linked to Islamist Group Now Threatening to Relaunch." News release, June 1, 2009.

Chernov Hwang, Julie. *Why Terrorists Quit: The Disengagement of Indonesian Jihadists*. Ithaca, NY: Cornell University Press, 2018.

Chowdhury, Arjun, and Ronald R. Krebs. "Making and Mobilizing Moderates: Rhetorical Strategy, Political Networks, and Counterterrorism." *Security Studies* 18, no. 3 (2009): 371–99.

Christakis, Nicholas A., and James H. Fowler. *Connected: How Your Friends' Friends' Friends Affect Everything You Feel, Think, and Do*. New York: Brown and Company, 2009.

Clark, Janine A. "Islamist Women in Yemen: Informal Nodes of Activism." In *Islamic Activism: A Social Movement Theory Approach*, edited by Quintan Wiktorowicz, pp. 164–84. Bloomington, IN: Indiana University Press, 2004.

Clauset, Aaron, Cosma Rohilla Shalizi, and M. E. J. Newman. "Power-Law Distributions in Empirical Data." *SIAM Review* 51, no. 4 (2009): 661–703.

Collins, Kathleen. "Ideas, Networks, and Islamist Movements: Evidence from Central Asia and the Caucasus." *World Politics* 60, no. 1 (2007): 64–96.

Crenshaw, Martha. "The Causes of Terrorism." *Comparative Politics* 13, no. 4 (July 1981): 379–399.

"How Terrorism Declines." *Terrorism and Political Violence* 3, no. 1 (1991): 69–87.

"Theories of Terrorism: Instrumental and Organisational Approaches." In *Inside Terrorist Organisations*, edited by David C. Rapoport, pp. 13–31. London: Frank Cass, 2001.

Creswell, John W. *Qualitative Inquiry & Research Design: Choosing among Five Approaches*. 2nd ed. Thousand Oaks, CA: Sage Publications, 2007.

Cronin, Audrey Kurth. *How Terrorism Ends: Understanding the Decline and Demise of Terrorist Campaigns*. Princeton, NJ: Princeton University Press, 2009.

della Porta, Donatella. *Social Movements, Political Violence, and the State: A Comparative Analysis of Italy and Germany*. Cambridge: Cambridge University Press, 1995.

"Leaving Underground Organizations: A Sociological Analysis of the Italian Case." In *Leaving Terrorism Behind: Individual and Collective Disengagement*, edited by Tore Bjørgo and John Horgan, pp. 66–87. New York: Routledge, 2009.

Clandestine Political Violence. New York: Cambridge University Press, 2013.

Dolnik, Adam. *Understanding Terrorist Innovation: Technologies, Tactics and Global Trends*. London: Routledge, 2007.

Dorussen, Han, and Hugh Ward. "Intergovernmental Organizations and the Kantian Peace: A Network Perspective." *Journal of Conflict Resolution* 52, no. 2 (2008): 189–212.

Downton Jr., James, and Paul Wehr. *The Persistent Activist: How Peace Commitment Develops and Survives.* Boulder, CO: Westview Press, 1997.

Ebaugh, Helen Rose. *The Gülen Movement: A Sociological Analysis of a Civic Movement Rooted in Moderate Islam.* London: Springer, 2010.

Eckstein, Harry. "Case Study and Theory in Political Science." In *Strategies of Inquiry,* Vol. 7 of *The Handbook of Political Science,* edited by Fred I. Greenstein and Nelson W. Polsby, pp. 79–138. Reading, MA: Addison-Wesley Publishing Company, 1975.

Eden, Lynn. *Whole World on Fire: Organizations, Knowledge, & Nuclear Weapons Devastation.* Ithaca, NY: Cornell University Press, 2004.

Effler, Erika Summers. *Laughing Saints and Righteous Heroes: Emotional Rhythms in Social Movement Groups.* Chicago, IL: University of Chicago Press, 2010.

Eilstrup-Sangiovanni, Mette. "Varieties of Cooperation: Government Networks in International Security." In *Networked Politics: Agency, Power, and Governance,* edited by Miles Kahler, pp. 194–227. Ithaca, NY: Cornell University Press, 2009.

Everton, Sean F. *Disrupting Dark Networks.* New York: Cambridge University Press, 2012.

Everton, Sean F., and Daniel Cunningham. "Terrorist Network Adaptation to a Changing Environment." In *Crime and Networks,* edited by Carlo Morselli, pp. 287–308. London: Routledge, 2013.

Feldman, Martha S. "Organizational Routines as a Source of Continuous Change." *Organization Science* 11, no. 6 (2000): 611–29.

Fenno, Jr., Richard F. *Home Style: House Members in Their Districts.* New York: Pearson, 2002.

Festinger, Leon, Henry W. Riecken, and Stanley Schacter. *When Prophecy Fails: A Social and Psychological Study of a Modern Group That Predicted the Destruction of the World.* New York: Harper & Row, 1964.

Findley, Michael G., and Joseph K. Young. "More Combatant Groups, More Terror?: Empirical Tests of an Outbidding Logic." *Terrorism and Political Violence* 24, no. 5 (2012): 706–21.

Foley, Frank. *Countering Terrorism in Britain and France: Institutions, Norms and the Shadow of the Past.* Cambridge: Cambridge University Press, 2013.

Forest, James J.F., ed. *Teaching Terror: Knowledge Transfer in the Terrorist World.* Lanham, MD: Rowman & Littlefield, 2006.

Freeman, Linton C. "Centrality in Social Networks: Conceptual Clarification." *Social Networks* 1, no. 3 (1979).

Garmezy, Norman. "Resilience in Children's Adaptation to Negative Life Events and Stressed Environments." *Pediatric Annals* 20, no. 9 (1991): 459–66.

Geertz, Clifford. "Thick Description: Toward an Interpretive Theory of Culture." In *The Interpretation of Cultures: Selected Essays by Clifford Geertz,* pp. 3–30. New York: Basic Books, 1973.

George, Alexander L. "Case Studies and Theory Development: The Method of Structured, Focused Comparisons." In *Diplomacy: New Approaches in History, Theory, and Policy,* edited by Paul Gordon Lauren, pp. 43–68. New York: Free Press, 1979.

George, Alexander L., and Andrew Bennett. *Case Studies and Theory Development in the Social Sciences.* Cambridge, MA: MIT Press, 2005.

Gerges, Fawaz A. "The Decline of Revolutionary Islam in Algeria and Egypt," *Survival*, 41, no. 1 (1999): 113–25.

ISIS: A History. Princeton, NJ: Princeton University Press, 2016.

Gilliat-Ray, Sophie. *Muslims in Britain: An Introduction*. New York: Cambridge University Press, 2010.

Glaser, Barney G., and Anselm L. Strauss. *The Discovery of Grounded Theory: Strategies for Qualitative Research*. New Brunswick, NJ: Aldine, 1967.

Goddard, Stacie E. "Brokering Peace: Networks, Legitimacy, and the Northern Ireland Peace Process." *International Studies Quarterly* 56 (2012): 501–15.

Goertz, Gary, and James Mahoney. *A Tale of Two Cultures: Qualitative and Quantitative Research in the Social Sciences*. Princeton, NJ: Princeton University Press, 2012.

Gould, Roger V. "Multiple Networks and Mobilization in the Paris Commune, 1871." *American Sociological Review* 56, no. 6 (1991): 716–29.

Granovetter, Mark S. "The Strength of Weak Ties." *American Journal of Sociology* 78, no. 6 (1973): 1360–80.

Hadden, Jennifer. *Networks in Contention: The Divisive Politics of Climate Change*. New York: Cambridge University Press, 2015.

Hafner-Burton, Emilie M., Miles Kahler, and Alexander H. Montgomery. "Network Analysis for International Relations." *International Organization* 63, no. 3 (Summer 2009): 559–92.

Hafner-Burton, Emilie M., and Alexander H. Montgomery. "Power Positions: International Organizations, Social Networks, and Conflict." *Journal of Conflict Resolution* 50, no. 1 (2006): 3–27.

Hamid, Sadek. "The Attraction of 'Authentic' Islam: Salafism and British Muslim Youth." In *Global Salafism: Islam's New Religious Movement*, edited by Roel Meijer, pp. 384–403. New York: Columbia University Press, 2009.

"Mapping Youth Work and Muslims in Britain." In *Youth Work and Islam: A Leap of Faith for Young People*, edited by Brian Belton and Sadek Hamid, pp. 83–97. Rotterdam: Sense Publishers, 2011.

Hamid, Shadi. *Temptations of Power: Islamists and Illiberal Democracy in a New Middle East*. New York: Oxford University Press, 2014.

Hamm, Mark S. *The Spectacular Few: Prisoner Radicalization and the Evolving Terrorist Threat*. New York: New York University Press, 2013.

Haykel, Bernard. "On the Nature of Salafi Thought and Action." In *Global Salafism: Islam's New Religious Movement*, edited by Roel Meijer, pp. 33–57. New York: Columbia University Press, 2009.

Hegghammer, Thomas. "Should I Stay or Should I Go? Explaining Variation in Western Jihadists' Choice between Domestic and Foreign Fighting." *American Political Science Review* 107, no. 1 (2013): 1–15.

Al-Hilali, Muhammad Taqi-ud-Din, and Muhammad Mushin Kahn. *Interpretation of the Meanings of the Noble Qur'an in the English Language*. Revised ed. Riyadh, Saudi Arabia: Maktaba Dar-us-Salam, 2007.

Hirschman, Albert O. *Exit, Voice, and Loyalty: Response to Decline in Firms, Organizations, and States*. Cambridge, MA: Harvard University Press, 1970.

Hocking, Jenny. "Counter-Terrorism and the Criminalisation of Politics: Australia's New Security Powers of Detention, Proscription and Control." *Australian Journal of Politics and History* 49, no. 3 (2003): 355–71.

Horgan, John. *The Psychology of Terrorism*. New York: Routledge, 2005.

Walking Away from Terrorism: Accounts of Disengagement from Radical and Extremist Movements. New York: Routledge, 2009.

Humphries, Mark D., and Kevin Gurney. "Network 'Small-World-Ness': A Quantitative Method for Determining Canonical Network Equivalence." *PLoSOne* 3, no. 4 (2008).

Hundeide, Karsten. "Becoming a Committed Insider." *Culture and Psychology* 9, no. 2 (2003): 107–27.

Husain, Ed. *The Islamist: Why I Joined Radical Islam in Britain, What I Saw Inside and Why I Left.* London: Penguin, 2007.

International Crisis Group. "Understanding Islamism." *Middle East/North Africa Report*, N°37 March 2, 2005.

Jackson, Brian A., John C. Baker, Kim Cragin, John Parachini, Horacio R. Trujillo, and Peter Chalk. *Aptitude for Destruction, Volume 1: Organizational Learning in Terrorist Groups and Its Implications for Combating Terrorism and Aptitude for Destruction.* Santa Monica, CA: RAND Corporation, 2005.

Aptitude for Destruction, Volume 2: Case Studies of Organizational Learning in Five Terrorist Groups. Santa Monica, CA: RAND Corporation, 2005.

Jasper, James M. *The Art of Moral Protest: Culture, Biography, and Creativity in Social Movements.* Chicago, IL: University of Chicago Press, 1997.

Jasper, James M., and Jane D. Poulsen. "Recruiting Strangers and Friends: Moral Shocks and Social Networks in Animal Rights and Anti-Nuclear Protests." *Social Problems* 42, no. 4 (1995): 493–512.

Jassal, Smita Tewari. "The Sohbet: Talking Islam in Turkey." *Sociology of Islam* 1, nos. 3–4 (2014): 188–208.

Jones, Nathan P. *Mexico's Illicit Drug Networks and the State Reaction.* Washington, DC: Georgetown University Press, 2016.

Kahler, Miles. *Networked Politics: Agency, Power, and Governance.* Ithaca, NY: Cornell University Press, 2009.

Kassimeris, George, and Leonie Jackson. "The Ideology and Discourse of the English Defence League: 'Not Racist, Not Violent, Just No Longer Silent'." *British Journal of Politics & International Relations* 17, no. 1 (2015): 171–88.

Keck, Margaret E., and Kathryn Sikkink. *Activists Beyond Borders: Advocacy Networks in International Politics.* Ithaca, NY: Cornell University Press, 1998.

Kenney, Michael. *From Pablo to Osama: Trafficking and Terrorist Networks, Government Bureaucracies, and Competitive Adaptation.* University Park, PA: Pennsylvania State University Press, 2007.

"'Dumb' yet Deadly: Local Knowledge and Poor Tradecraft among Islamist Militants in Britain and Spain." *Studies in Conflict and Terrorism* 33, no. 10 (2010): 911–32.

"Hotbed of Radicalization or Something Else?: An Ethnographic Exploration of a Muslim Neighborhood in Ceuta." *Terrorism and Political Violence* 23, no. 4 (2011): 537–59.

"Learning from the 'Dark Side': Identifying, Accessing, and Interviewing Illicit Non-State Actors." In *Conducting Terrorism Field Research: A Guide*, edited by Adam Dolnik, pp. 26–45. New York: Routledge, 2013.

Kenney, Michael, John Horgan, Cale Horne, Peter Vining, Kathleen M. Carley, Michael W. Bigrigg, Mia Bloom, and Kurt Braddock, "Organisational Adaptation in an Activist Network: Social Networks, Leadership, and Change in al-Muhajiroun." *Applied Ergonomics* 44, no. 5 (September 2013), pp. 739–47.

Kenney, Michael, and Stephen Coulthart. "The Methodological Challenges of Extracting Dark Networks: Minimizing False Positives through Ethnography." In *Illuminating Dark Networks*, edited by Luke M. Gerdes, pp. 52–70. New York: Cambridge University Press, 2015.

Kettle, Louise, and Andrew Mumford. "Terrorist Learning: A New Analytical Framework." *Studies in Conflict & Terrorism* 40, no. 7 (2017): 523–38.

Khagram, Sanjeev, James V. Riker, and Kathryn Sikkink. *Restructuring World Politics: Transnational Social Movements, Networks, and Norms*. Minneapolis, MN: University of Minnesota Press, 2002.

Khosrokhavar, Farhad. "Radicalization in Prison: The French Case." *Politics, Religion and Ideology* 14, no. 2 (2013): 284–306.

Kim, Hyojoung, and Peter S. Bearman. "The Structure and Dynamics of Movement Participation." *American Sociological Review* 62, no. 1 (1997): 70–93.

King, Gary, Robert O. Keohane, and Sidney Verba. *Designing Social Inquiry: Scientific Inference in Qualitative Research*. Princeton, NJ: Princeton University Press, 1994.

Kinsella, David. "The Black Market in Small Arms: Examining a Social Network." *Contemporary Security Policy* 27, no. 1 (2006): 100–17.

Klandermans, Bert. *The Social Psychology of Protest*. Cambridge, MA: Blackwell, 1997.

Klausen, Jytte. *The Cartoons that Shook the World*. New Haven, CT: Yale University Press, 2009.

———. "Tweeting the Jihad: Social Media Networks of Western Foreign Fighters in Syria and Iraq." *Studies in Conflict and Terrorism* 38, no. 1 (2015): 1–22.

Knoke, David. *Political Networks: The Structural Perspective*. New York: Cambridge University Press, 1990.

Krebs, Valdis E. "Mapping Networks of Terrorist Cells." *Connections* 24, no. 3 (2002): 43–52.

Kurtz, Don L. "Controlled Burn: The Gendering of Stress and Burnout in Modern Policing." *Feminist Criminology* 3, no. 3 (2008): 216–38.

Kydd, Andrew H., and Barbara F. Walter. "The Strategies of Terrorism." *International Security* 31, no. 1 (2006): 49–80.

Lake, David A., and Wendy H. Wong. "The Politics of Networks: Interests, Power, and Human Rights Norms." In *Networked Politics: Agency, Power, and Governance*, edited by Miles Kahler, pp. 127–50. Ithaca, NY: Cornell University Press, 2009.

Lambert, Robert. *Countering Al-Qaeda in London: Police and Muslims in Partnership*. New York: Columbia University Press, 2013.

Langone, Michael D. "Responding to Jihadism: A Cultic Studies Perspective." *Cultic Studies Review* 5, no. 2 (2006): 1–39.

Lave, Jean, and Etienne Wenger. *Situated Learning: Legitimate Peripheral Participation*. New York: Cambridge University Press, 1991.

Lee, Jenny S. Y., and Syed Akhtar. "Effects of the Workplace Social Context and Job Content on Nurse Burnout." *Human Resource Management* 50, no. 2 (2011): 227–45.

Legrand, Tim, and Lee Jarvis. "Enemies of the State: Proscription Powers and Their Use in the United Kingdom." *British Politics* 9, no. 4 (2014): 450–71.

Lewis, Philip. *Young, British and Muslim*. New York: Continuum, 2007.

Lia, Brynjar. *Architect of Global Jihad: The Life of Al-Qaida Strategist Abu Mus'ab Al Suri*. New York: Columbia University Press, 2008.

Lofland, John. *Doomsday Cult: A Study of Conversion, Proselytization, and Maintenance of Faith*. Englewood Cliffs, NJ: Prentice-Hall, 1966.

Lofland, John, and Rodney Stark. "Becoming a World-Saver: A Theory of Conversion to a Deviant Perspective." *American Sociological Review* 30, no. 6 (1965): 862–75.

London Metropolitan Police. "Four Charged with Terror Offences." Press release, July 19, 2012, http://content.met.police.uk/News/Four-charged-with-terror-offences/1400010136294/1257246745756.

Lowles, Nick, and Joe Mulhall. "Gateway to Terror: Anjem Choudary and the Al-Muhajiroun Network." London: HOPE not hate, 2013.

McAdam, Doug. "Recruitment to High-Risk Activism: The Case of Freedom Summer." *American Journal of Sociology* 92, no. 1 (1986): 64–90.

——— . *Freedom Summer*. New York: Oxford University Press, 1988.

McAdam, Doug, and Ronnelle Paulsen. "Specifying the Relationship between Social Ties and Activism." *American Journal of Sociology* 99, no. 3 (1993): 640–67.

McCants, William. *The ISIS Apocalypse: The History, Strategy, and Doomsday Vision of the Islamic State*. New York: St Martin's Press, 2015.

McCauley, Clark, and Sophia Moskalenko. "Mechanisms of Political Radicalization: Pathways Toward Terrorism," *Terrorism and Political Violence* 20, no. 3 (2008): 415–433.

——— . *Friction: How Radicalization Happens to Them and Us*. New York: Oxford University Press, 2011.

McClurg, Scott D., and David Lazer. "Political Networks." *Social Networks* 36, (2014): 1–4.

McClurg, Scott D., and Joseph K. Young. "Editors' Introduction: A Relational Political Science." *PS: Political Science and Politics* 44, no. 1 (2011): 39–43.

McFadden, Paula, Anne Campbell, and Brian Taylor. "Resilience and Burnout in Child Protection Social Work: Individual and Organisational Themes from a Systematic Literature Review." *The British Journal of Social Work* 45, no. 5 (2015): 1546–63.

Maher, Shiraz. *Salafi-Jihadism: The History of an Idea*. New York: Oxford University Press, 2016.

Malet, David. *Foreign Fighters: Transnational Identity in Civil Conflicts*. New York: Oxford University Press, 2015.

Malinowski, Bronislaw. *Argonauts of the Western Pacific: An Account of Native Enterprise and Adventure in the Archipelagoes of Melanesian New Guinea*. Prospect Heights, IL: Waveland Press, 1984 [1922].

Malthener, Stefan. *Mobilizing the Faithful: Militant Islamist Groups and Their Constituencies*. Frankfurt: Campus Verlag, 2001.

Manning, Ruth, and Courtney La Bau. "In and Out of Extremism." London: Quilliam Foundation, 2015.

Maoz, Zeev. *Networks of Nations: The Evolution, Structure, and Impact of International Networks, 1816–2001*. New York: Cambridge University Press, 2011.

March, James G. "Exploration and Exploitation in Organizational Learning." *Organization Science* 2, no. 1 (1991): 71–87.

Meijer, Roel. "Commanding Right and Forbidding Wrong as a Principle of Social Action: The Case of the Egyptian Al-Jama's Al-Islamiyya." In *Global Salafism: Islam's New Religious Movement*, edited by Roel Meijer, pp. 189–220. New York: Columbia University Press, 2009.

Mendelsohn, Barak. *The Al-Qaeda Franchise: The Expansion of Al-Qaeda and Its Consequences.* New York: Oxford University Press, 2016.

Mische, Ann. *Partisan Publics: Communication and Contention across Brazilian Youth Activist Networks.* Princeton, NJ: Princeton University Press, 2008.

Moghadam, Assaf. *Nexus of Global Jihad: Understanding Cooperation among Terrorist Actors.* New York: Columbia University Press, 2017.

Moghaddam, Fathali M. "The Staircase to Terrorism: A Psychological Exploration." *American Psychologist* 60, no. 2 (Feb–Mar 2005): 161–9.

Montgomery, Alexander H. "Ringing in Proliferation: How to Dismantle an Atomic Bomb Network." *International Security* 30, no. 2 (2005): 153–87.

Morrison, John F. "Splitting to Survive: Understanding Terrorist Group Fragmentation." *Journal of Criminological Research, Policy and Practice* 3, no. 3 (2017): 222–32.

Morton, Jesse and Mitchell Silber. "NYPD vs. Revolution Muslim: The Inside Story of the Defeat of a Local Radicalization Hub." *CTC Sentinel* (April 2018): 1–7.

Nawaz, Maajid, and Tom Bromley. *Radical.* London: WH Allen, 2013.

Nepstad, Sharon Erickson. "Persistent Resistance: Commitment and Community in the Plowshares Movement." *Social Problems* 51, no. 1 (2004): 43–60.

Neumann, Peter R. "The Trouble with Radicalization." *International Affairs* 89, no. 4 (2013): 873–93.

"Foreign Fighter Total in Syria/Iraq Now Exceeds 20,000; Surpasses Afghanistan Conflict in the 1980s." *ICSR Insight* (2015). http://icsr.info/2015/01/foreign-fighter-total-syriairaq-now-exceeds-20000-surpasses-afghanistan-conflict-1980s/.

Nexon, Daniel H., and Thomas Wright. "What's at Stake in the American Empire Debate." *American Political Science Review* 101, no. 2 (2007): 253–71.

Nicolini, Davide, Silvia Gherardi, and Dvora Yanow, eds. *Knowing in Organizations: A Practice-Based Approach.* Armonk, NY: M.E. Sharpe, 2003.

O'Neill, Sean, and Daniel McGrory. *The Suicide Factory: Abu Hamza and the Finsbury Park Mosque.* London: Harper Perennial, 2006.

Orlikowski, Wanda J. "Knowing in Practice: Enacting a Collective Capability in Distributed Organizing." *Organization Science* 13, no. 3 (2002): 249–73.

Orr, Julian E. *Talking About Machines: An Ethnography of a Modern Job.* Ithaca, NY: Cornell University Press, 1996.

Padgett, John F., and Christopher K. Ansell. "Robust Action and the Rise of the Medici, 1400–34." *American Journal of Sociology* 98, no. 6 (1993): 1259–319.

Pantucci, Raffaello. *'We Love Death as You Love Life': Britain's Suburban Terrorists.* London: Hurst & Company, 2015.

Pedahzur, Ami, and Arie Perliger. "The Changing Nature of Suicide Attacks: A Social Network Perspective." *Social Forces* 84, no. 4 (2006): 1987–2008.

Pupcenoks, Juris, and Ryan McCabe. "The Rise of the Fringe: Right Wing Populists, Islamists and Politics in the UK." *Journal of Muslim Minority Affairs* 33, no. 2 (2013): 171–84.

Raab, Jörg, and H. Brinton Milward. "Dark Networks as Problems." *Journal of Public Administration Research and Theory* 13, no. 4 (2003): 413–39.

Ranstorp, Magnus, and Magnus Normark, eds. *Understanding Terrorism Innovation and Learning: Al-Qaeda and Beyond.* Abingdon: Routledge, 2015.

Rapoport, David C. "The Four Waves of Modern Terrorism." In *Attacking Terrorism: Elements of a Grand Strategy*, edited by Audrey Kurth Cronin and James M. Ludes, pp. 46–73. Washington, DC: Georgetown University Press, 2004.

Rashwan, Diaa. "The Renunciation of Violence by Egyptian Jihadi Organizations." In *Leaving Terrorism Behind*, edited by Tore Bjørgo and John Horgan, pp. 113–31. New York: Routledge, 2009.

Rasmussen, Maria J., and Mohammed M. Hafez, eds. *Terrorist Innovations in Weapons of Mass Effect: Preconditions, Causes, and Predictive Indicators*. Ft. Belvoir, VA: Defense Threat Reduction Agency, 2010.

Raymond, Catherine Zara. "Al Muhajiroun and Islam4UK: The Group Behind the Ban." London: International Centre for the Study of Radicalisation and Political Violence, King's College, 2010.

Reinares, Fernando. "Exit from Terrorism: A Qualitative Empirical Study on Disengagement and Deradicalization among Members of ETA." *Terrorism and Political Violence* 23, no. 5 (2011): 780–803.

Richards, Lyn. *Handling Qualitative Data: A Practical Guide*. 3rd ed. London: Sage Publications, 2015.

Richardson, James T., Jan van der Lans, and Frans Derks. "Leaving and Labeling: Voluntary and Coerced Disaffiliation from Religious Social Movements." *Research in Social Movements, Conflicts and Change* 9 (1986): 97–126.

Robben, Antonius C. G. M. "Ethnographic Seduction, Transference, and Resistance in Dialogues About Terror and Violence in Argentina." *Ethos* 24, no. 1 (1996): 71–106.

Robbins, Thomas. *Cults, Converts and Charisma: The Sociology of New Religious Movements*. Thousand Oaks, CA: Sage Publications, 1988.

Roberts, Joanne. "Limits to Communities of Practice." *Journal of Management Studies* 43, no. 3 (2006): 623–39.

Ronson, Jon. "*Tottenham Ayatollah*." Channel Four, RDF Media, April 8, 1997.

    Them: Adventures with Extremists. London: Picador, 2001.

Ross, Jeffrey Ian, and Ted Robert Gurr. "Why Terrorism Subsides: A Comparative Study of Canada and the United States." *Comparative Politics* 21, no. 4 (1989): 405–26.

Sageman, Marc. *Understanding Terror Networks*. Philadelphia, PA: University of Pennsylvania Press, 2004.

    Misunderstanding Terrorism. Philadelphia, PA: University of Pennsylvania Press, 2017.

    Turning to Political Violence: The Emergence of Terrorism. Philadelphia, PA: University of Pennsylvania Press, 2017.

Schatz, Edward, ed. *Political Ethnography: What Immersion Contributes to the Study of Power*. Chicago, IL: University of Chicago Press, 2009.

Shane, Scott. *Objective Troy: A Terrorist, a President, and the Rise of the Drone*. New York: Tim Duggan Books, 2015.

Shapiro, Jacob N. *The Terrorist's Dilemma: Managing Violent Covert Organizations*. Princeton, NJ: Princeton University Press, 2013.

Shapiro, Julie B. "The Politicization of the Designation of Foreign Terrorist Organizations: The Effect on the Separation of Powers." *Cardozo Public Law, Policy and Ethics Journal* 6, no. 1 (Spring 2008): 547–600.

Silber, Mitchell D., and Arvin Bhatt. "Radicalization in the West: The Homegrown Threat." New York: Police Department, City of New York, 2007.

Simcox, Robin, Hannah Stuart, and Houriya Ahmed. *Islamist Terrorism: The British Connections*. London: The Centre for Social Cohesion, 2010.

Simmel, Georg. *The Sociology of Georg Simmel*. Translated, edited, and introduced by Kurt H. Wolff. New York: Free Press, 1950.

Snow, David A., Louis A. Zurcher, and Sheldon Ekland-Olson. "Social Networks and Social Movements: A Microstructural Approach to Differential Recruitment." *American Sociological Review* 45, no. 5 (1980): 787–801.

Sprinzak, Ehud. "The Psychopolitical Formation of Extreme Left Terrorism in a Democracy: The Case of the Weathermen." In *Origins of Terrorism: Psychologies, Ideologies, Theologies, States of Mind*, edited by Walter Reich, pp. 65–85. Washington, DC: Woodrow Wilson Center Press, 1998.

Staniland, Paul. *Networks of Rebellion: Explaining Insurgent Cohesion and Collapse*. Ithaca, NY: Cornell University Press, 2014.

Stark, Rodney. *The Rise of Christianity: A Sociologist Reconsiders History*. Princeton, NJ: Princeton University Press, 1996.

Stark, Rodney, and William Sims Bainbridge. "Networks of Faith: Interpersonal Bonds and Recruitment to Cults and Sects." *American Journal of Sociology* 85, no. 6 (1980): 1376–95.

Sutcliffe, Kathleen M., and Timothy J. Vogus. "Organizing for Resilience." In *Positive Organizational Scholarship: Foundations of a New Discipline*, edited by Kim S. Cameron, Jane E. Dutton and Robert E. Quinn, pp. 94–121. San Francisco, CA: Berrett-Koehler Publishers, 2003.

Taji-Farouki, Suha. *A Fundamental Quest: Hizb Al-Tahrir and the Search for the Islamic Caliphate*. London: Grey Seal, 1996.

"Islamists and the Threat of Jihad: Hizb Al-Tahrir and Al-Muhajiroun on Israel and the Jews." *Middle Eastern Studies* 36, no. 4 (2000): 21–46.

Taub, Ben. "Journey to Jihad: Why Are Teen-Agers Joining ISIS?" *The New Yorker*, June 1, 2015.

Taylor, Max, and John Horgan. "A Conceptual Framework for Addressing Psychological Process in the Development of the Terrorist." *Terrorism and Political Violence* 18, no. 4 (2006): 585–601.

Treadwell, James, and Jon Garland. "Masculinity, Marginalization and Violence: A Case Study of the English Defence League." *British Journal of Criminology* 51, no. 4 (2011): 621–34.

United Kingdom Crown Prosecution Service. "The Counter-Terrorism Division of the Crown Prosecution Service (CPS) – Cases Concluded in 2015." www.cps.gov.uk/publications/prosecution/ctd_2015.html.

"Men Jailed for Supporting Terrorism." Press release, February 2, 2017, www.cps.gov.uk/news/latest_news/men_jailed_for_supporting_terrorism/.

United Kingdom Home Office. "Terror Organisation Proscribed." Press release, November 9, 2011, www.homeoffice.gov.uk/media-centre/news/mac-proscription.

"Proscribed Terrorist Organizations." July 6, 2012 and May 3, 2017.

US Department of State. "State Department Terrorist Designations of El Shafee Elsheikh, Anjem Choudary, Sami Bouras, Shane Dominic Crawford, and Mark John Taylor." Press release, March 30, 2017, www.state.gov/r/pa/prs/ps/2017/03/269306.htm.

"State Department Terrorist Designations of Siddhartha Dhar and Abdelatif Gaini." Press release, January 23, 2018, www.state.gov/r/pa/prs/ps/2018/01/277594.htm.

Uzzi, Brian, and Jarrett Spiro. "Collaboration and Creativity: The Small World Problem." *American Journal of Sociology* 111, no. 2 (2005): 447–504.

Valente, Thomas W. *Social Networks and Health: Models, Methods, and Applications.* New York: Oxford University Press, 2010.

Vidino, Lorenzo. "Sharia4: From Confrontational Activism to Militancy." *Perspectives on Terrorism* 9, no. 2 (April 2015): 2–16.

Wang, Dan J., and Sarah A. Soule. "Social Movement Organizational Collaboration: Networks of Learning and the Diffusion of Protest Tactics, 1960–1995." *American Journal of Sociology* 117, no. 6 (2012): 1674–722.

Wasserman, Stanley, and Katherine Faust. *Social Network Analysis: Methods and Applications.* New York: Cambridge University Press, 1994.

Watts, Duncan J. "Networks, Dynamics, and the Small-World Phenomenon." *American Journal of Sociology* 105, no. 2 (1999): 493–527.

Six Degrees: The Science of a Connected Age. New York: Norton, 2003.

"The 'New' Science of Networks." *Annual Review of Sociology* 30, no. 1 (2004): 243–70.

Watts, Duncan J., and Steven H. Strogatz. "Collective Dynamics of 'Small-World' Networks." *Nature* 393, no. 6684 (1998): 440–42.

Weber, Max. *The Theory of Social and Economic Organization.* Translated by A. M. Henderson and Talcott Parsons. New York: Free Press, 1964.

Weeks, Douglas. "Radicals and Reactionaries: The Polarisation of Community and Government in the Name of Public Safety and Security." Doctoral Dissertation, University of St Andrews, 2012.

Weine, Stevan. "Building Community Resilience to Violent Extremism." *Georgetown Journal of International Affairs* 14 (Summer/Fall 2013): 81–9.

Wenger, Etienne. *Communities of Practice: Learning, Meaning, and Identity.* Cambridge: Cambridge University Press, 1998.

Wenger, Etienne, Richard A. McDermott, and William Snyder. *Cultivating Communities of Practice: A Guide to Managing Knowledge.* Boston, MA: Harvard Business School Press, 2002.

Wickham-Crowley, Timothy P. *Guerrillas and Revolution in Latin America: A Comparative Study of Insurgents and Regimes since 1956.* Princeton, NJ: Princeton University Press, 1992.

Wiktorowicz, Quintan. *Radical Islam Rising: Muslim Extremism in the West.* Lanham, MD: Rowman & Littlefield, 2005.

"The Salafi Movement: Violence and the Fragmentation of Community." In *Muslim Networks: From Hajj to Hip Hop*, edited by Miriam Cooke and Bruce B. Lawrence, pp. 208–34. Chapel Hill, NC: University of North Carolina Press, 2005.

"Anatomy of the Salafi Movement." *Studies in Conflict and Terrorism* 29, no. 3 (2006): 207–39.

Wiktorowicz, Quintan, and Karl Kaltenthaler. "The Rationality of Radical Islam." *Political Science Quarterly* 121, no. 2 (2006): 295–319.

Williams, Phil. "Transnational Criminal Networks." In *Networks and Netwars*, edited by John Arquilla and David Ronfeldt, pp. 61–98. Santa Monica, CA: RAND Corporation, 2001.

Wiltfang, Gregory L., and Doug McAdam. "The Costs and Risks of Social Activism: A Study of Sanctuary Movement Activism." *Social Forces* 69, no. 4 (1991): 987–1010.

Wong, Wendy H. *Internal Affairs: How the Structure of NGOs Transforms Human Rights.* Ithaca, NY: Cornell University Press, 2012.

Wood, Elisabeth Jean. "Ethical Challenges of Field Research in Conflict Zones." *Qualitative Sociology* 29, no. 3 (2006): 373–86.

Wright, Lawrence. "The Rebellion Within: An Al Qaeda Mastermind Questions Terrorism." *The New Yorker,* June 2, 2008.

Xu, Jennifer, and Hsinchun Chen. "The Topology of Dark Networks." *Communications of the ACM* 51, no. 10 (2008).

Yanow, Dvora. "Dear Author, Dear Reader: The Third Hermeneutic in Writing and Reviewing Ethnography." In *Political Ethnography: What Immersion Contributes to the Study of Power,* edited by Edward Schatz, pp. 275–302. Chicago, IL: University of Chicago Press, 2009.

Index

Recent Books in the Series (continued from p. ii)